TO EVERYONE WHO LOVES AND
SUPPORTS MY VIDEOS, I HOPE YOU
ENJOY THIS AS MUCH AS I DO.

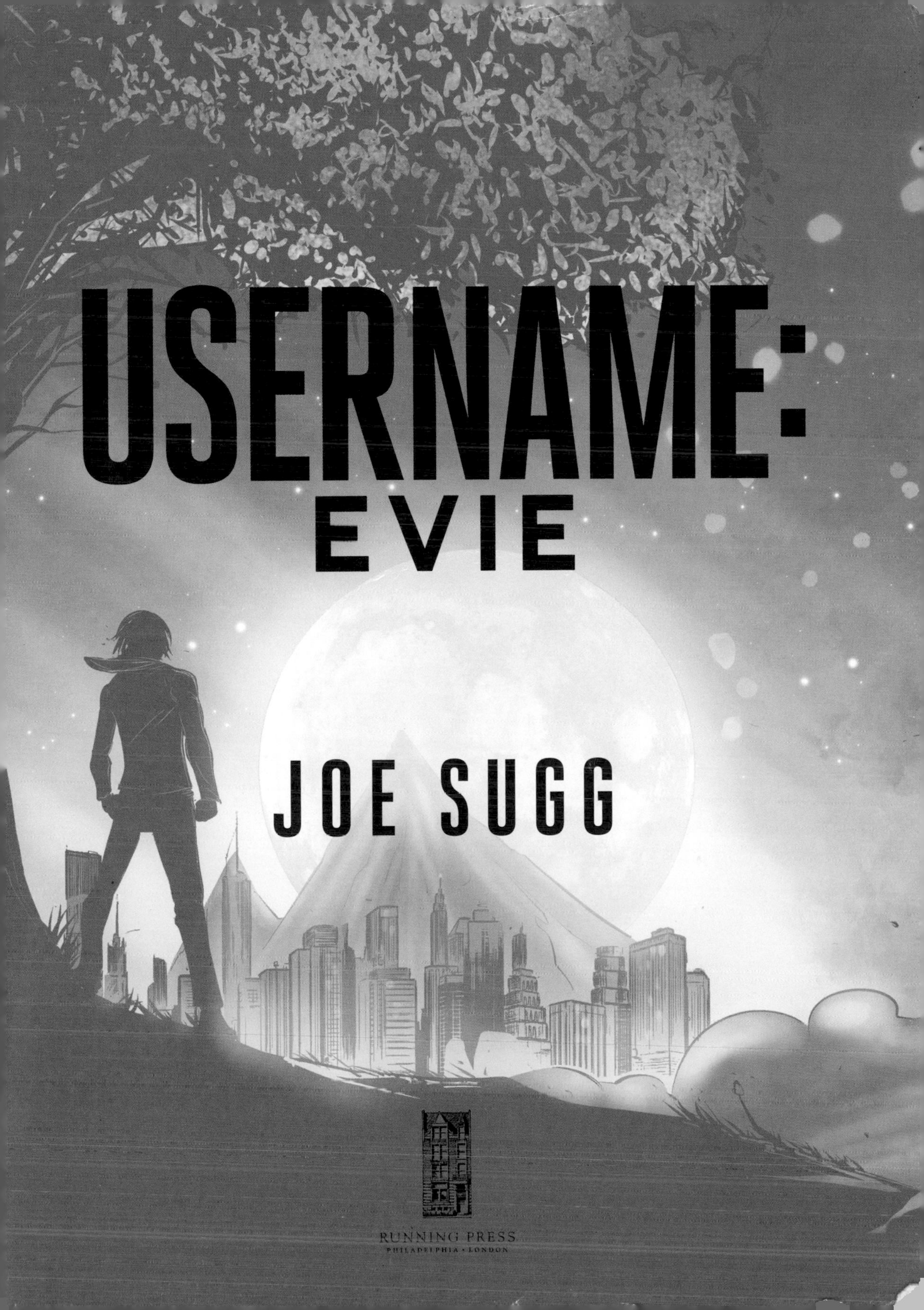

USERNAME: EVIE

JOE SUGG

RUNNING PRESS
PHILADELPHIA • LONDON

First published in the UK in 2015 by Hodder & Stoughton a member of the Hachette Book Group
First published in the United States in 2015 by Running Press Book Publishers
A Member of the Perseus Books Group

Printed in the United States

ISBN 978-0-7624-6010-6

Library of Congress Control Number: 2015946625
E-book ISBN 978-0-7624-6011-3

9 8 7 6 5 4
Digit on the right indicates the number of this printing

Artwork by Amrit Birdi
Colorist: Joaquin Pereyra
Letterist: Mindy Lopkin

Running Press Book Publishers
2300 Chestnut Street
Philadelphia, PA 19103-4371

Visit us on the web!
www.runningpress.com

HELLO THERE

MY NAME IS JOE SUGG, OTHERWISE KNOWN AS THATCHERJOE ON YOUTUBE.

FIRST OFF, I'D JUST LIKE TO SAY A MASSIVE THANK YOU FOR CHOOSING TO BUY MY FIRST EVER GRAPHIC NOVEL — MY FIRST EVER BOOK, IN FACT! I AM SO FLIPPIN' PLEASED WITH IT AND I HOPE YOU WILL BE TOO.

YOU MIGHT BE WONDERING WHERE THE INSPIRATION CAME FROM TO CREATE A GRAPHIC NOVEL. WELL, IT GOES RIGHT BACK TO GROWING UP OBSESSED WITH COMICS LIKE *THE BEANO* AND *THE DANDY* — I STILL HAVE ALL MY OLD COPIES CLOGGING UP THE ATTIC BACK HOME... SORRY, DAD. FAST-FORWARD TO 16-YEAR-OLD SUGG IN SIXTH FORM AT CORSHAM SCHOOL BEING SET A MEDIA STUDIES ASSIGNMENT TO CREATE A TRAILER FOR AN APOCALYPTIC/DYSTOPIAN FILM. NOW, NORMALLY I WAS THE SORT OF KID IN SCHOOL WHO LEFT HIS HOMEWORK UNTIL THE LAST MINUTE. BUT THIS PROJECT WAS EXACTLY THE KIND OF THING I WAS INTERESTED IN AND FOR THE FIRST TIME IN MY LIFE NOT ONLY DID I DO THE HOMEWORK THE DAY IT WAS SET, I ACTUALLY DID EXTRA WORK IN MY SPARE TIME! AS IT HAPPENS, ONE OF MY MEDIA STUDIES TEACHERS LENT ME A WELL-KNOWN GRAPHIC NOVEL AND I WAS INSPIRED TO CREATE MY OWN GRAPHIC NOVEL TO ACCOMPANY THE TRAILER. SEE, STARTING TO MAKE SENSE, RIGHT?

AS MANY OF YOU WILL KNOW, AFTER I'D COMPLETED MY A-LEVELS I DECIDED TO DO AN APPRENTICESHIP AS A ROOF THATCHER WITH MY UNCLE GARY. I LOVED IT (EXCEPT FOR THE FROSTY MORNINGS) AND HAVE ALWAYS SAID IT'S GOOD TO KNOW I HAVE A FALL-BACK CAREER AND TRADE, BUT AT THE TIME I FELT I NEEDED TO FIND OTHER WAYS TO CHANNEL MY CREATIVITY. AROUND THE SAME TIME MY SISTER,

ZOE, HAD STARTED A YOUTUBE CHANNEL AND AFTER APPEARING IN A COUPLE OF HER VIDEOS, I DECIDED YOUTUBE WOULD BE THE PLACE TO PUT ALL THE CREATIVE STUFF I HAD INSIDE MY BRAIN.

THAT WAS BACK IN 2011 AND NOW — AS I SIT HERE WRITING THIS INTRODUCTION — I LIVE IN LONDON, AND TRYING TO MAKE PEOPLE LAUGH IN SHORT VIDEOS ON THE INTERNET IS MY FULL-TIME JOB — AMAZING! BEFORE I KNEW IT MY AUDIENCE GREW AND GREW AND NOW IT'S LARGER THAN I COULD HAVE EVER ANTICIPATED. THE SUCCESS OF MY CHANNEL HAS GIVEN ME SO MANY AMAZING OPPORTUNITIES, NOT LEAST ALLOWING ME TO CREATE MY OWN PIECE OF ART IN THE FORM OF THIS GRAPHIC NOVEL. I HONESTLY REMEMBER HAVING A MINI FLASHBACK AT THE START OF THIS PROCESS TO THE DAYS OF READING *THE BEANO*, AND LATER SPENDING HOURS ON SOME DODGY ILLUSTRATOR SOFTWARE TRYING TO CREATE A GRAPHIC NOVEL FRONT COVER FOR AN A-LEVEL MEDIA STUDIES PROJECT.

BUT, MORE IMPORTANT THAN ALL THAT STUFF YOU'VE JUST READ, THE BIGGEST INSPIRATION FOR THIS BOOK ARE THE AMAZING PEOPLE (YEP, THAT'S YOU) THAT TAKE TIME OUT OF THEIR DAY NOT JUST TO SUPPORT MY SILLY LITTLE VIDEOS, BUT TO SUPPORT ME IN EVERYTHING I DO. SO MANY OF THE THINGS YOU'LL SEE AND READ IN THE FOLLOWING PAGES ARE INSPIRED BY ISSUES THAT MY VIEWERS ARE HAVING, OR THINGS YOU'RE GOING THROUGH AND HAVE SHARED WITH ME.

SO, FINALLY, I'D LIKE TO SAY ENJOY THE ADVENTURE THAT IS *USERNAME: EVIE*, YOU'LL NEVER KNOW JUST HOW MUCH I APPRECIATE WHAT YOU'VE DONE FOR ME AND THIS IS A LITTLE SOMETHING FROM ME TO YOU — THIS ISN'T MY GRAPHIC NOVEL, IT'S OURS.

ALL THE BEST,

JOE

P.S. GUYS, UNDER *NO* CIRCUMSTANCES SHOULD YOU CLIMB INTO A FRIDGE, JUMP OFF A ROOFTOP, OR DO ANY OF THE OTHER DANGEROUS THINGS THAT EVIE DOES...

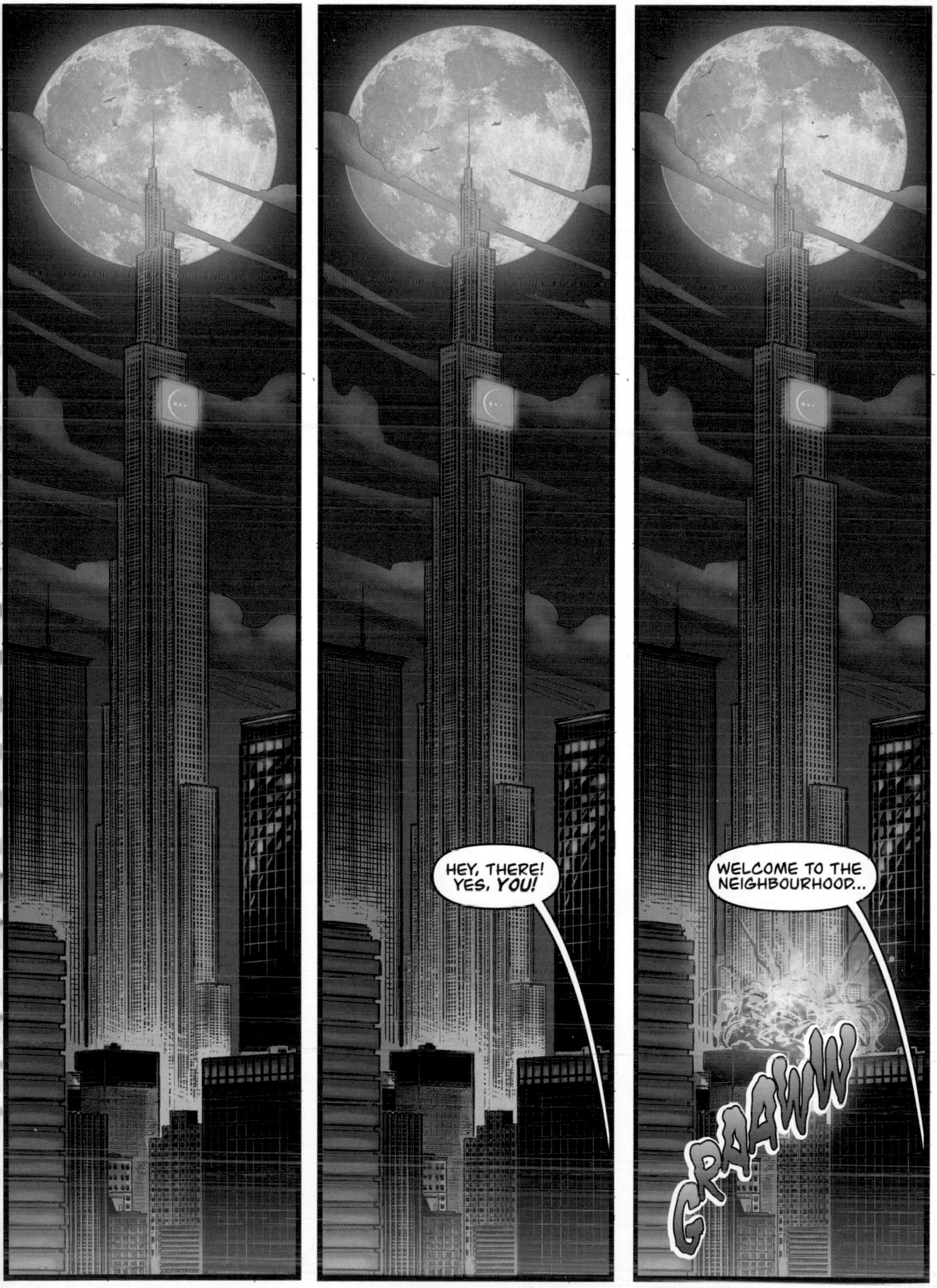
HEY, THERE! YES, YOU!
WELCOME TO THE NEIGHBOURHOOD...
GRAAWW

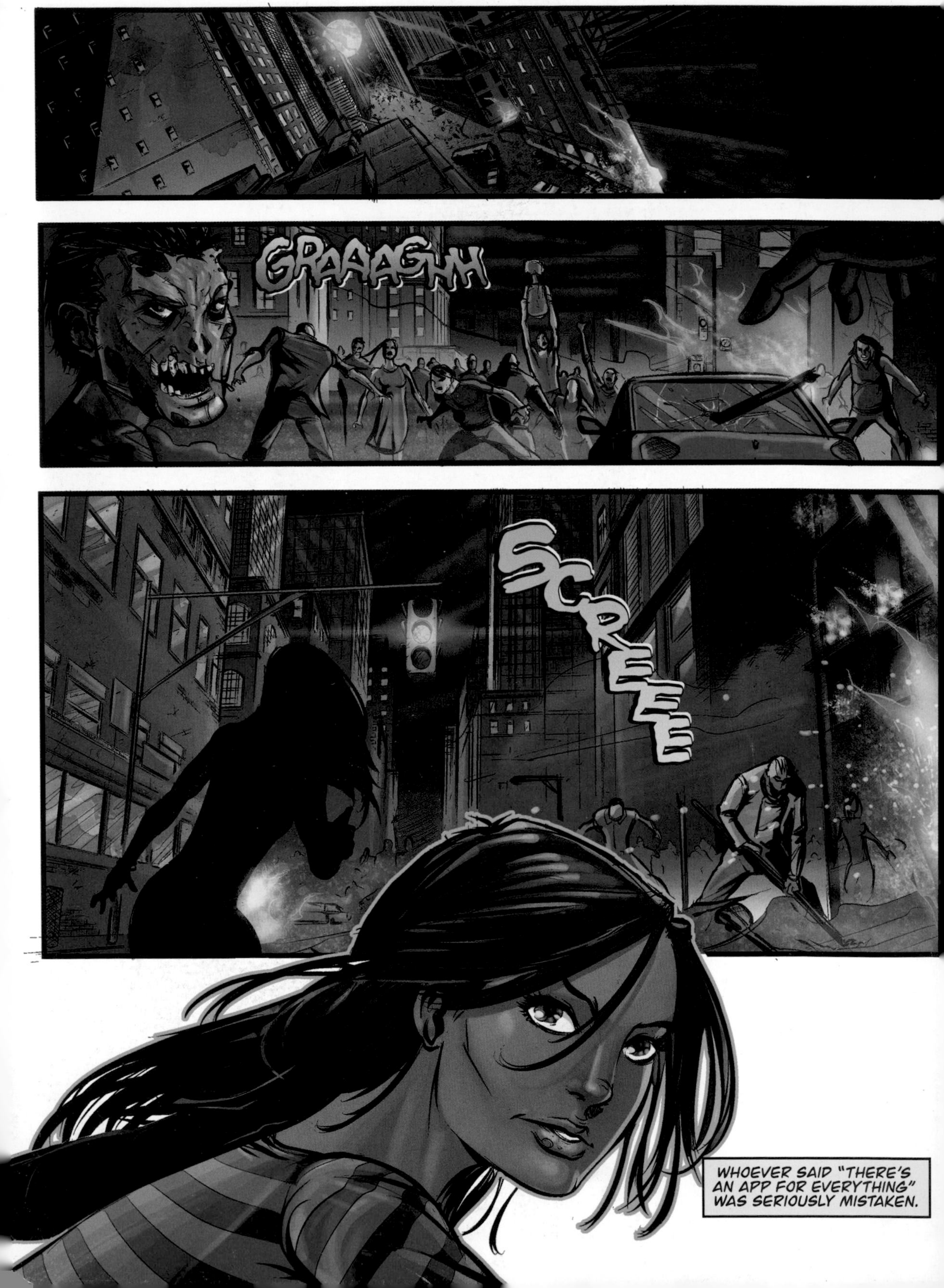
GRAAAGHH
SCREEEE
WHOEVER SAID "THERE'S AN APP FOR EVERYTHING" WAS SERIOUSLY MISTAKEN.

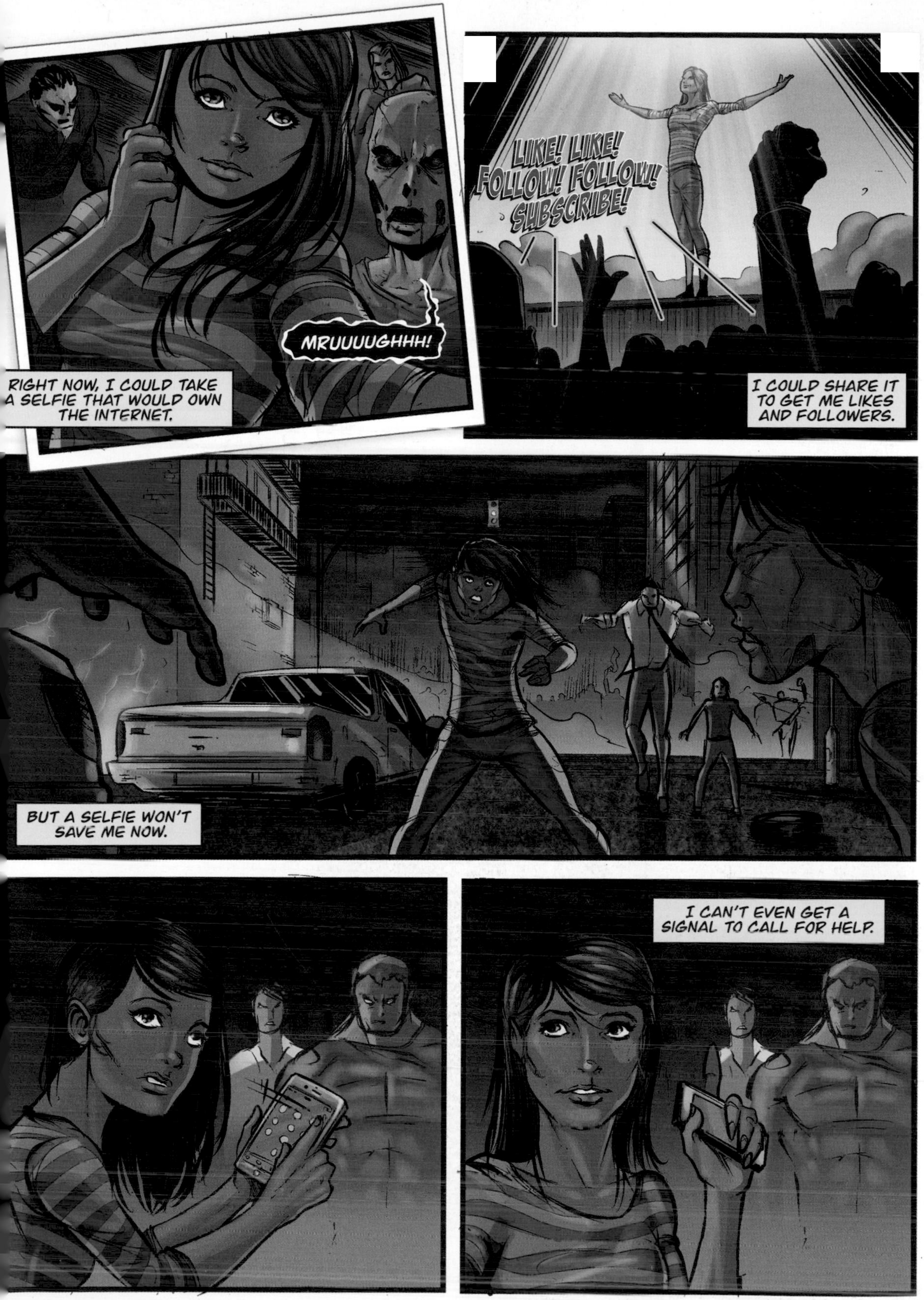
MRUUUUGHHH!
RIGHT NOW, I COULD TAKE A SELFIE THAT WOULD OWN THE INTERNET.
LIKE! LIKE! FOLLOW! FOLLOW! SUBSCRIBE!
I COULD SHARE IT TO GET ME LIKES AND FOLLOWERS.
BUT A SELFIE WON'T SAVE ME NOW.
I CAN'T EVEN GET A SIGNAL TO CALL FOR HELP.

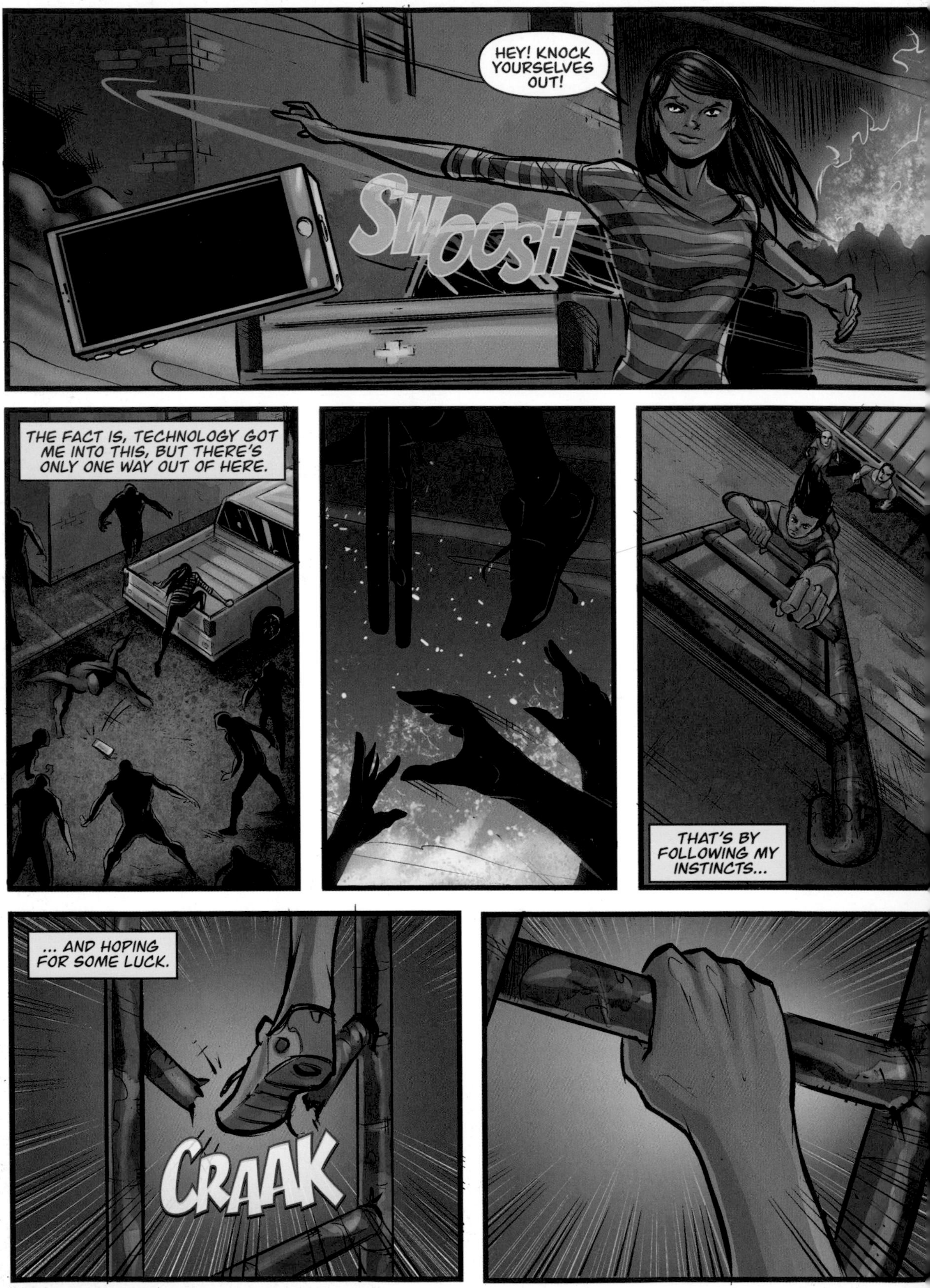
HEY! KNOCK YOURSELVES OUT!
SWOOSH
THE FACT IS, TECHNOLOGY GOT ME INTO THIS, BUT THERE'S ONLY ONE WAY OUT OF HERE.
THAT'S BY FOLLOWING MY INSTINCTS...
... AND HOPING FOR SOME LUCK.
CRAAK

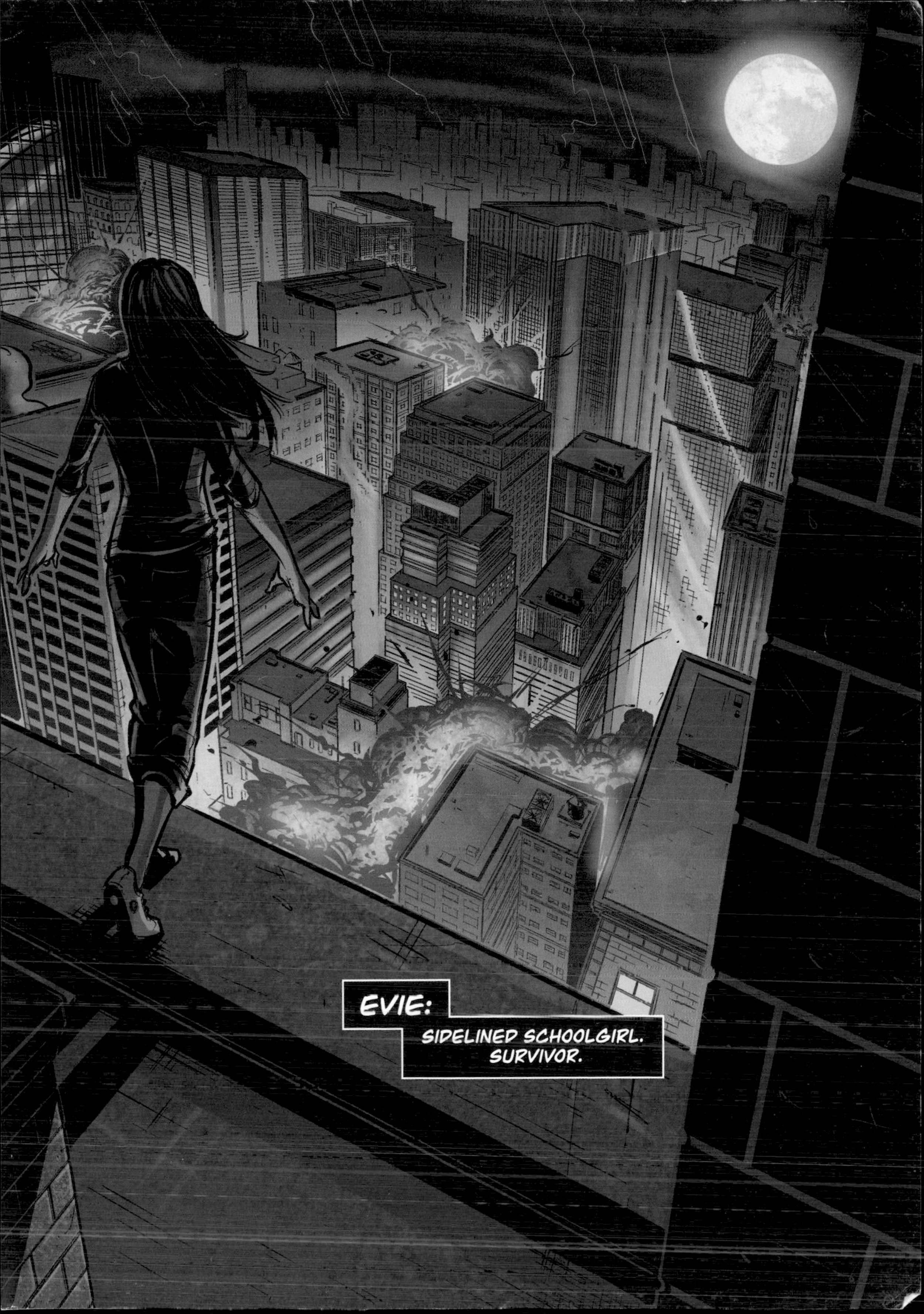
EVIE:
SIDELINED SCHOOLGIRL.
SURVIVOR.

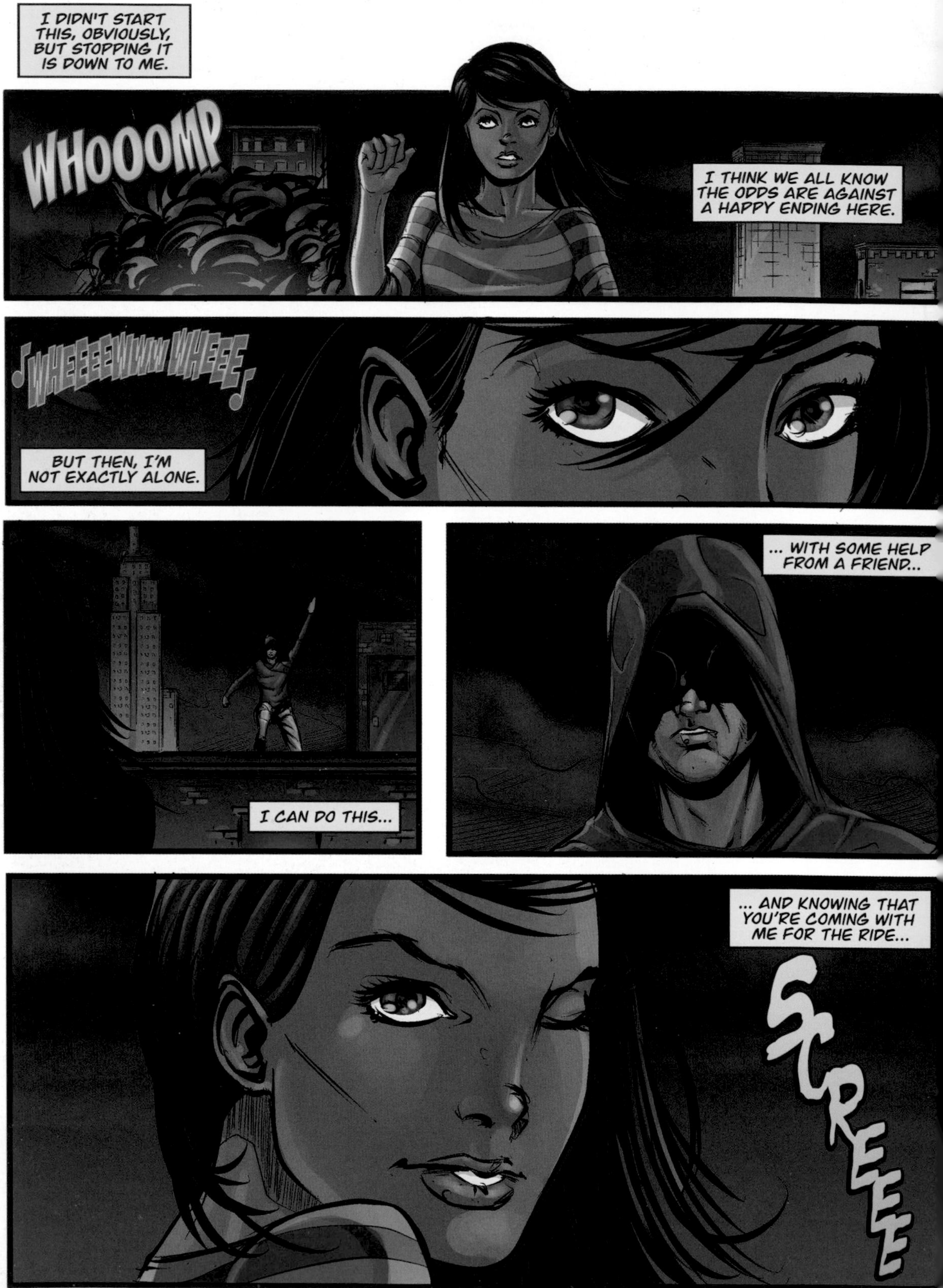
I DIDN'T START THIS, OBVIOUSLY, BUT STOPPING IT IS DOWN TO ME.
WHOOOMP
I THINK WE ALL KNOW THE ODDS ARE AGAINST A HAPPY ENDING HERE.
WHEEEEWWW WHEEE
BUT THEN, I'M NOT EXACTLY ALONE.
I CAN DO THIS...
... WITH SOME HELP FROM A FRIEND...
... AND KNOWING THAT YOU'RE COMING WITH ME FOR THE RIDE...
SCREEEE

HURRY! THEY'RE COMING!
GRAAAAGHH
SO FOR NOW, LET'S NOT RELY ON PHONES OR APPS...
... AND INSTEAD TAKE A LEAP OF FAITH.
IN CASE I COME TO A HORRIBLE END HERE, GUYS, YOU SHOULD KNOW HOW IT ALL BEGAN...

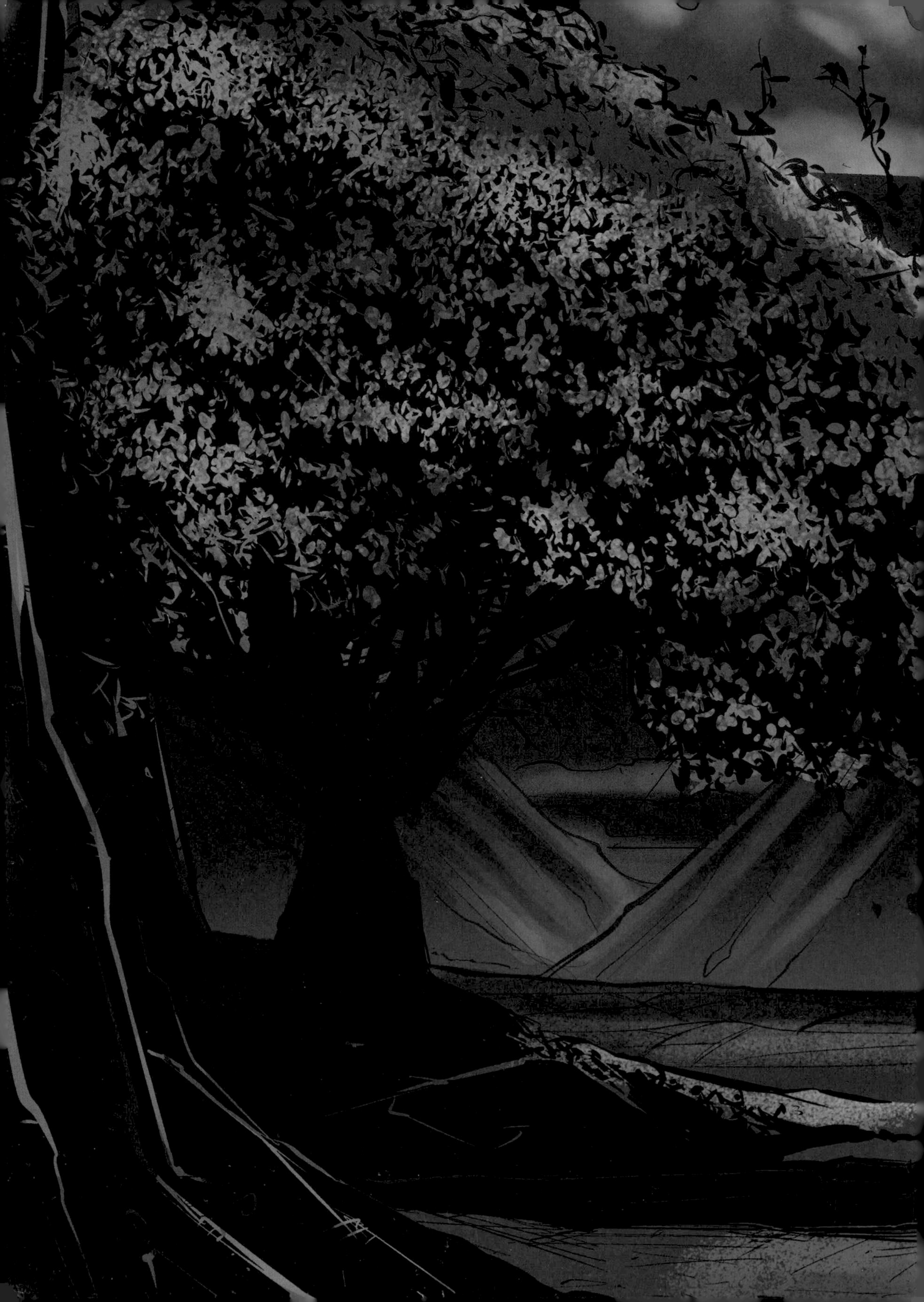

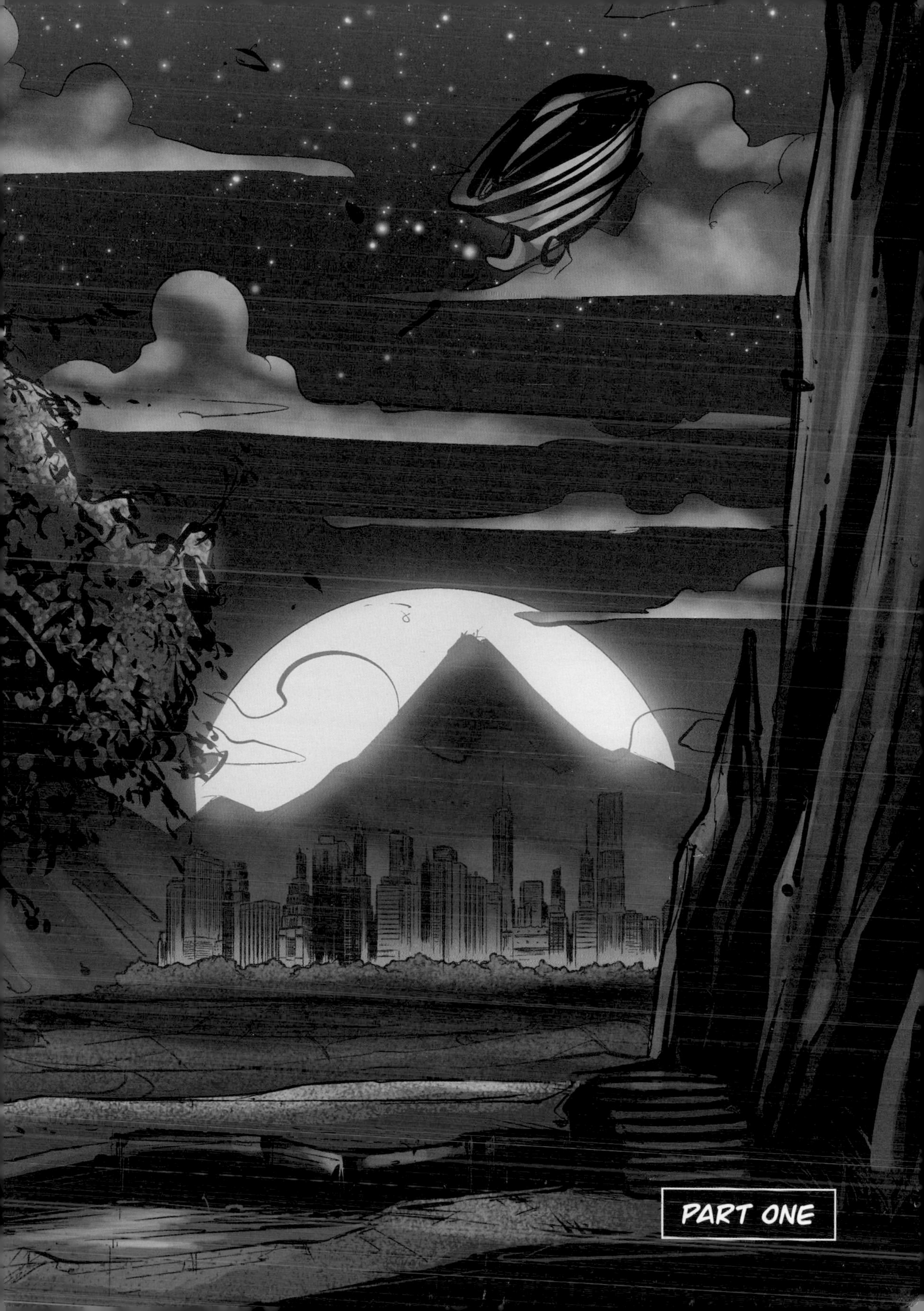
PART ONE

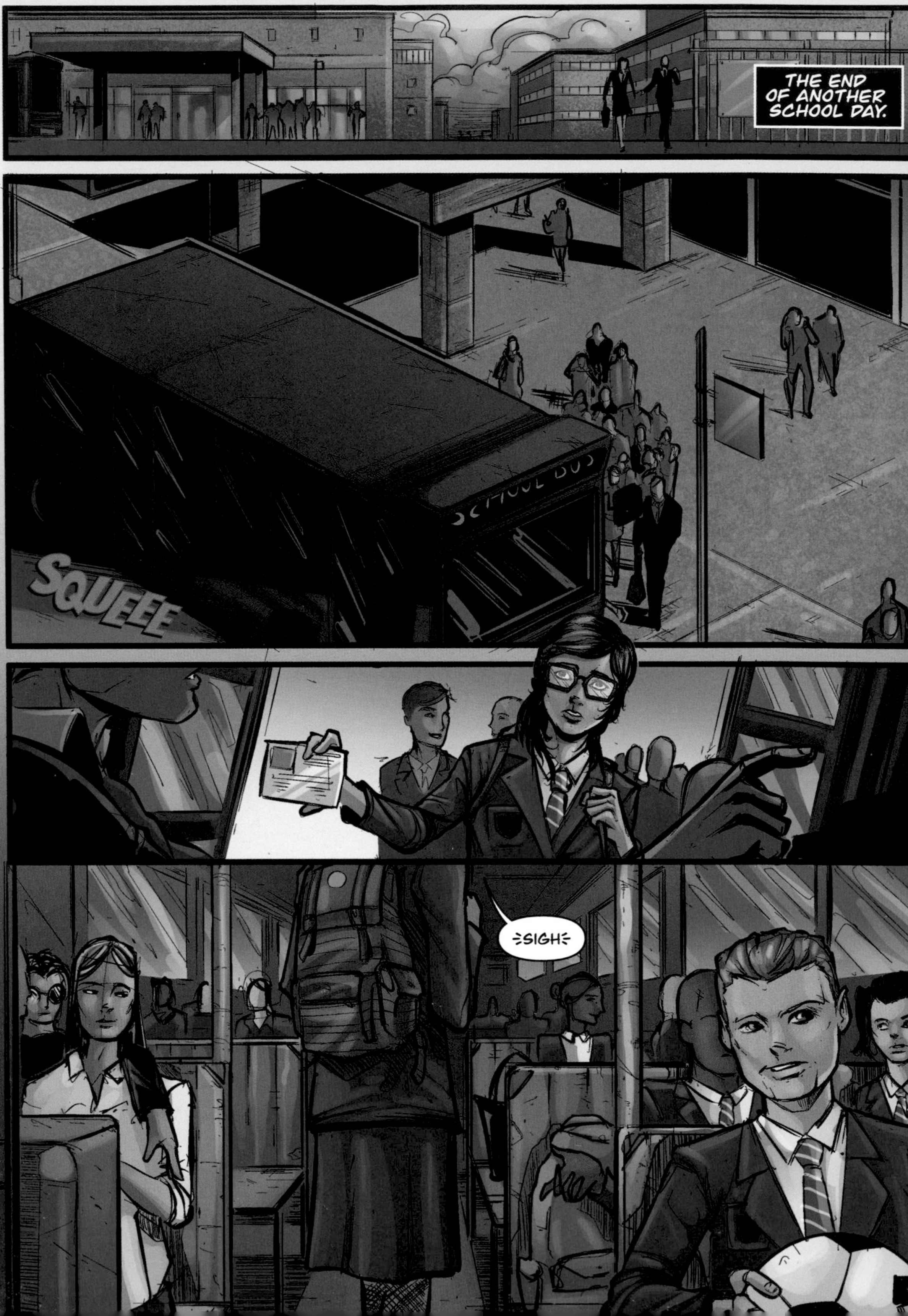
THE END OF ANOTHER SCHOOL DAY.
SQUEEE
SIGH

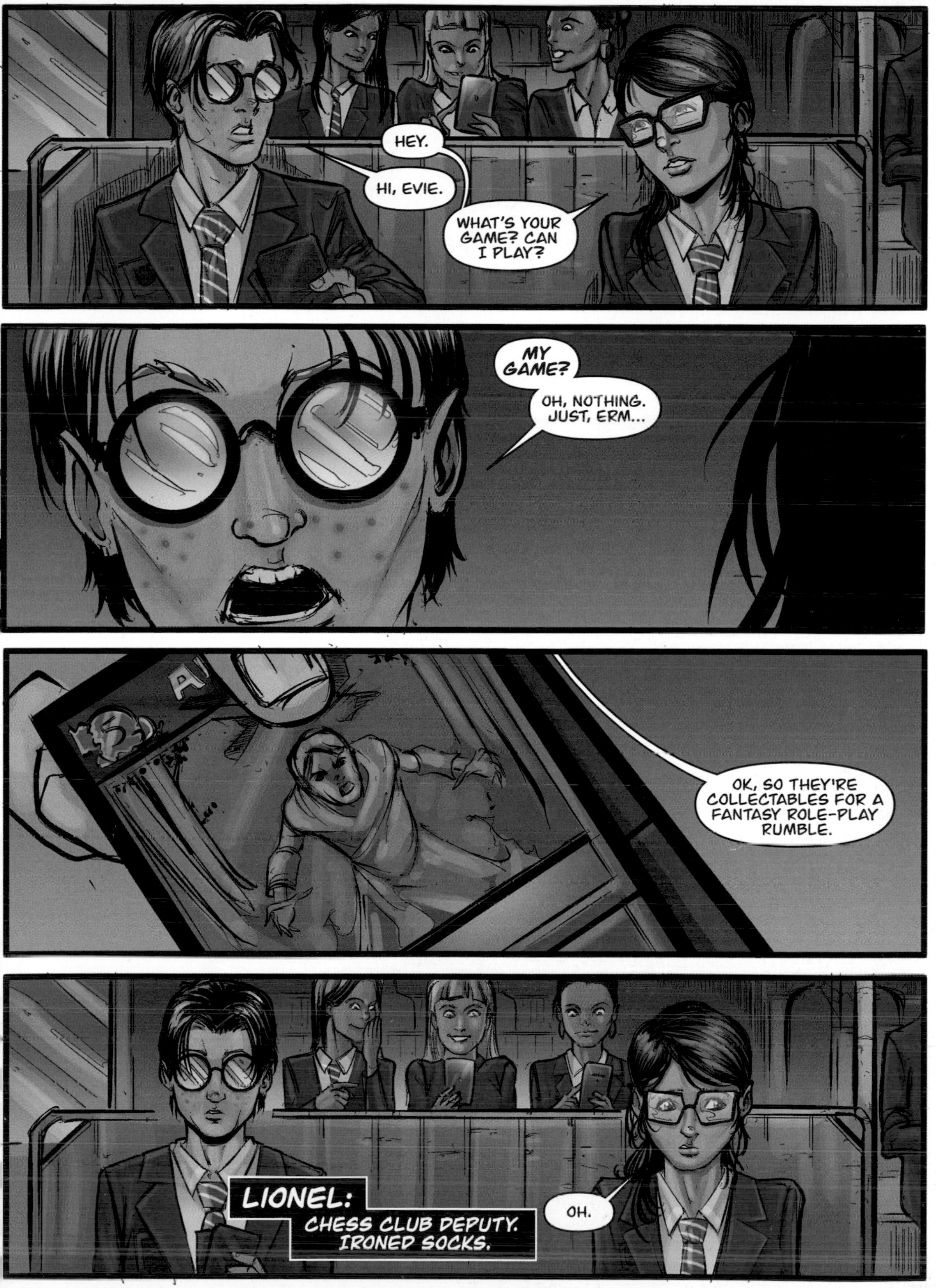
HEY.
HI, EVIE.
WHAT'S YOUR GAME? CAN I PLAY?
MY GAME?
OH, NOTHING. JUST, ERM...
OK, SO THEY'RE COLLECTABLES FOR A FANTASY ROLE-PLAY RUMBLE.
LIONEL:
CHESS CLUB DEPUTY. IRONED SOCKS.
OH.

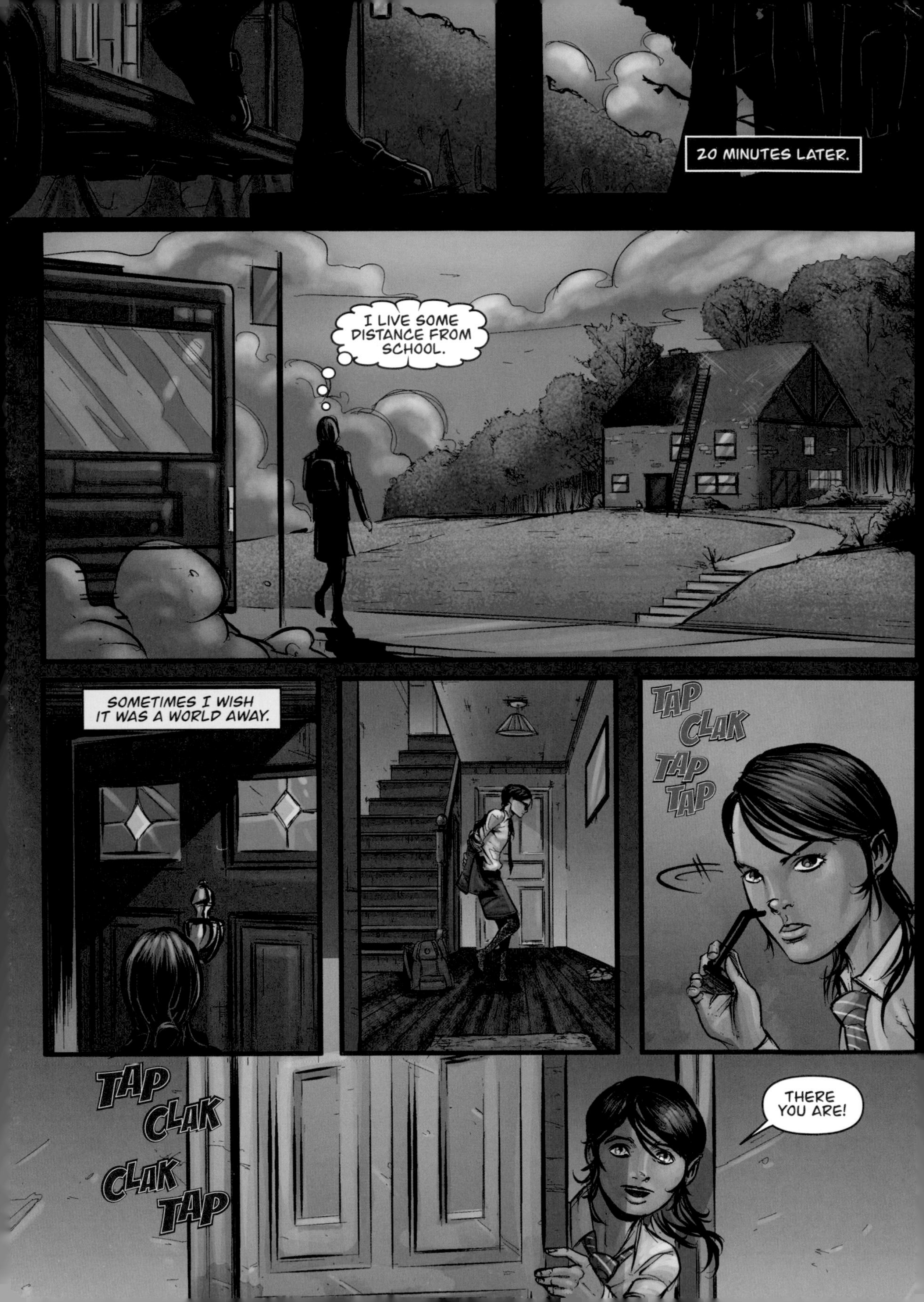
20 MINUTES LATER.
I LIVE SOME DISTANCE FROM SCHOOL.
SOMETIMES I WISH IT WAS A WORLD AWAY.
TAP CLAK TAP TAP
TAP CLAK CLAK TAP
THERE YOU ARE!

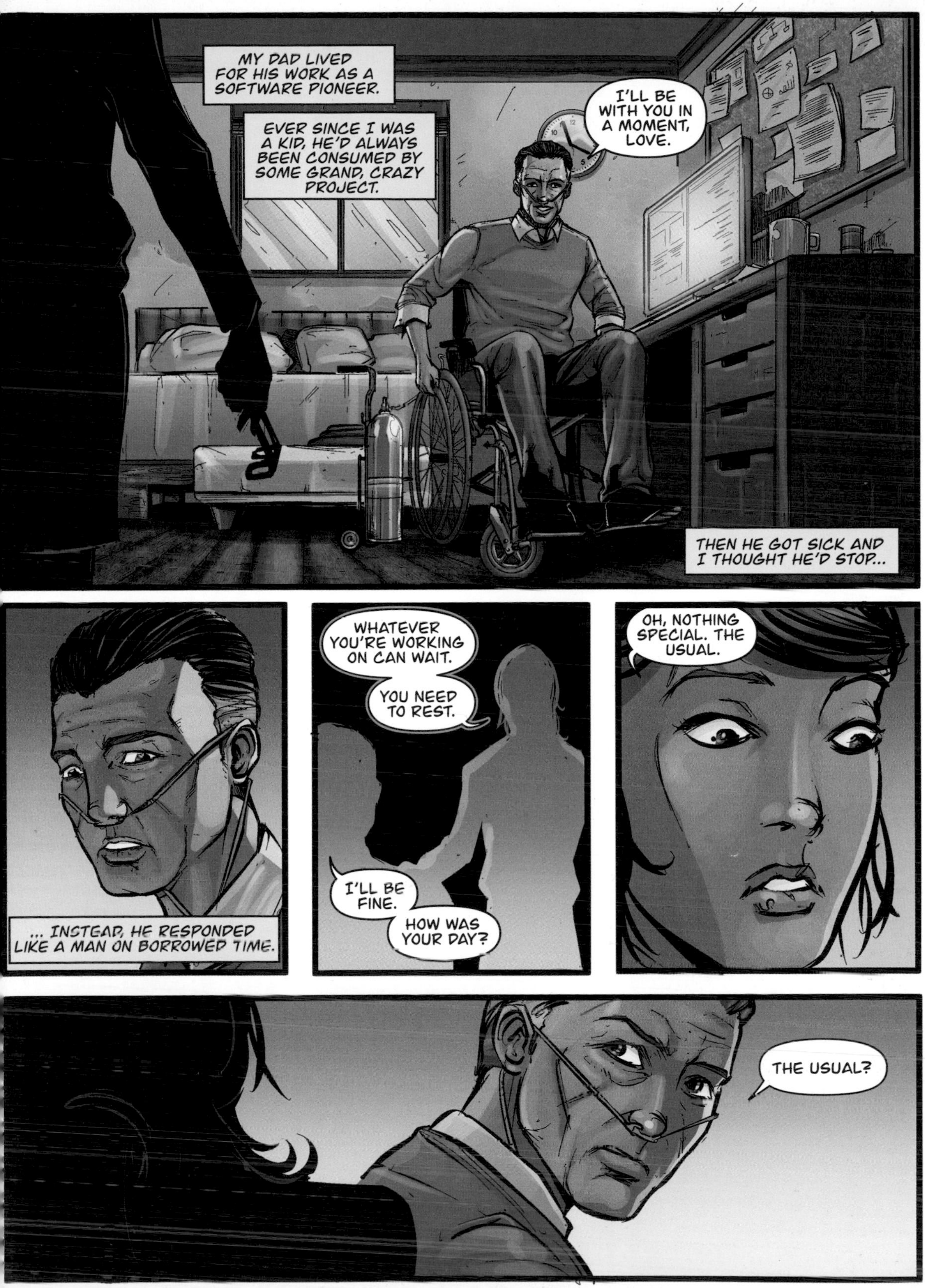
MY DAD LIVED FOR HIS WORK AS A SOFTWARE PIONEER.
EVER SINCE I WAS A KID, HE'D ALWAYS BEEN CONSUMED BY SOME GRAND, CRAZY PROJECT.
I'LL BE WITH YOU IN A MOMENT, LOVE.
THEN HE GOT SICK AND I THOUGHT HE'D STOP...
... INSTEAD, HE RESPONDED LIKE A MAN ON BORROWED TIME.
WHATEVER YOU'RE WORKING ON CAN WAIT.
YOU NEED TO REST.
I'LL BE FINE.
HOW WAS YOUR DAY?
OH, NOTHING SPECIAL. THE USUAL.
THE USUAL?

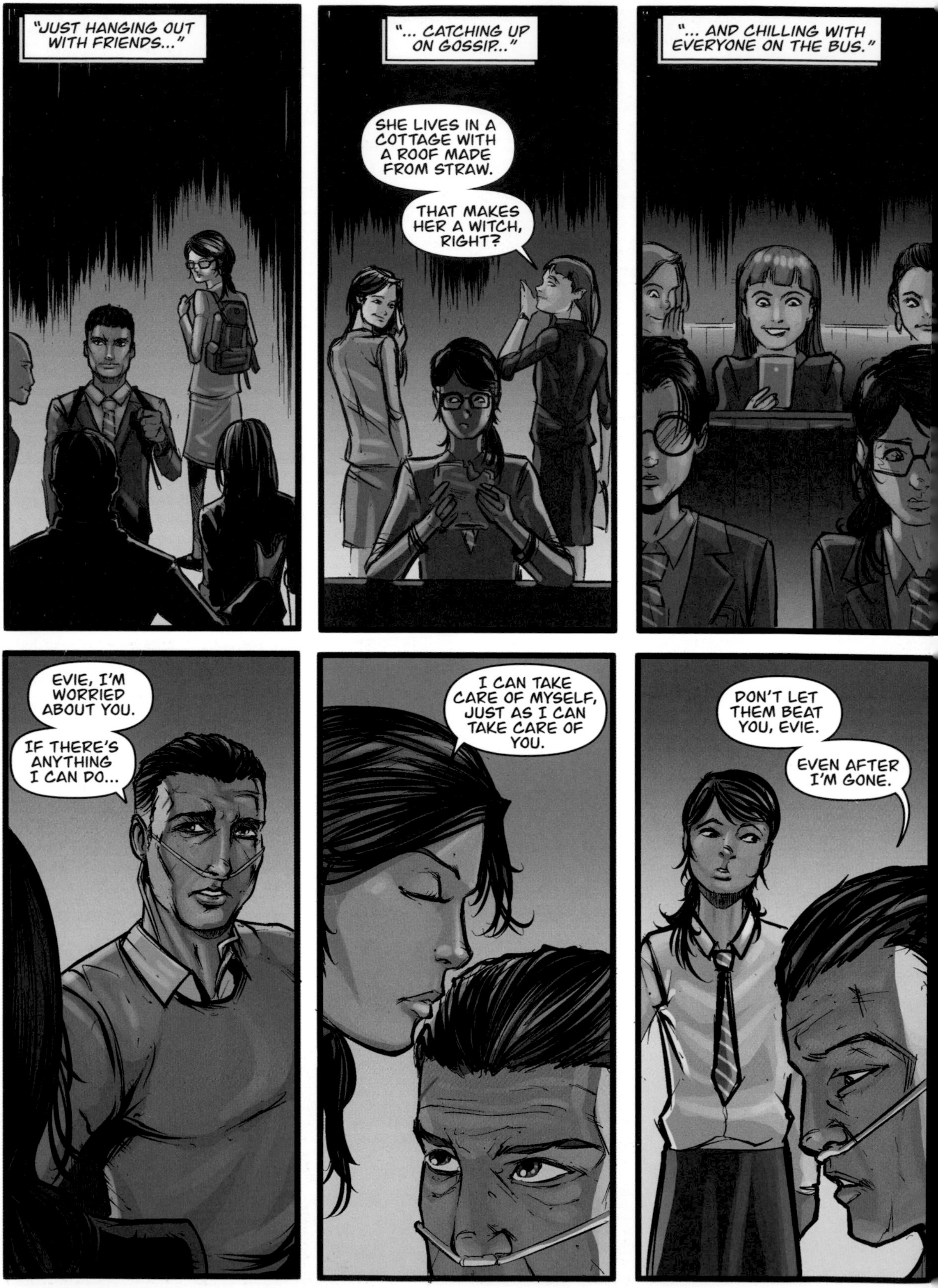
"JUST HANGING OUT WITH FRIENDS..."
"... CATCHING UP ON GOSSIP..."
SHE LIVES IN A COTTAGE WITH A ROOF MADE FROM STRAW.
THAT MAKES HER A WITCH, RIGHT?
"... AND CHILLING WITH EVERYONE ON THE BUS."
EVIE, I'M WORRIED ABOUT YOU.
IF THERE'S ANYTHING I CAN DO...
I CAN TAKE CARE OF MYSELF, JUST AS I CAN TAKE CARE OF YOU.
DON'T LET THEM BEAT YOU, EVIE.
EVEN AFTER I'M GONE.

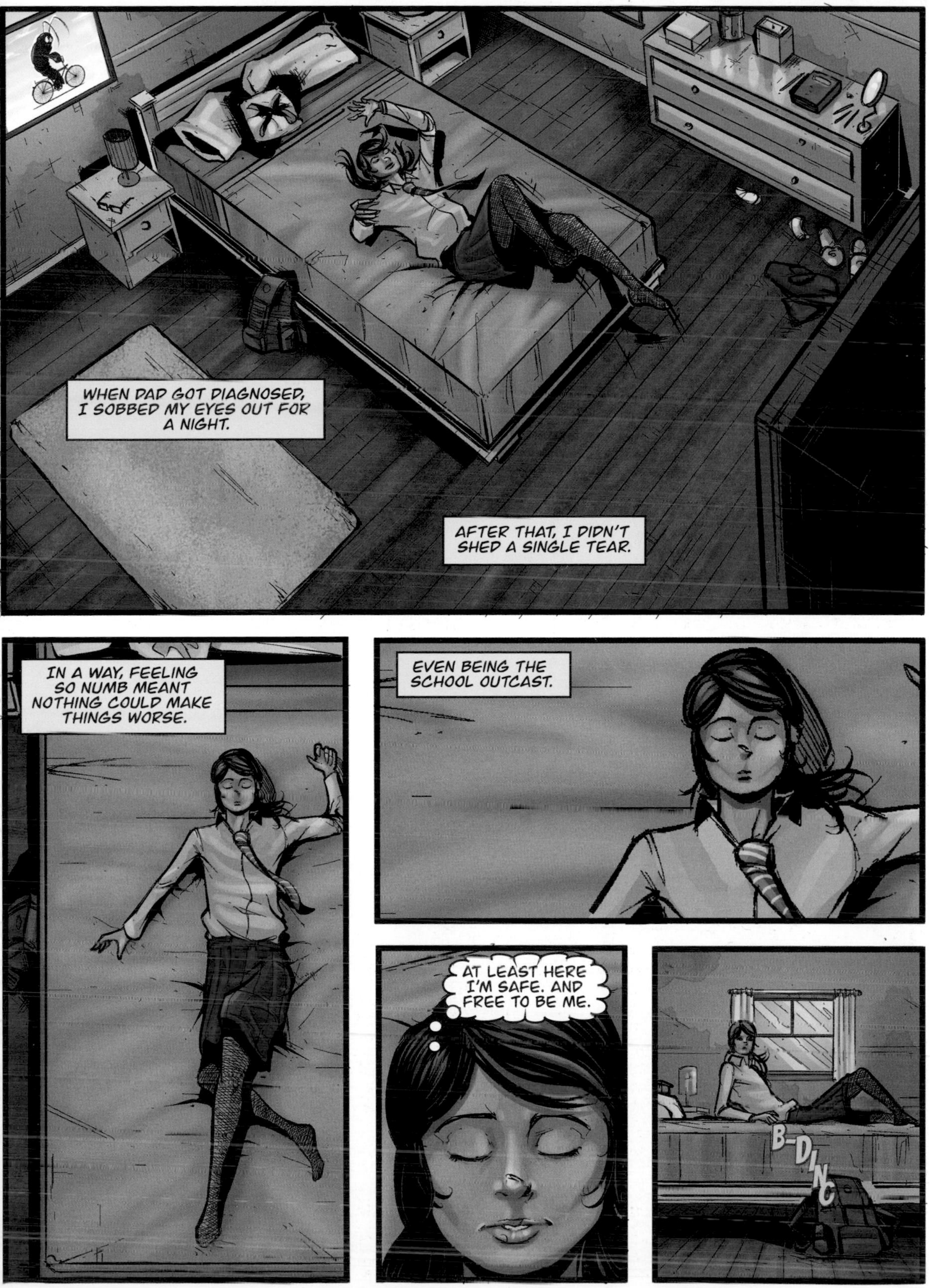

WHEN DAD GOT DIAGNOSED, I SOBBED MY EYES OUT FOR A NIGHT.
AFTER THAT, I DIDN'T SHED A SINGLE TEAR.
IN A WAY, FEELING SO NUMB MEANT NOTHING COULD MAKE THINGS WORSE.
EVEN BEING THE SCHOOL OUTCAST.
AT LEAST HERE I'M SAFE. AND FREE TO BE ME.
B-DING

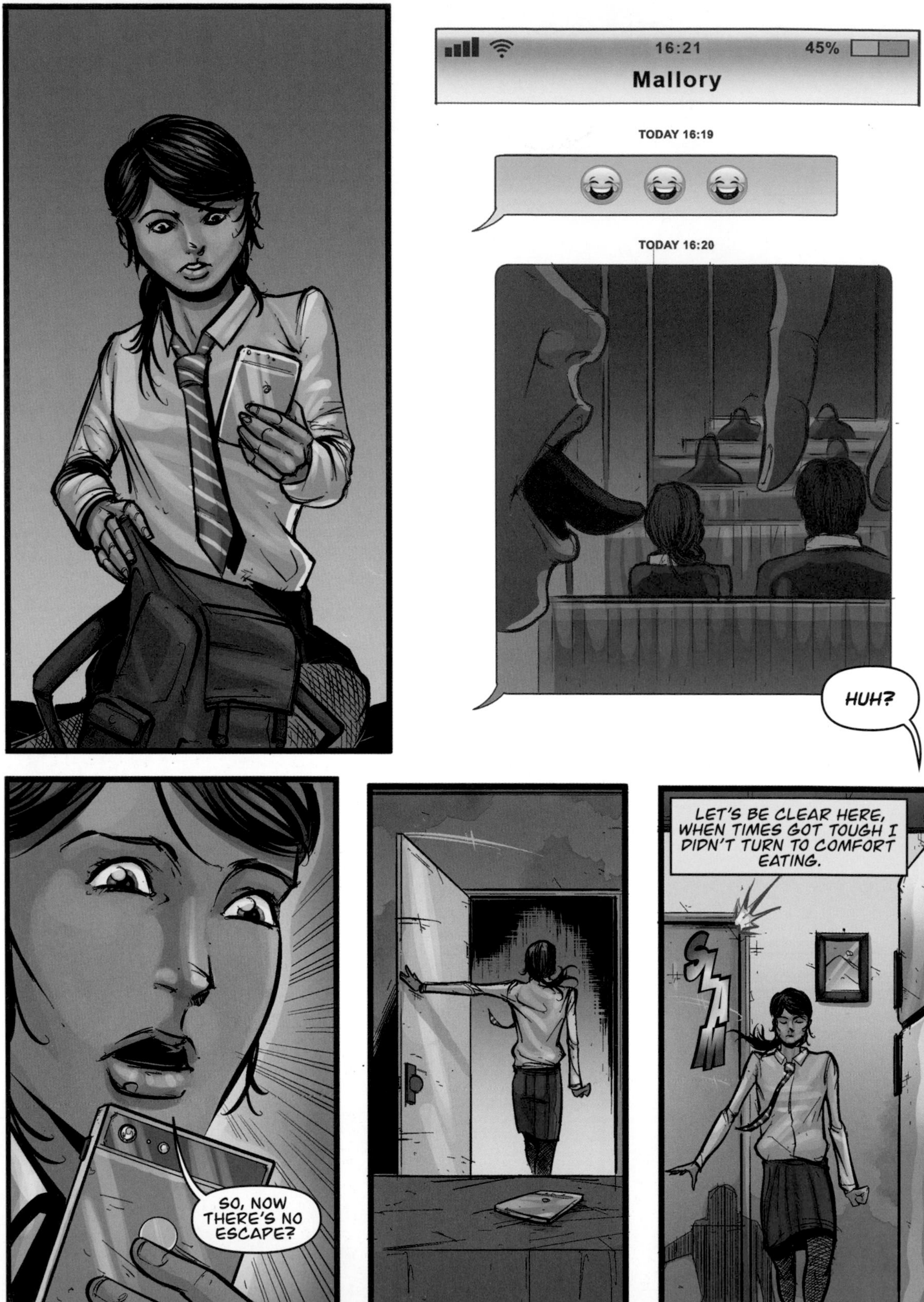
16:21
45%
Mallory
TODAY 16:19
TODAY 16:20
HUH?
SO, NOW THERE'S NO ESCAPE?
LET'S BE CLEAR HERE, WHEN TIMES GOT TOUGH I DIDN'T TURN TO COMFORT EATING.

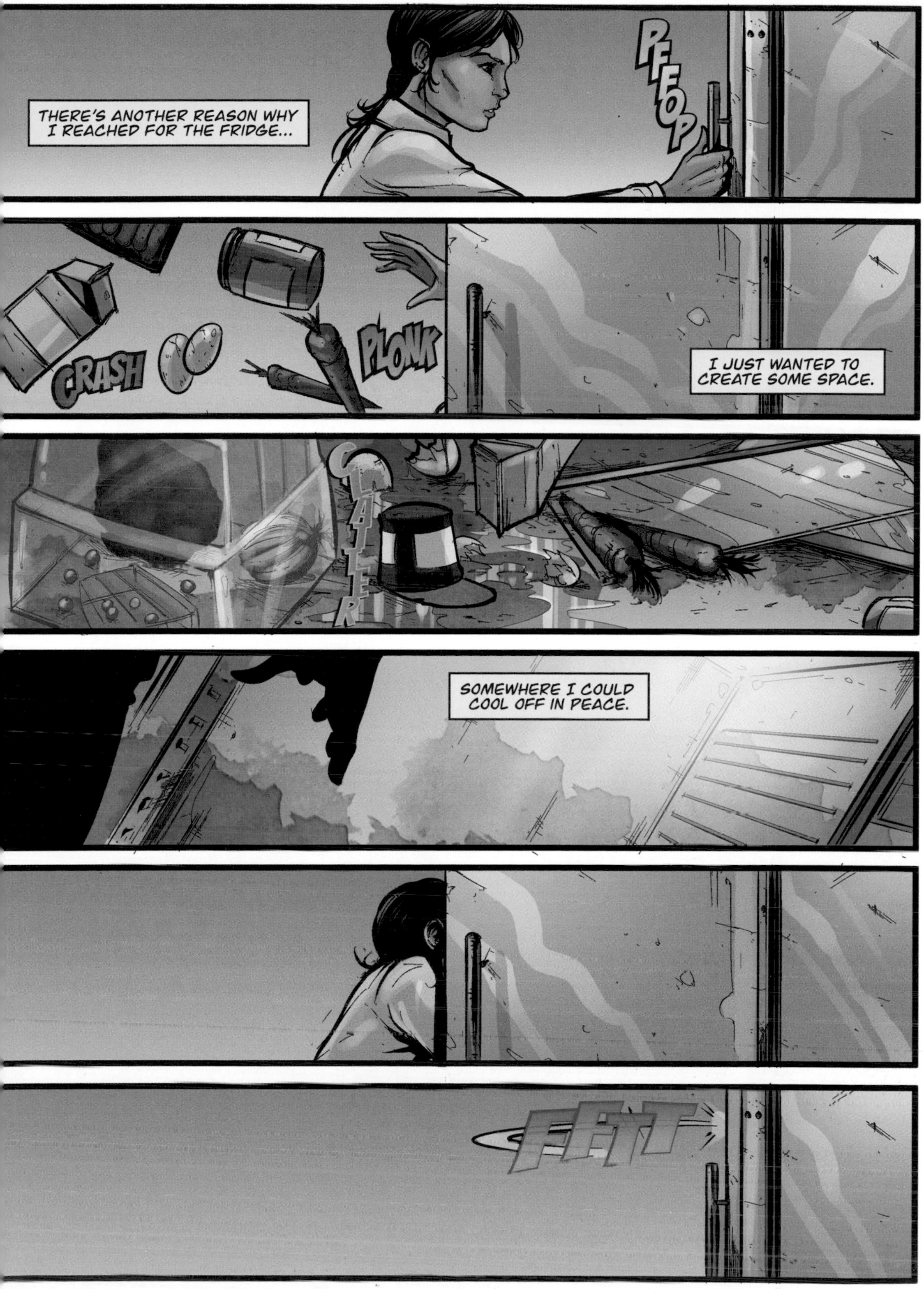
THERE'S ANOTHER REASON WHY I REACHED FOR THE FRIDGE...
PFFOP
CRASH
PLONK
I JUST WANTED TO CREATE SOME SPACE.
CLATTER
SOMEWHERE I COULD COOL OFF IN PEACE.
FFTT

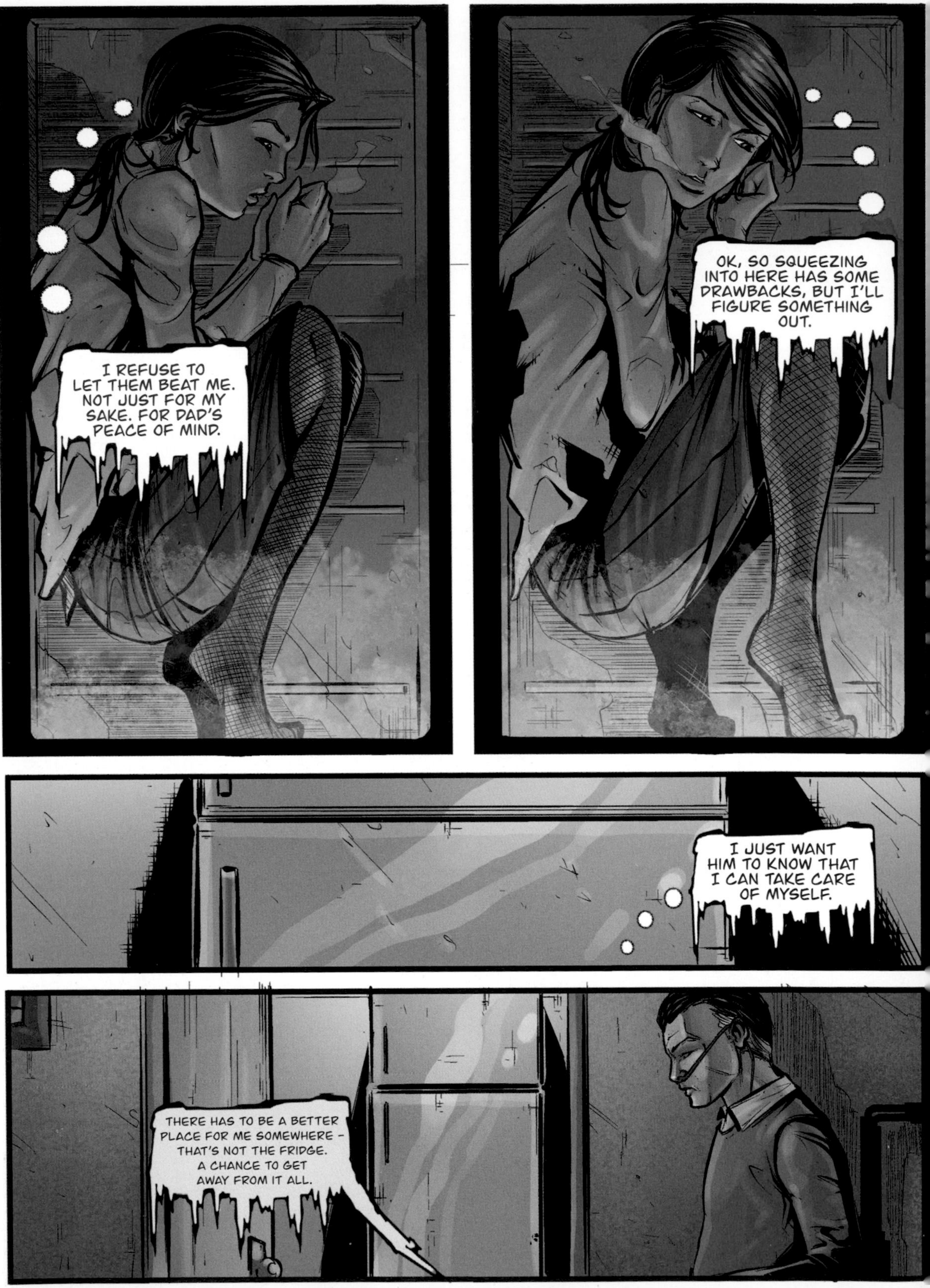
I REFUSE TO LET THEM BEAT ME. NOT JUST FOR MY SAKE. FOR DAD'S PEACE OF MIND.
OK, SO SQUEEZING INTO HERE HAS SOME DRAWBACKS, BUT I'LL FIGURE SOMETHING OUT.
I JUST WANT HIM TO KNOW THAT I CAN TAKE CARE OF MYSELF.
THERE HAS TO BE A BETTER PLACE FOR ME SOMEWHERE - THAT'S NOT THE FRIDGE. A CHANCE TO GET AWAY FROM IT ALL.

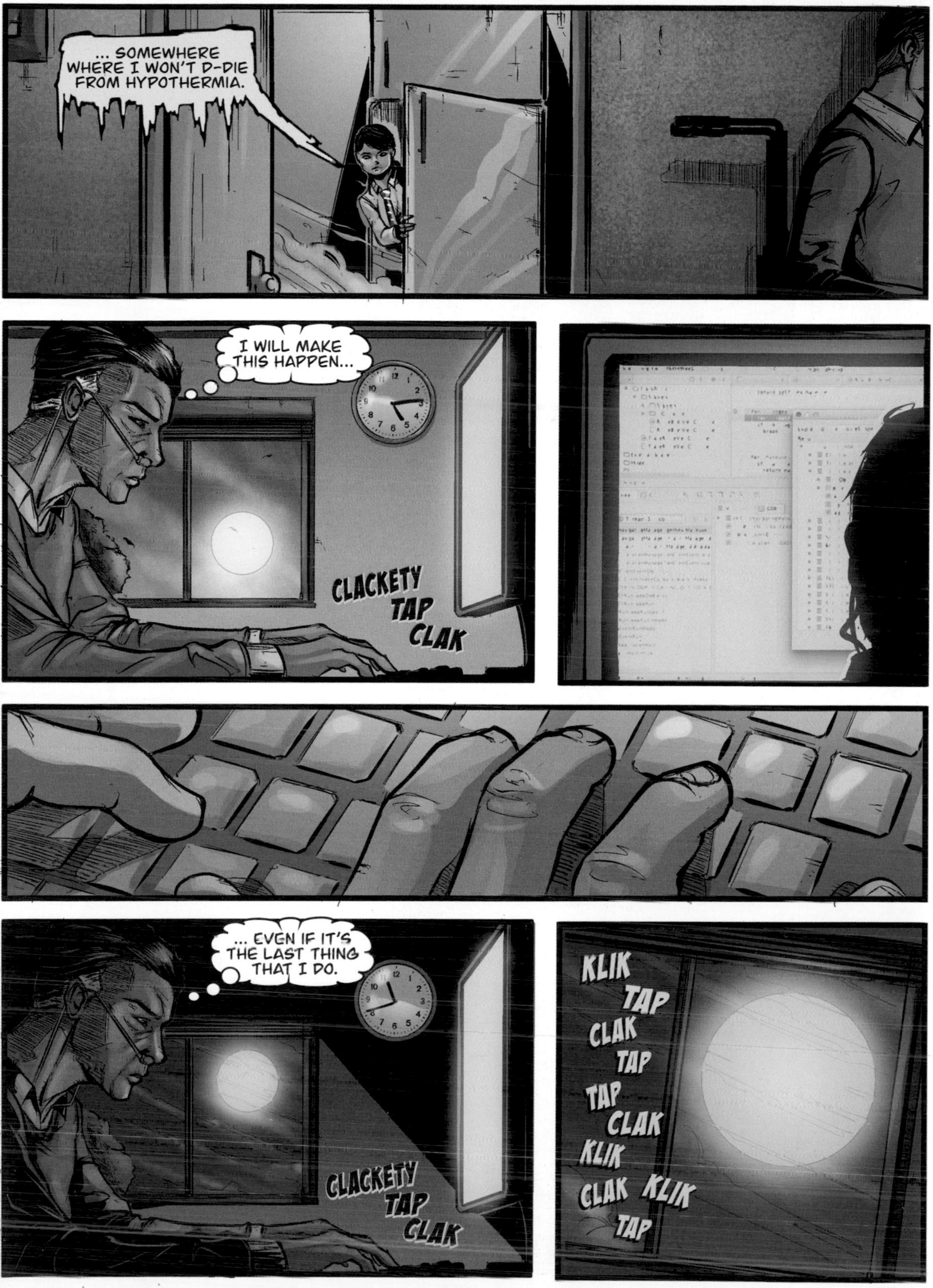
... SOMEWHERE WHERE I WON'T D-DIE FROM HYPOTHERMIA.
I WILL MAKE THIS HAPPEN...
CLACKETY TAP CLAK
... EVEN IF IT'S THE LAST THING THAT I DO.
CLACKETY TAP CLAK
KLIK TAP CLAK TAP TAP CLAK KLIK CLAK KLIK TAP

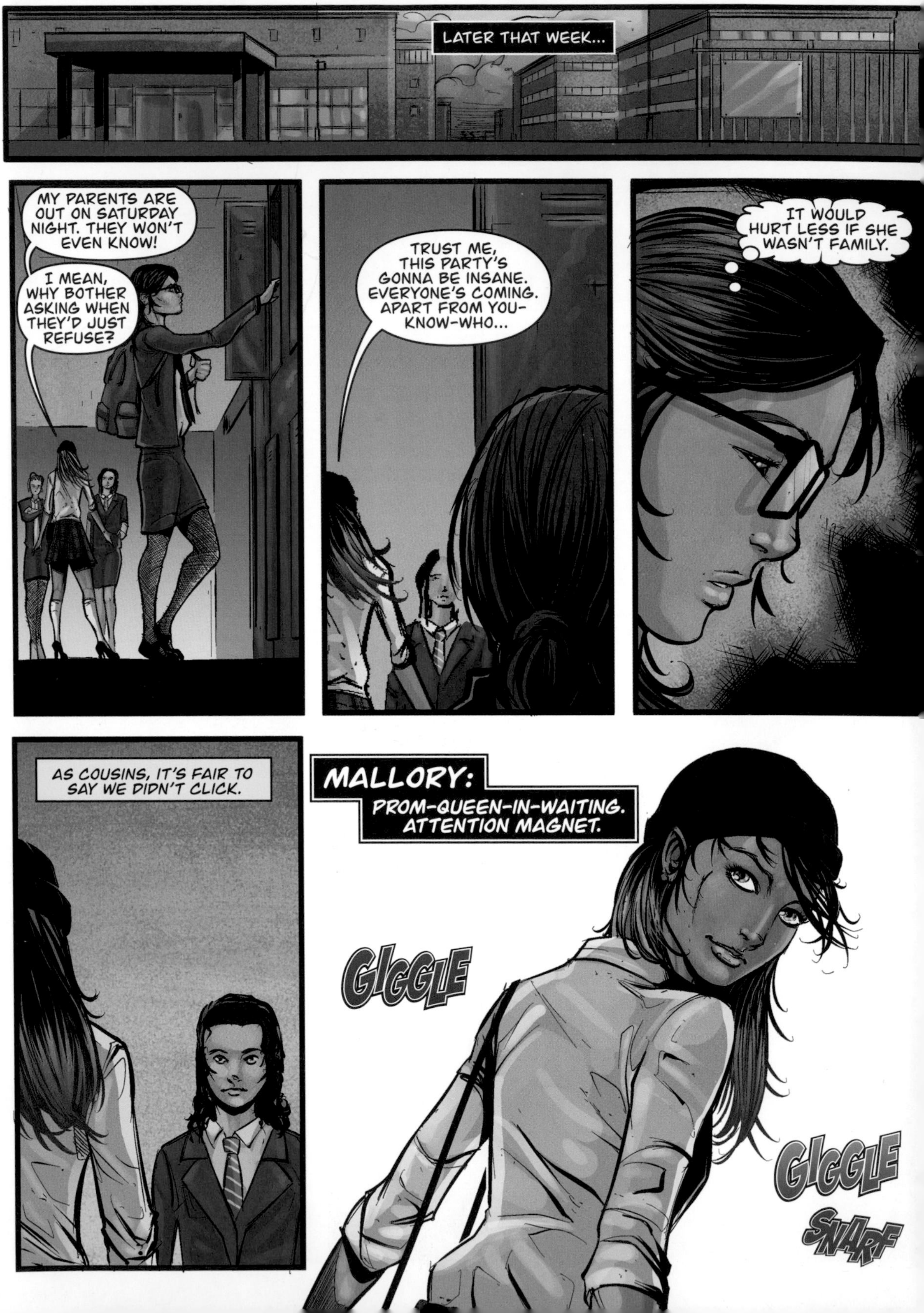
LATER THAT WEEK...
MY PARENTS ARE OUT ON SATURDAY NIGHT. THEY WON'T EVEN KNOW!
I MEAN, WHY BOTHER ASKING WHEN THEY'D JUST REFUSE?
TRUST ME, THIS PARTY'S GONNA BE INSANE. EVERYONE'S COMING. APART FROM YOU-KNOW-WHO...
IT WOULD HURT LESS IF SHE WASN'T FAMILY.
AS COUSINS, IT'S FAIR TO SAY WE DIDN'T CLICK.
MALLORY:
PROM-QUEEN-IN-WAITING. ATTENTION MAGNET.
GIGGLE
GIGGLE
SNARF

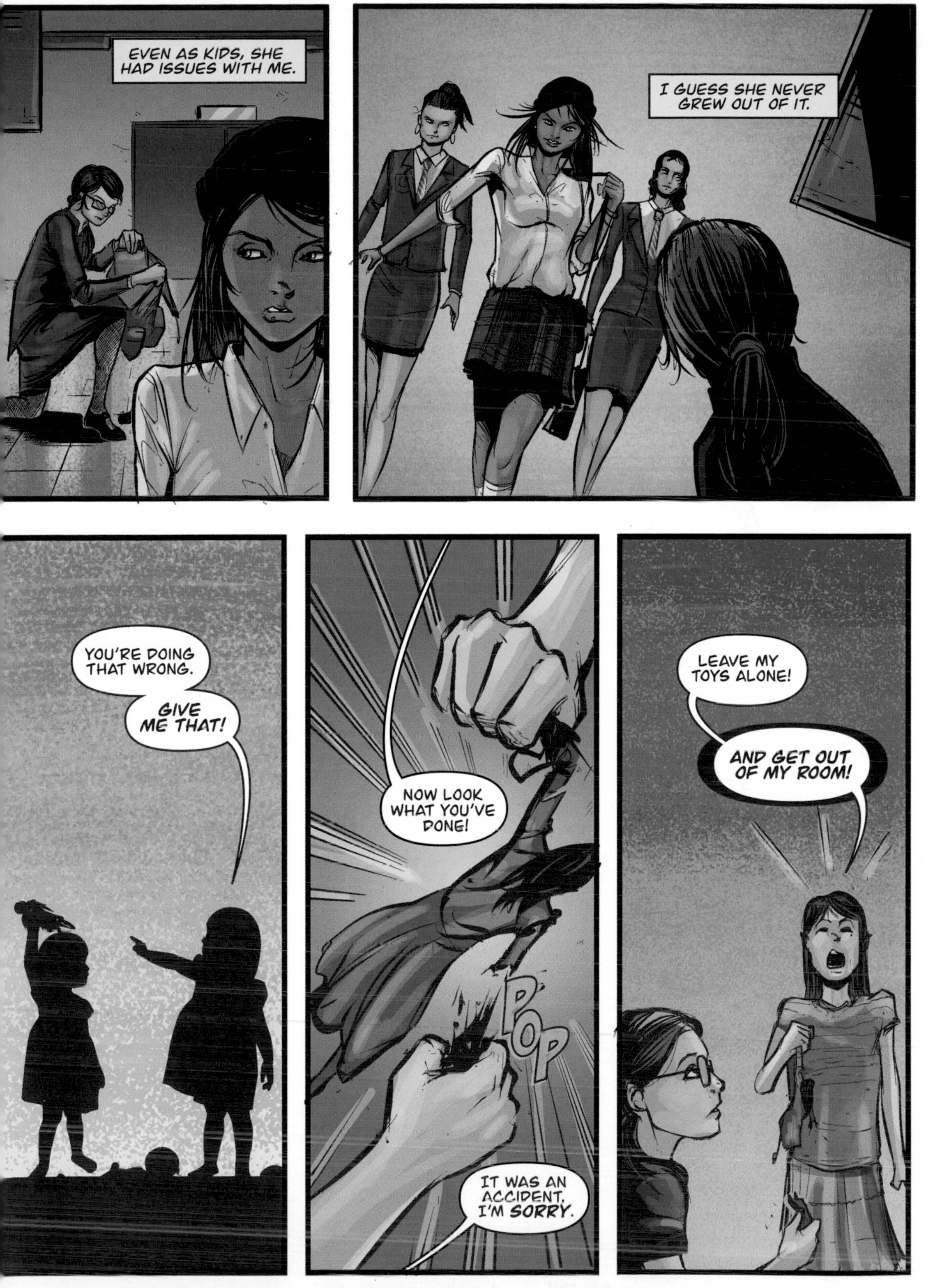
EVEN AS KIDS, SHE HAD ISSUES WITH ME.
I GUESS SHE NEVER GREW OUT OF IT.
YOU'RE DOING THAT WRONG.
GIVE ME THAT!
NOW LOOK WHAT YOU'VE DONE!
POP
IT WAS AN ACCIDENT. I'M SORRY.
LEAVE MY TOYS ALONE!
AND GET OUT OF MY ROOM!

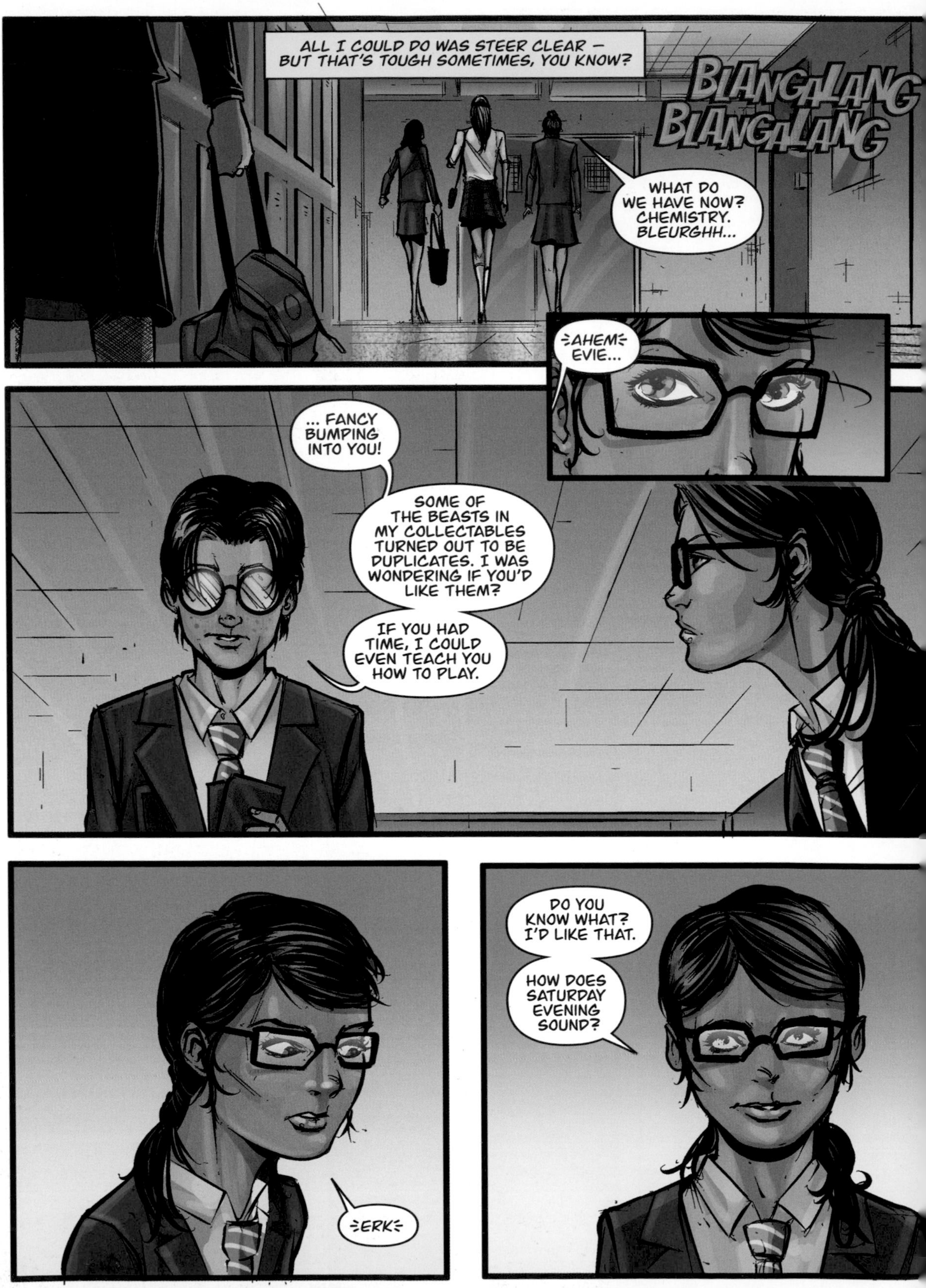
ALL I COULD DO WAS STEER CLEAR — BUT THAT'S TOUGH SOMETIMES, YOU KNOW?
BLANGALANG BLANGALANG
WHAT DO WE HAVE NOW? CHEMISTRY. BLEURGHH...
AHEM EVIE...
... FANCY BUMPING INTO YOU!
SOME OF THE BEASTS IN MY COLLECTABLES TURNED OUT TO BE DUPLICATES. I WAS WONDERING IF YOU'D LIKE THEM?
IF YOU HAD TIME, I COULD EVEN TEACH YOU HOW TO PLAY.
ERK
DO YOU KNOW WHAT? I'D LIKE THAT.
HOW DOES SATURDAY EVENING SOUND?

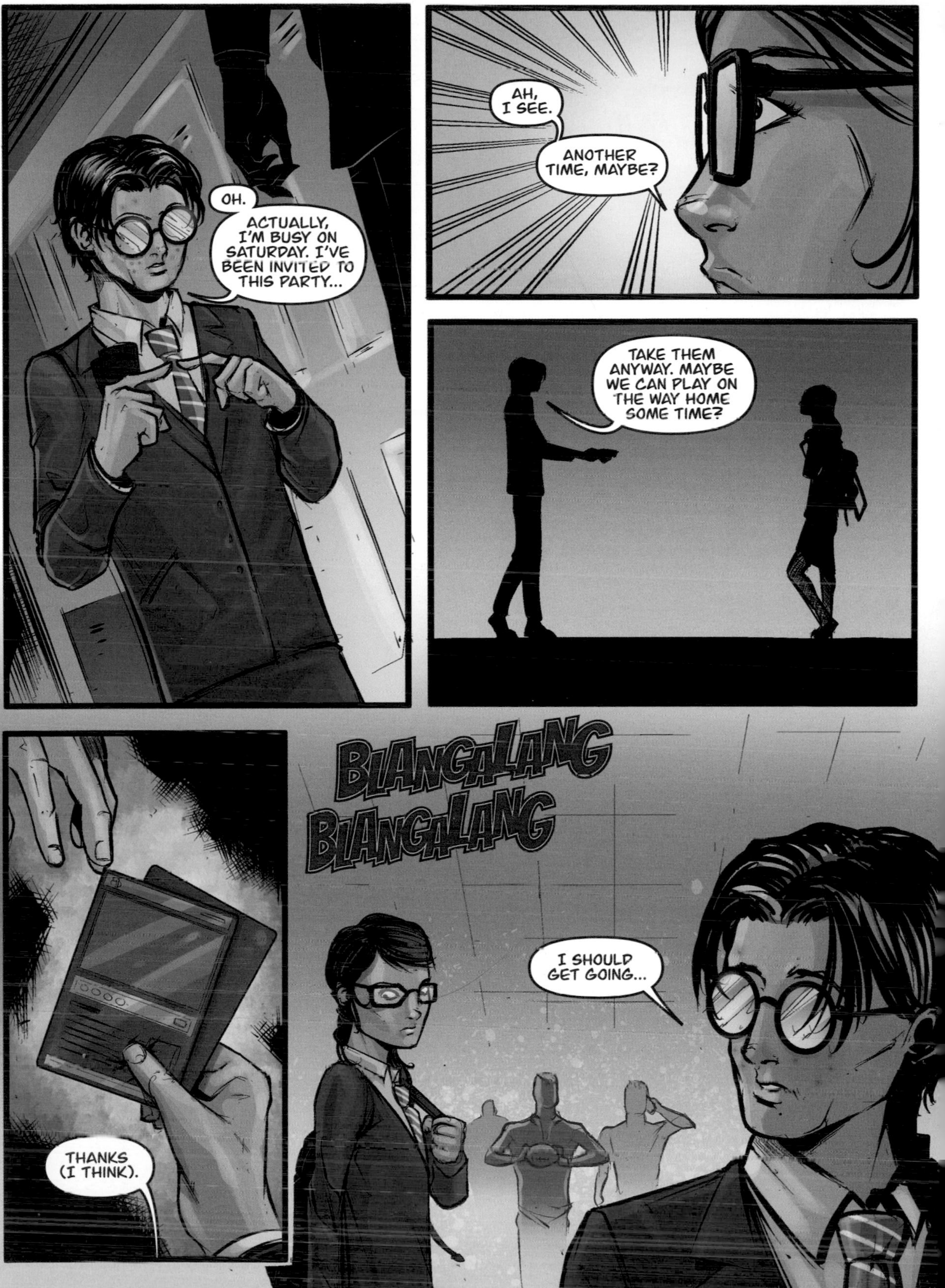
OH.
ACTUALLY, I'M BUSY ON SATURDAY. I'VE BEEN INVITED TO THIS PARTY...
AH, I SEE.
ANOTHER TIME, MAYBE?
TAKE THEM ANYWAY. MAYBE WE CAN PLAY ON THE WAY HOME SOME TIME?
THANKS (I THINK).
BLANGALANG
BLANGALANG
I SHOULD GET GOING...

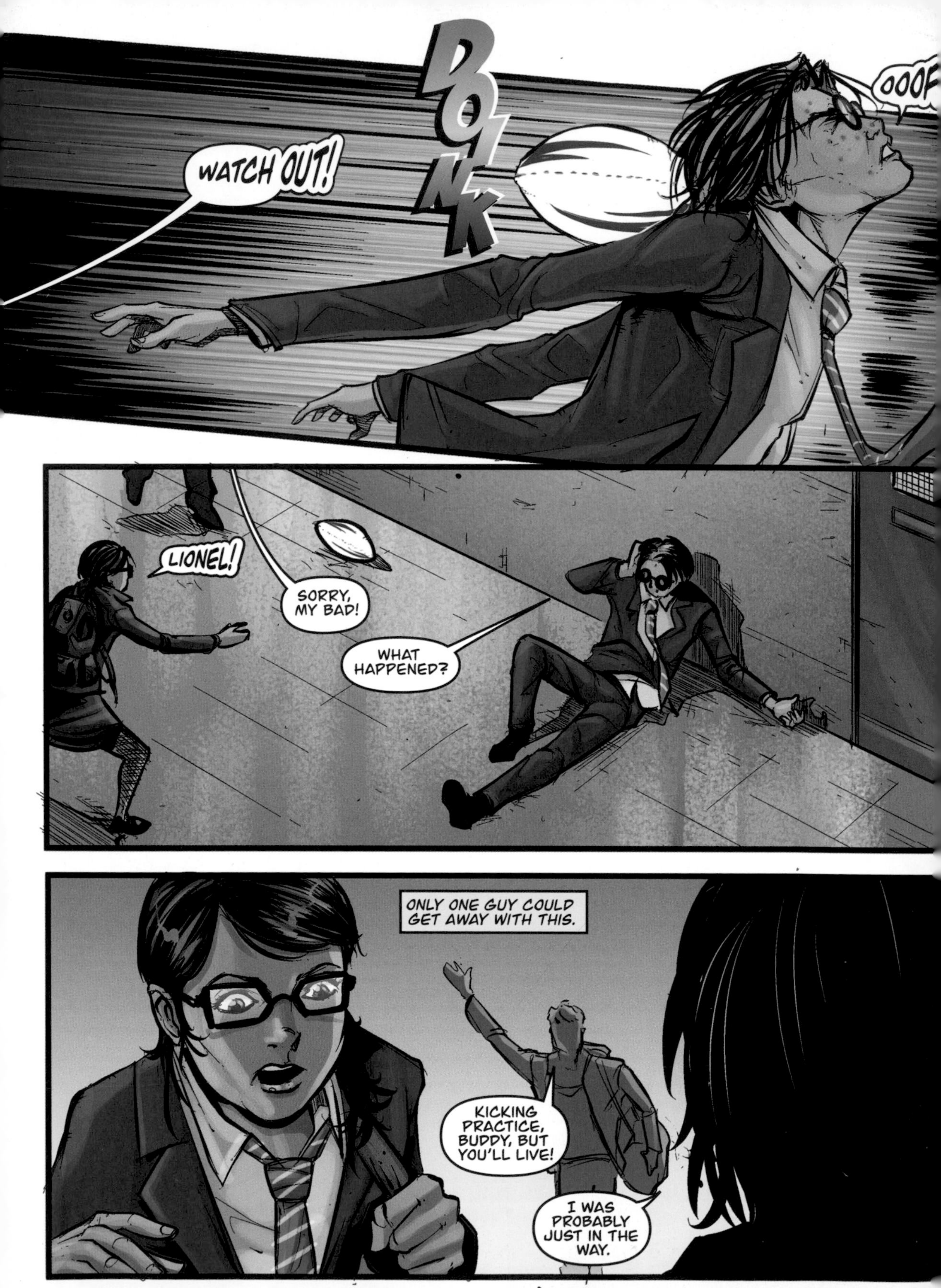
WATCH OUT!
DOINK
OOOF
LIONEL!
SORRY, MY BAD!
WHAT HAPPENED?
ONLY ONE GUY COULD GET AWAY WITH THIS.
KICKING PRACTICE, BUDDY, BUT YOU'LL LIVE!
I WAS PROBABLY JUST IN THE WAY.

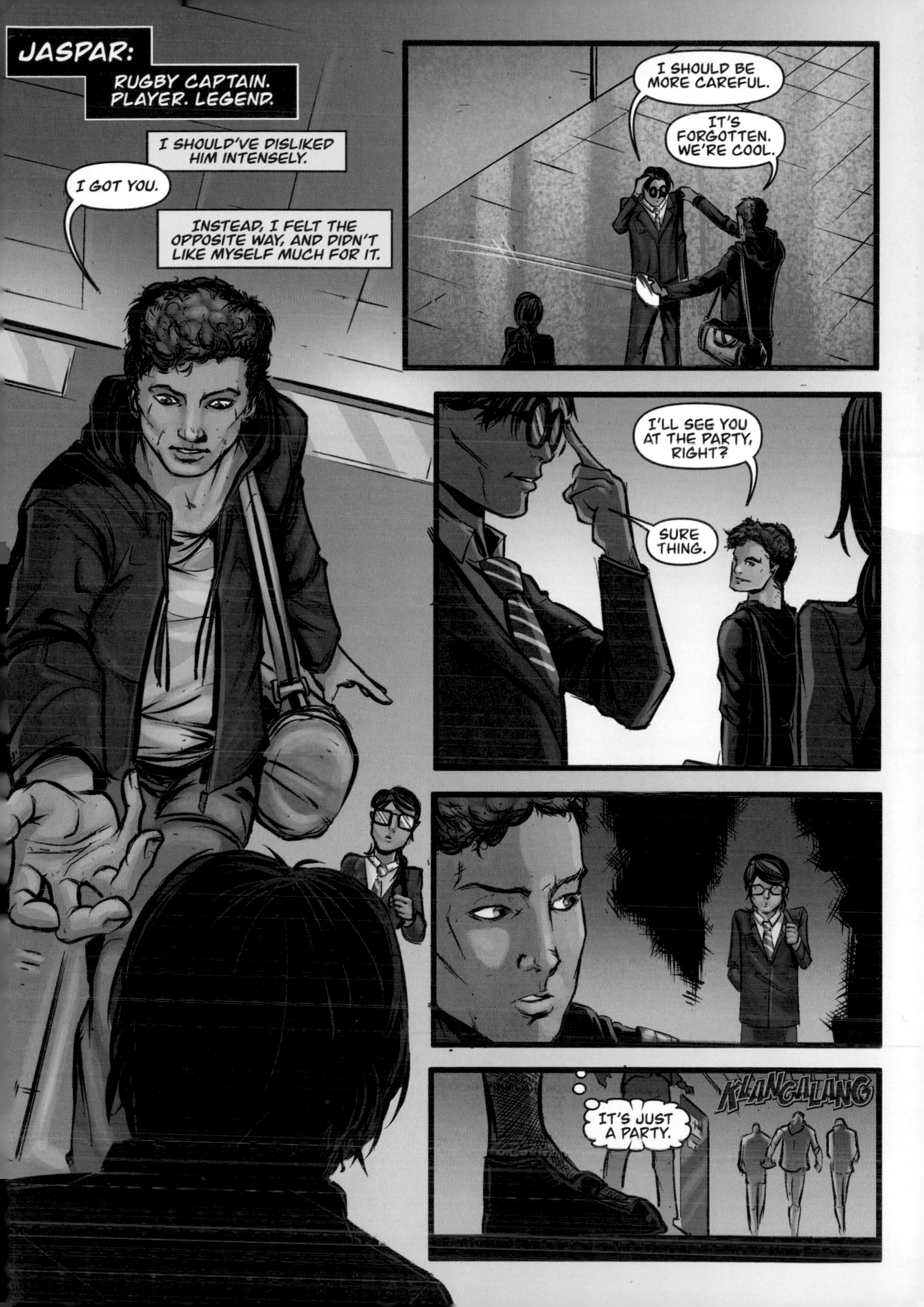
JASPAR:
RUGBY CAPTAIN. PLAYER. LEGEND.
I SHOULD'VE DISLIKED HIM INTENSELY.
I GOT YOU.
INSTEAD, I FELT THE OPPOSITE WAY, AND DIDN'T LIKE MYSELF MUCH FOR IT.
I SHOULD BE MORE CAREFUL.
IT'S FORGOTTEN. WE'RE COOL.
I'LL SEE YOU AT THE PARTY, RIGHT?
SURE THING.
IT'S JUST A PARTY.
KLANGALANG

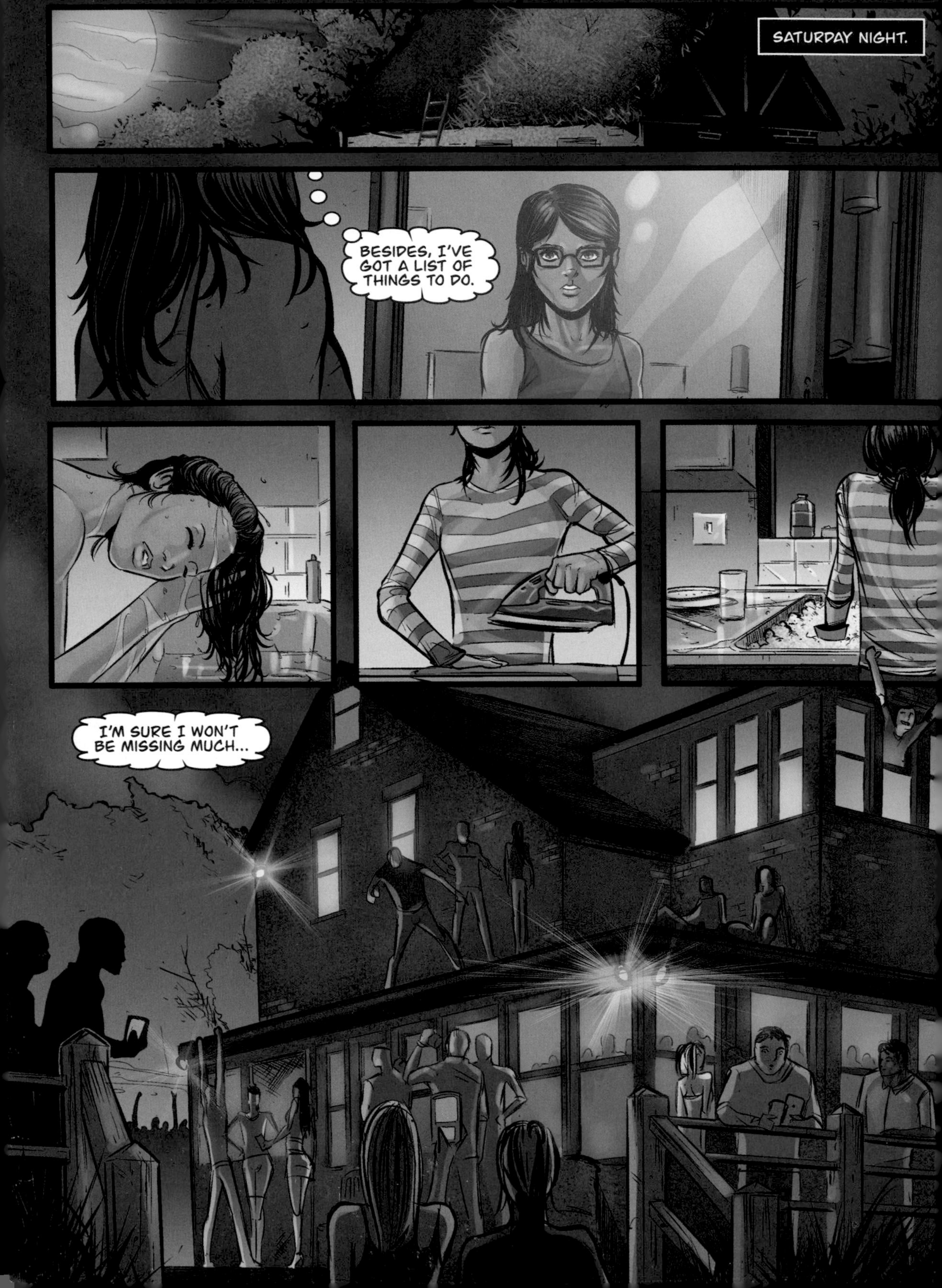
SATURDAY NIGHT.
BESIDES, I'VE GOT A LIST OF THINGS TO DO.
I'M SURE I WON'T BE MISSING MUCH...

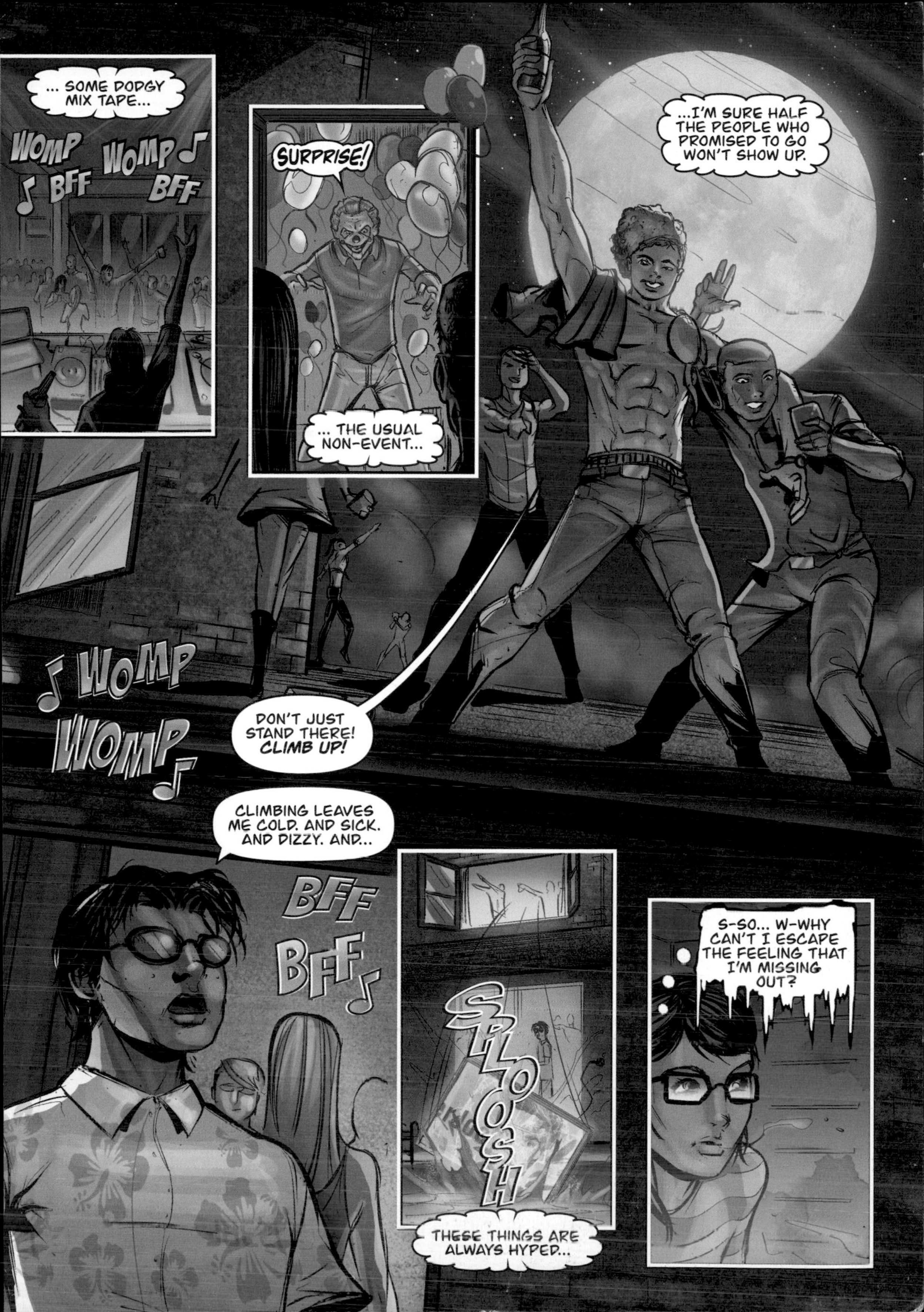
... SOME DODGY MIX TAPE...
WOMP BFF WOMP BFF
SURPRISE!
... THE USUAL NON-EVENT...
...I'M SURE HALF THE PEOPLE WHO PROMISED TO GO WON'T SHOW UP.
WOMP WOMP
DON'T JUST STAND THERE! CLIMB UP!
CLIMBING LEAVES ME COLD. AND SICK. AND DIZZY. AND...
BFF BFF
SPLOOSH
THESE THINGS ARE ALWAYS HYPED...
S-SO... W-WHY CAN'T I ESCAPE THE FEELING THAT I'M MISSING OUT?

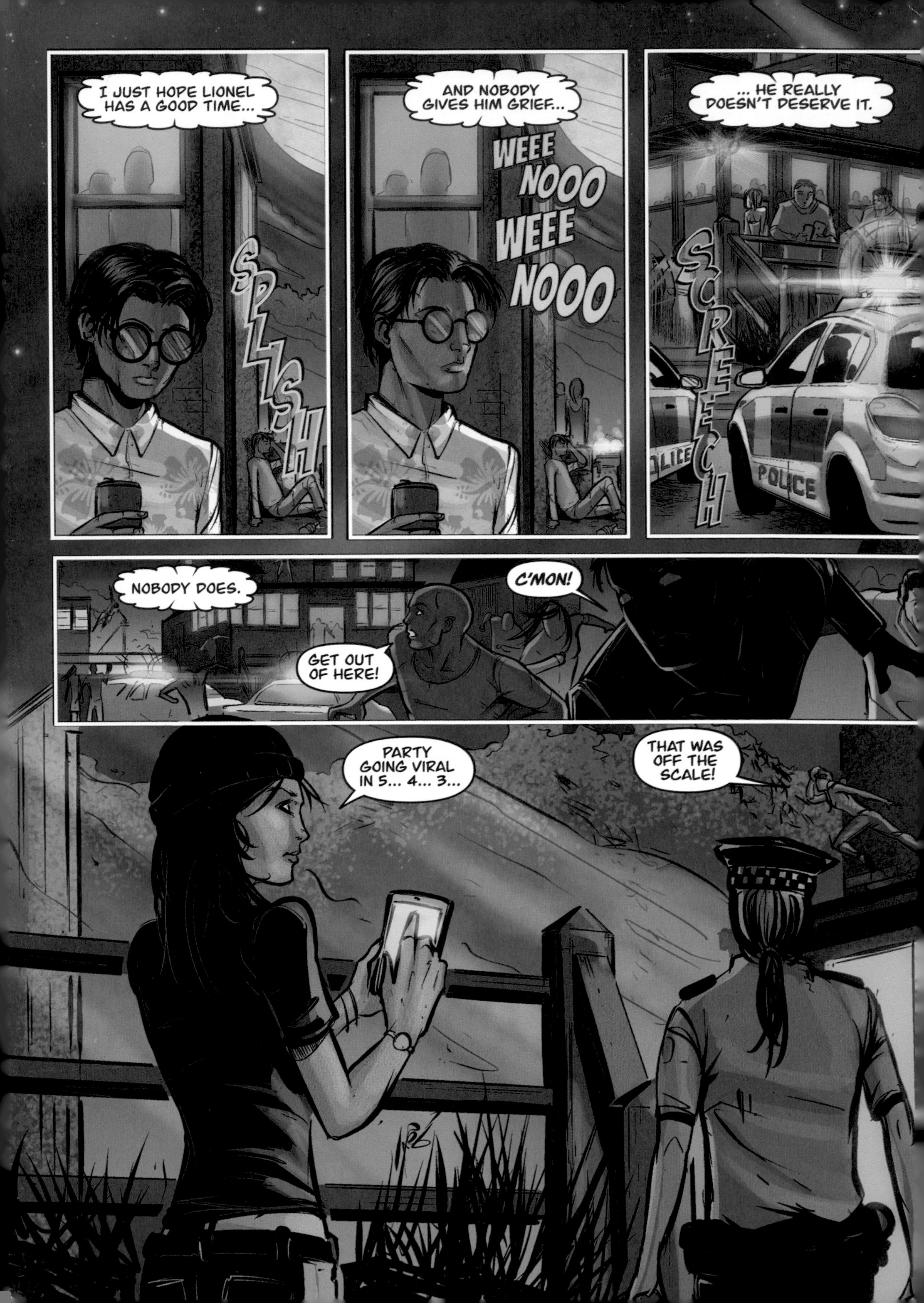
I JUST HOPE LIONEL HAS A GOOD TIME...
SPLISH
AND NOBODY GIVES HIM GRIEF...
WEEE NOOO WEEE NOOO
... HE REALLY DOESN'T DESERVE IT.
SCREECH
POLICE
POLICE
NOBODY DOES.
C'MON!
GET OUT OF HERE!
PARTY GOING VIRAL IN 5... 4... 3...
THAT WAS OFF THE SCALE!

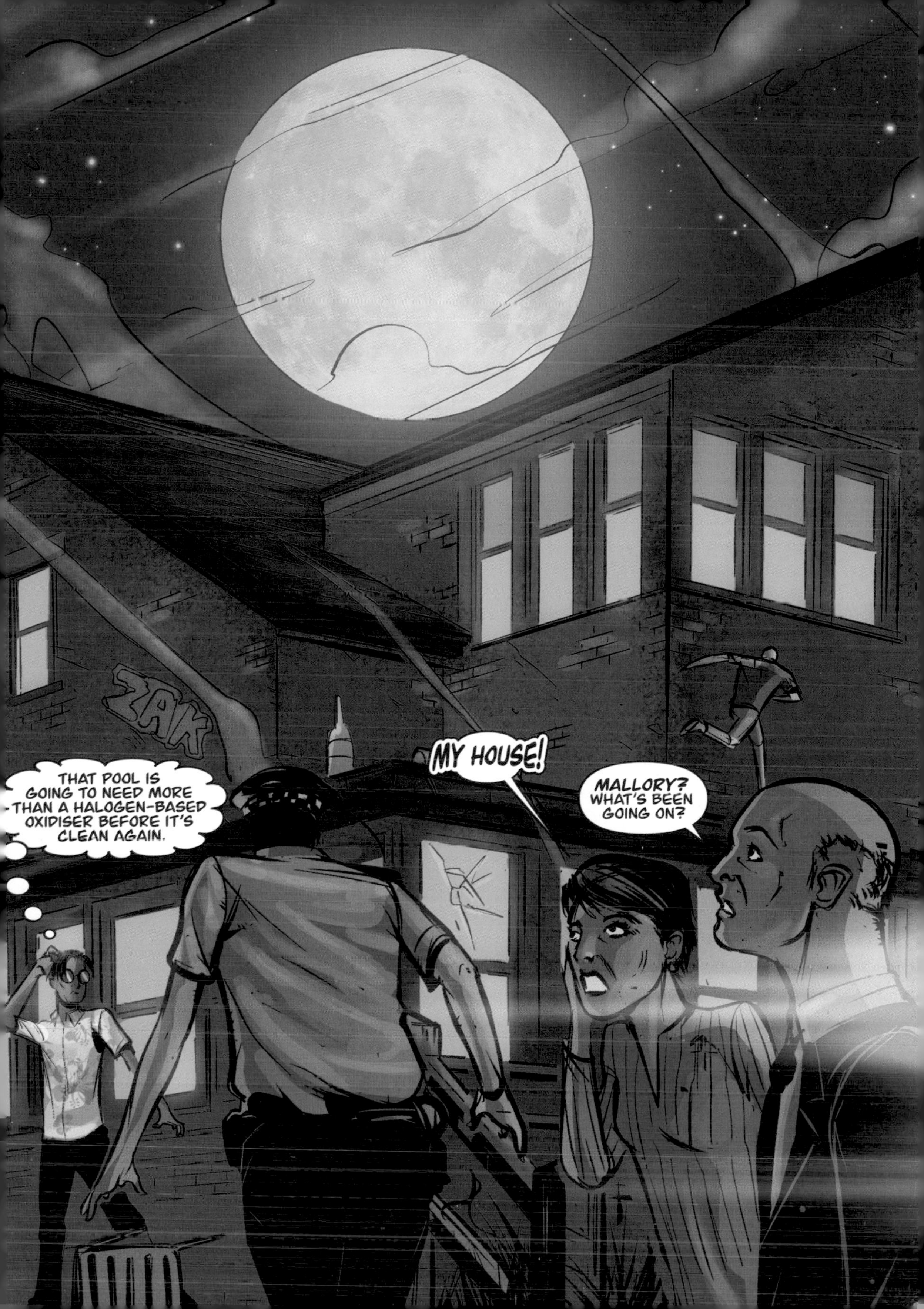
THAT POOL IS GOING TO NEED MORE THAN A HALOGEN-BASED OXIDISER BEFORE IT'S CLEAN AGAIN.
MY HOUSE!
MALLORY? WHAT'S BEEN GOING ON?
ZAK

FRIDGE, YOU'VE BEEN GOOD TO ME WHEN TIMES ARE TOUGH, BUT THERE HAS TO BE A SAFER PLACE...

...I CAN'T FEEL MY TOES.

CLAK
TAP
TAP
KLIK

DAD, I WAS THINKING. COULD WE HAVE A ROAST DINNER SOON?

EVER SINCE YOU WERE LITTLE, YOU'VE ASKED FOR THAT WHENEVER YOU NEED CHEERING UP...

DON'T LET THEM GET YOU DOWN, EVIE.

BE PROUD OF WHO YOU ARE, AND NEVER LOSE SIGHT OF THE FACT THAT YOU ARE LOVED.

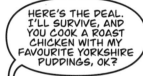

HERE'S THE DEAL. I'LL SURVIVE, AND YOU COOK A ROAST CHICKEN WITH MY FAVOURITE YORKSHIRE PUDDINGS, OK?

I'LL MAKE THE BEST YOU EVER TASTED.

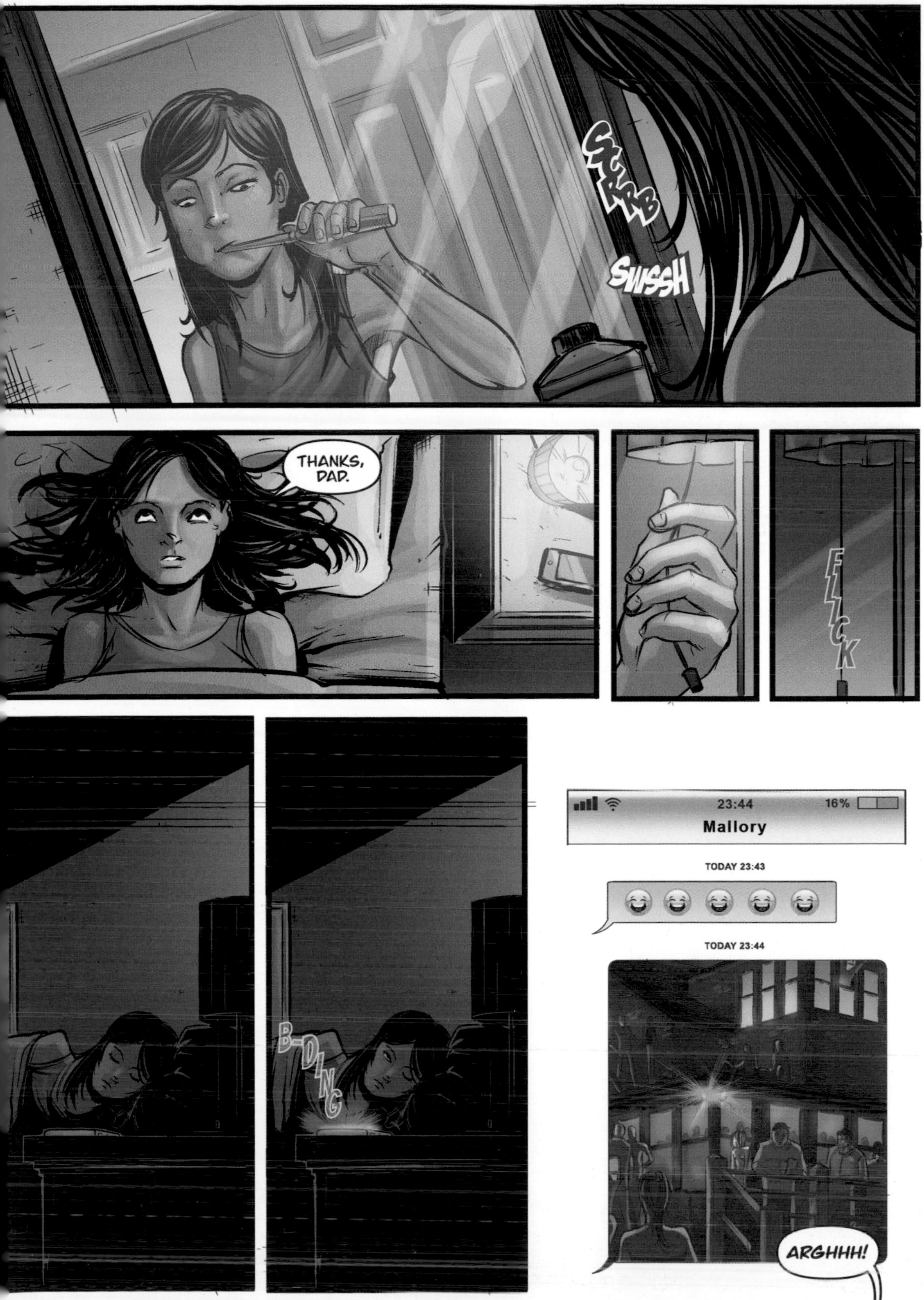
SCRRB
SWSSH
THANKS, DAD.
FLICK
B-DING
23:44
16%
Mallory
TODAY 23:43
TODAY 23:44
ARGHHH!

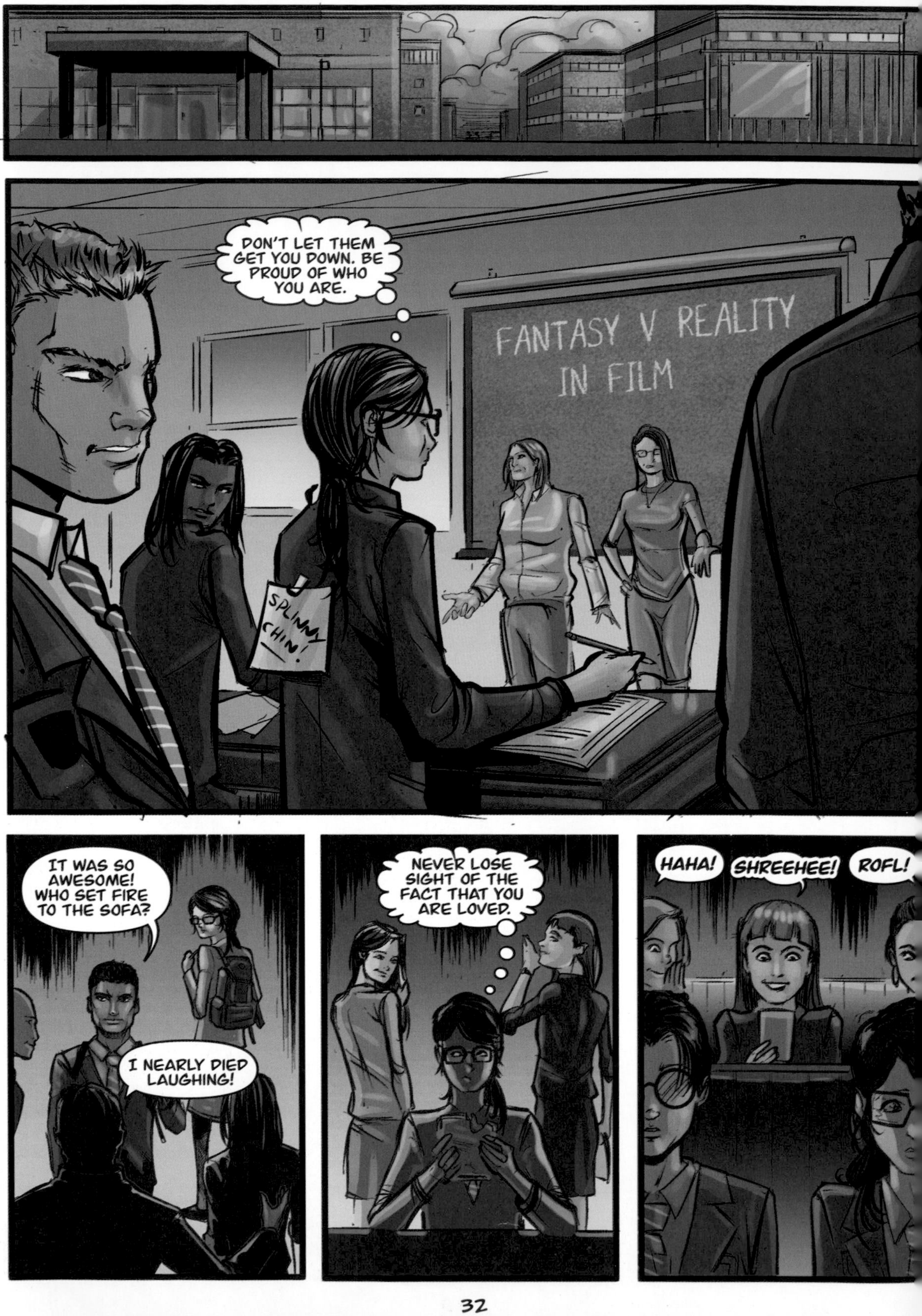
DON'T LET THEM GET YOU DOWN. BE PROUD OF WHO YOU ARE.
FANTASY V REALITY IN FILM
SPLINNY CHIN!
IT WAS SO AWESOME! WHO SET FIRE TO THE SOFA?
I NEARLY DIED LAUGHING!
NEVER LOSE SIGHT OF THE FACT THAT YOU ARE LOVED.
HAHA!
SHREEHEE!
ROFL!

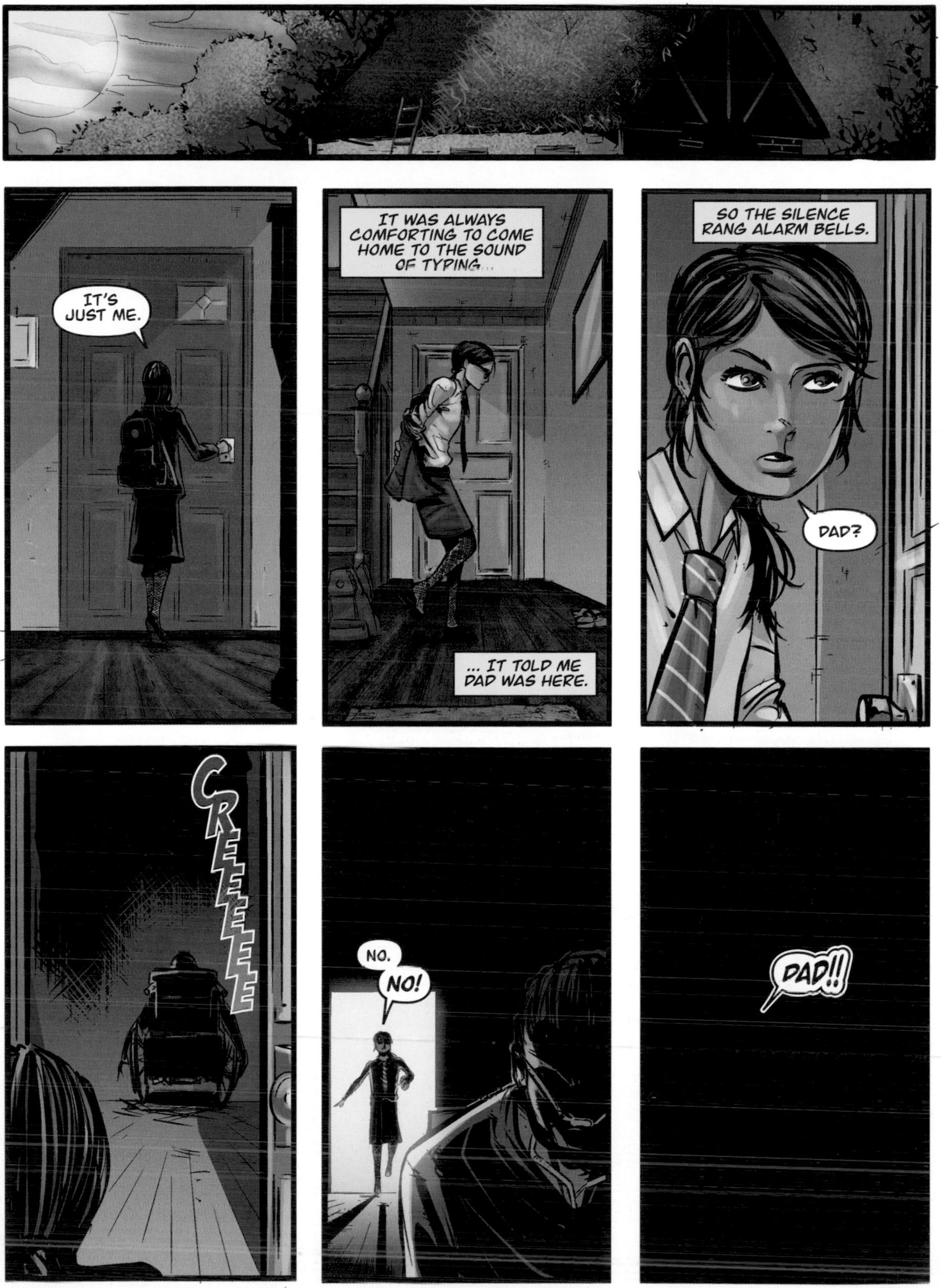
IT'S JUST ME.
IT WAS ALWAYS COMFORTING TO COME HOME TO THE SOUND OF TYPING...
... IT TOLD ME DAD WAS HERE.
SO THE SILENCE RANG ALARM BELLS.
DAD?
CREEEEEE
NO.
NO!
DAD!!

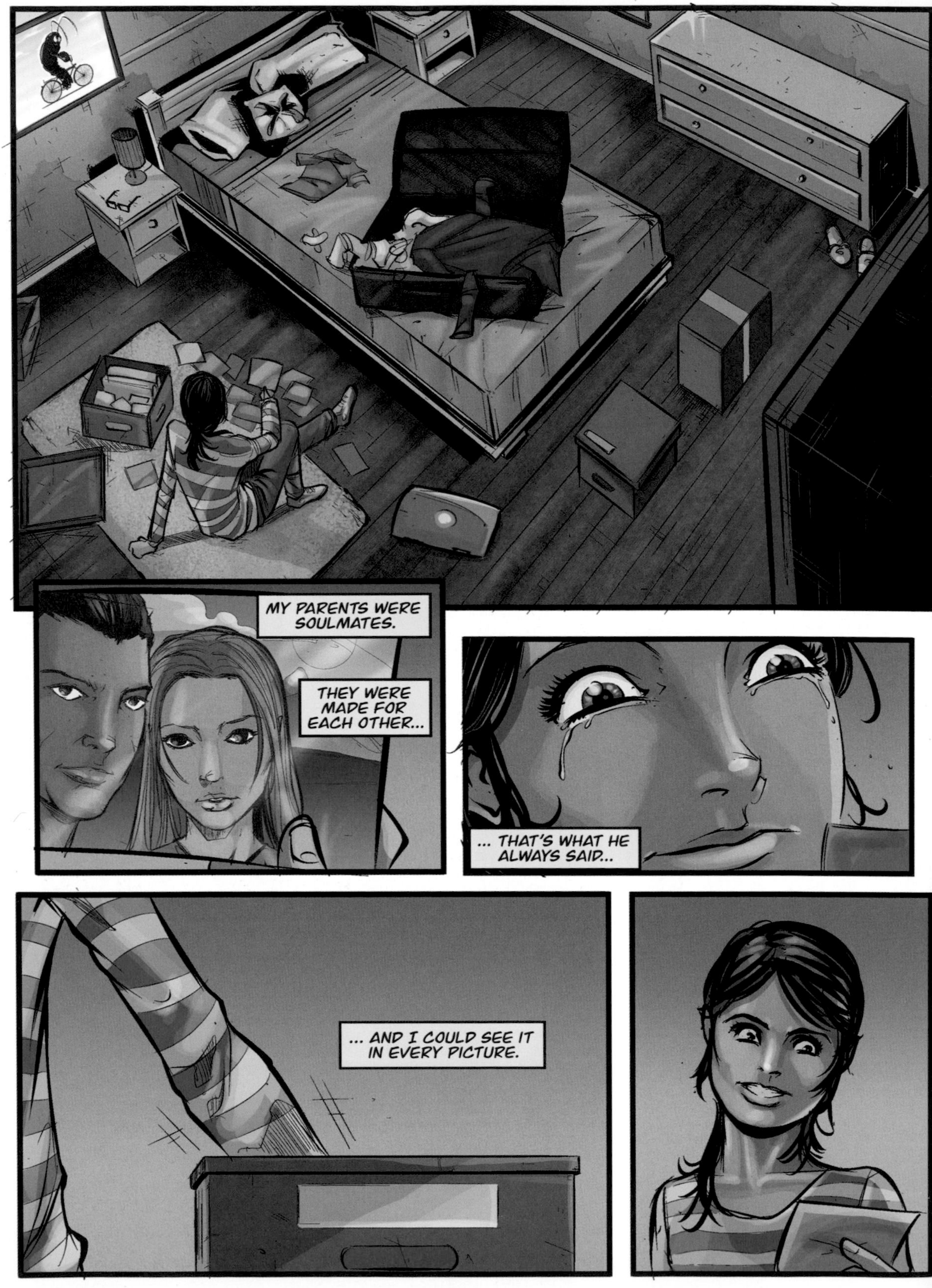
MY PARENTS WERE SOULMATES.
THEY WERE MADE FOR EACH OTHER...
... THAT'S WHAT HE ALWAYS SAID...
... AND I COULD SEE IT IN EVERY PICTURE.

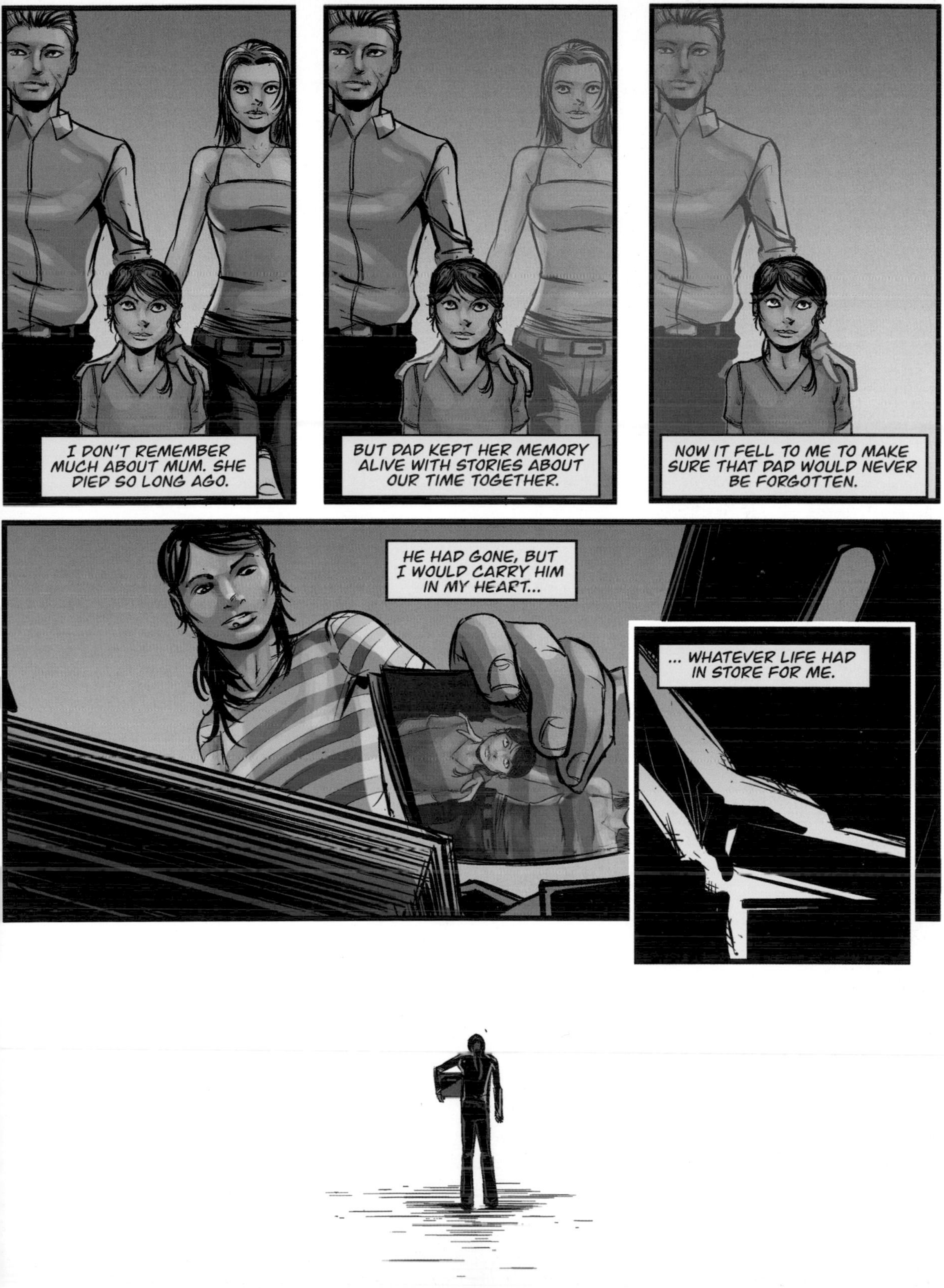
I DON'T REMEMBER MUCH ABOUT MUM. SHE DIED SO LONG AGO.
BUT DAD KEPT HER MEMORY ALIVE WITH STORIES ABOUT OUR TIME TOGETHER.
NOW IT FELL TO ME TO MAKE SURE THAT DAD WOULD NEVER BE FORGOTTEN.
HE HAD GONE, BUT I WOULD CARRY HIM IN MY HEART...
... WHATEVER LIFE HAD IN STORE FOR ME.

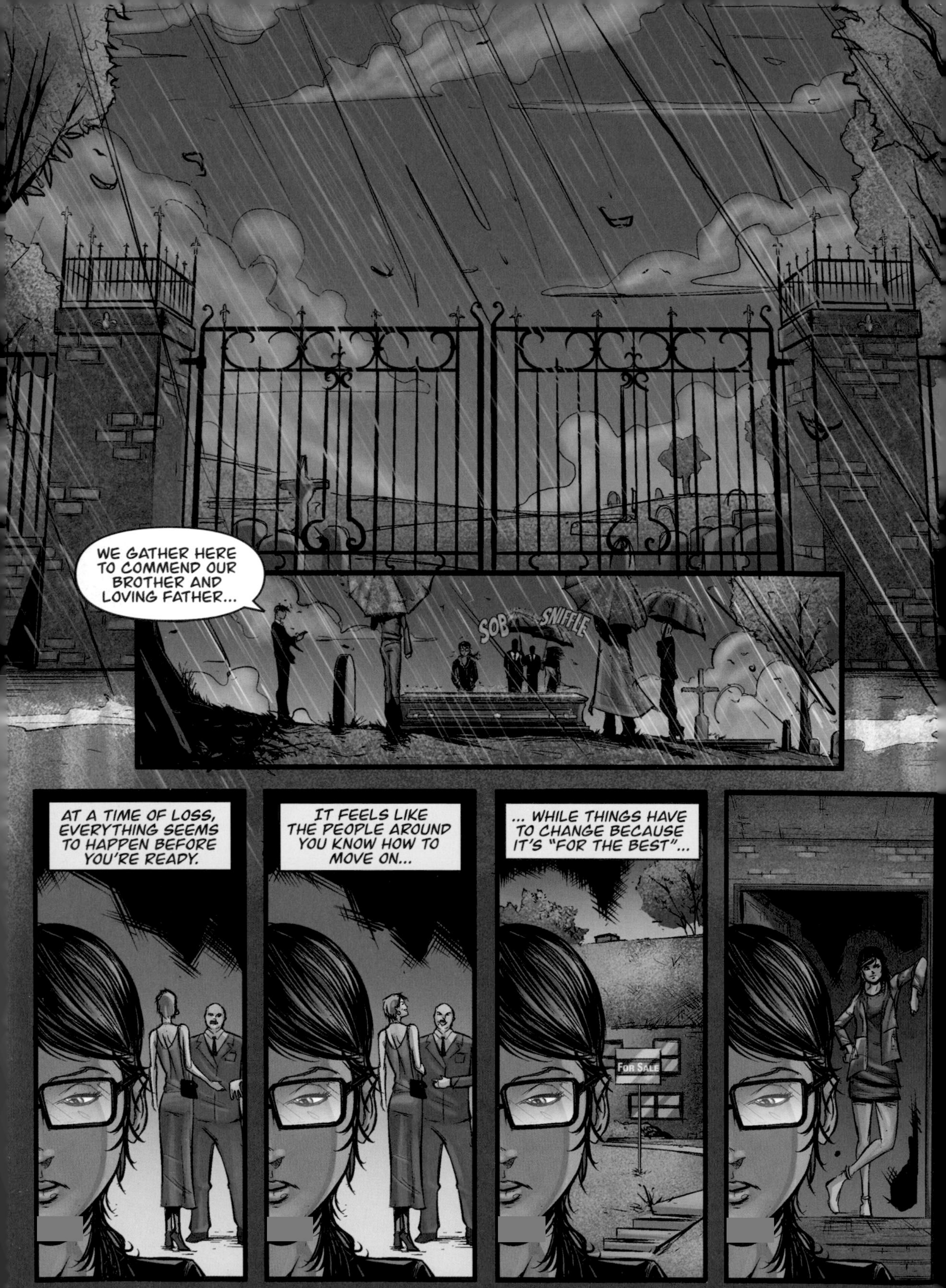
WE GATHER HERE TO COMMEND OUR BROTHER AND LOVING FATHER...
SOB
SNIFFLE
AT A TIME OF LOSS, EVERYTHING SEEMS TO HAPPEN BEFORE YOU'RE READY.
IT FEELS LIKE THE PEOPLE AROUND YOU KNOW HOW TO MOVE ON...
... WHILE THINGS HAVE TO CHANGE BECAUSE IT'S "FOR THE BEST"...
FOR SALE

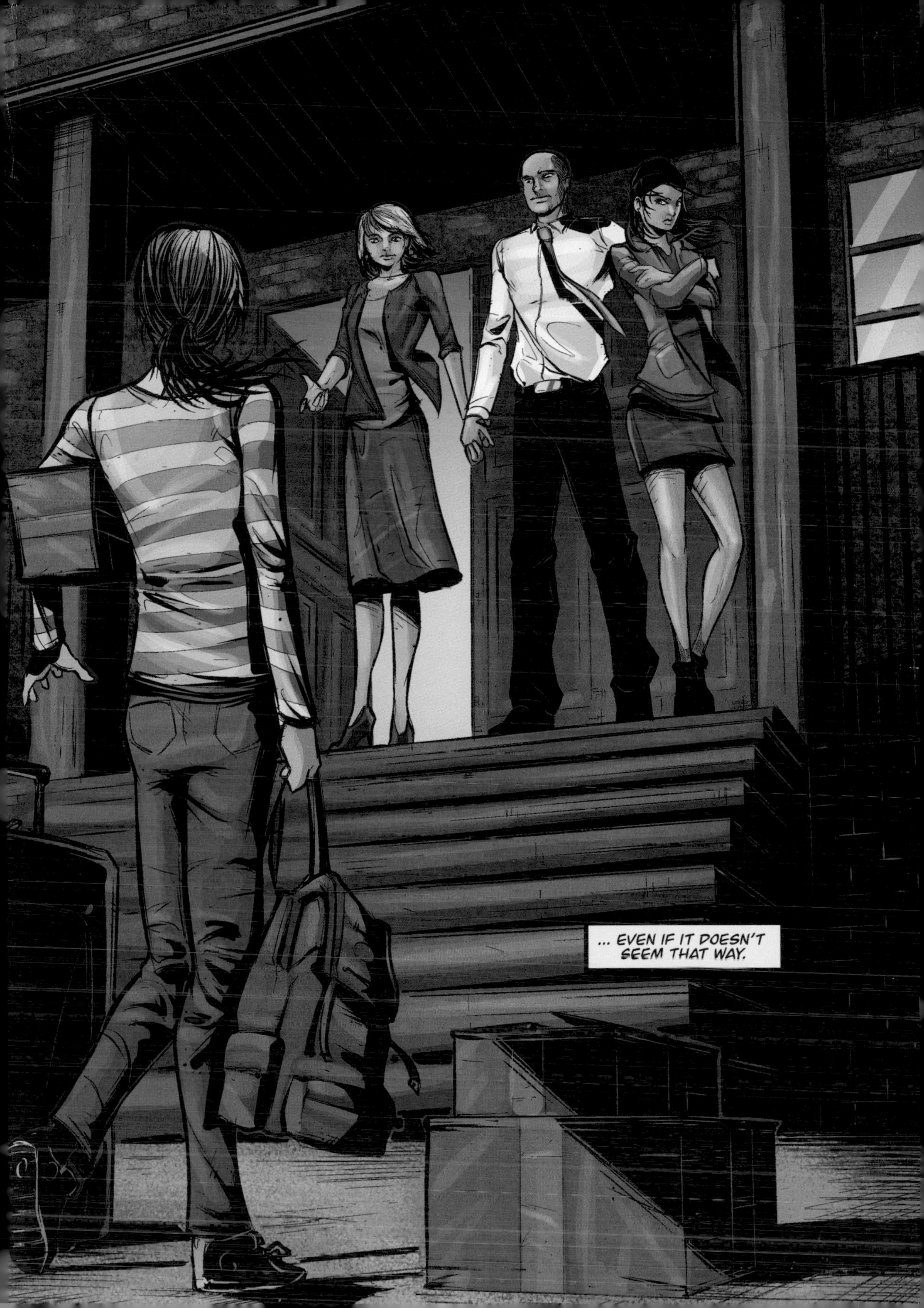
... EVEN IF IT DOESN'T SEEM THAT WAY.

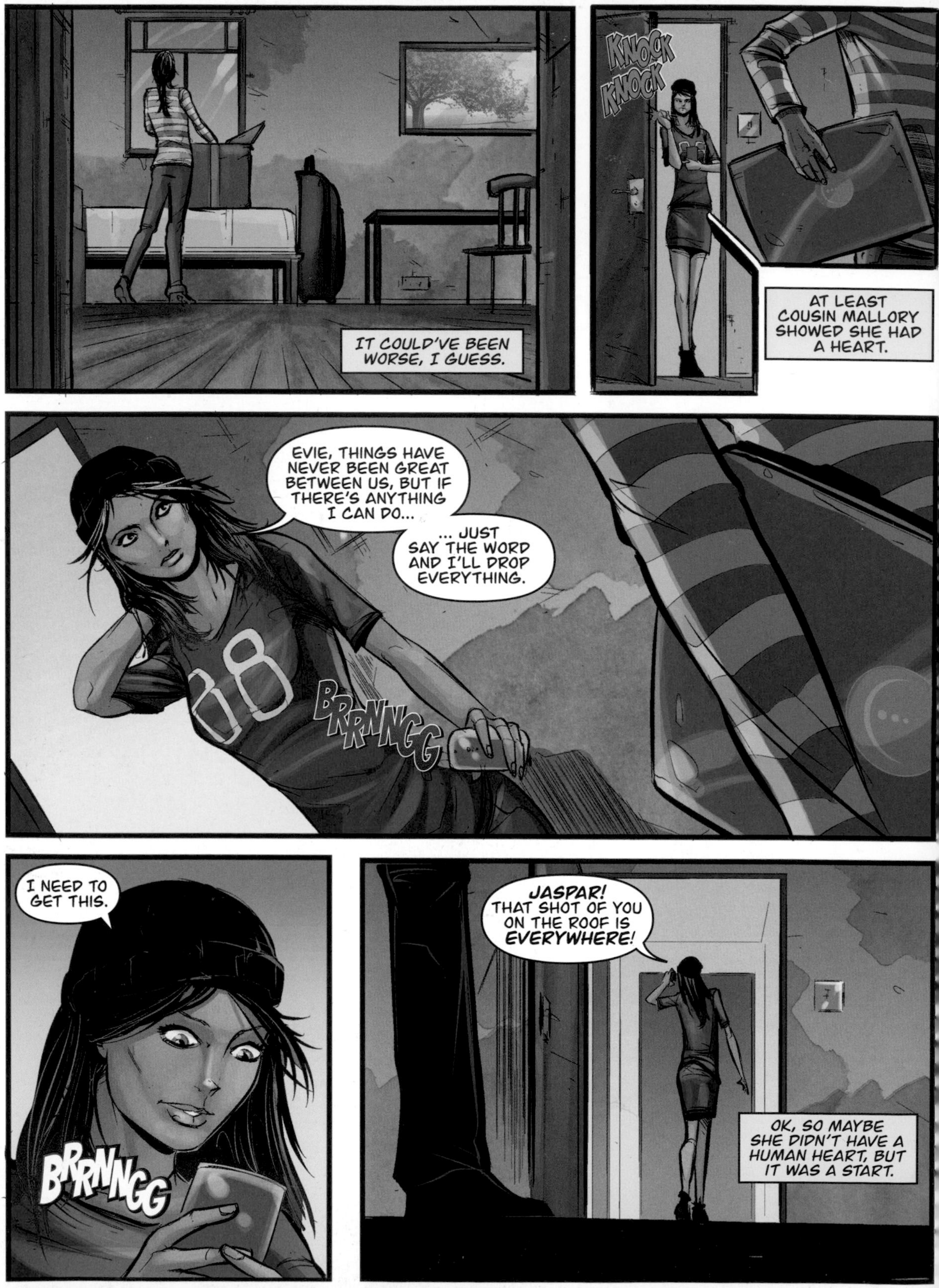
IT COULD'VE BEEN WORSE, I GUESS.
KNOCK KNOCK
AT LEAST COUSIN MALLORY SHOWED SHE HAD A HEART.
EVIE, THINGS HAVE NEVER BEEN GREAT BETWEEN US, BUT IF THERE'S ANYTHING I CAN DO...
... JUST SAY THE WORD AND I'LL DROP EVERYTHING.
BRRNNGG
I NEED TO GET THIS.
BRRNNGG
JASPAR! THAT SHOT OF YOU ON THE ROOF IS EVERYWHERE!
OK, SO MAYBE SHE DIDN'T HAVE A HUMAN HEART, BUT IT WAS A START.

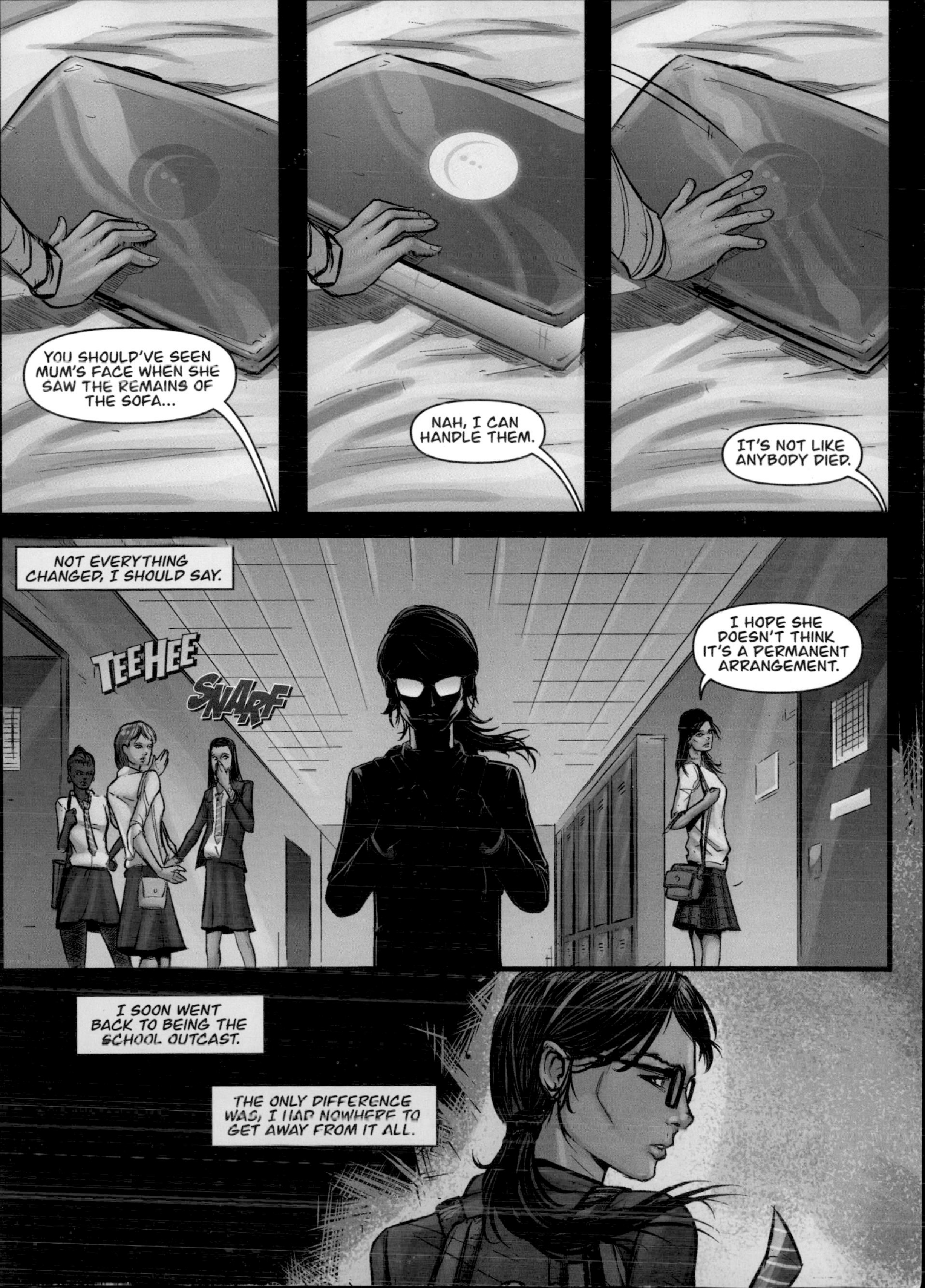
YOU SHOULD'VE SEEN MUM'S FACE WHEN SHE SAW THE REMAINS OF THE SOFA...
NAH, I CAN HANDLE THEM.
IT'S NOT LIKE ANYBODY DIED.
NOT EVERYTHING CHANGED, I SHOULD SAY.
TEEHEE
SNARF
I HOPE SHE DOESN'T THINK IT'S A PERMANENT ARRANGEMENT.
I SOON WENT BACK TO BEING THE SCHOOL OUTCAST.
THE ONLY DIFFERENCE WAS, I HAD NOWHERE TO GET AWAY FROM IT ALL.

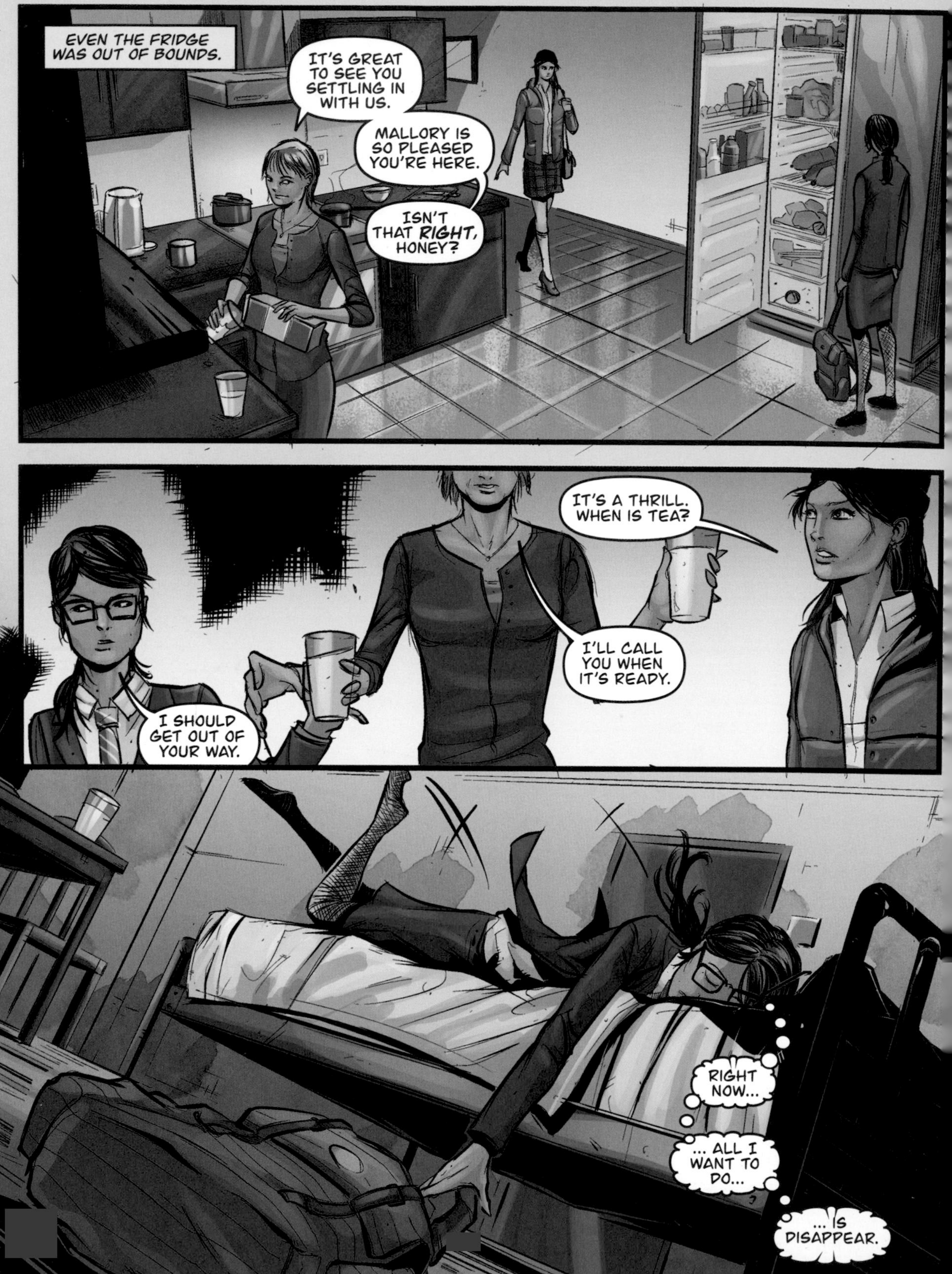
EVEN THE FRIDGE WAS OUT OF BOUNDS.
IT'S GREAT TO SEE YOU SETTLING IN WITH US.
MALLORY IS SO PLEASED YOU'RE HERE.
ISN'T THAT RIGHT, HONEY?
IT'S A THRILL. WHEN IS TEA?
I'LL CALL YOU WHEN IT'S READY.
I SHOULD GET OUT OF YOUR WAY.
RIGHT NOW...
... ALL I WANT TO DO...
... IS DISAPPEAR.

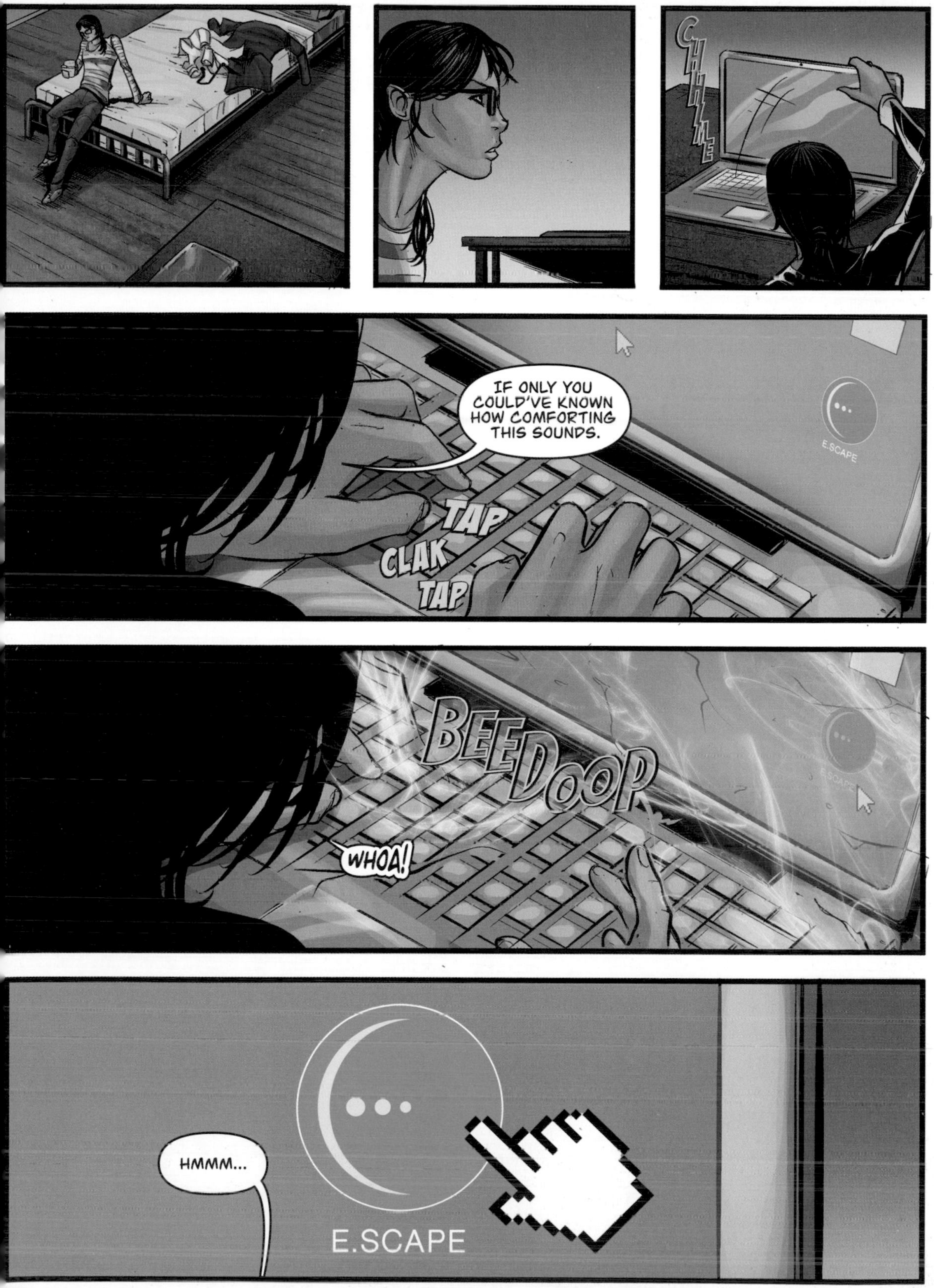
IF ONLY YOU COULD'VE KNOWN HOW COMFORTING THIS SOUNDS.
E.SCAPE
TAP
CLAK
TAP
BEEDOOP
E.SCAPE
WHOA!
HMMM...
E.SCAPE

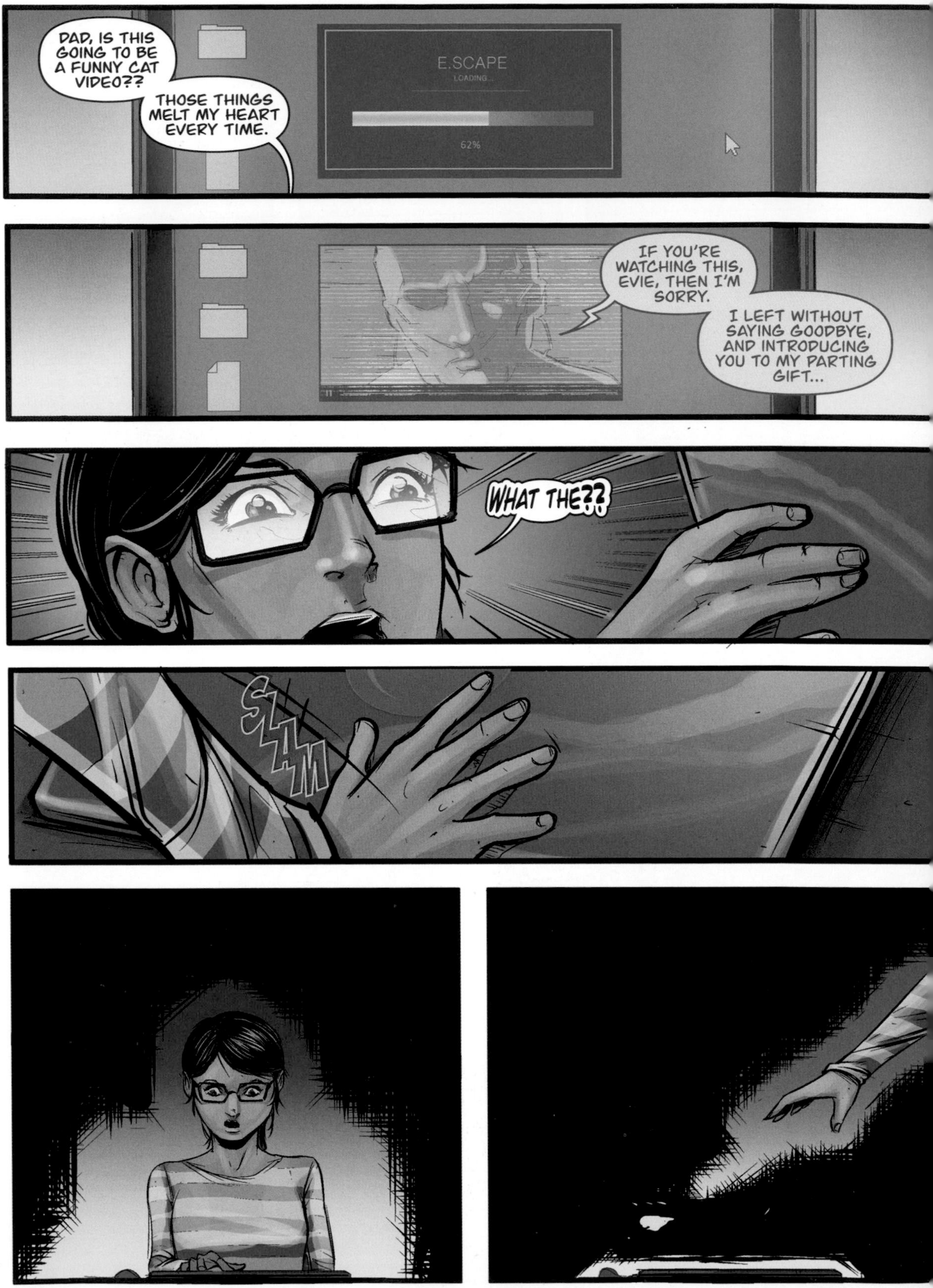
DAD, IS THIS GOING TO BE A FUNNY CAT VIDEO??
THOSE THINGS MELT MY HEART EVERY TIME.
E.SCAPE
LOADING...
62%
IF YOU'RE WATCHING THIS, EVIE, THEN I'M SORRY.
I LEFT WITHOUT SAYING GOODBYE, AND INTRODUCING YOU TO MY PARTING GIFT...
WHAT THE??
SLAM

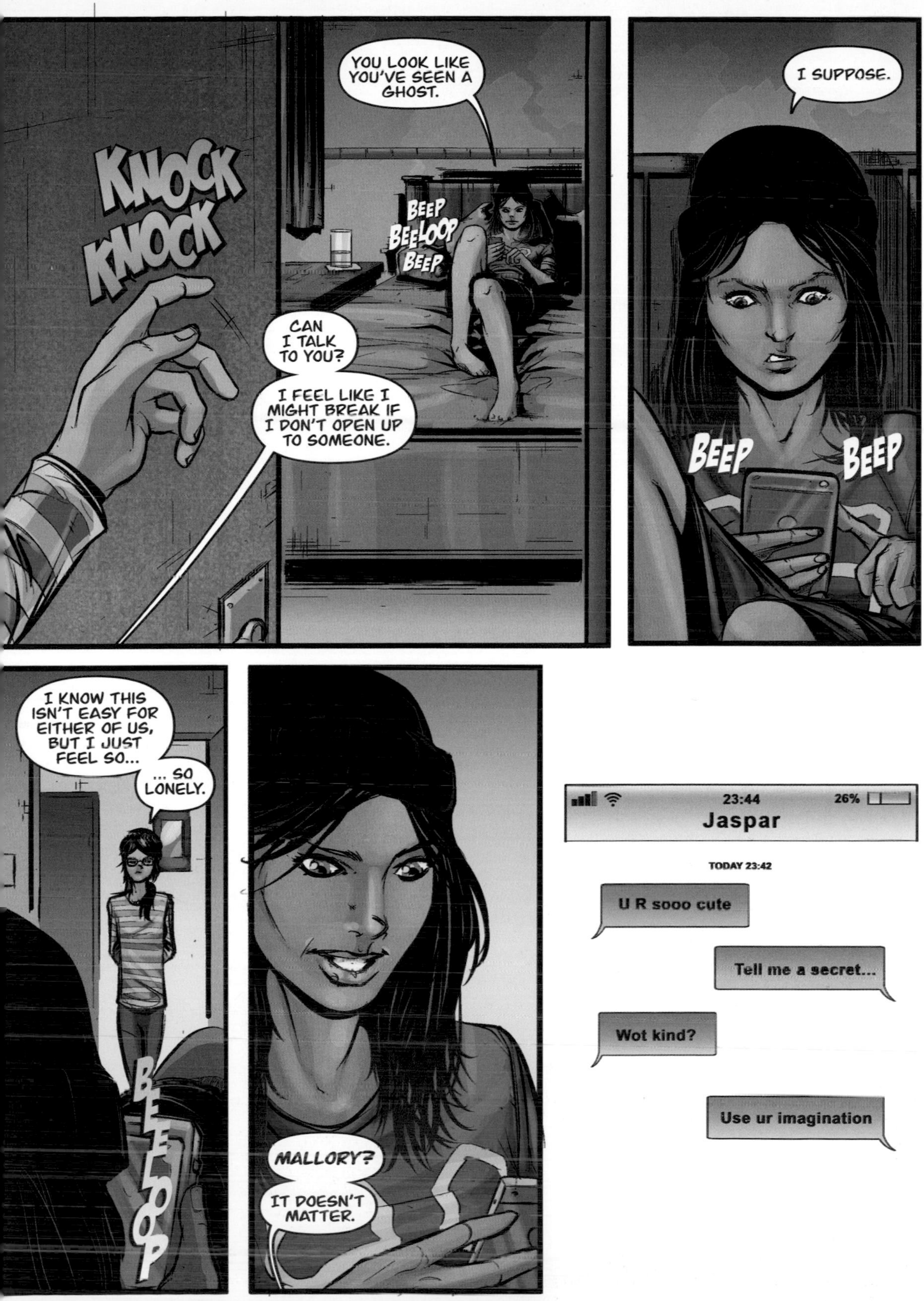
KNOCK KNOCK
YOU LOOK LIKE YOU'VE SEEN A GHOST.
BEEP BEELOOP BEEP
CAN I TALK TO YOU?
I FEEL LIKE I MIGHT BREAK IF I DON'T OPEN UP TO SOMEONE.
I SUPPOSE.
BEEP
BEEP
I KNOW THIS ISN'T EASY FOR EITHER OF US, BUT I JUST FEEL SO...
... SO LONELY.
BEELOOP
MALLORY?
IT DOESN'T MATTER.
23:44
26%
Jaspar
TODAY 23:42
U R sooo cute
Tell me a secret...
Wot kind?
Use ur imagination

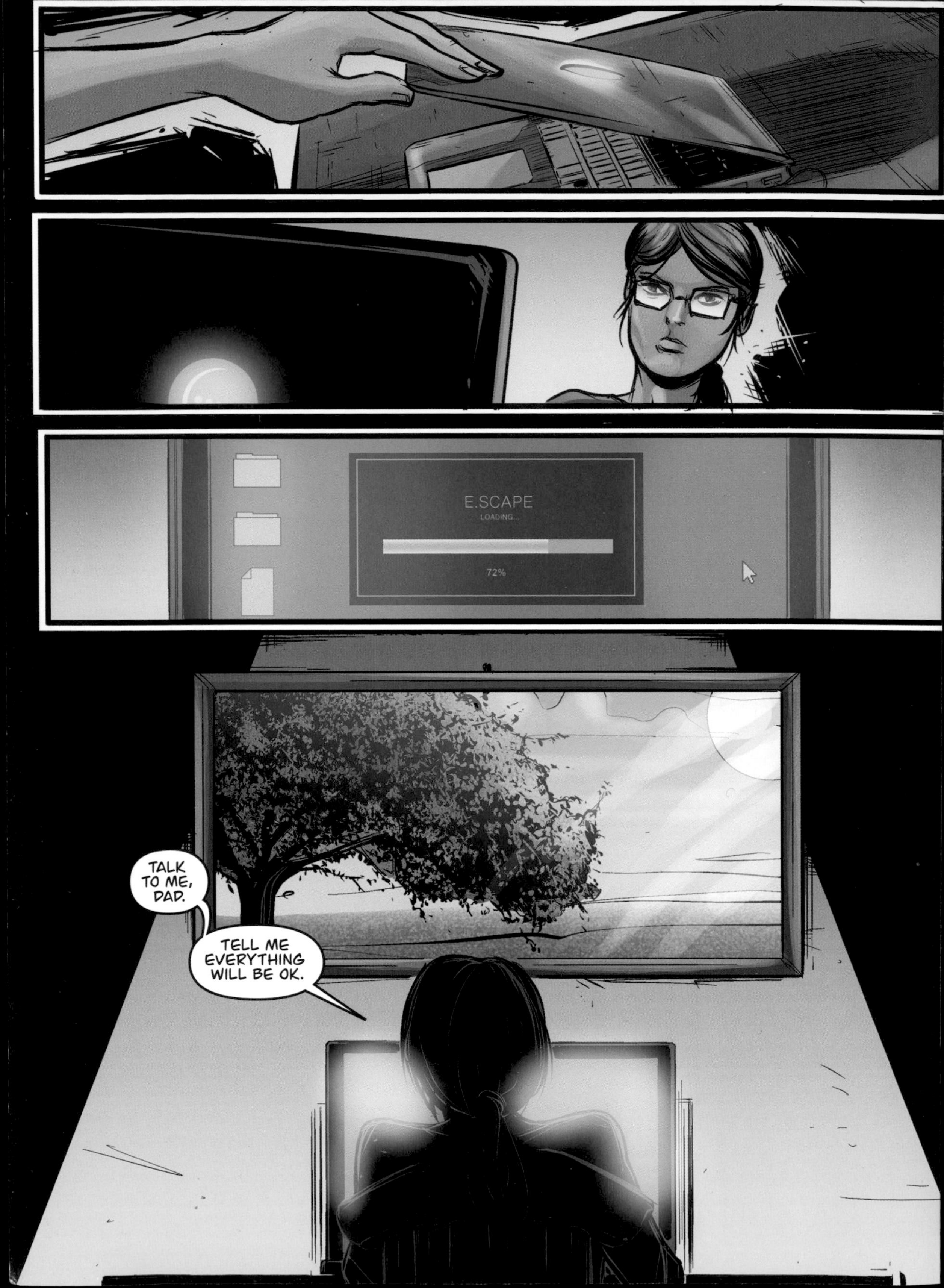
E.SCAPE
72%
TALK TO ME, DAD.
TELL ME EVERYTHING WILL BE OK.

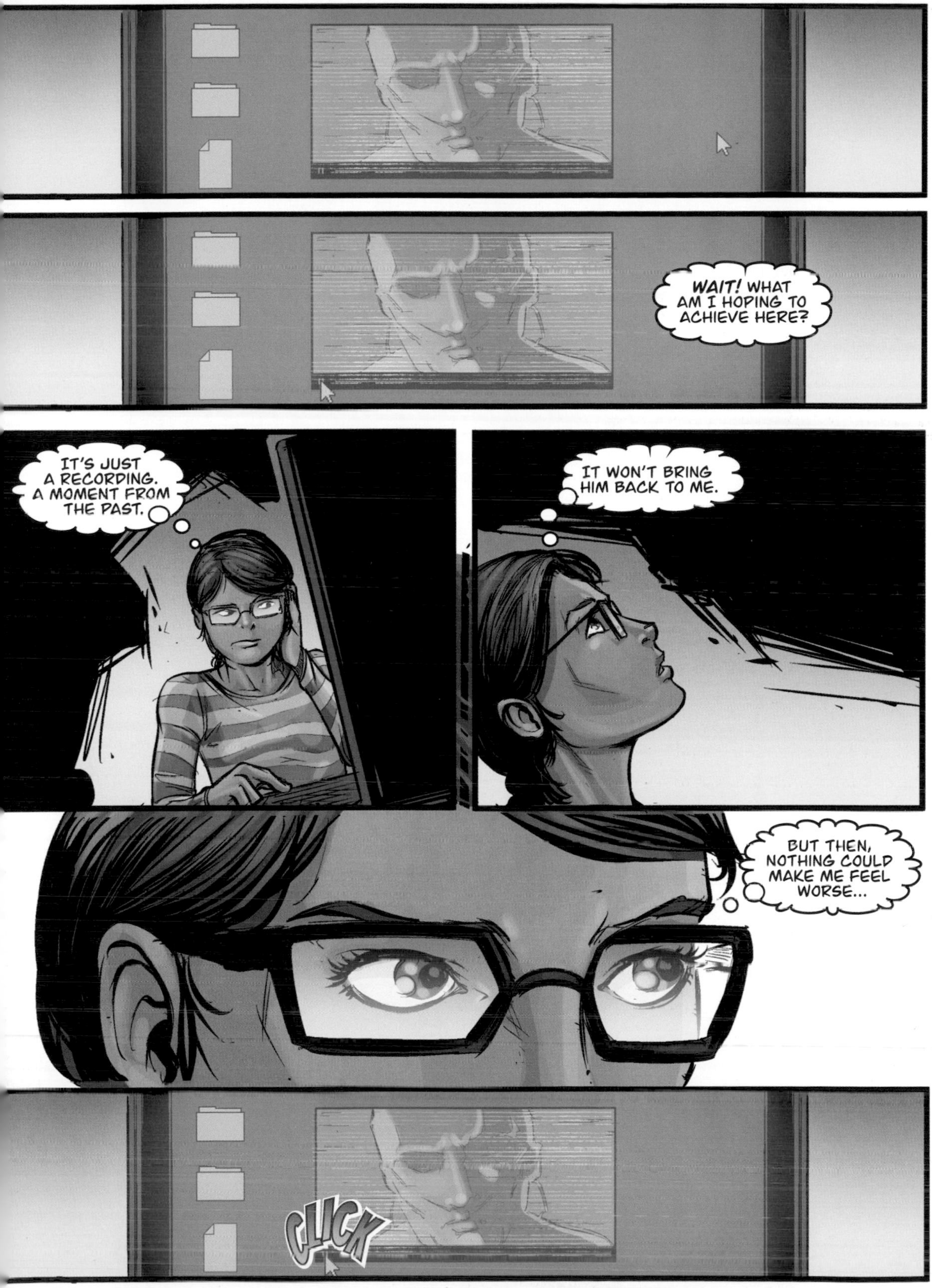
WAIT! WHAT AM I HOPING TO ACHIEVE HERE?
IT'S JUST A RECORDING. A MOMENT FROM THE PAST.
IT WON'T BRING HIM BACK TO ME.
BUT THEN, NOTHING COULD MAKE ME FEEL WORSE...
CLICK

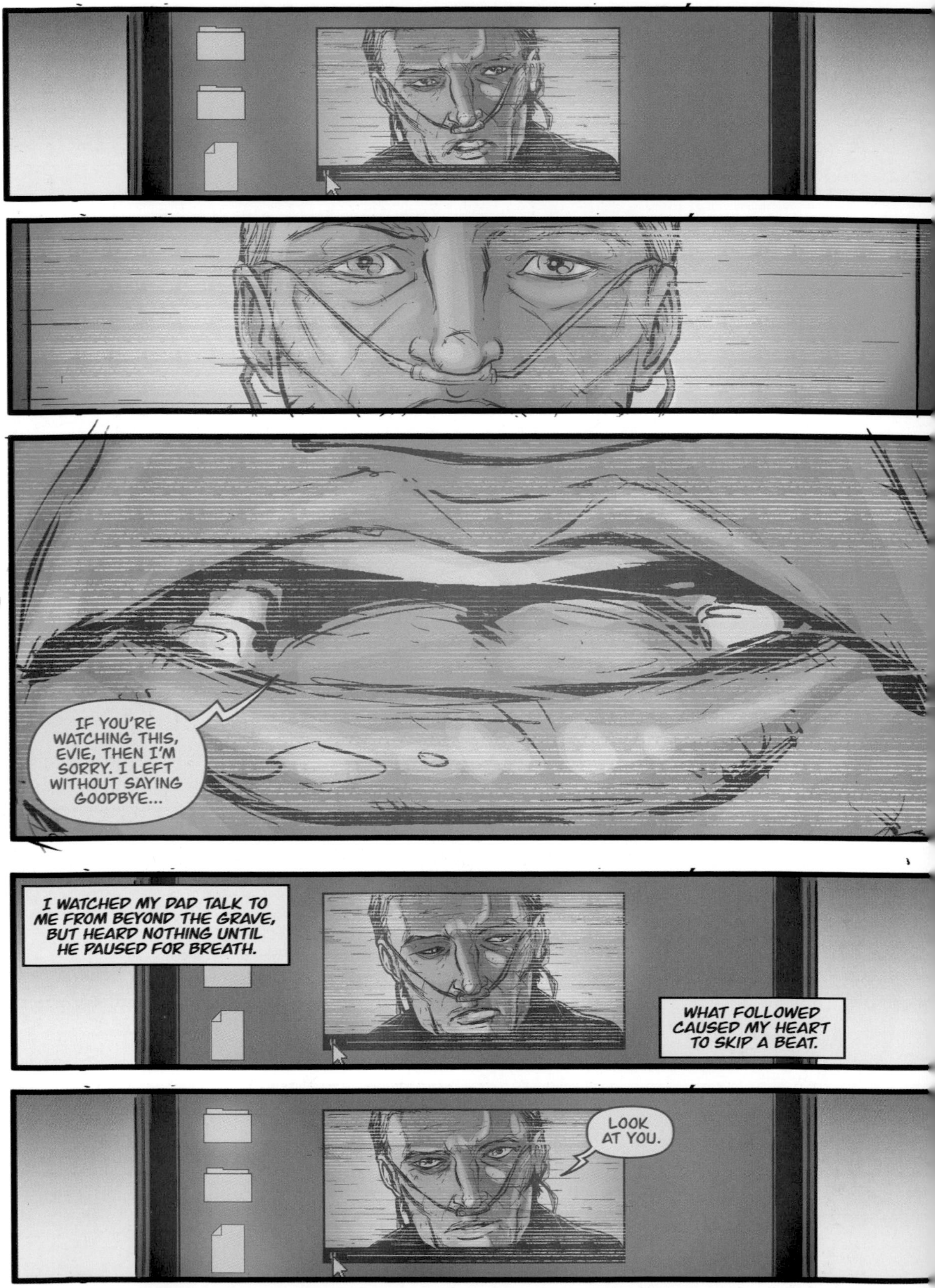
IF YOU'RE WATCHING THIS, EVIE, THEN I'M SORRY. I LEFT WITHOUT SAYING GOODBYE...
I WATCHED MY DAD TALK TO ME FROM BEYOND THE GRAVE, BUT HEARD NOTHING UNTIL HE PAUSED FOR BREATH.
WHAT FOLLOWED CAUSED MY HEART TO SKIP A BEAT.
LOOK AT YOU.

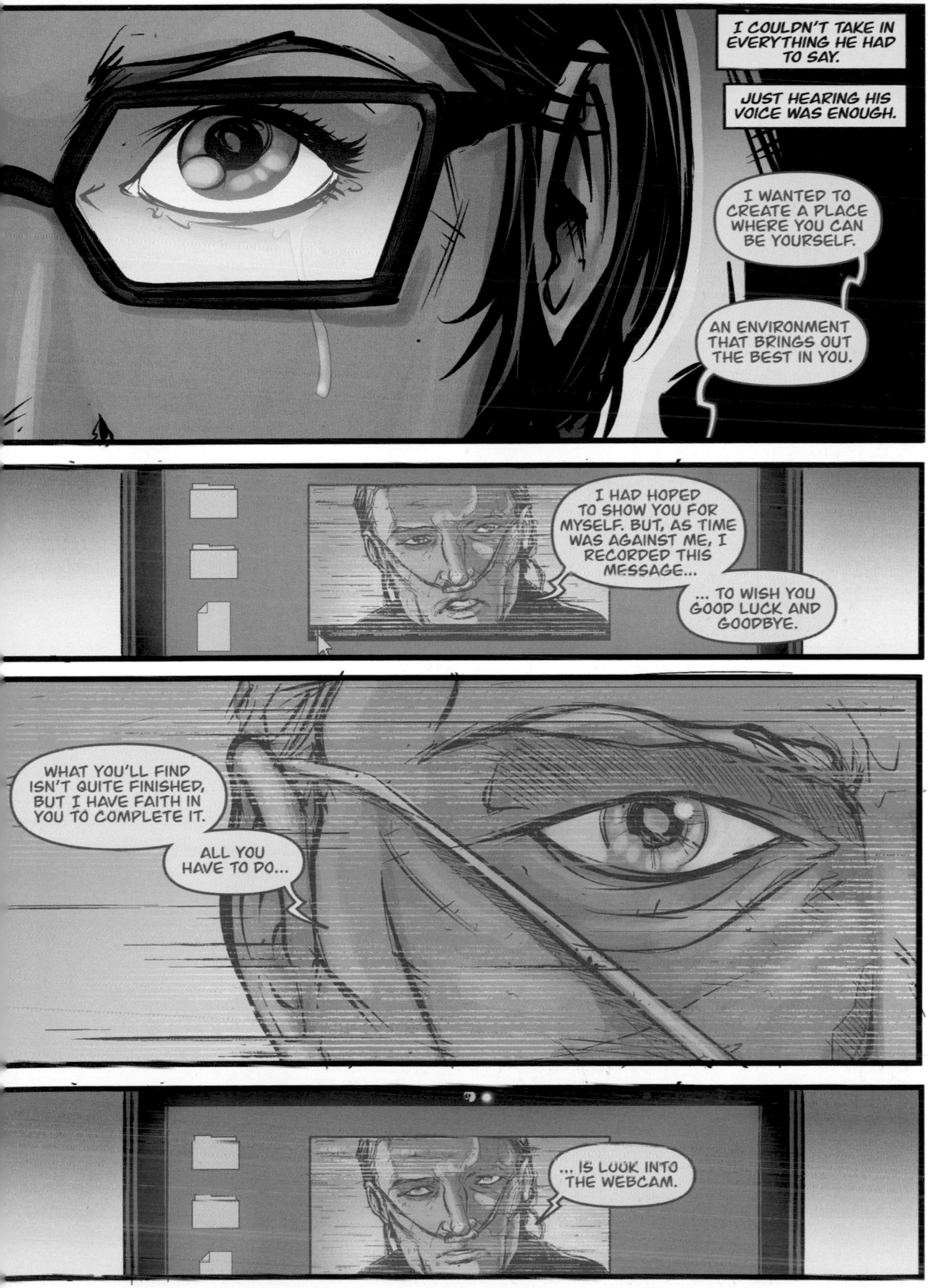
I COULDN'T TAKE IN EVERYTHING HE HAD TO SAY.
JUST HEARING HIS VOICE WAS ENOUGH.
I WANTED TO CREATE A PLACE WHERE YOU CAN BE YOURSELF.
AN ENVIRONMENT THAT BRINGS OUT THE BEST IN YOU.
I HAD HOPED TO SHOW YOU FOR MYSELF. BUT, AS TIME WAS AGAINST ME, I RECORDED THIS MESSAGE...
... TO WISH YOU GOOD LUCK AND GOODBYE.
WHAT YOU'LL FIND ISN'T QUITE FINISHED, BUT I HAVE FAITH IN YOU TO COMPLETE IT.
ALL YOU HAVE TO DO...
... IS LOOK INTO THE WEBCAM.

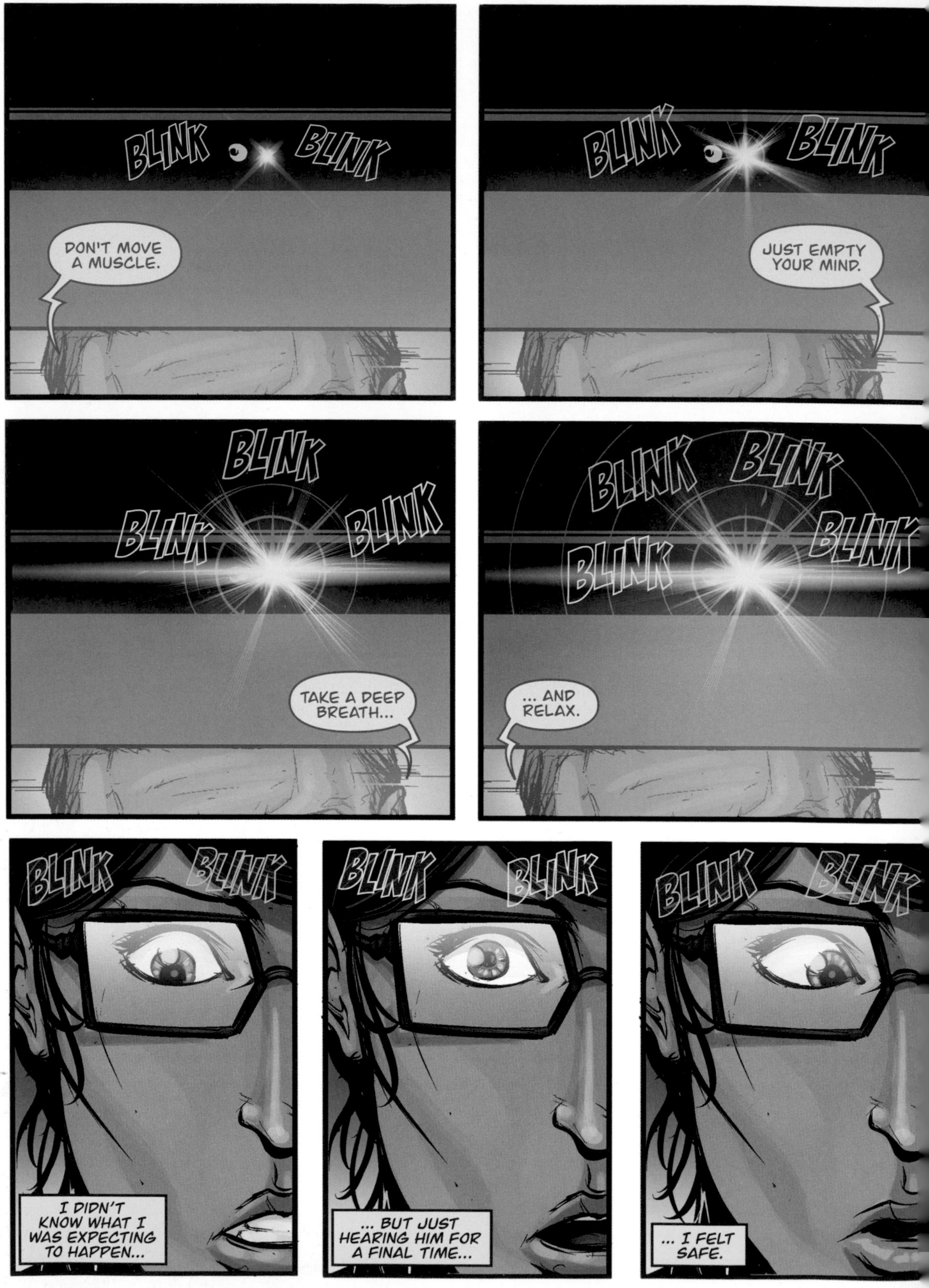
BLINK
BLINK
DON'T MOVE A MUSCLE.
BLINK
BLINK
JUST EMPTY YOUR MIND.
BLINK
BLINK
BLINK
TAKE A DEEP BREATH...
BLINK
BLINK
BLINK
BLINK
... AND RELAX.
BLINK
BLINK
I DIDN'T KNOW WHAT I WAS EXPECTING TO HAPPEN...
BLINK
BLINK
... BUT JUST HEARING HIM FOR A FINAL TIME...
BLINK
BLINK
... I FELT SAFE.

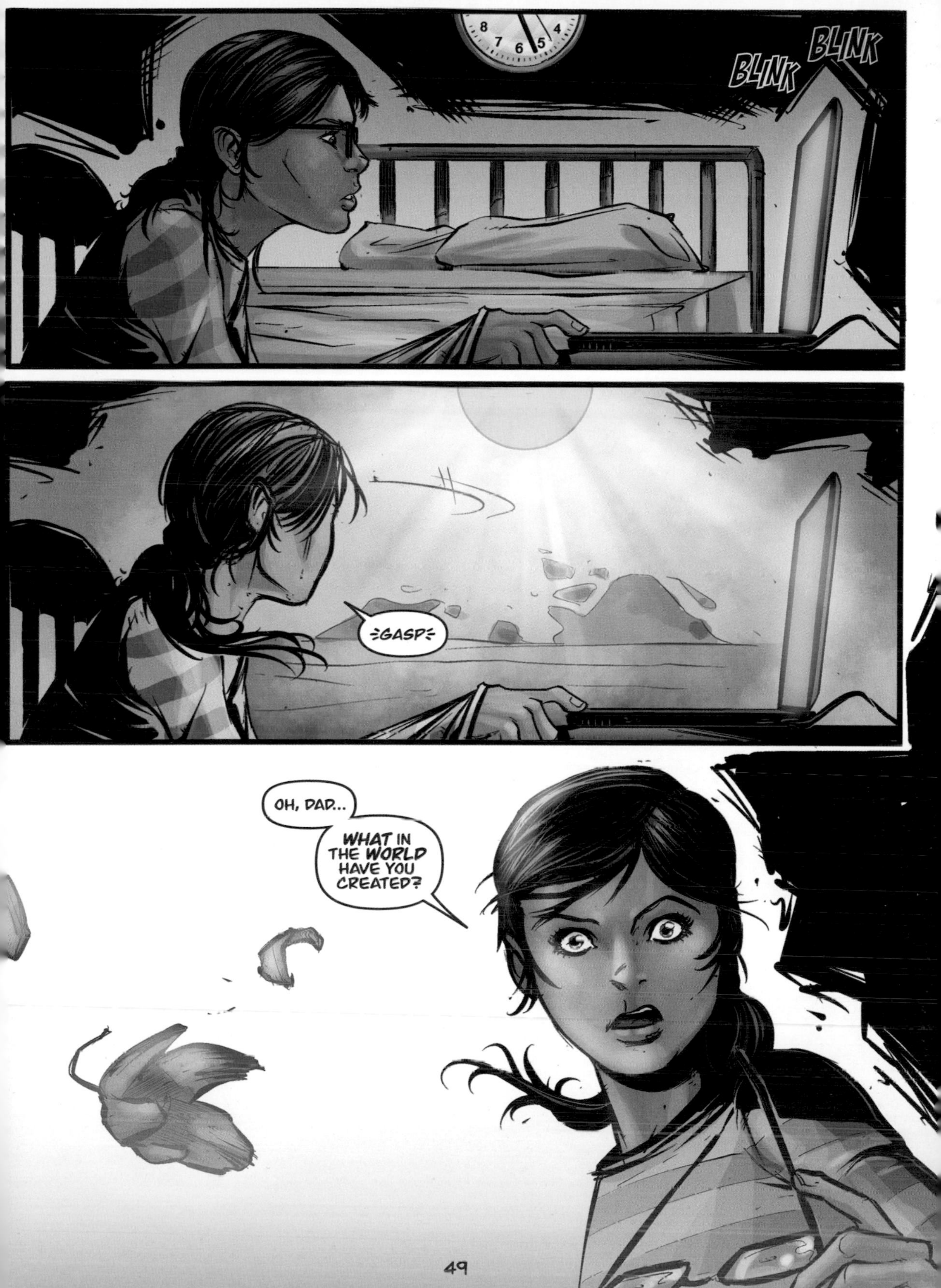
BLINK
BLINK
GASP
OH, DAD...
WHAT IN THE WORLD HAVE YOU CREATED?

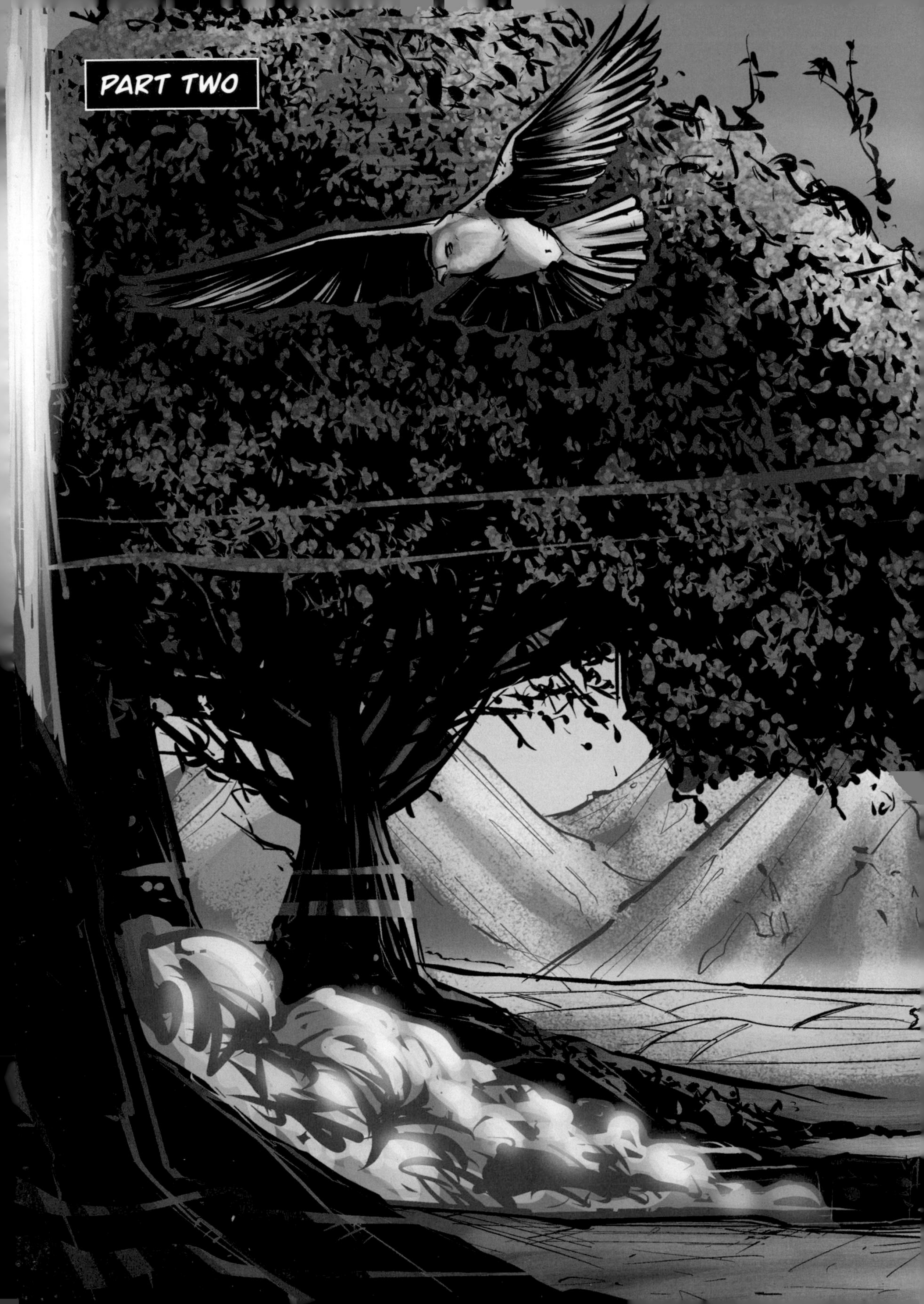
PART TWO

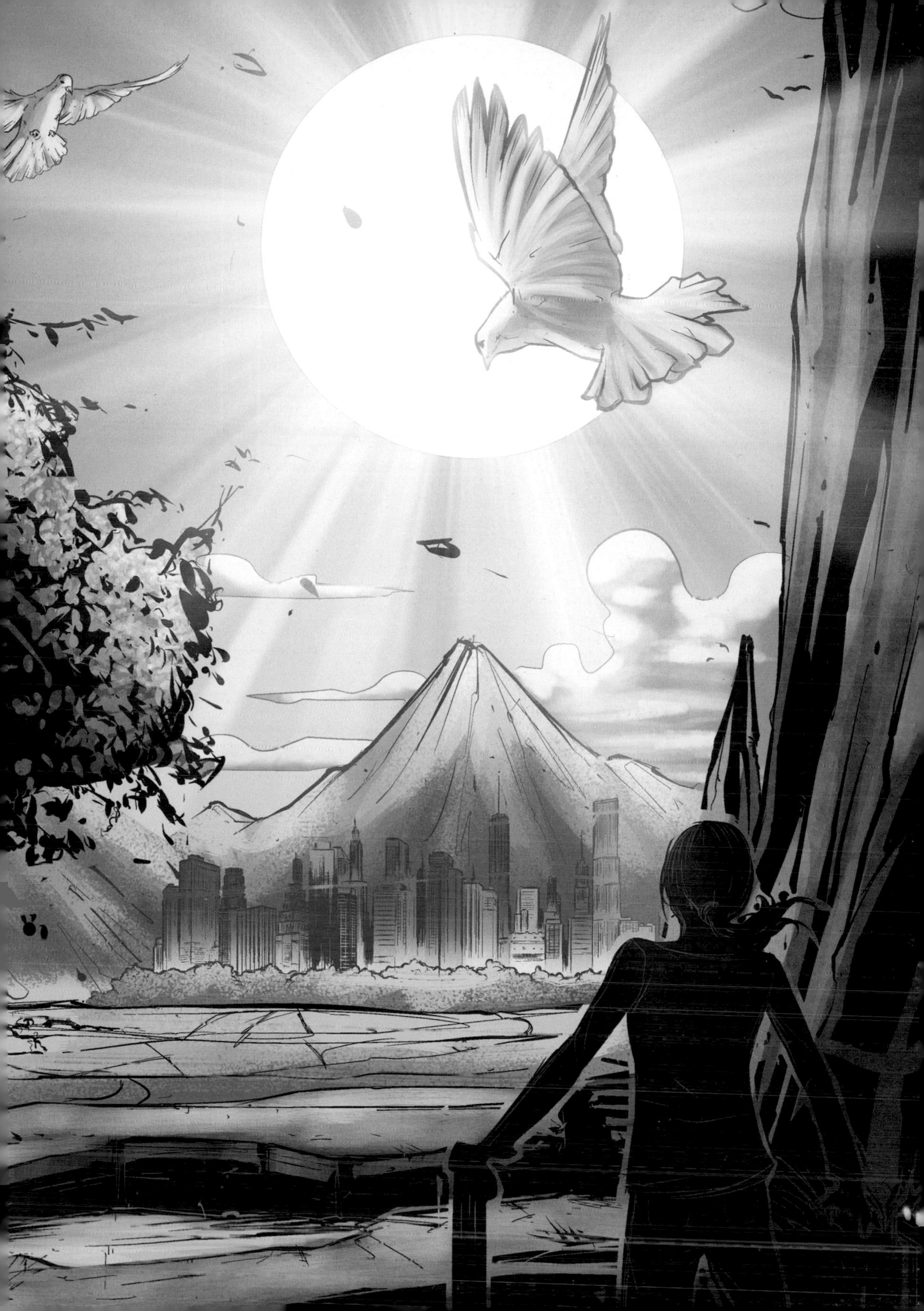

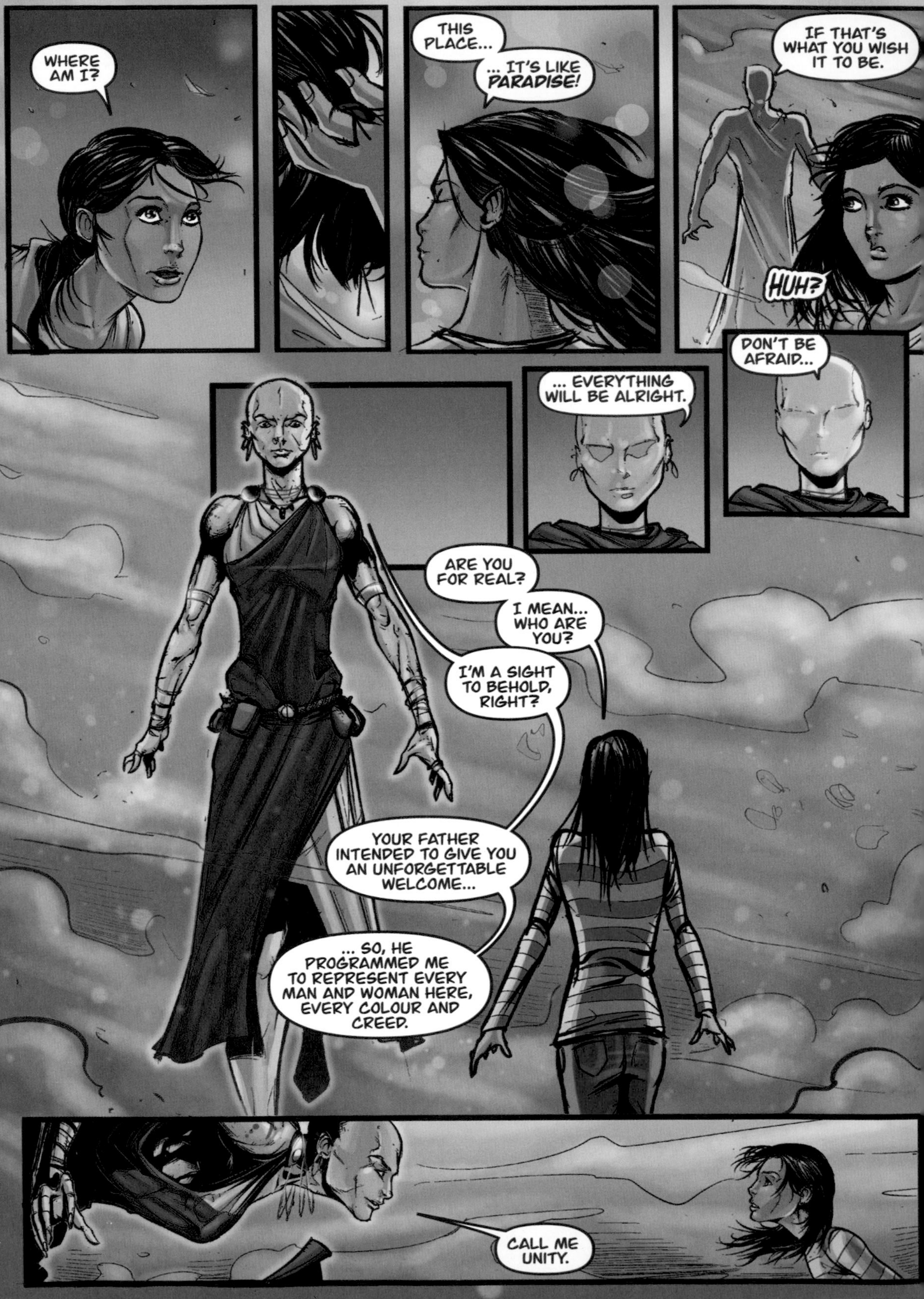
WHERE AM I?
THIS PLACE...
... IT'S LIKE PARADISE!
IF THAT'S WHAT YOU WISH IT TO BE.
HUH?
DON'T BE AFRAID...
... EVERYTHING WILL BE ALRIGHT.
ARE YOU FOR REAL?
I MEAN... WHO ARE YOU?
I'M A SIGHT TO BEHOLD, RIGHT?
YOUR FATHER INTENDED TO GIVE YOU AN UNFORGETTABLE WELCOME...
... SO, HE PROGRAMMED ME TO REPRESENT EVERY MAN AND WOMAN HERE, EVERY COLOUR AND CREED.
CALL ME UNITY.

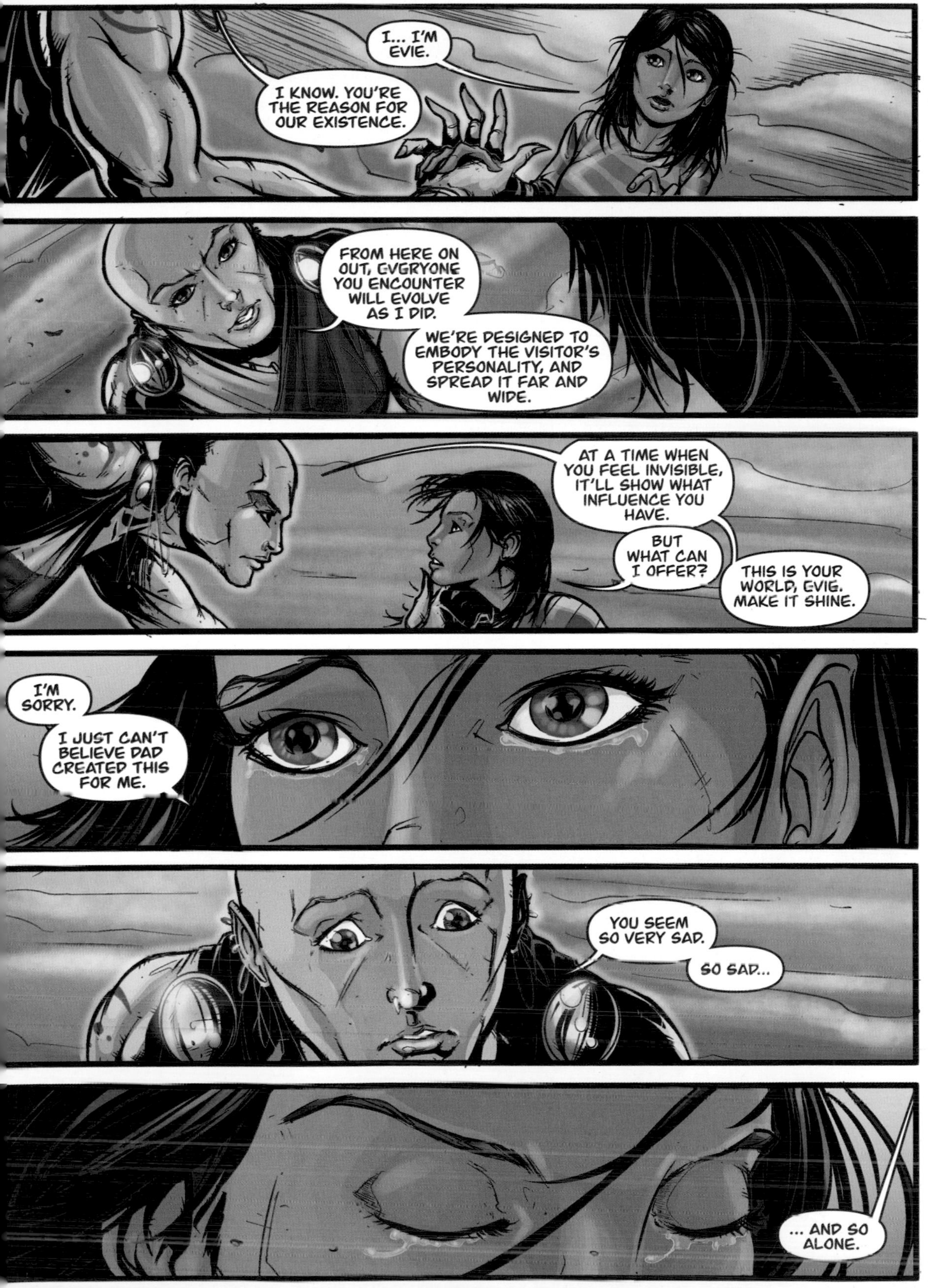
I... I'M EVIE.
I KNOW. YOU'RE THE REASON FOR OUR EXISTENCE.
FROM HERE ON OUT, EVERYONE YOU ENCOUNTER WILL EVOLVE AS I DID.
WE'RE DESIGNED TO EMBODY THE VISITOR'S PERSONALITY, AND SPREAD IT FAR AND WIDE.
AT A TIME WHEN YOU FEEL INVISIBLE, IT'LL SHOW WHAT INFLUENCE YOU HAVE.
BUT WHAT CAN I OFFER?
THIS IS YOUR WORLD, EVIE. MAKE IT SHINE.
I'M SORRY.
I JUST CAN'T BELIEVE DAD CREATED THIS FOR ME.
YOU SEEM SO VERY SAD.
SO SAD...
... AND SO ALONE.

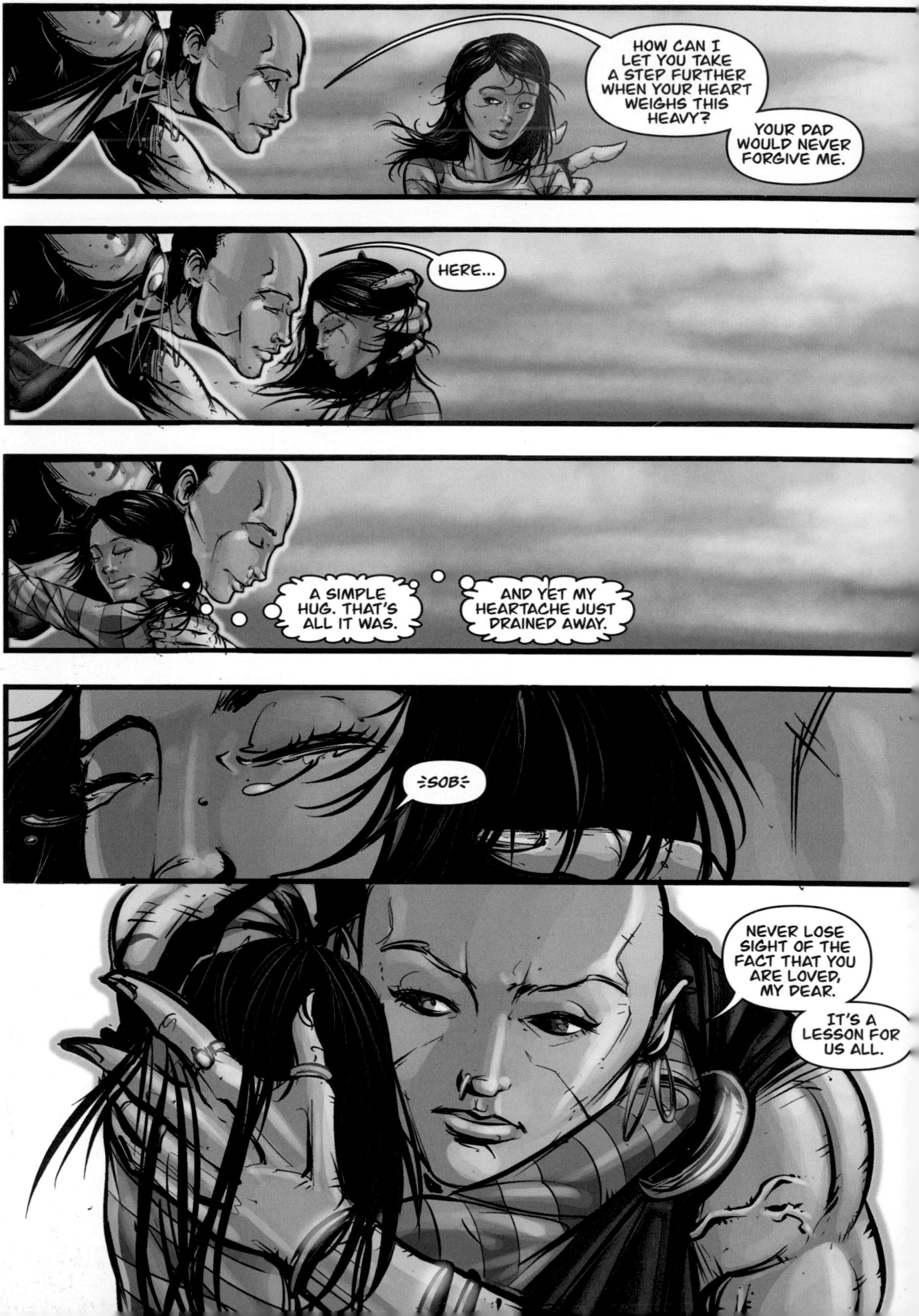
HOW CAN I LET YOU TAKE A STEP FURTHER WHEN YOUR HEART WEIGHS THIS HEAVY?
YOUR DAD WOULD NEVER FORGIVE ME.
HERE...
A SIMPLE HUG. THAT'S ALL IT WAS.
AND YET MY HEARTACHE JUST DRAINED AWAY.
SOB
NEVER LOSE SIGHT OF THE FACT THAT YOU ARE LOVED, MY DEAR.
IT'S A LESSON FOR US ALL.

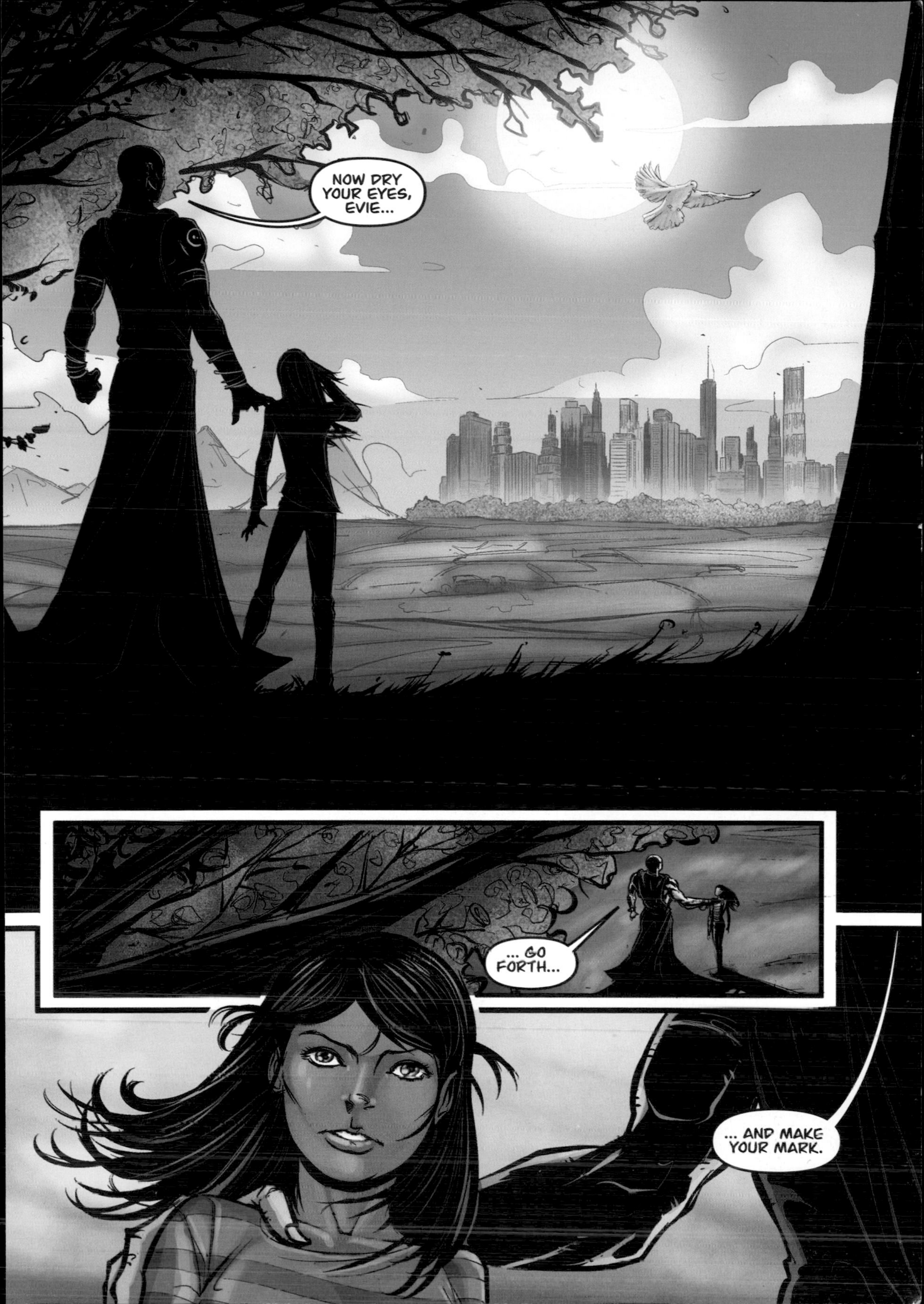
NOW DRY YOUR EYES, EVIE...
... GO FORTH...
... AND MAKE YOUR MARK.

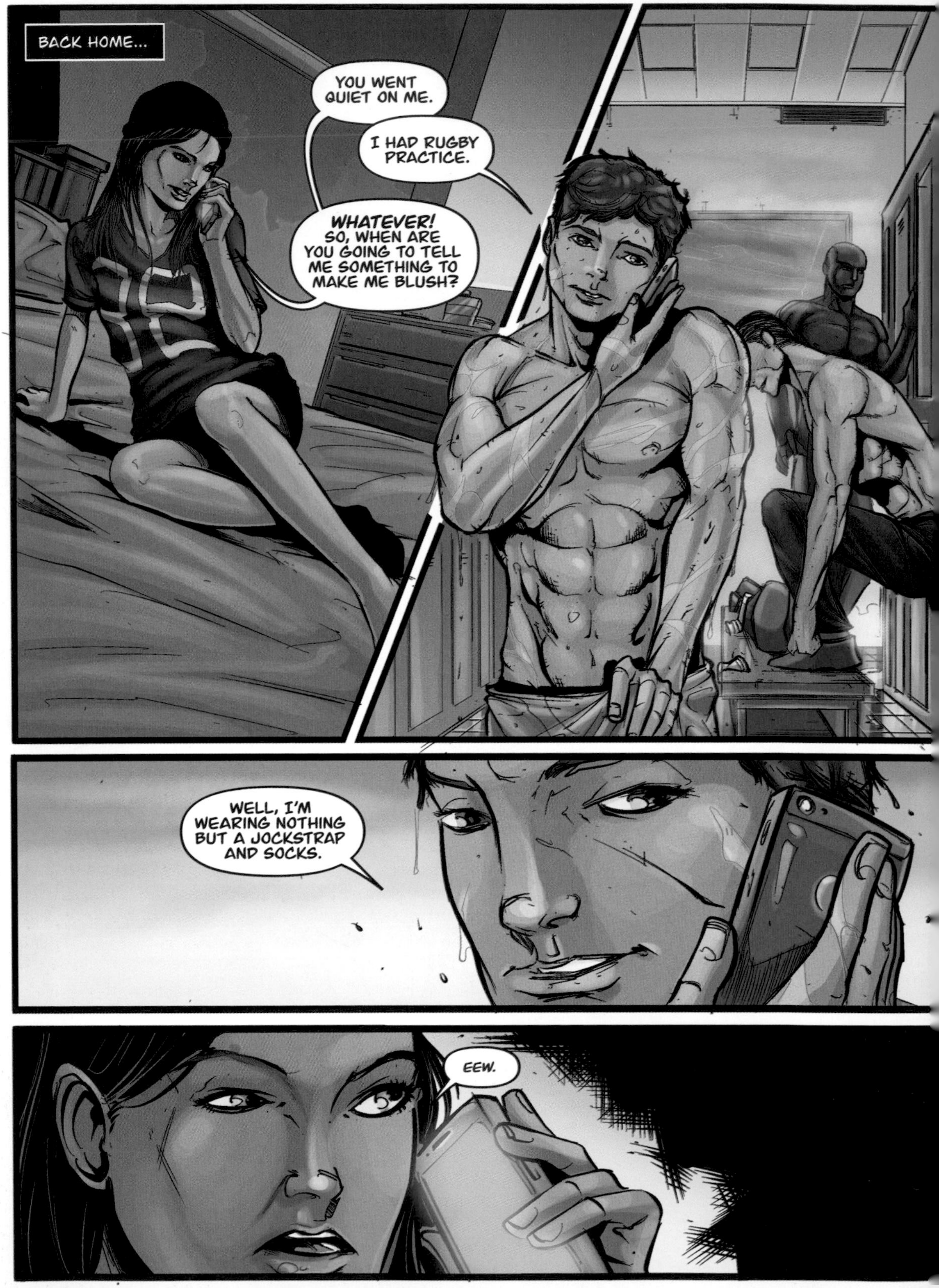
BACK HOME...
YOU WENT QUIET ON ME.
I HAD RUGBY PRACTICE.
WHATEVER! SO, WHEN ARE YOU GOING TO TELL ME SOMETHING TO MAKE ME BLUSH?
WELL, I'M WEARING NOTHING BUT A JOCKSTRAP AND SOCKS.
EEW.

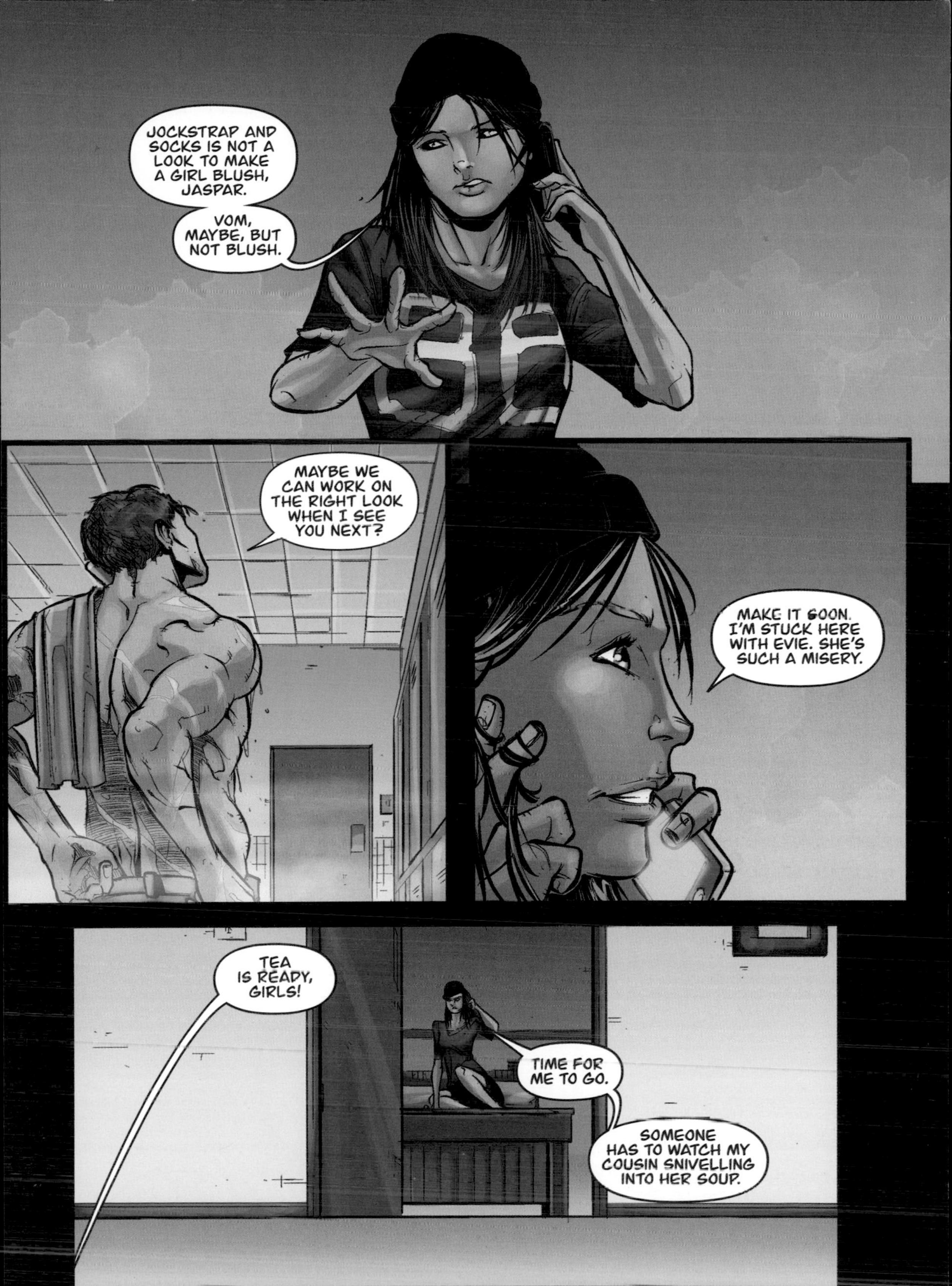
JOCKSTRAP AND SOCKS IS NOT A LOOK TO MAKE A GIRL BLUSH, JASPAR.
VOM, MAYBE, BUT NOT BLUSH.
MAYBE WE CAN WORK ON THE RIGHT LOOK WHEN I SEE YOU NEXT?
MAKE IT SOON. I'M STUCK HERE WITH EVIE. SHE'S SUCH A MISERY.
TEA IS READY, GIRLS!
TIME FOR ME TO GO.
SOMEONE HAS TO WATCH MY COUSIN SNIVELLING INTO HER SOUP.

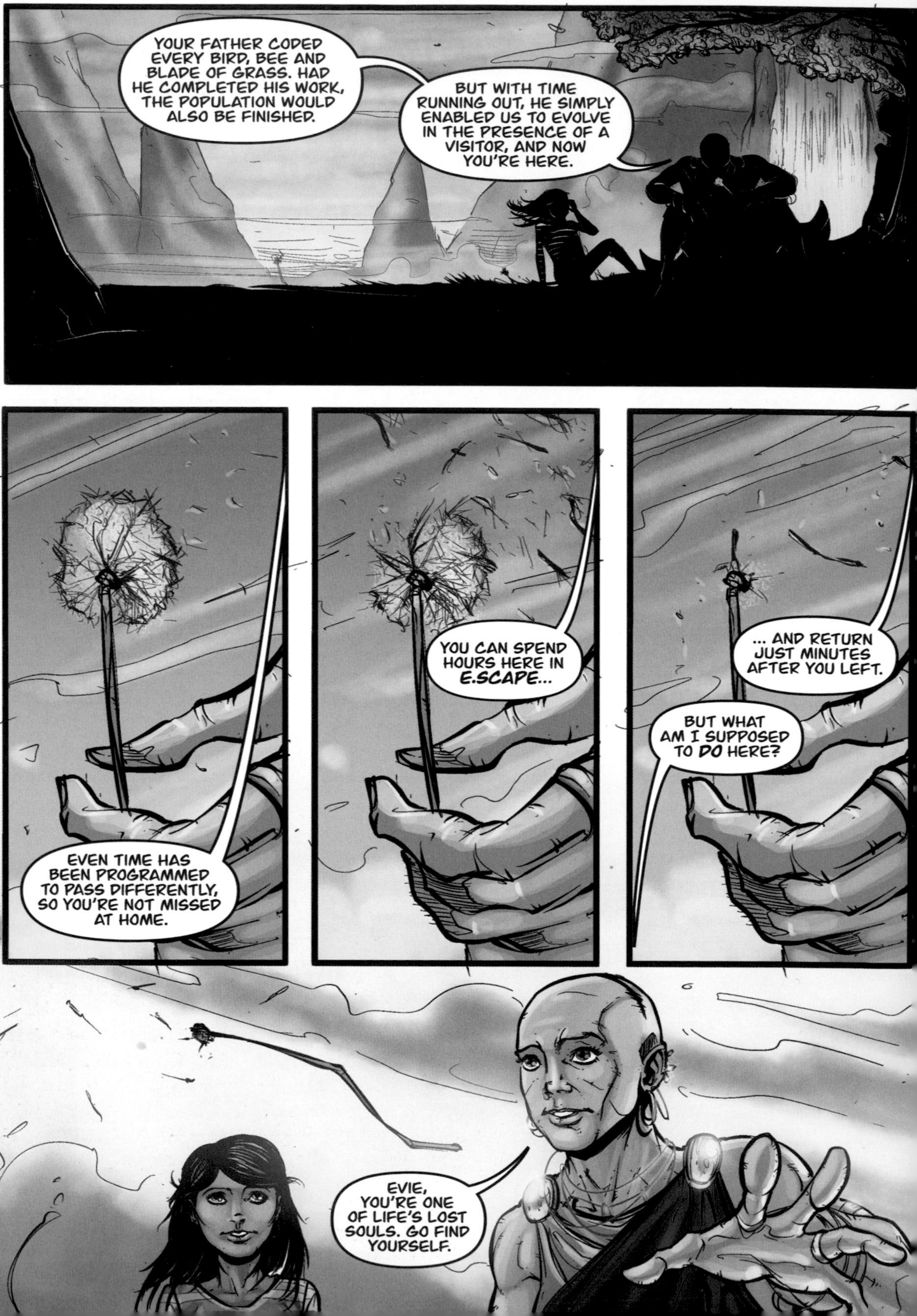
YOUR FATHER CODED EVERY BIRD, BEE AND BLADE OF GRASS. HAD HE COMPLETED HIS WORK, THE POPULATION WOULD ALSO BE FINISHED.
BUT WITH TIME RUNNING OUT, HE SIMPLY ENABLED US TO EVOLVE IN THE PRESENCE OF A VISITOR, AND NOW YOU'RE HERE.
EVEN TIME HAS BEEN PROGRAMMED TO PASS DIFFERENTLY, SO YOU'RE NOT MISSED AT HOME.
YOU CAN SPEND HOURS HERE IN **E.SCAPE**...
... AND RETURN JUST MINUTES AFTER YOU LEFT.
BUT WHAT AM I SUPPOSED TO ***DO*** HERE?
EVIE, YOU'RE ONE OF LIFE'S LOST SOULS. GO FIND YOURSELF.

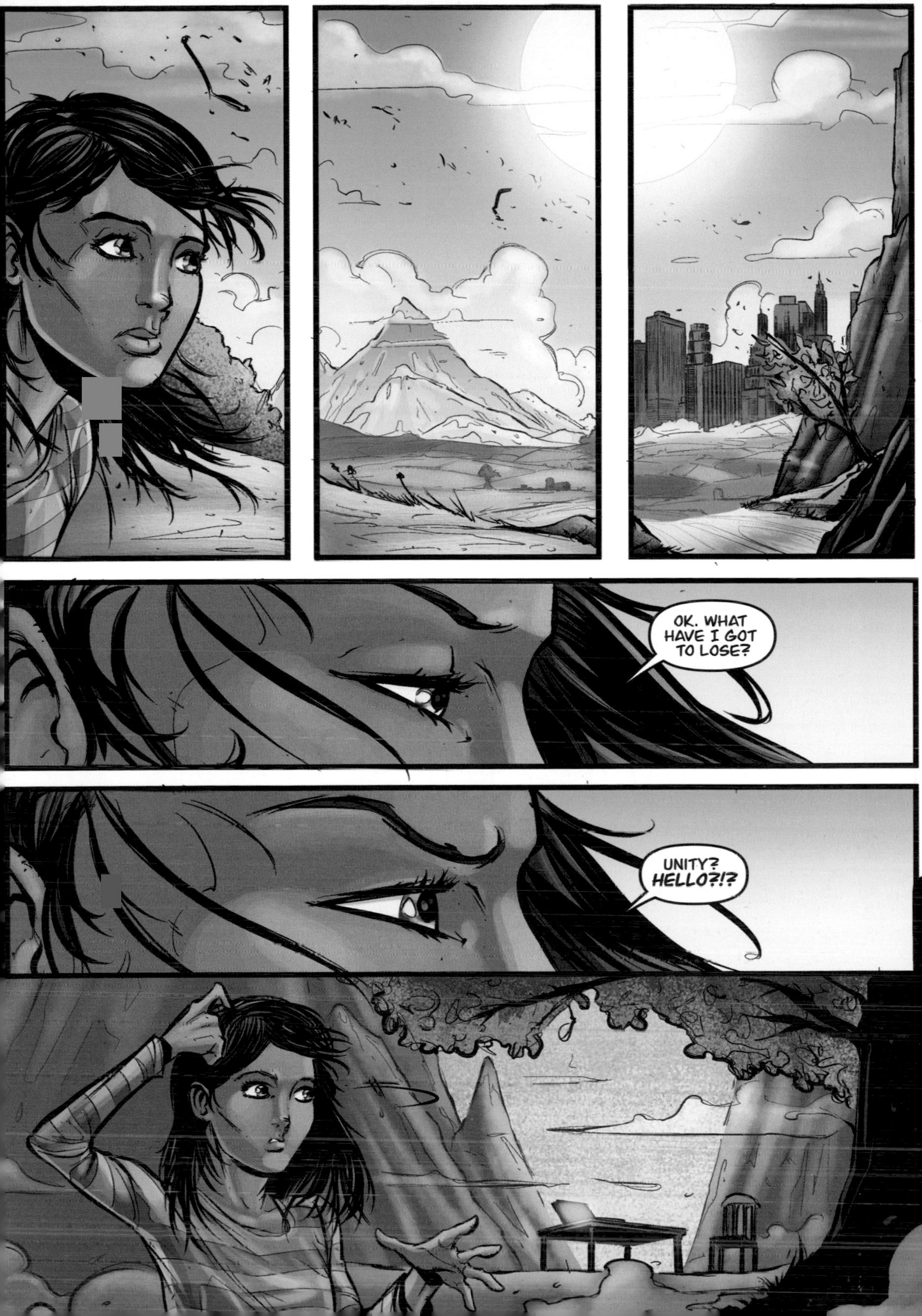
OK. WHAT HAVE I GOT TO LOSE?
UNITY? HELLO?!?

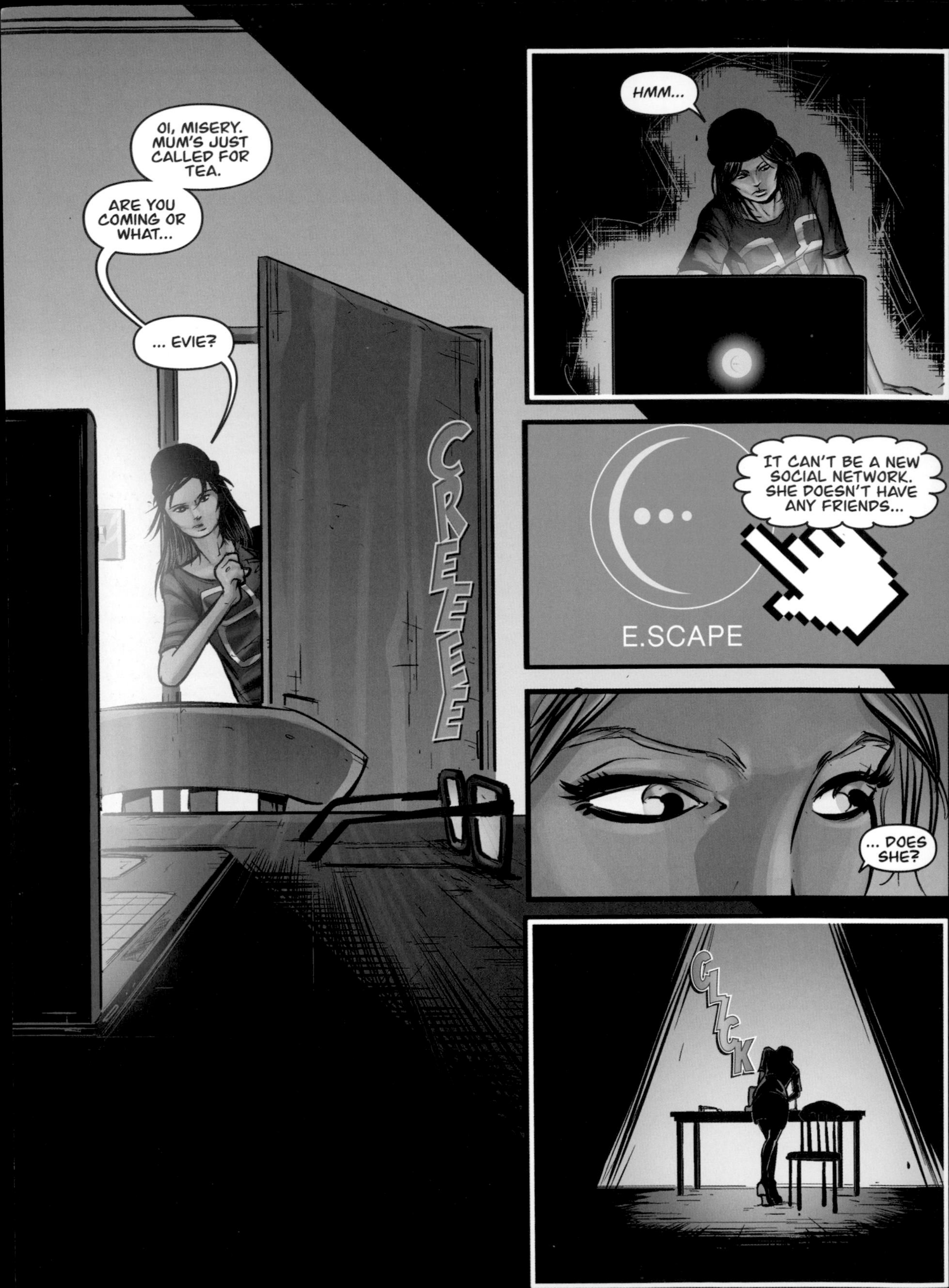
OI, MISERY. MUM'S JUST CALLED FOR TEA.
ARE YOU COMING OR WHAT...
... EVIE?
CREEEEE
HMM...
E.SCAPE
IT CAN'T BE A NEW SOCIAL NETWORK. SHE DOESN'T HAVE ANY FRIENDS...
... DOES SHE?
CLICK

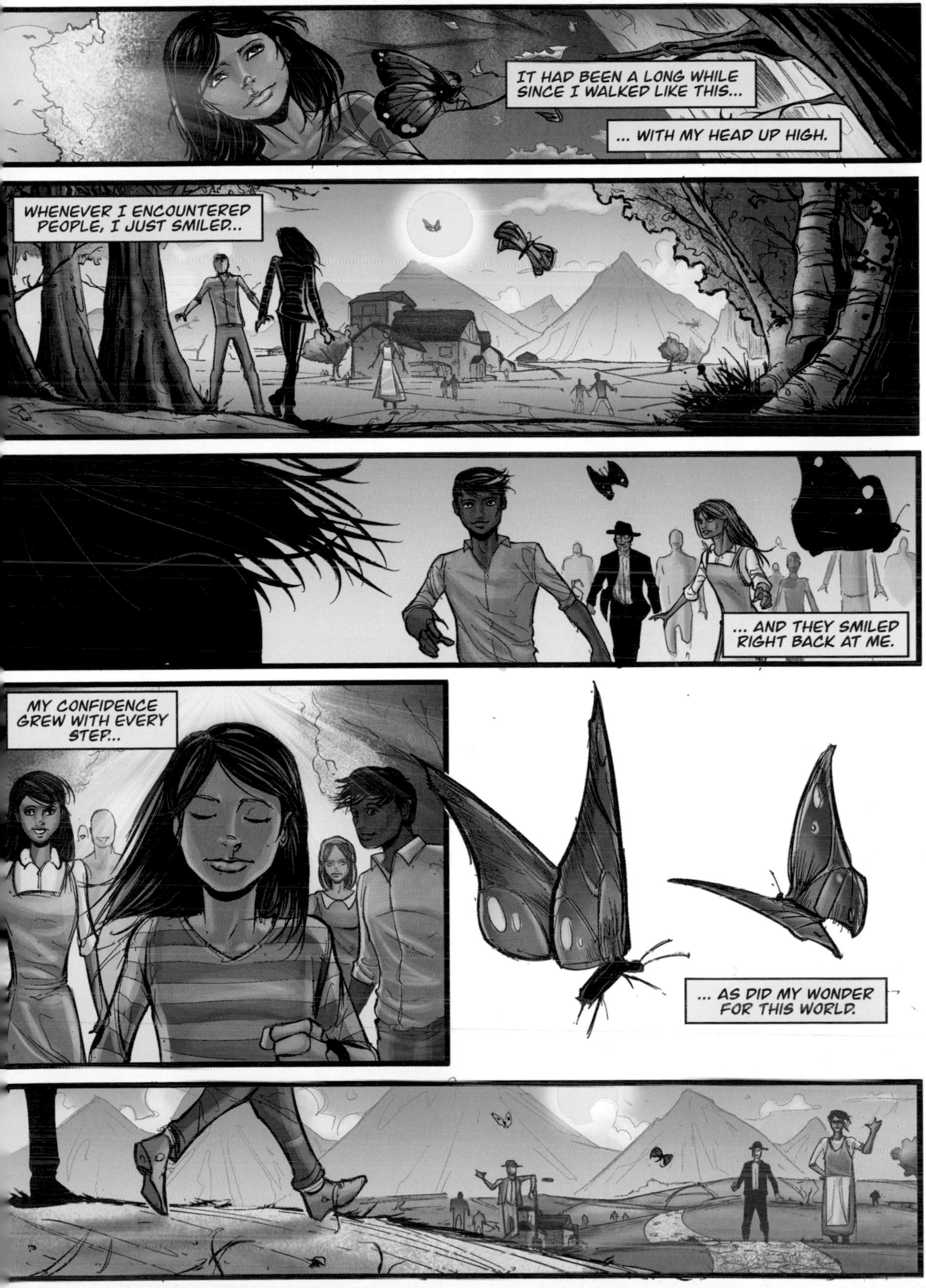
IT HAD BEEN A LONG WHILE SINCE I WALKED LIKE THIS...
... WITH MY HEAD UP HIGH.
WHENEVER I ENCOUNTERED PEOPLE, I JUST SMILED...
... AND THEY SMILED RIGHT BACK AT ME.
MY CONFIDENCE GREW WITH EVERY STEP...
... AS DID MY WONDER FOR THIS WORLD.

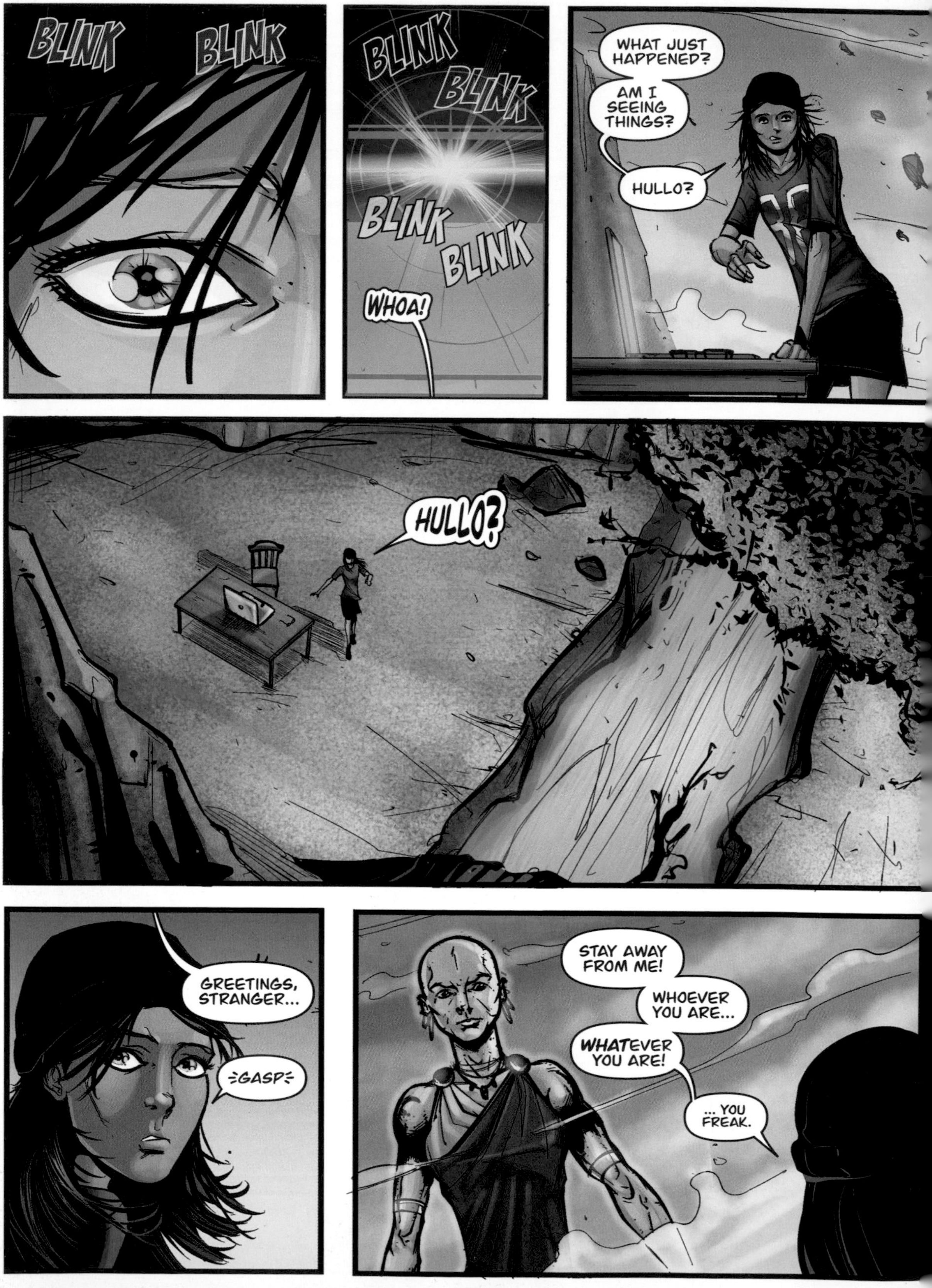
BLINK
BLINK
BLINK
BLINK
BLINK
BLINK
WHOA!
WHAT JUST HAPPENED?
AM I SEEING THINGS?
HULLO?
HULLO?
GREETINGS, STRANGER...
GASP
STAY AWAY FROM ME!
WHOEVER YOU ARE...
WHATEVER YOU ARE!
... YOU FREAK.

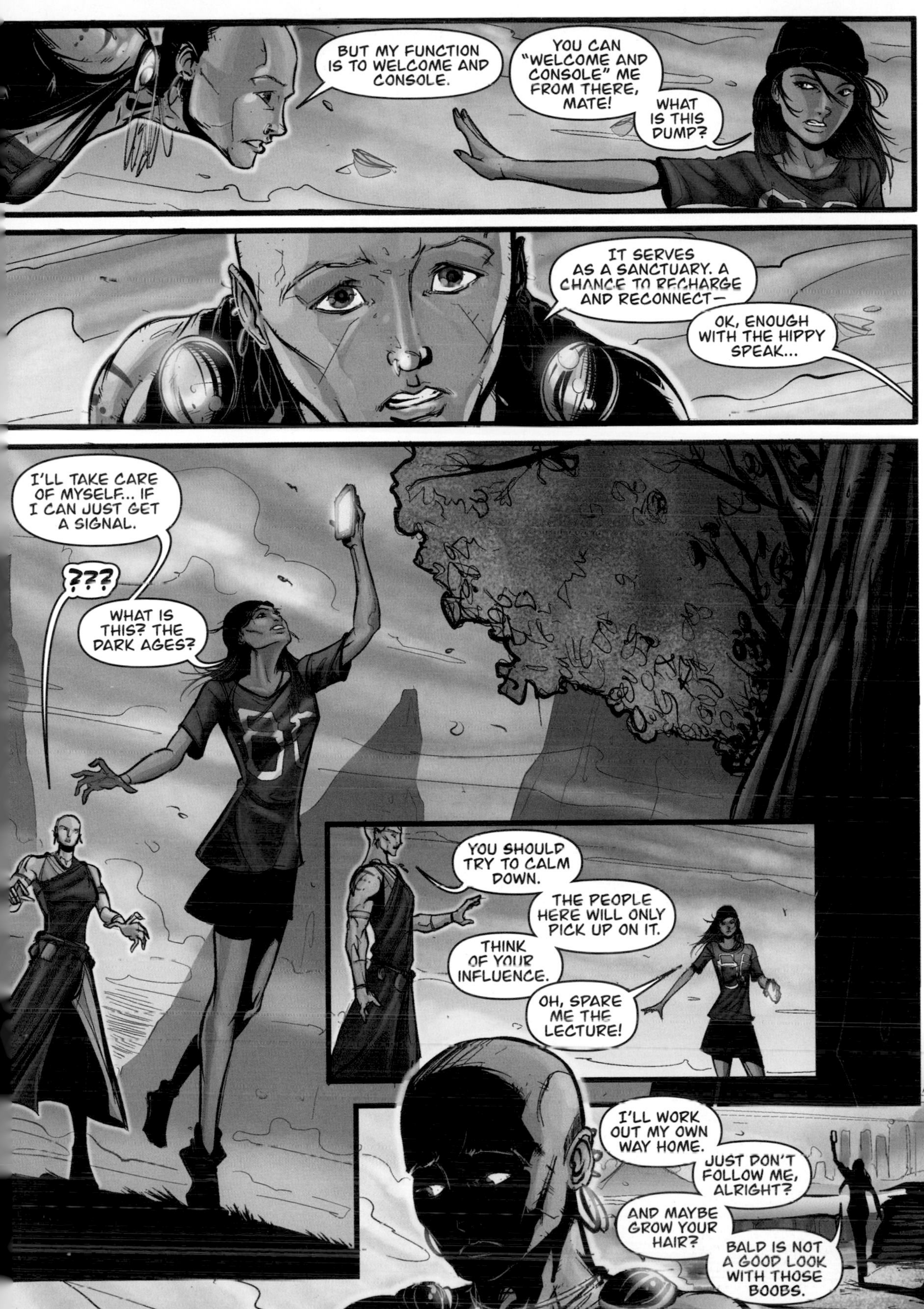
BUT MY FUNCTION IS TO WELCOME AND CONSOLE.
YOU CAN "WELCOME AND CONSOLE" ME FROM THERE, MATE!
WHAT IS THIS DUMP?
IT SERVES AS A SANCTUARY. A CHANCE TO RECHARGE AND RECONNECT—
OK, ENOUGH WITH THE HIPPY SPEAK...
I'LL TAKE CARE OF MYSELF... IF I CAN JUST GET A SIGNAL.
???
WHAT IS THIS? THE DARK AGES?
YOU SHOULD TRY TO CALM DOWN.
THE PEOPLE HERE WILL ONLY PICK UP ON IT.
THINK OF YOUR INFLUENCE.
OH, SPARE ME THE LECTURE!
I'LL WORK OUT MY OWN WAY HOME.
JUST DON'T FOLLOW ME, ALRIGHT?
AND MAYBE GROW YOUR HAIR?
BALD IS NOT A GOOD LOOK WITH THOSE BOOBS.

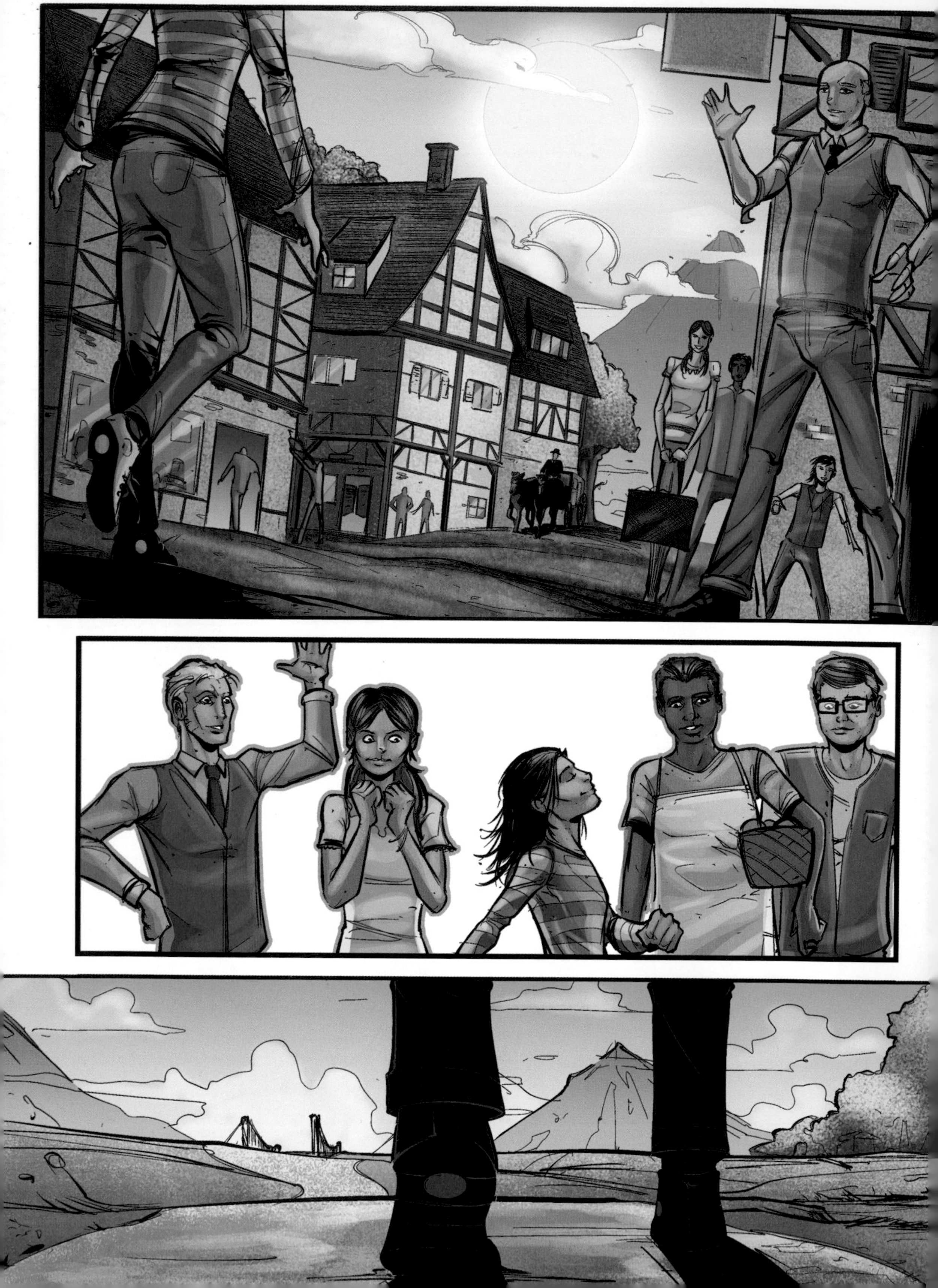

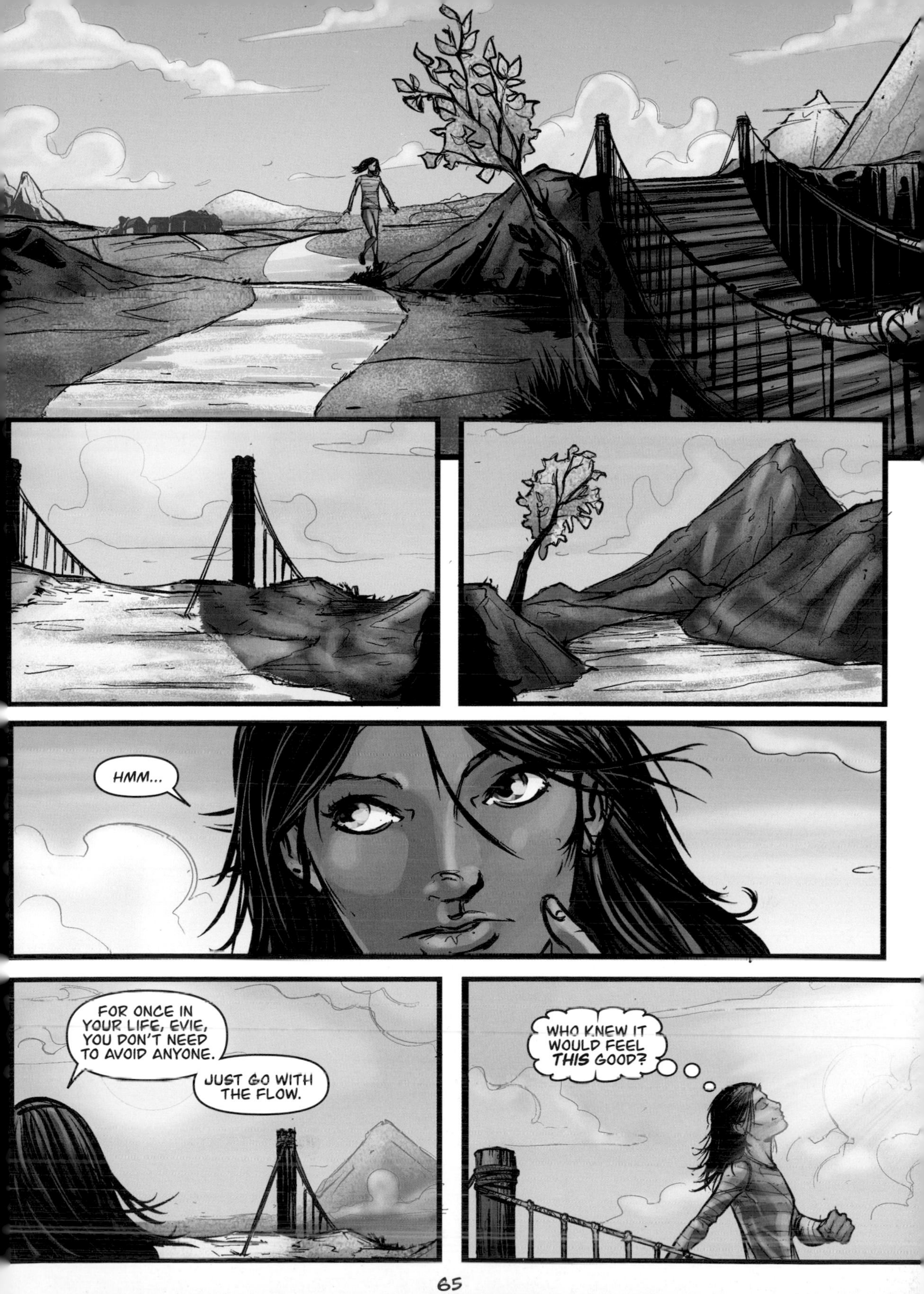
HMM...
FOR ONCE IN YOUR LIFE, EVIE, YOU DON'T NEED TO AVOID ANYONE.
JUST GO WITH THE FLOW.
WHO KNEW IT WOULD FEEL THIS GOOD?

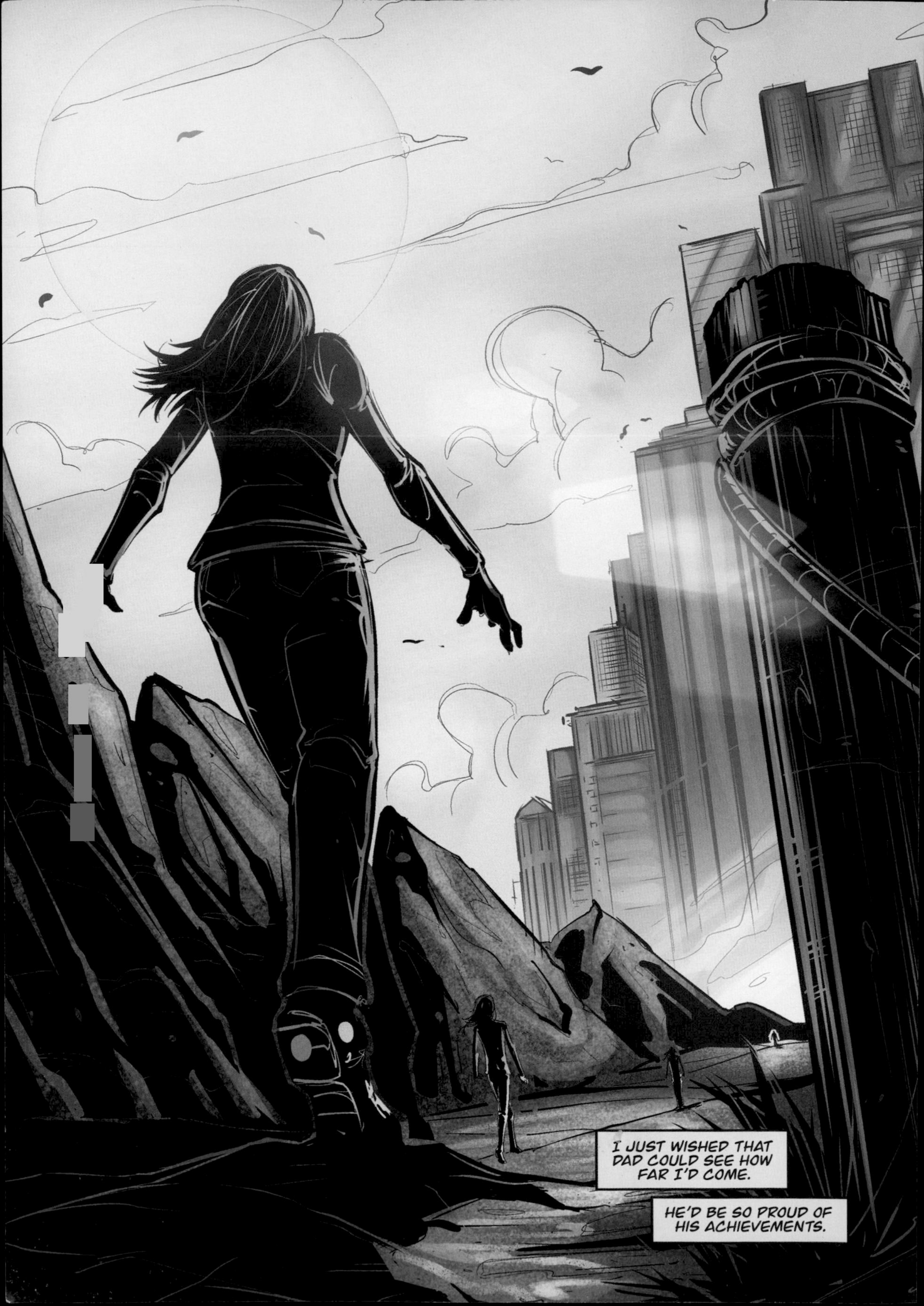
I JUST WISHED THAT DAD COULD SEE HOW FAR I'D COME.
HE'D BE SO PROUD OF HIS ACHIEVEMENTS.

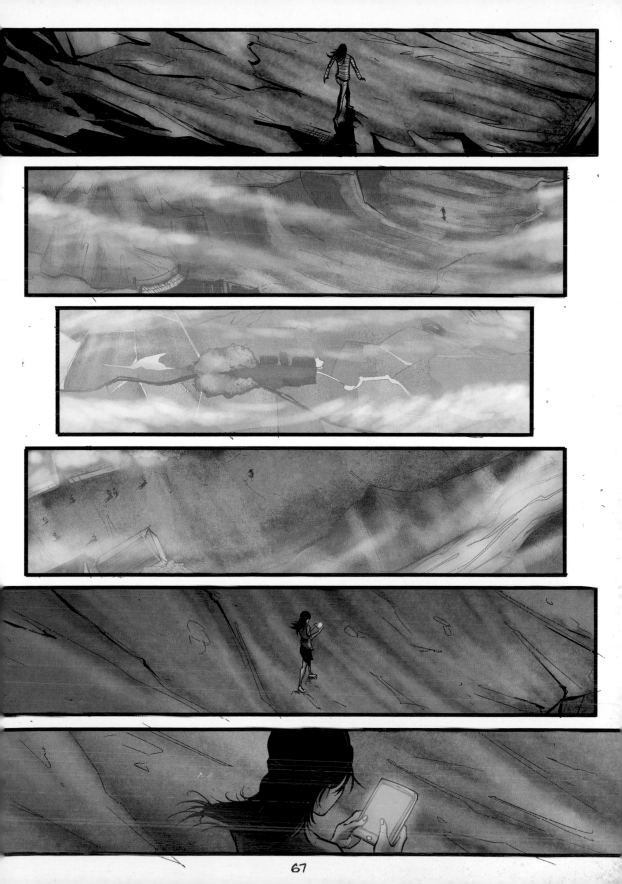

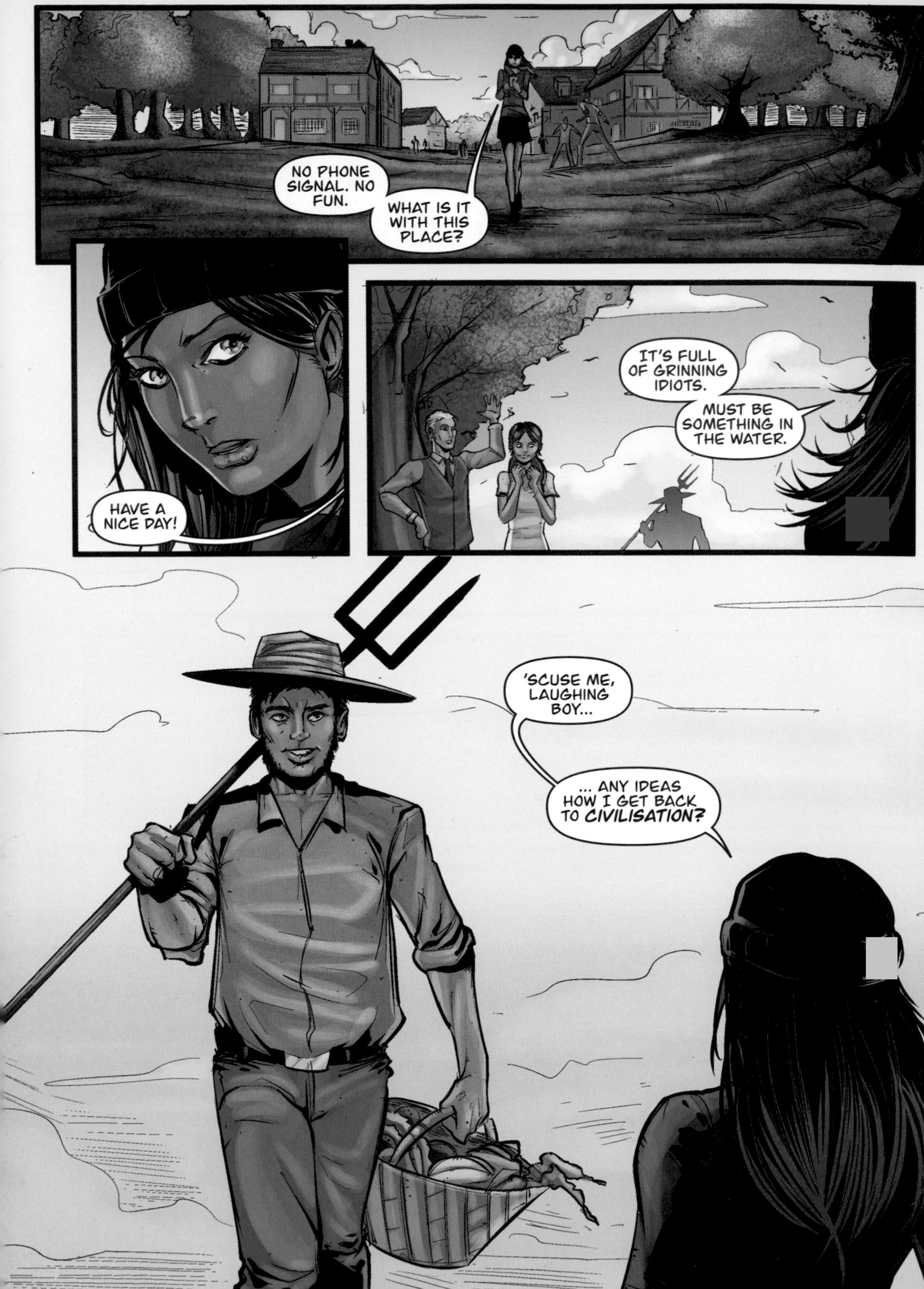
NO PHONE SIGNAL. NO FUN.
WHAT IS IT WITH THIS PLACE?
HAVE A NICE DAY!
IT'S FULL OF GRINNING IDIOTS.
MUST BE SOMETHING IN THE WATER.
'SCUSE ME, LAUGHING BOY...
... ANY IDEAS HOW I GET BACK TO CIVILISATION?

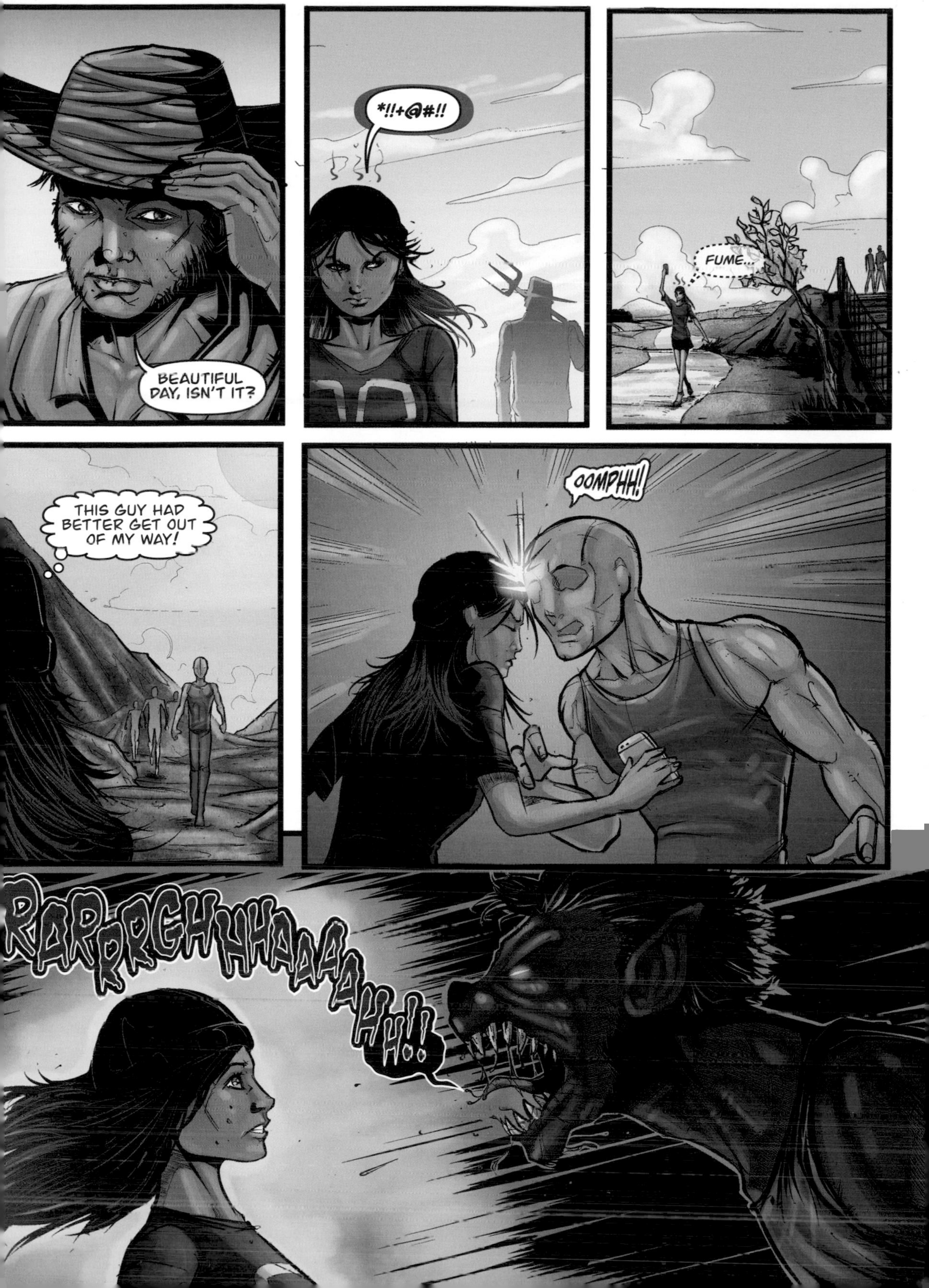
BEAUTIFUL DAY, ISN'T IT?
*!!+@#!!
FUME...
THIS GUY HAD BETTER GET OUT OF MY WAY!
OOMPHH!
RARRRGHHHAAAAAHH!!

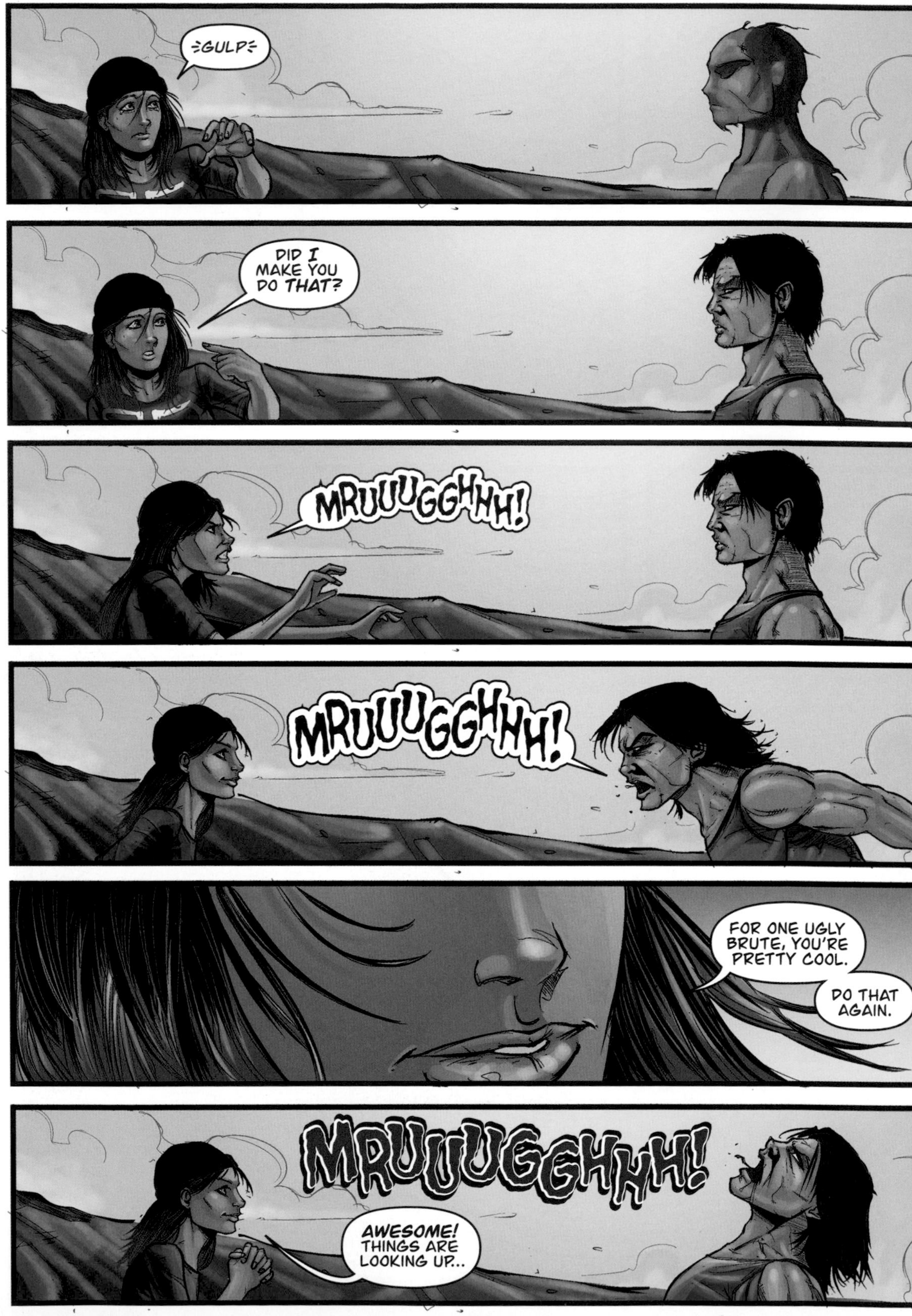

=GULP=
DID I MAKE YOU DO THAT?
MRUUUGGHHH!
MRUUUGGHHH!
FOR ONE UGLY BRUTE, YOU'RE PRETTY COOL.
DO THAT AGAIN.
MRUUUGGHHH!
AWESOME! THINGS ARE LOOKING UP...

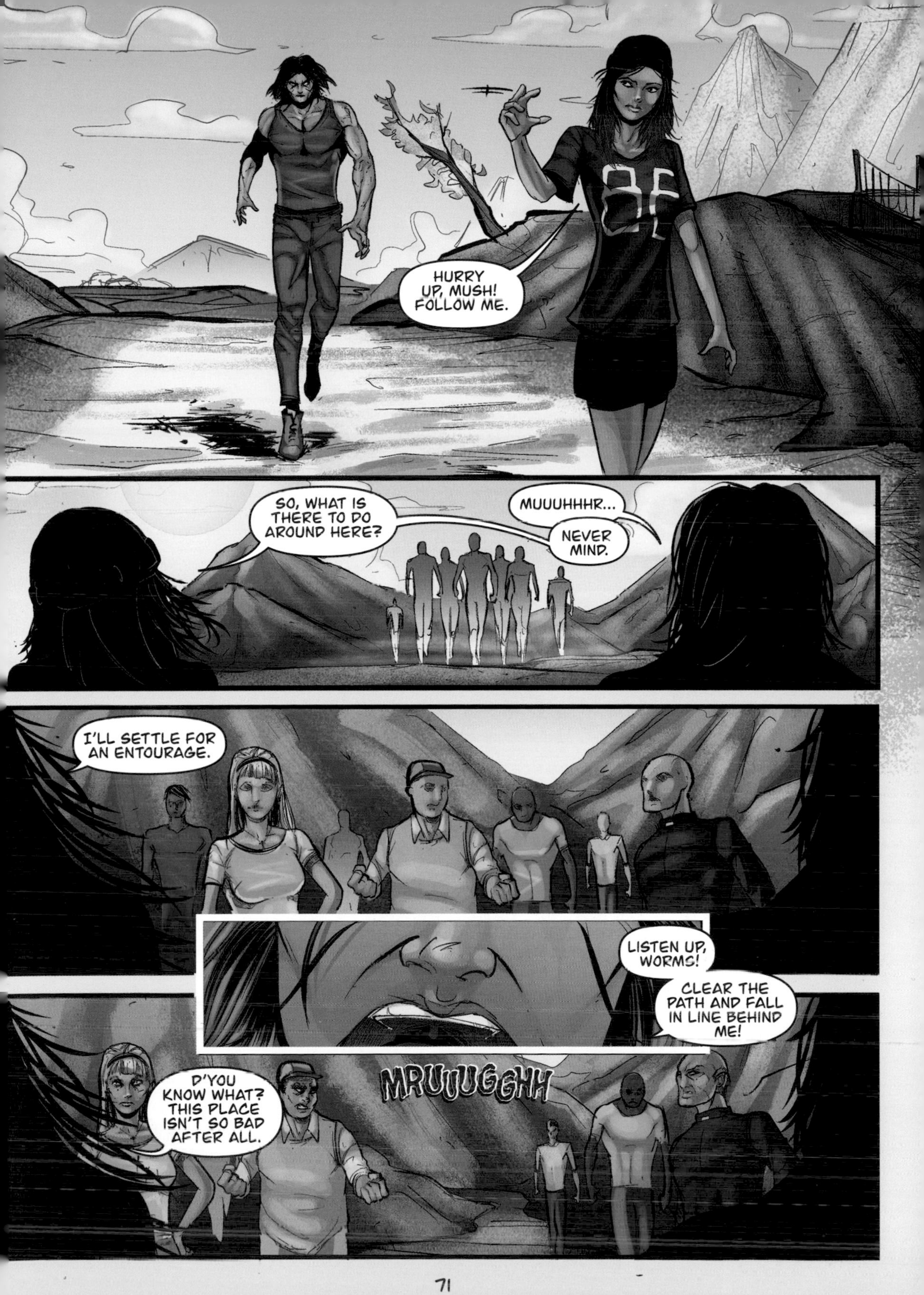
HURRY UP, MUSH! FOLLOW ME.
SO, WHAT IS THERE TO DO AROUND HERE?
MUUUHHHR...
NEVER MIND.
I'LL SETTLE FOR AN ENTOURAGE.
LISTEN UP, WORMS!
CLEAR THE PATH AND FALL IN LINE BEHIND ME!
MRUUUGGHH
D'YOU KNOW WHAT? THIS PLACE ISN'T SO BAD AFTER ALL.

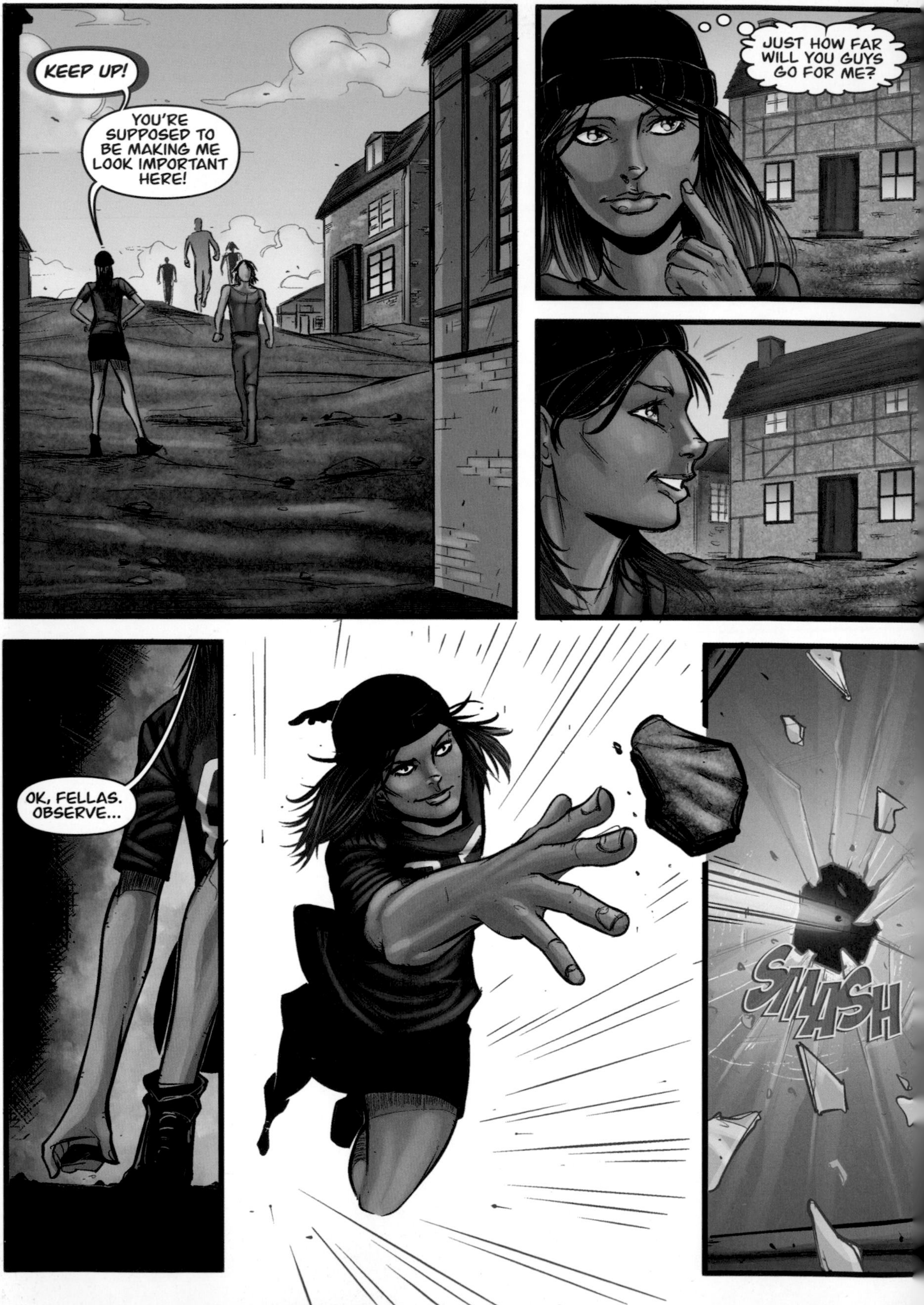
KEEP UP!
YOU'RE SUPPOSED TO BE MAKING ME LOOK IMPORTANT HERE!
JUST HOW FAR WILL YOU GUYS GO FOR ME?
OK, FELLAS. OBSERVE...
SMASH

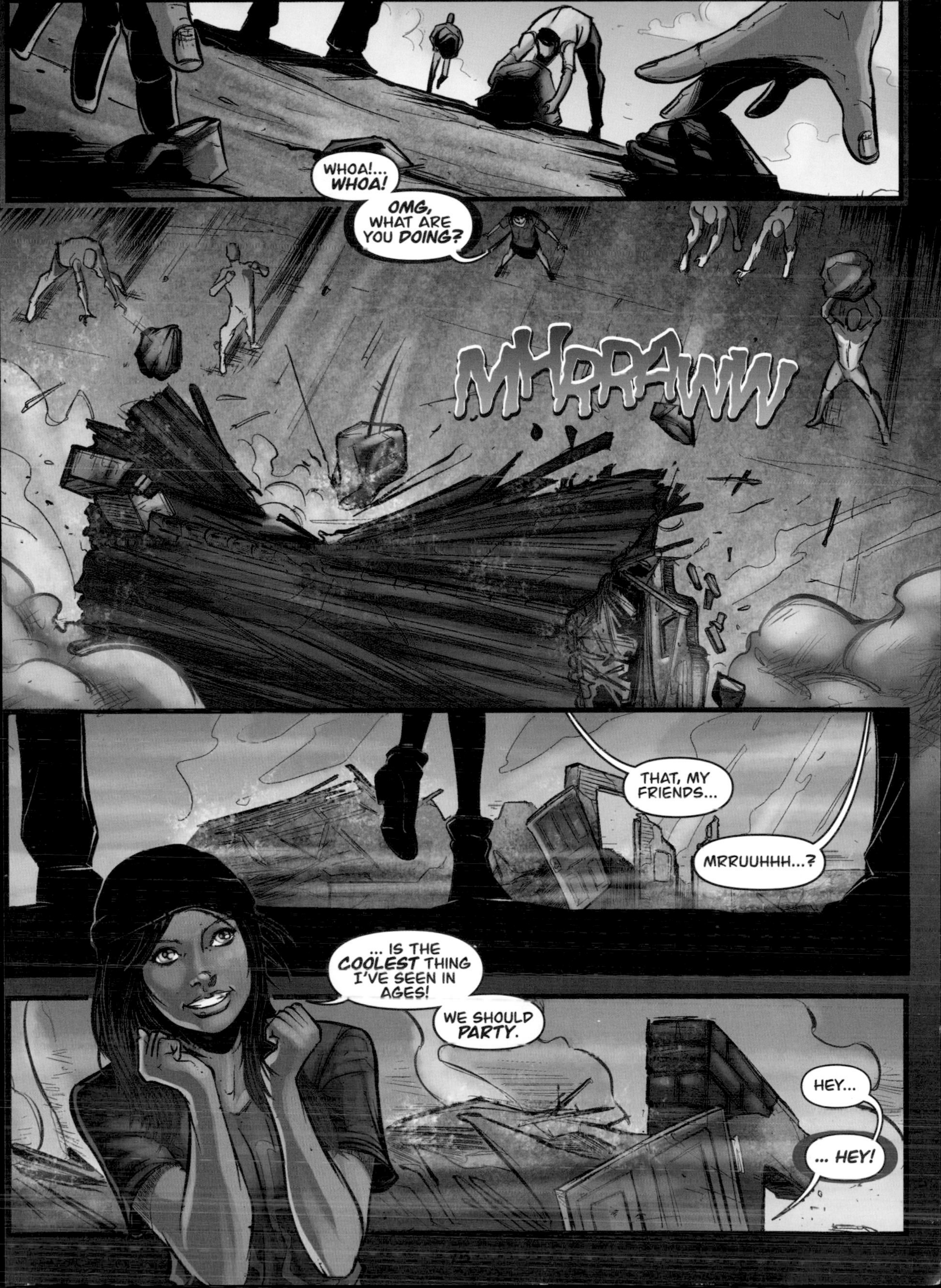
WHOA!... WHOA!
OMG, WHAT ARE YOU DOING?
MHRRAWW
THAT, MY FRIENDS...
MRRUUHHH...?
... IS THE COOLEST THING I'VE SEEN IN AGES!
WE SHOULD PARTY.
HEY...
... HEY!

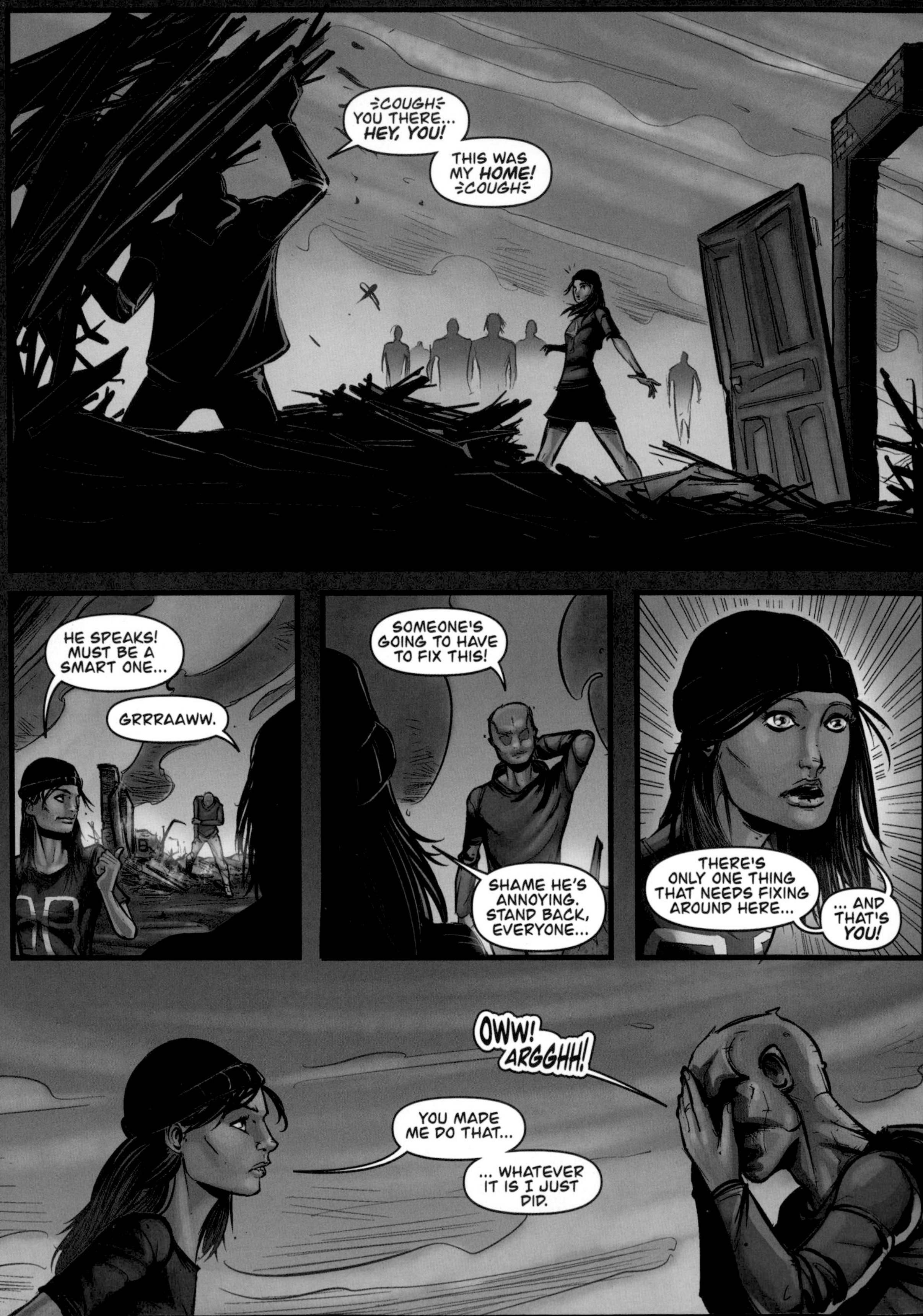

COUGH YOU THERE... HEY, YOU!
THIS WAS MY HOME! COUGH
HE SPEAKS! MUST BE A SMART ONE...
GRRRAAWW.
SOMEONE'S GOING TO HAVE TO FIX THIS!
SHAME HE'S ANNOYING. STAND BACK, EVERYONE...
THERE'S ONLY ONE THING THAT NEEDS FIXING AROUND HERE...
... AND THAT'S YOU!
OWW! ARGGHH!
YOU MADE ME DO THAT...
... WHATEVER IT IS I JUST DID.

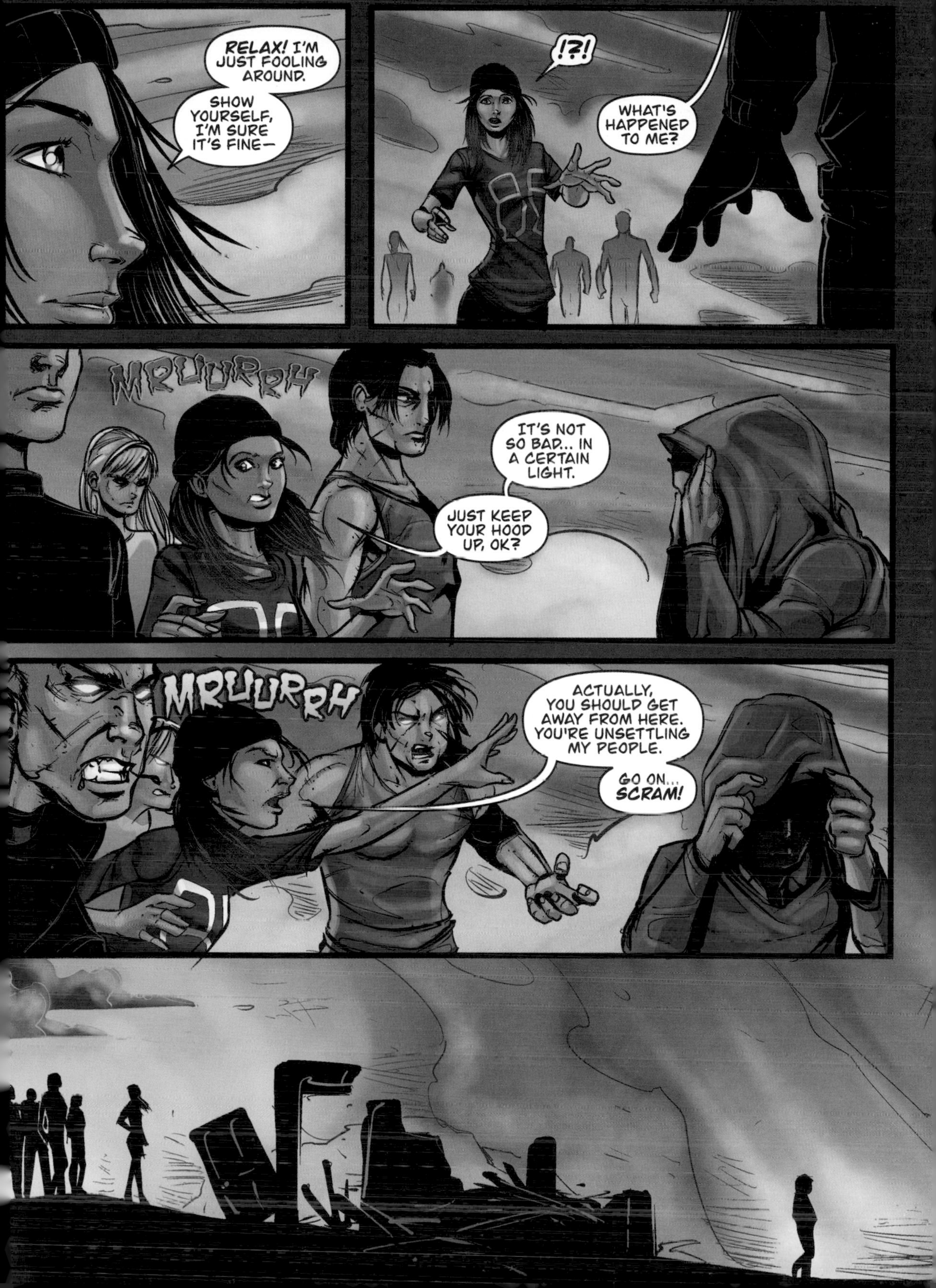
RELAX! I'M JUST FOOLING AROUND.
SHOW YOURSELF, I'M SURE IT'S FINE—
!?!
WHAT'S HAPPENED TO ME?
MRUURRH
IT'S NOT SO BAD... IN A CERTAIN LIGHT.
JUST KEEP YOUR HOOD UP, OK?
MRUURRH
ACTUALLY, YOU SHOULD GET AWAY FROM HERE. YOU'RE UNSETTLING MY PEOPLE.
GO ON... SCRAM!

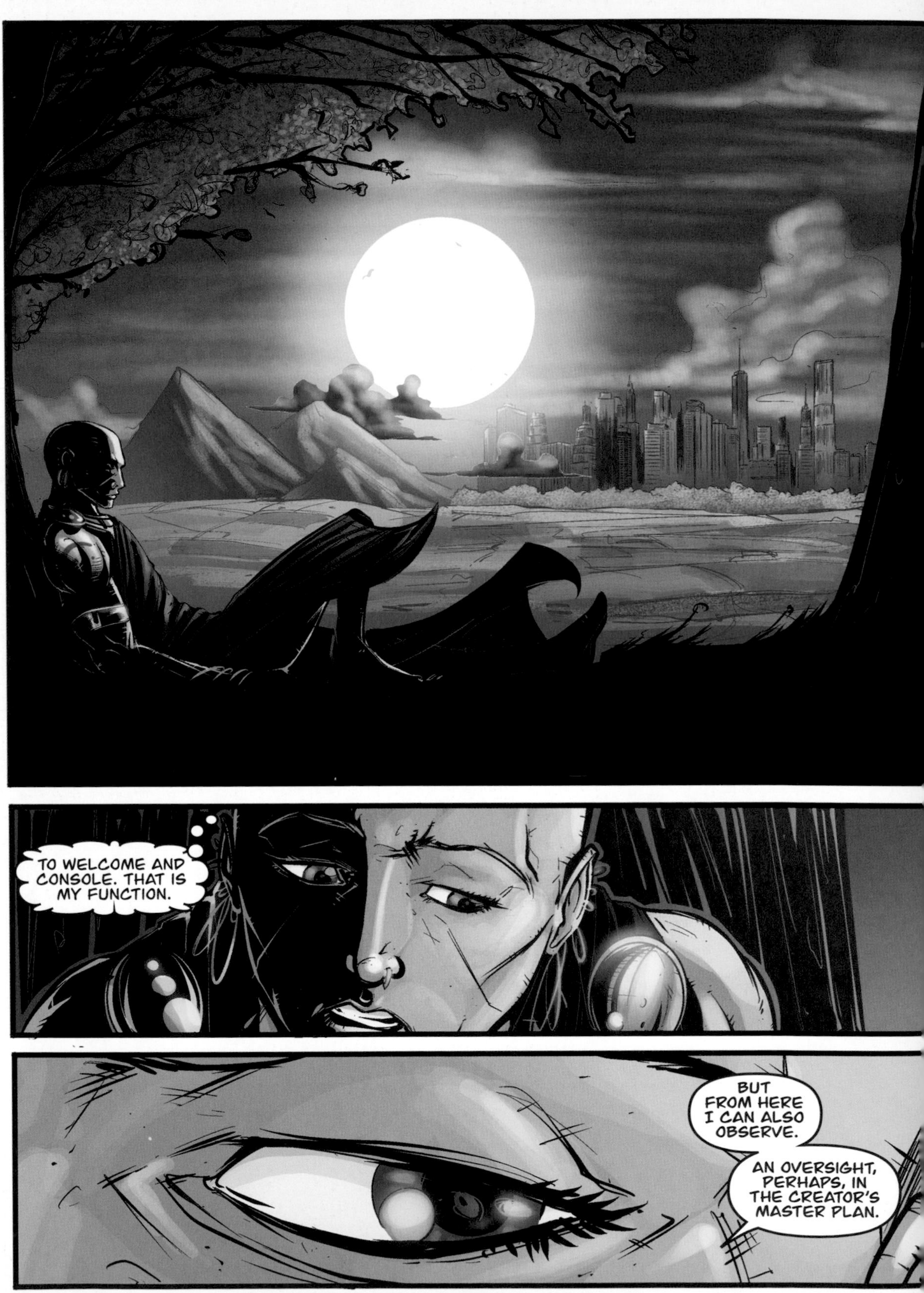
TO WELCOME AND CONSOLE. THAT IS MY FUNCTION.
BUT FROM HERE I CAN ALSO OBSERVE.
AN OVERSIGHT, PERHAPS, IN THE CREATOR'S MASTER PLAN.

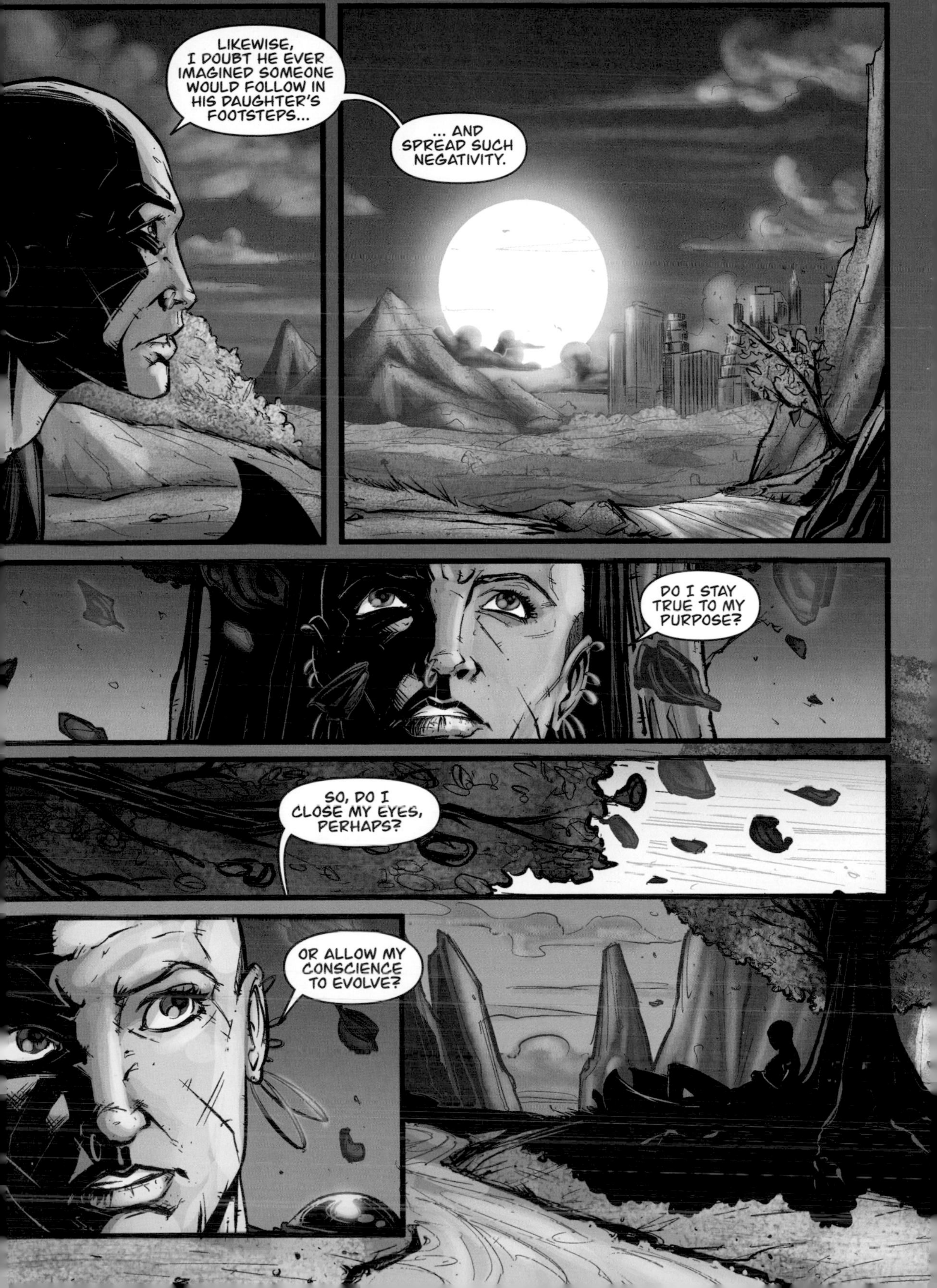
LIKEWISE, I DOUBT HE EVER IMAGINED SOMEONE WOULD FOLLOW IN HIS DAUGHTER'S FOOTSTEPS...
... AND SPREAD SUCH NEGATIVITY.
DO I STAY TRUE TO MY PURPOSE?
SO, DO I CLOSE MY EYES, PERHAPS?
OR ALLOW MY CONSCIENCE TO EVOLVE?

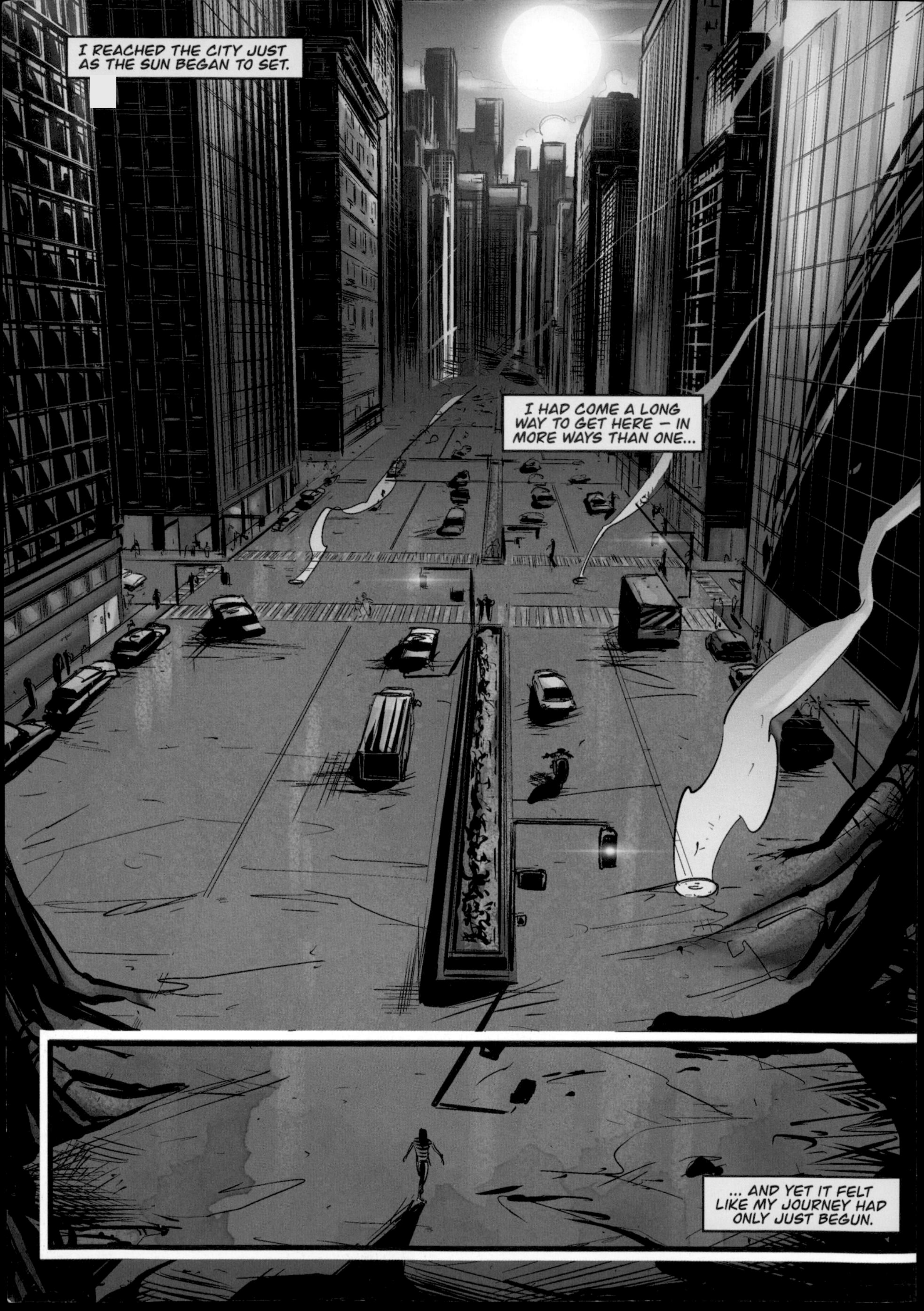
I REACHED THE CITY JUST AS THE SUN BEGAN TO SET.
I HAD COME A LONG WAY TO GET HERE – IN MORE WAYS THAN ONE...
... AND YET IT FELT LIKE MY JOURNEY HAD ONLY JUST BEGUN.

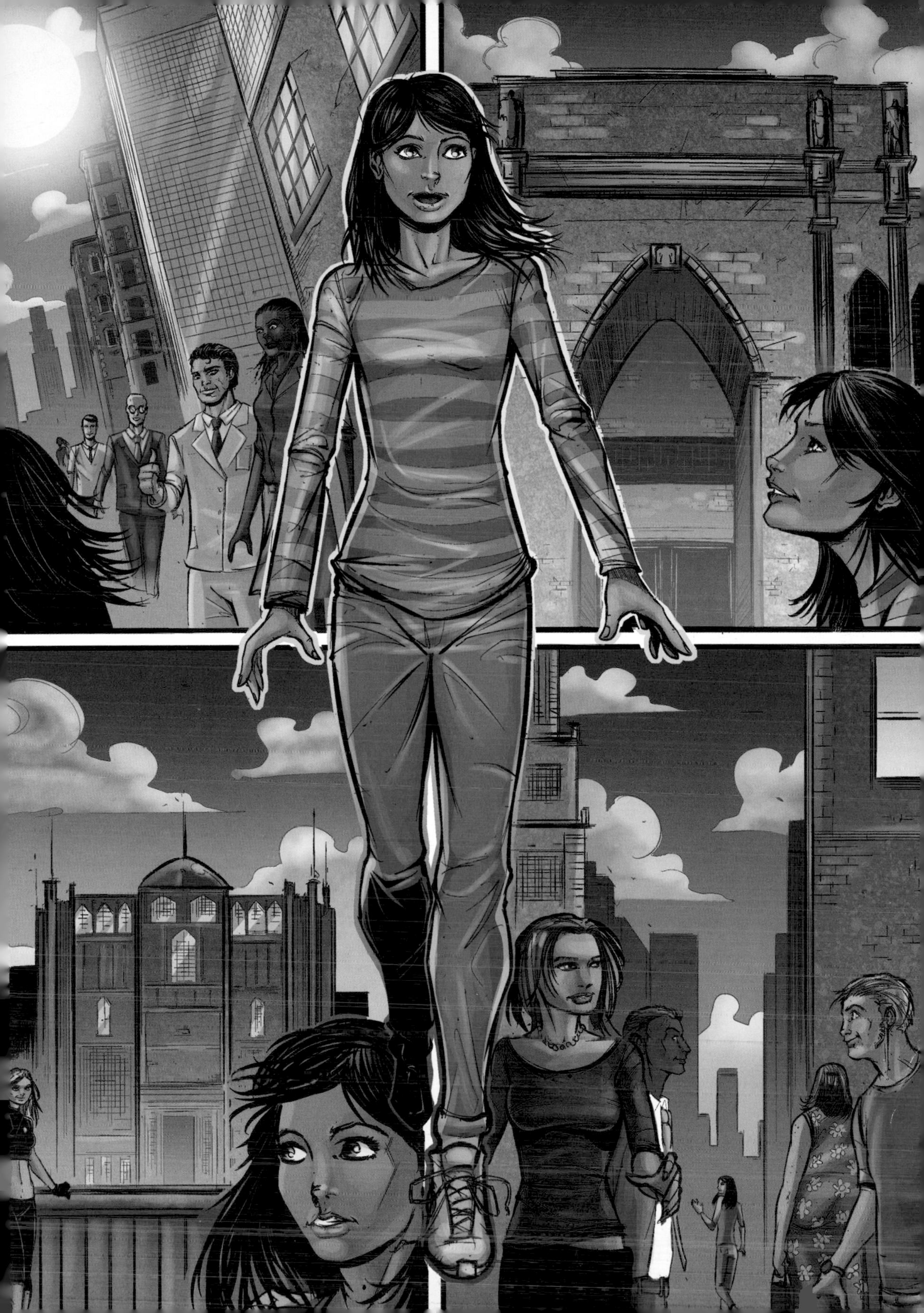

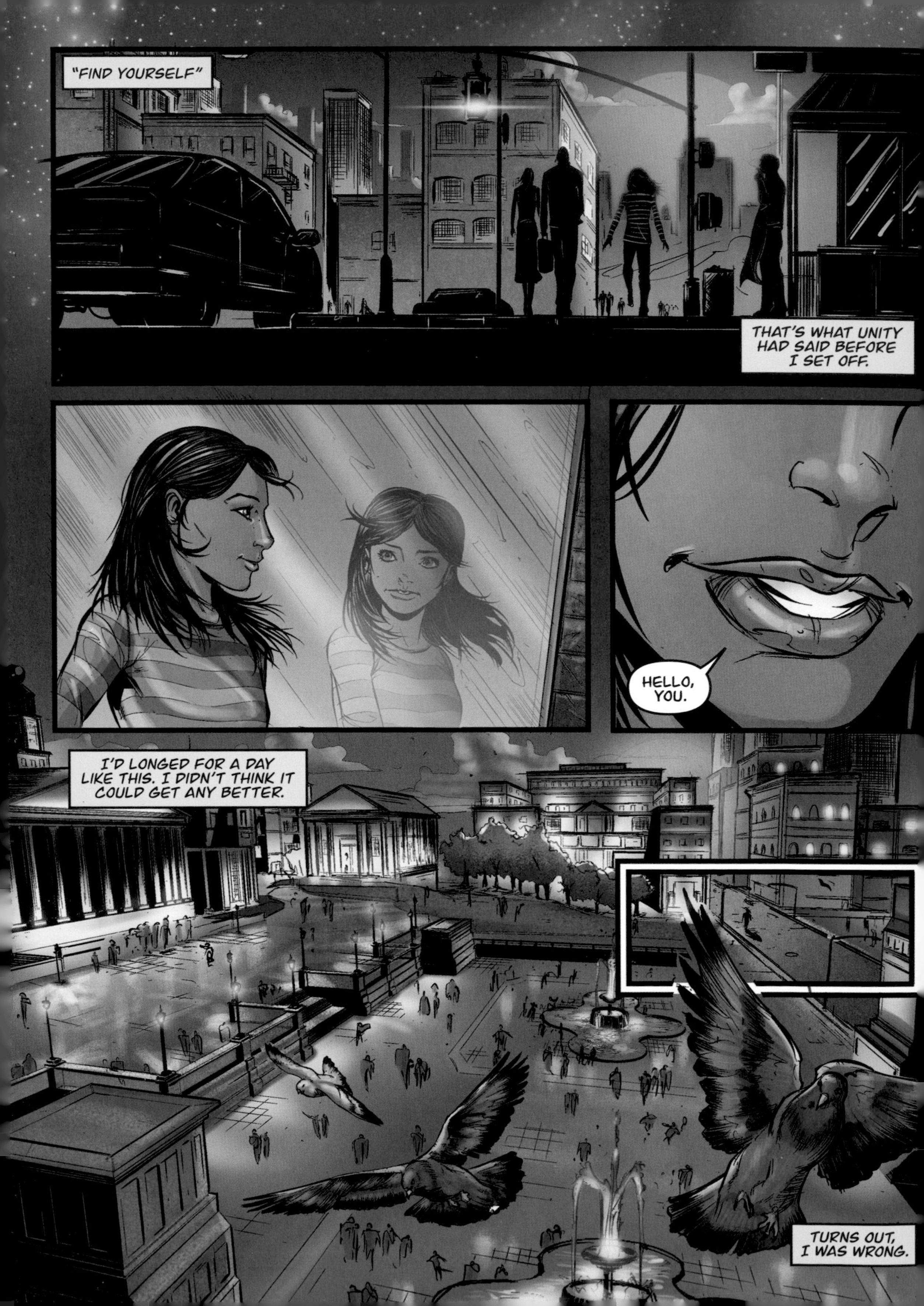
"FIND YOURSELF"
THAT'S WHAT UNITY HAD SAID BEFORE I SET OFF.
HELLO, YOU.
I'D LONGED FOR A DAY LIKE THIS. I DIDN'T THINK IT COULD GET ANY BETTER.
TURNS OUT, I WAS WRONG.

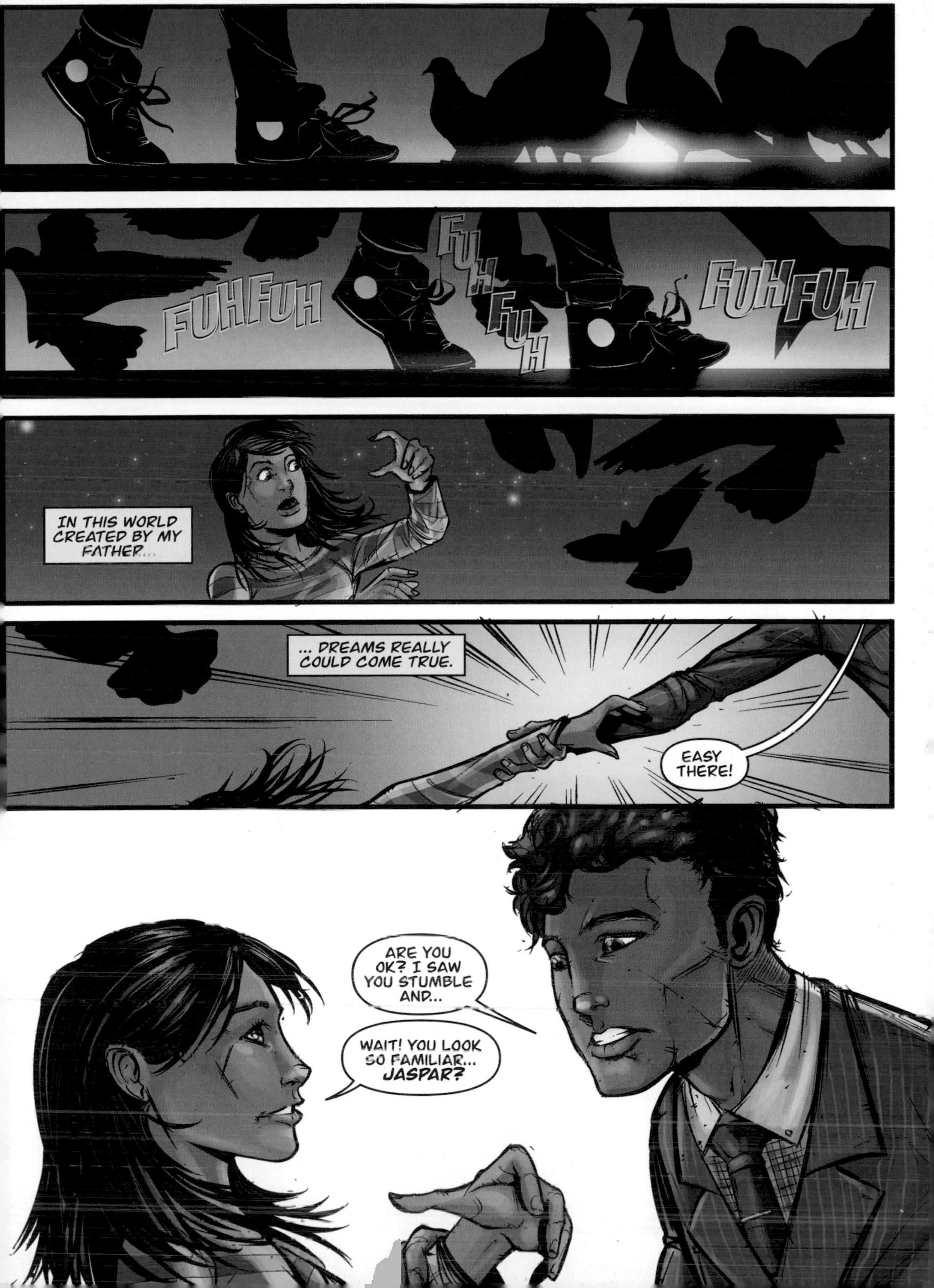

FUHFUH
FUH FUH
FUHFUH
IN THIS WORLD CREATED BY MY FATHER...
... DREAMS REALLY COULD COME TRUE.
EASY THERE!
ARE YOU OK? I SAW YOU STUMBLE AND...
WAIT! YOU LOOK SO FAMILIAR... JASPAR?

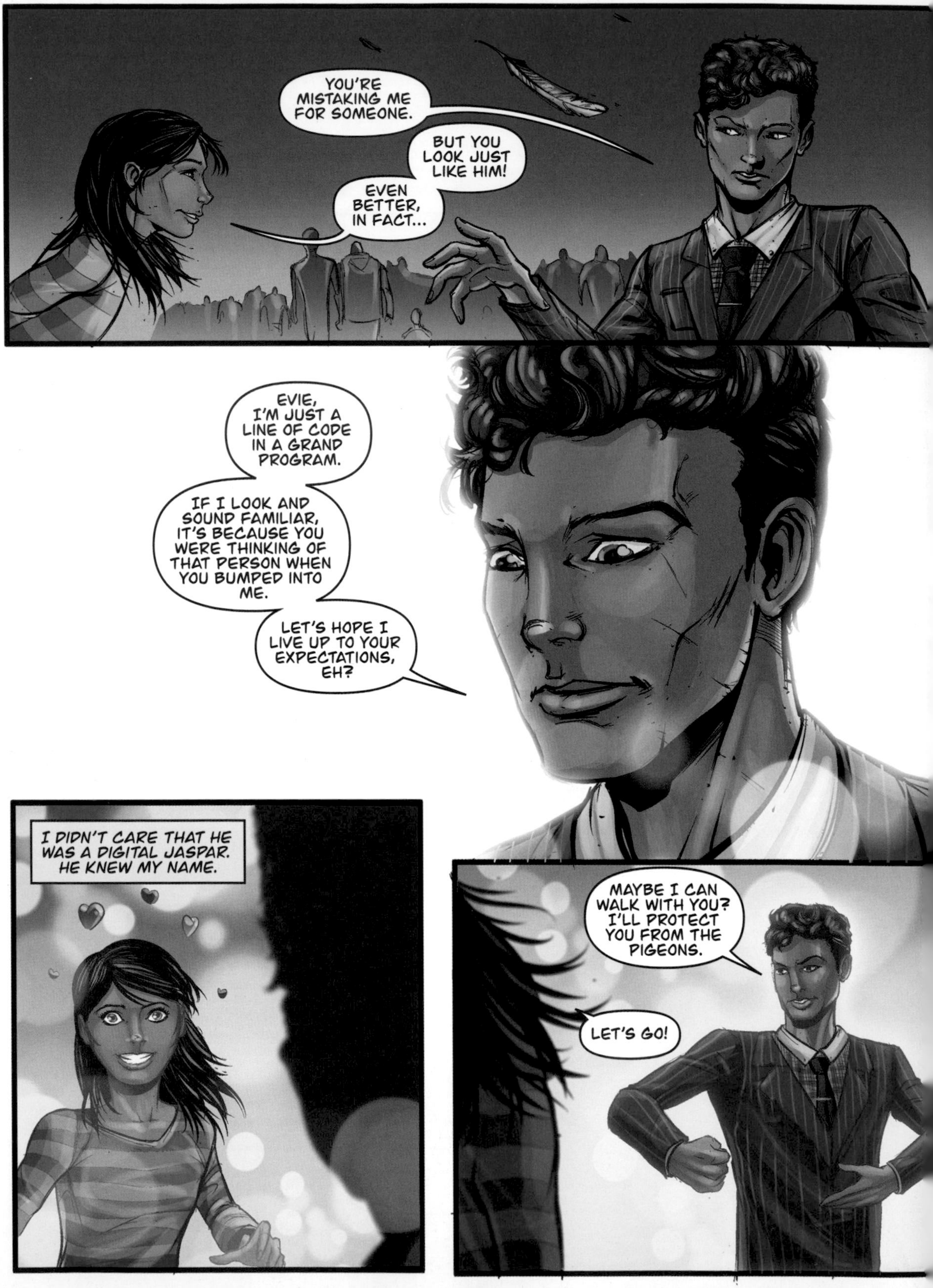
YOU'RE MISTAKING ME FOR SOMEONE.
BUT YOU LOOK JUST LIKE HIM!
EVEN BETTER, IN FACT...
EVIE, I'M JUST A LINE OF CODE IN A GRAND PROGRAM.
IF I LOOK AND SOUND FAMILIAR, IT'S BECAUSE YOU WERE THINKING OF THAT PERSON WHEN YOU BUMPED INTO ME.
LET'S HOPE I LIVE UP TO YOUR EXPECTATIONS, EH?
I DIDN'T CARE THAT HE WAS A DIGITAL JASPAR. HE KNEW MY NAME.
MAYBE I CAN WALK WITH YOU? I'LL PROTECT YOU FROM THE PIGEONS.
LET'S GO!

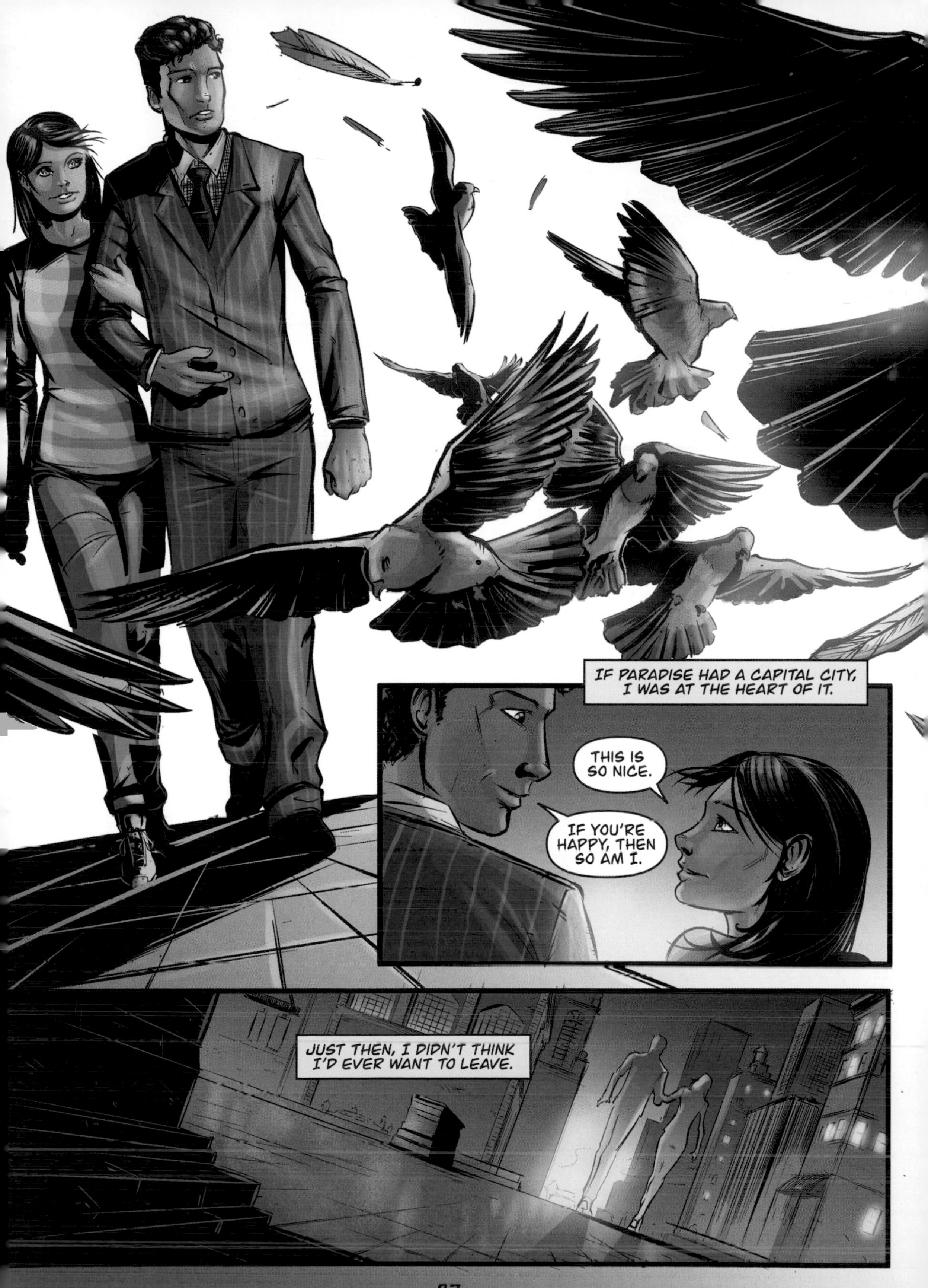
IF PARADISE HAD A CAPITAL CITY, I WAS AT THE HEART OF IT.
THIS IS SO NICE.
IF YOU'RE HAPPY, THEN SO AM I.
JUST THEN, I DIDN'T THINK I'D EVER WANT TO LEAVE.

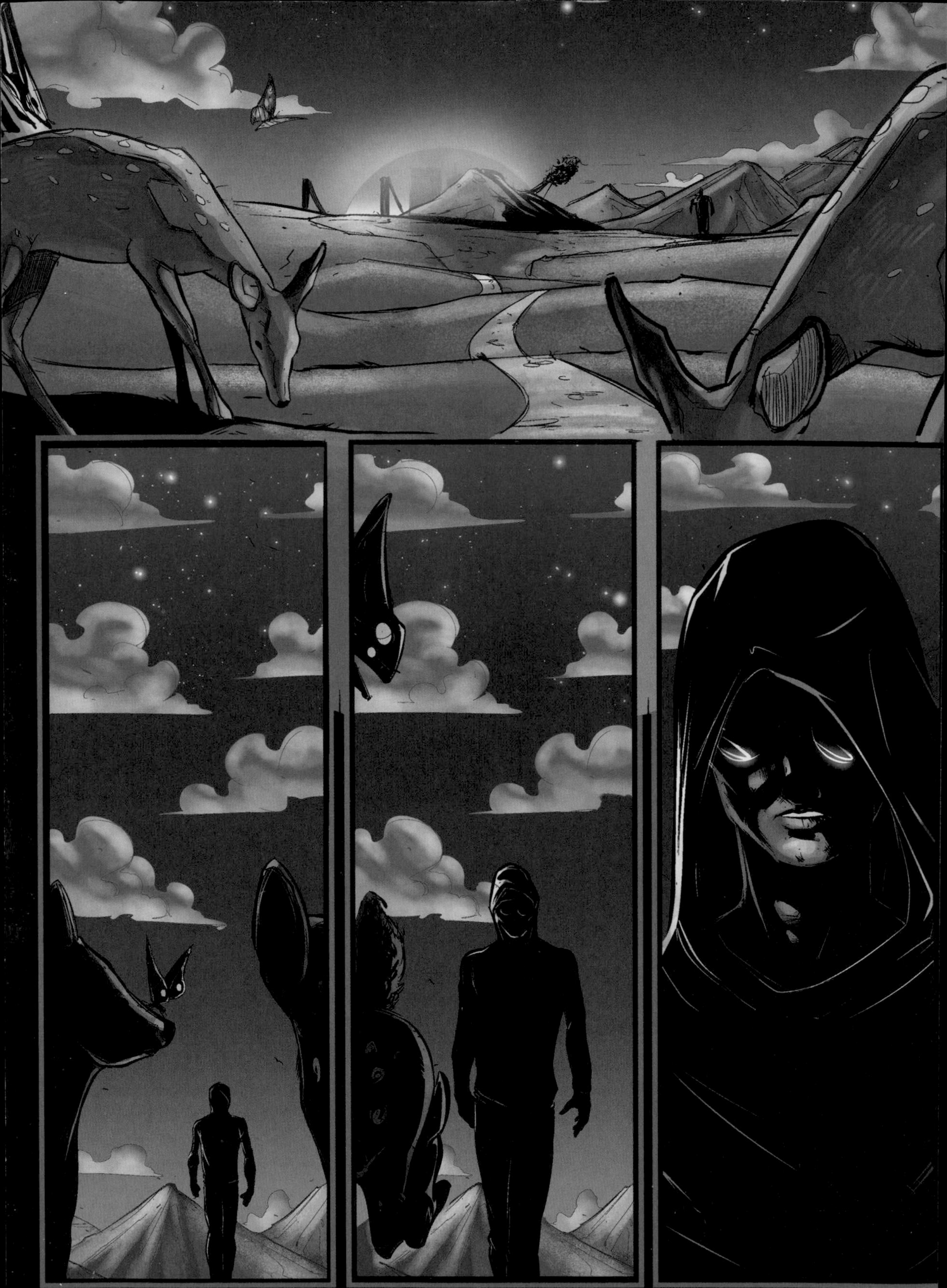

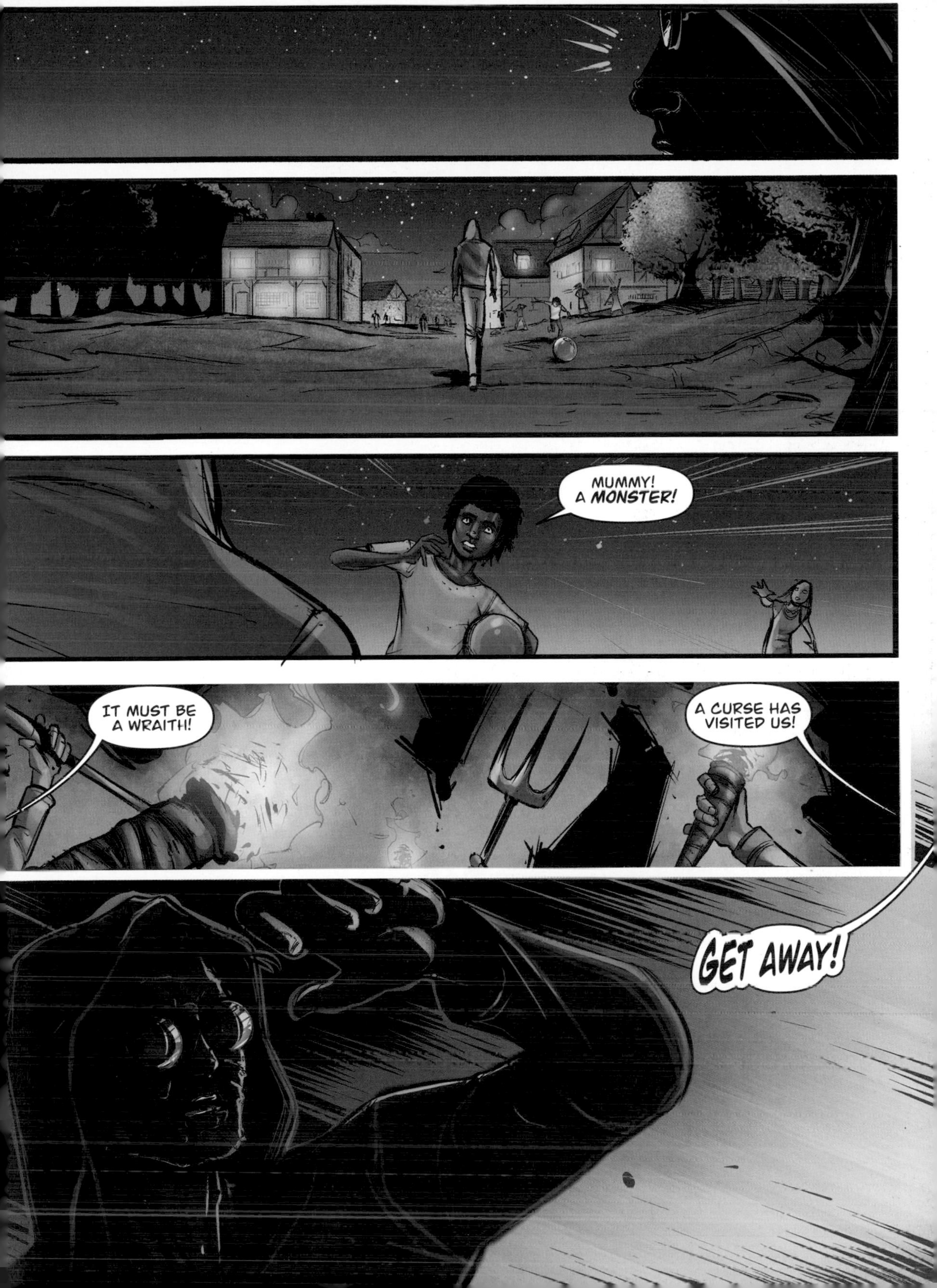
MUMMY! A MONSTER!
IT MUST BE A WRAITH!
A CURSE HAS VISITED US!
GET AWAY!

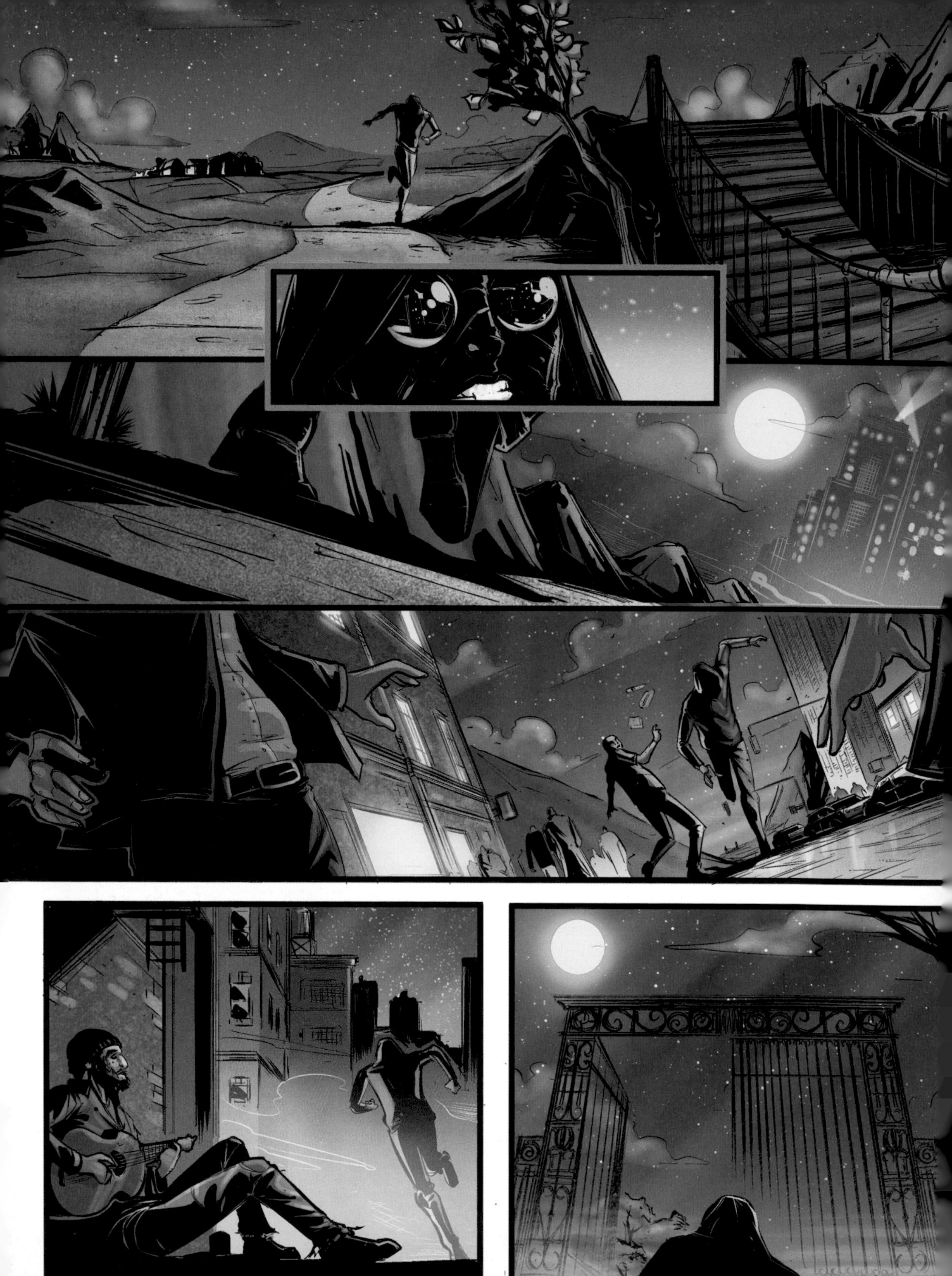

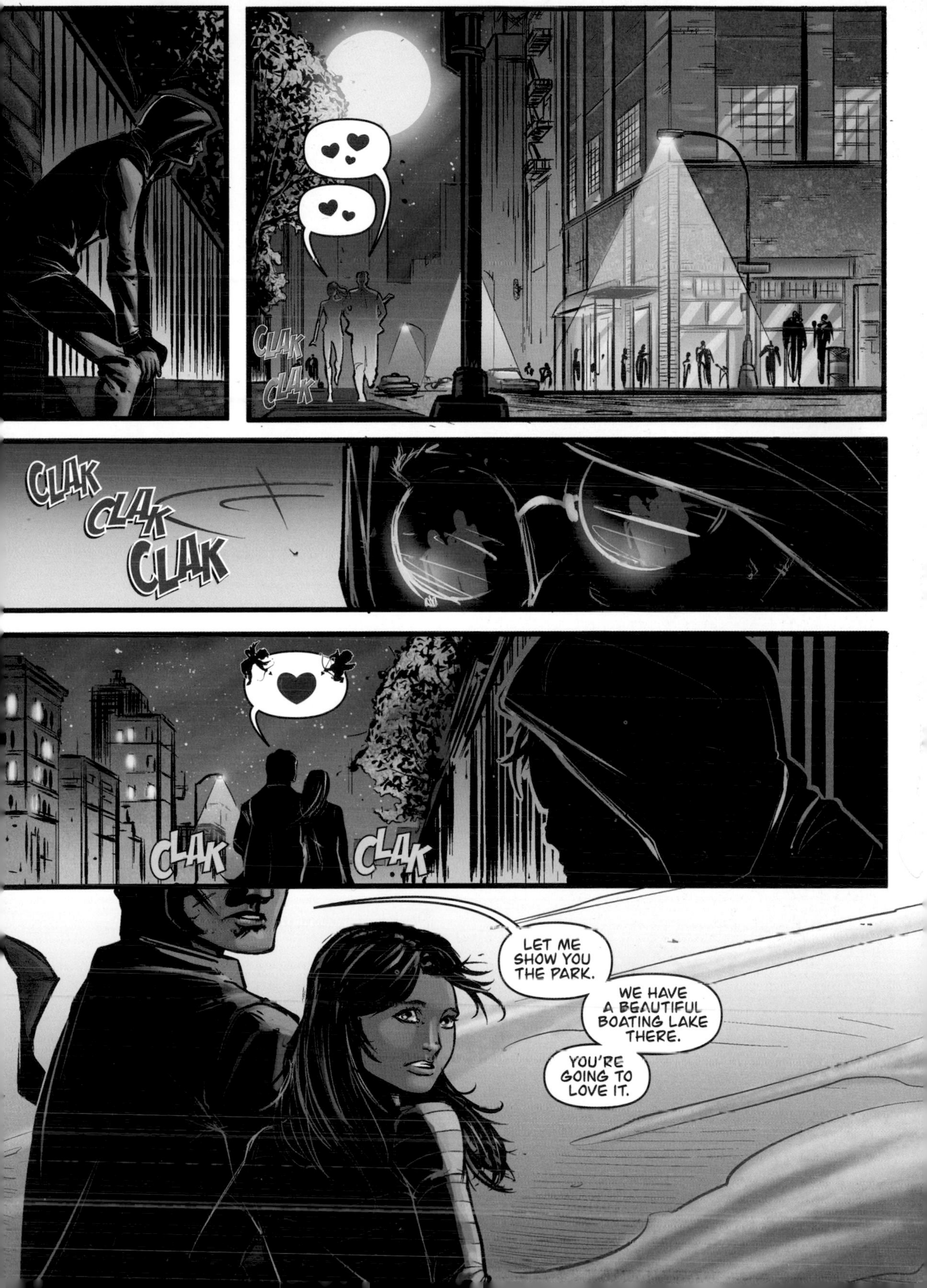
CLAK CLAK
CLAK CLAK CLAK
CLAK
CLAK
LET ME SHOW YOU THE PARK.
WE HAVE A BEAUTIFUL BOATING LAKE THERE.
YOU'RE GOING TO LOVE IT.

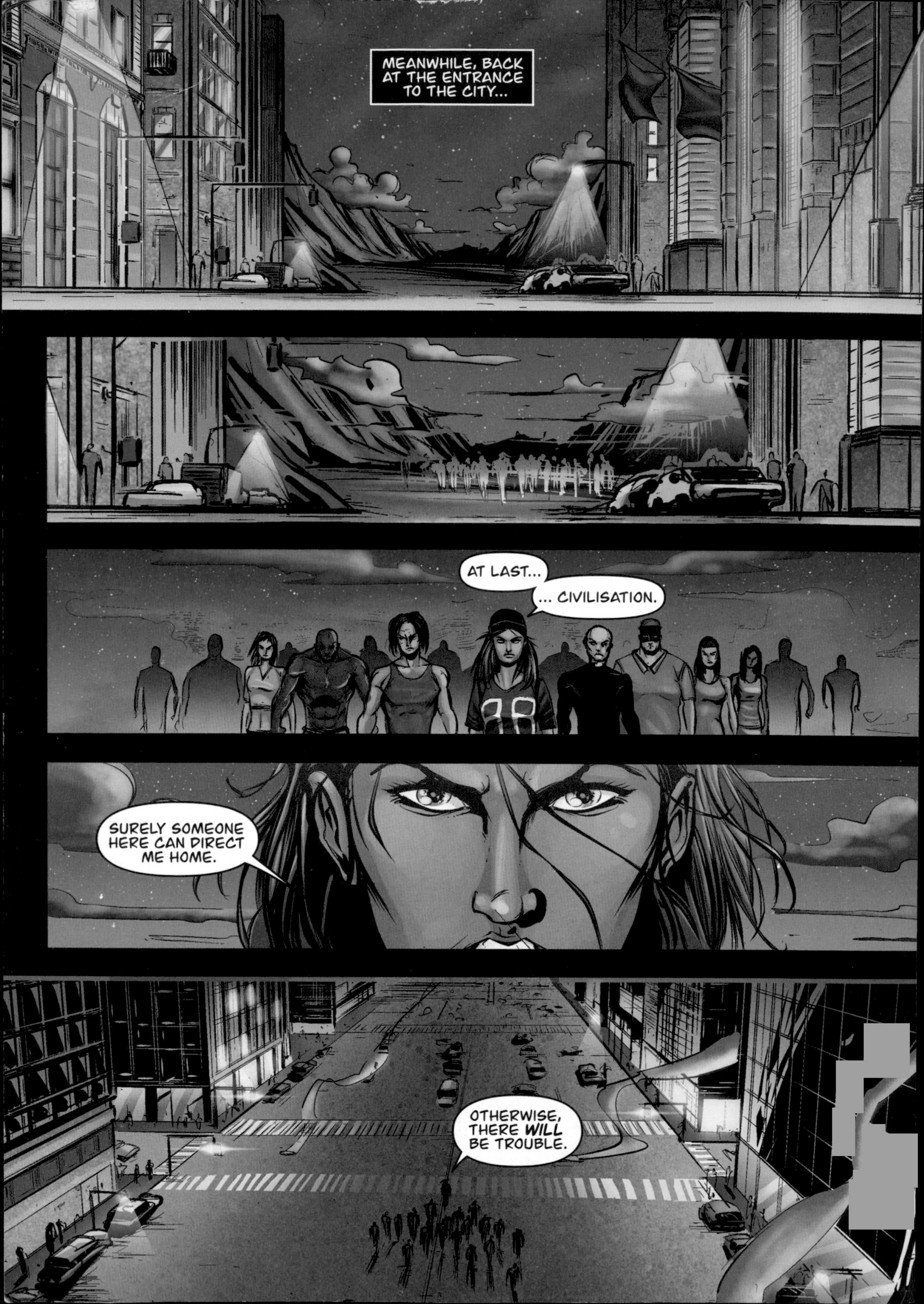
MEANWHILE, BACK AT THE ENTRANCE TO THE CITY...
AT LAST...
... CIVILISATION.
SURELY SOMEONE HERE CAN DIRECT ME HOME.
OTHERWISE, THERE **WILL** BE TROUBLE.

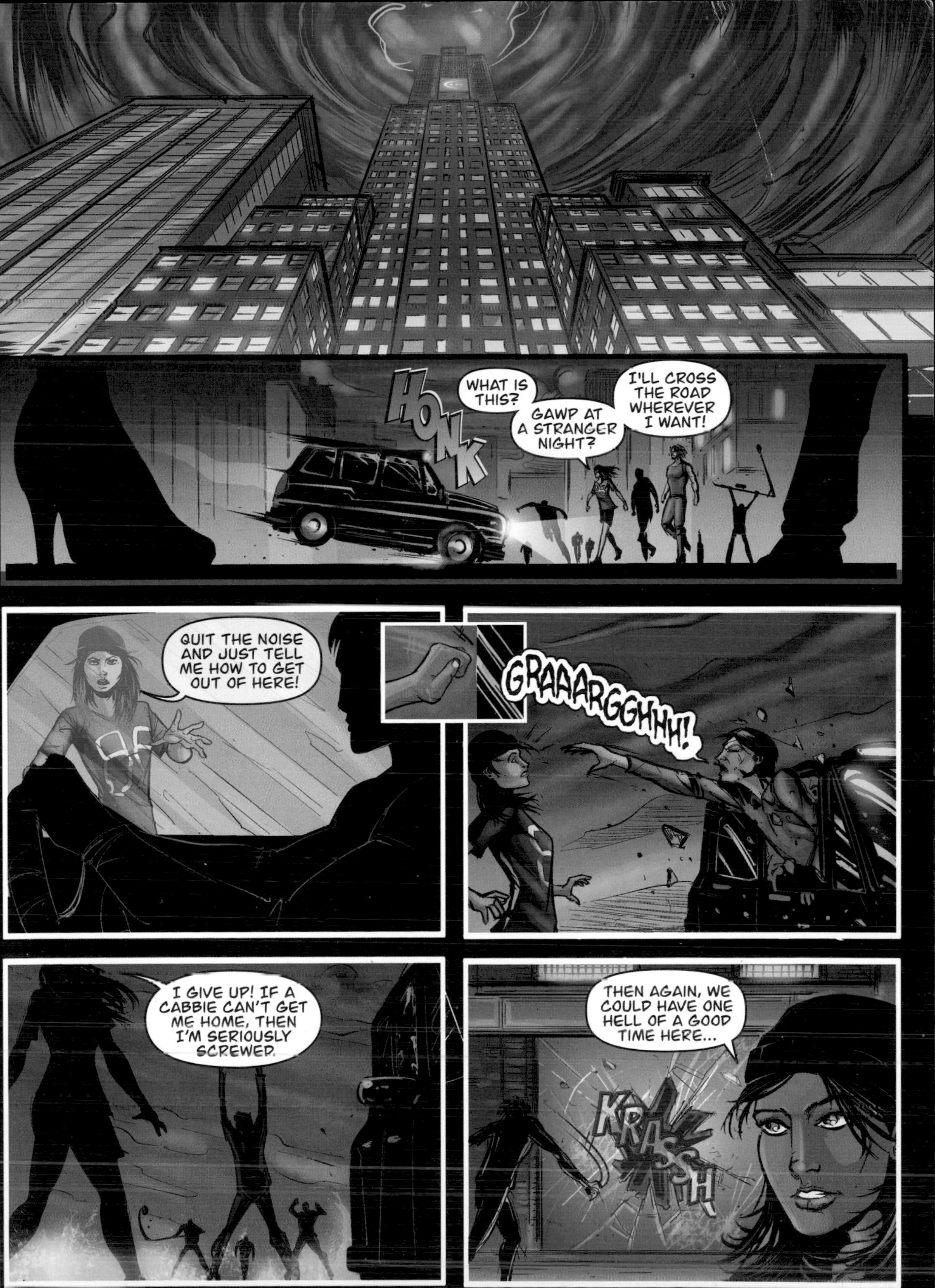
HONK
WHAT IS THIS?
GAWP AT A STRANGER NIGHT?
I'LL CROSS THE ROAD WHEREVER I WANT!
QUIT THE NOISE AND JUST TELL ME HOW TO GET OUT OF HERE!
GRAAAARGGHHH!
I GIVE UP! IF A CABBIE CAN'T GET ME HOME, THEN I'M SERIOUSLY SCREWED.
THEN AGAIN, WE COULD HAVE ONE HELL OF A GOOD TIME HERE...
KRASSH

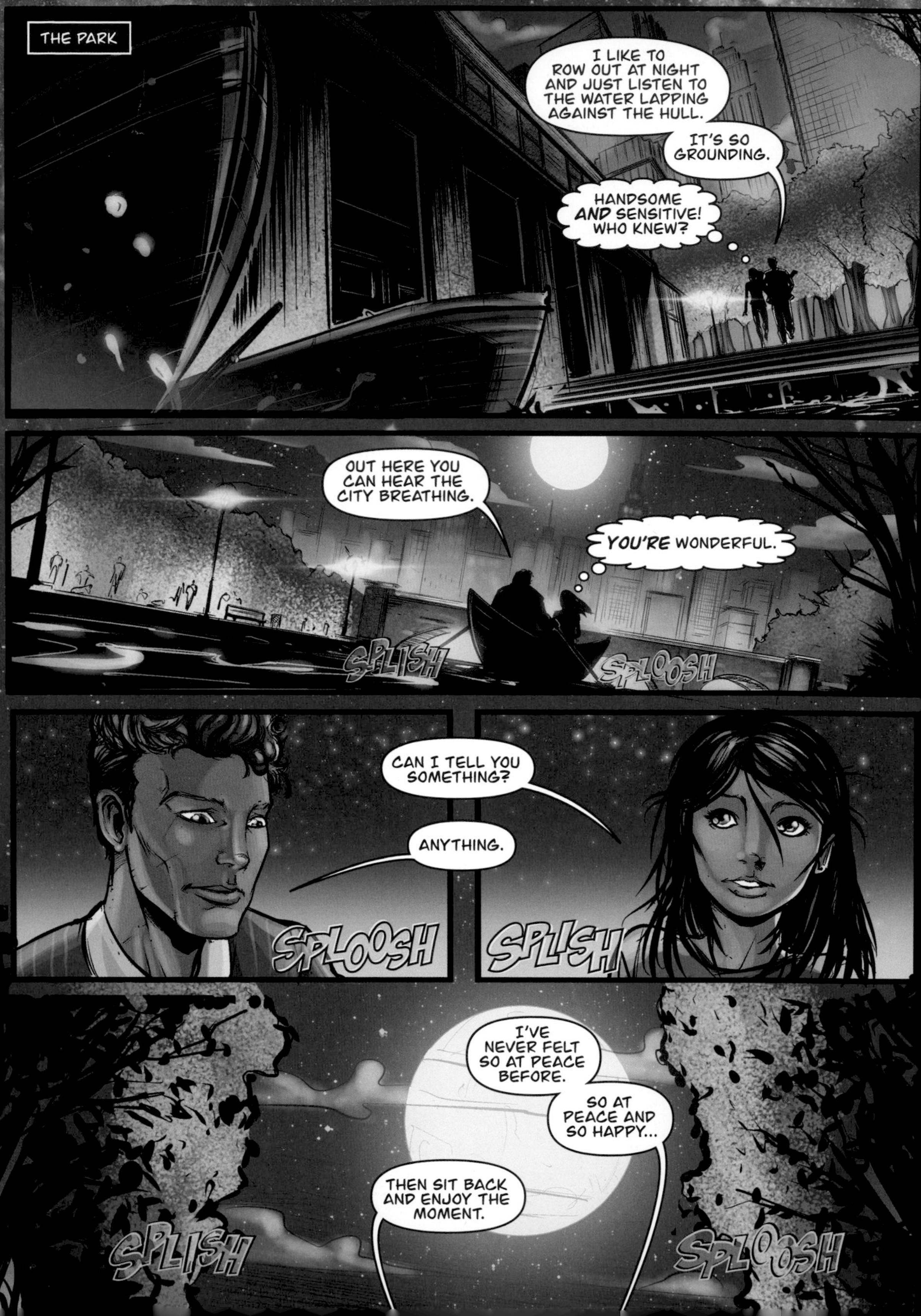
THE PARK
I LIKE TO ROW OUT AT NIGHT AND JUST LISTEN TO THE WATER LAPPING AGAINST THE HULL.
IT'S SO GROUNDING.
HANDSOME AND SENSITIVE! WHO KNEW?
OUT HERE YOU CAN HEAR THE CITY BREATHING.
YOU'RE WONDERFUL.
SPLISH
SPLOOSH
CAN I TELL YOU SOMETHING?
ANYTHING.
SPLOOSH
SPLISH
I'VE NEVER FELT SO AT PEACE BEFORE.
SO AT PEACE AND SO HAPPY...
THEN SIT BACK AND ENJOY THE MOMENT.
SPLISH
SPLOOSH

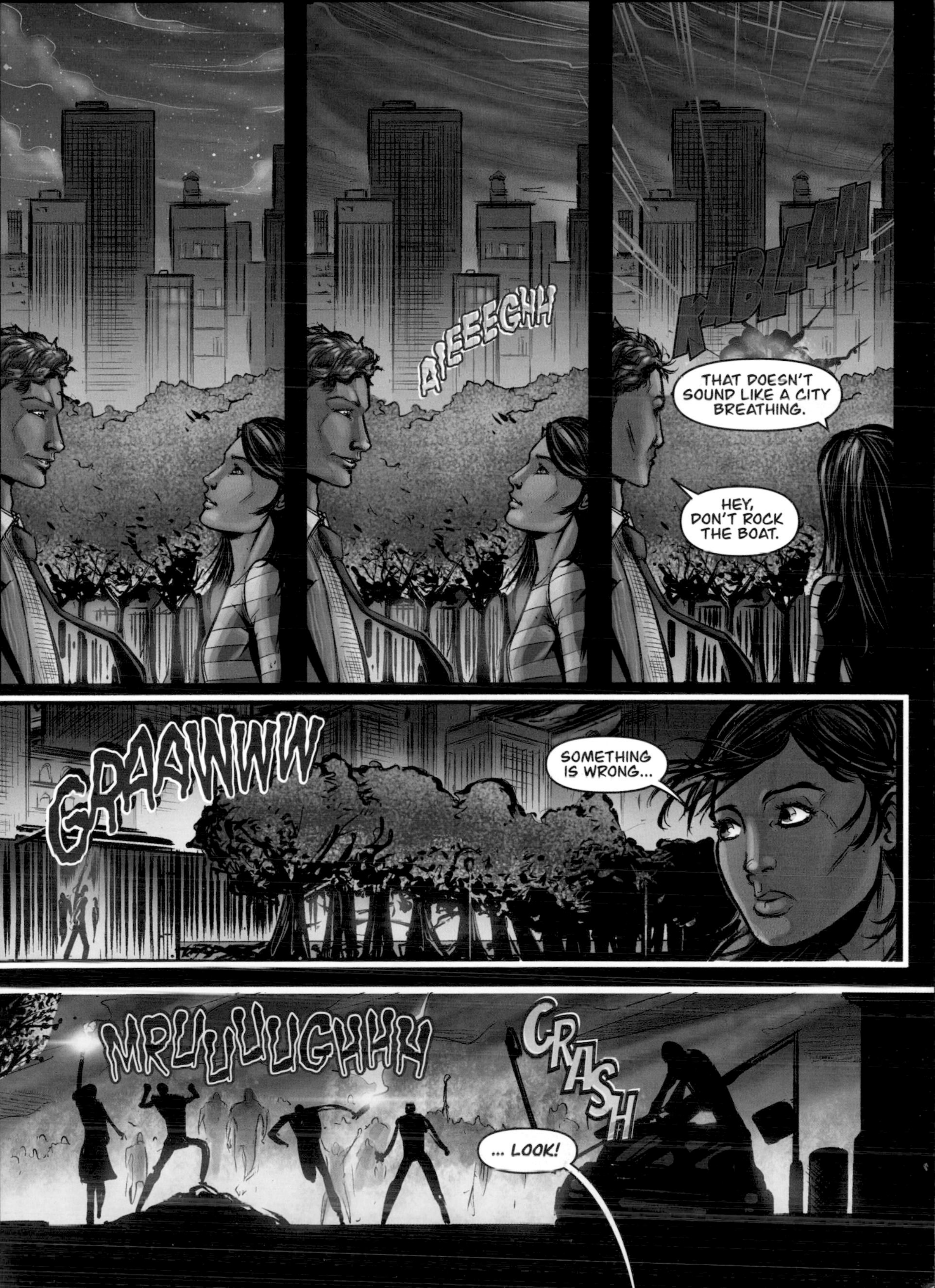
AIEEEEGHH
KABLAAM
THAT DOESN'T SOUND LIKE A CITY BREATHING.
HEY, DON'T ROCK THE BOAT.
GRAAWWW
SOMETHING IS WRONG...
MRUUUUGHHH
CRASH
... LOOK!

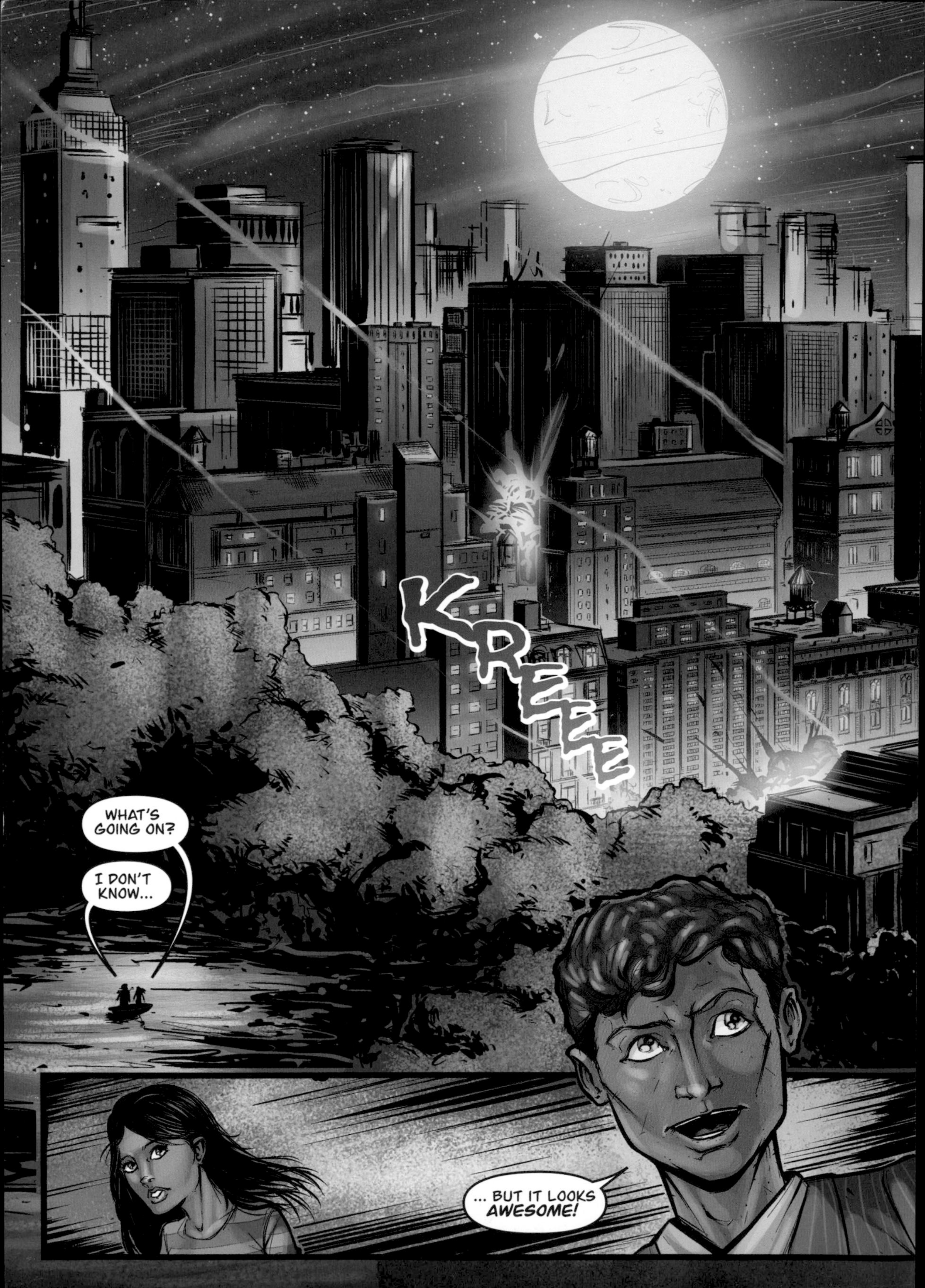
KREEEE
WHAT'S GOING ON?
I DON'T KNOW...
... BUT IT LOOKS AWESOME!

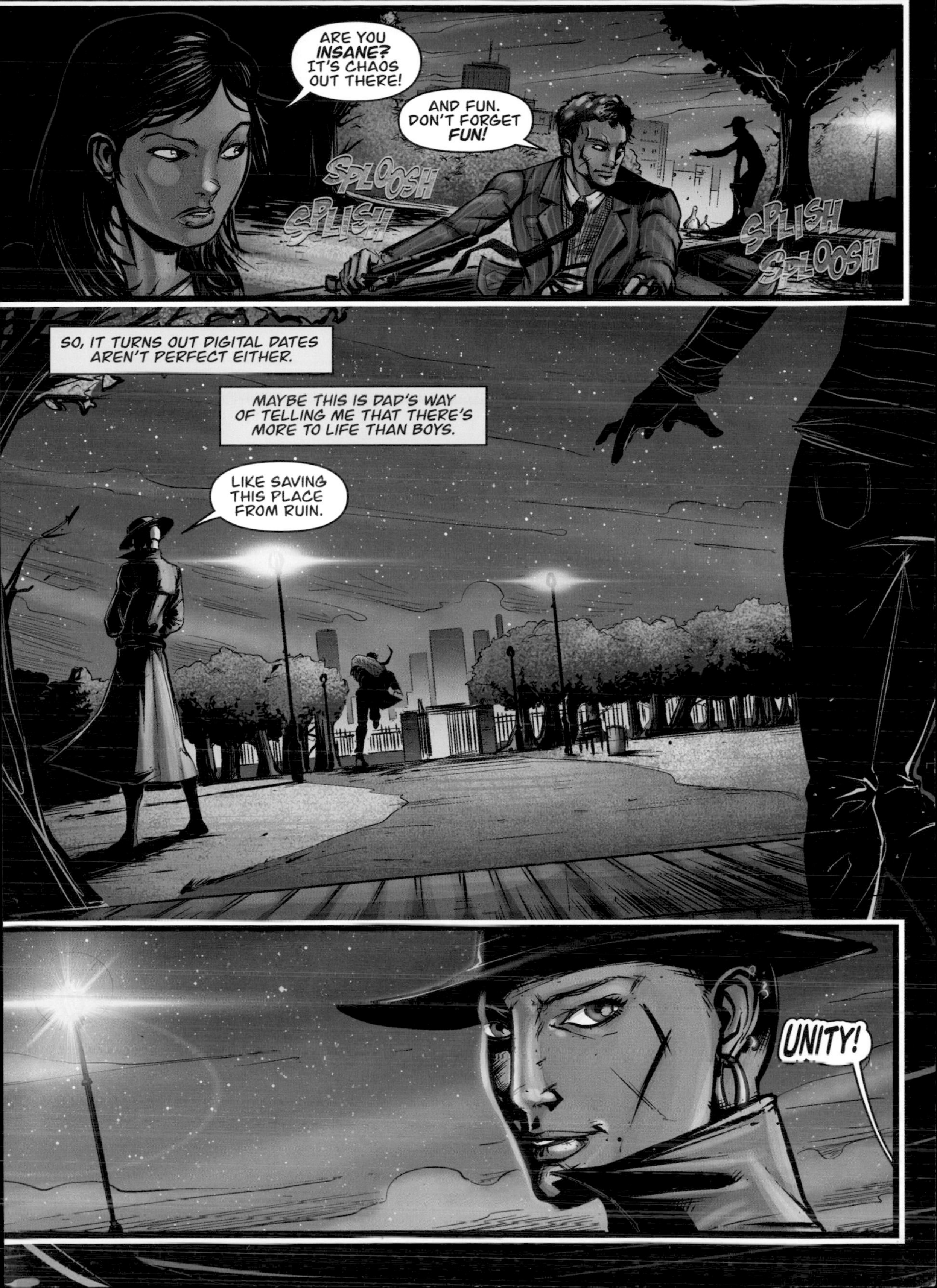

ARE YOU INSANE? IT'S CHAOS OUT THERE!
AND FUN. DON'T FORGET FUN!
SPLOOSH
SPLISH
SPLISH
SPLOOSH
SO, IT TURNS OUT DIGITAL DATES AREN'T PERFECT EITHER.
MAYBE THIS IS DAD'S WAY OF TELLING ME THAT THERE'S MORE TO LIFE THAN BOYS.
LIKE SAVING THIS PLACE FROM RUIN.
UNITY!

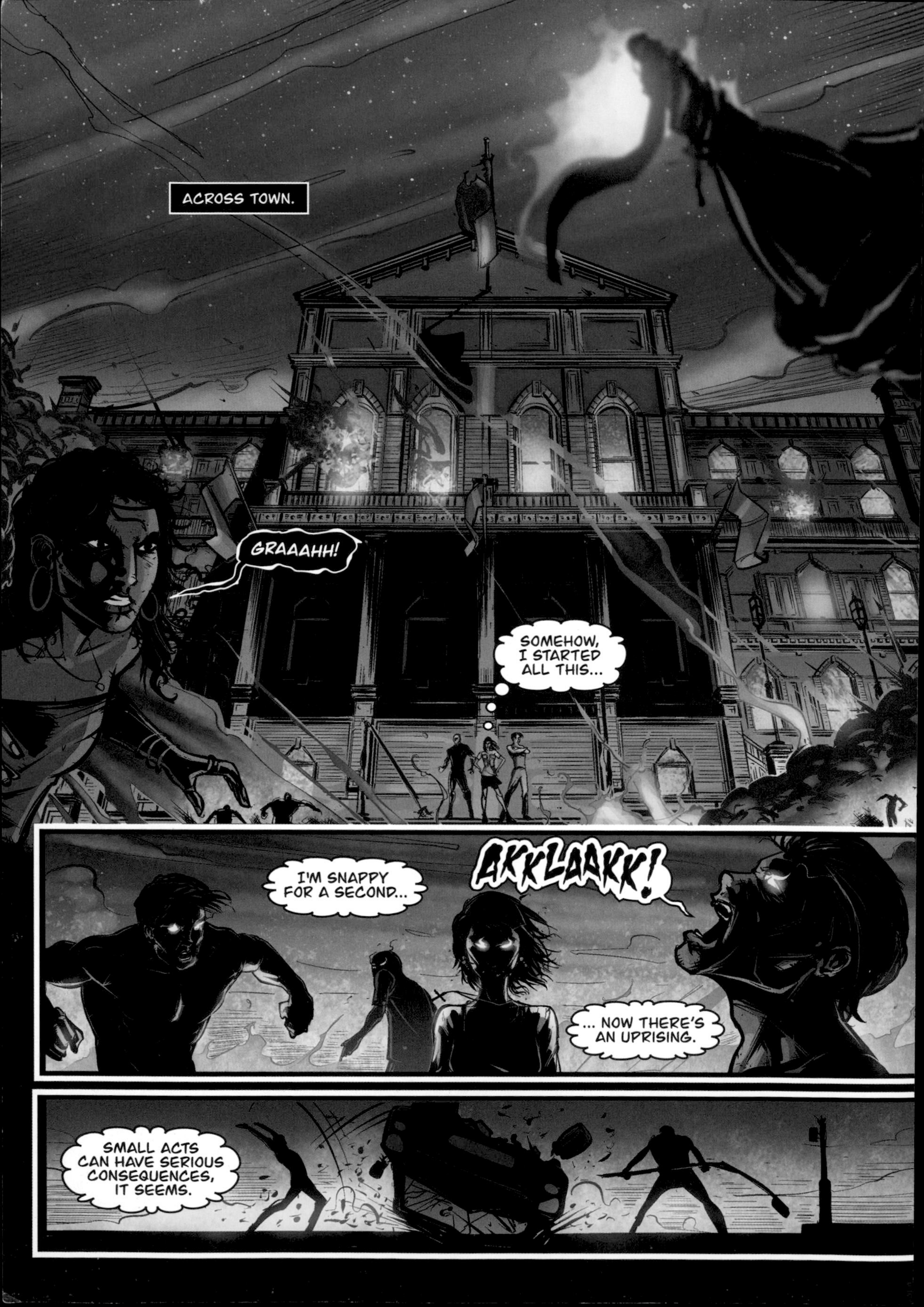
ACROSS TOWN.
GRAAAHH!
SOMEHOW, I STARTED ALL THIS...
I'M SNAPPY FOR A SECOND...
AKKLAAKK!
... NOW THERE'S AN UPRISING.
SMALL ACTS CAN HAVE SERIOUS CONSEQUENCES, IT SEEMS.

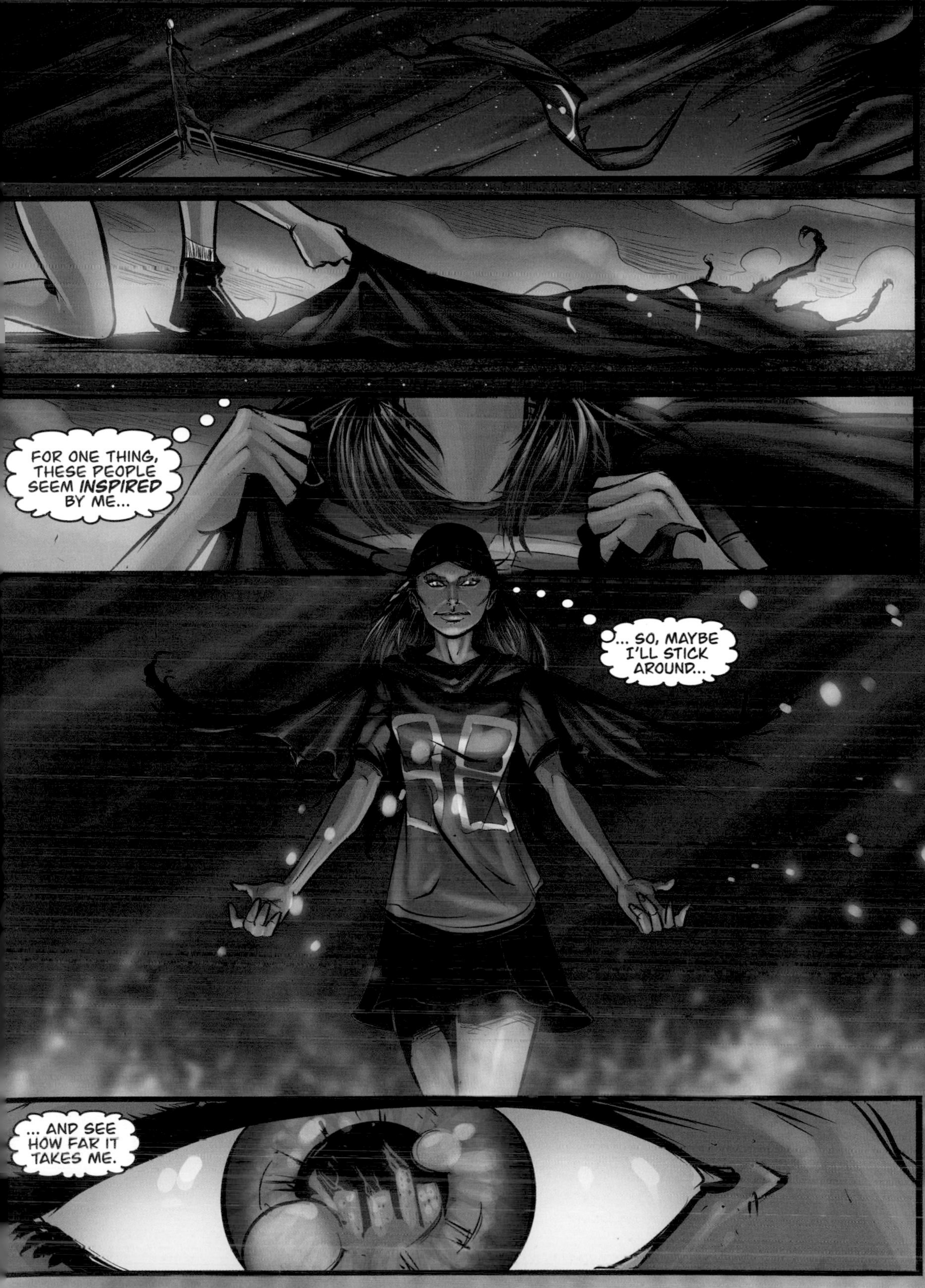
FOR ONE THING, THESE PEOPLE SEEM INSPIRED BY ME...
... SO, MAYBE I'LL STICK AROUND...
... AND SEE HOW FAR IT TAKES ME.

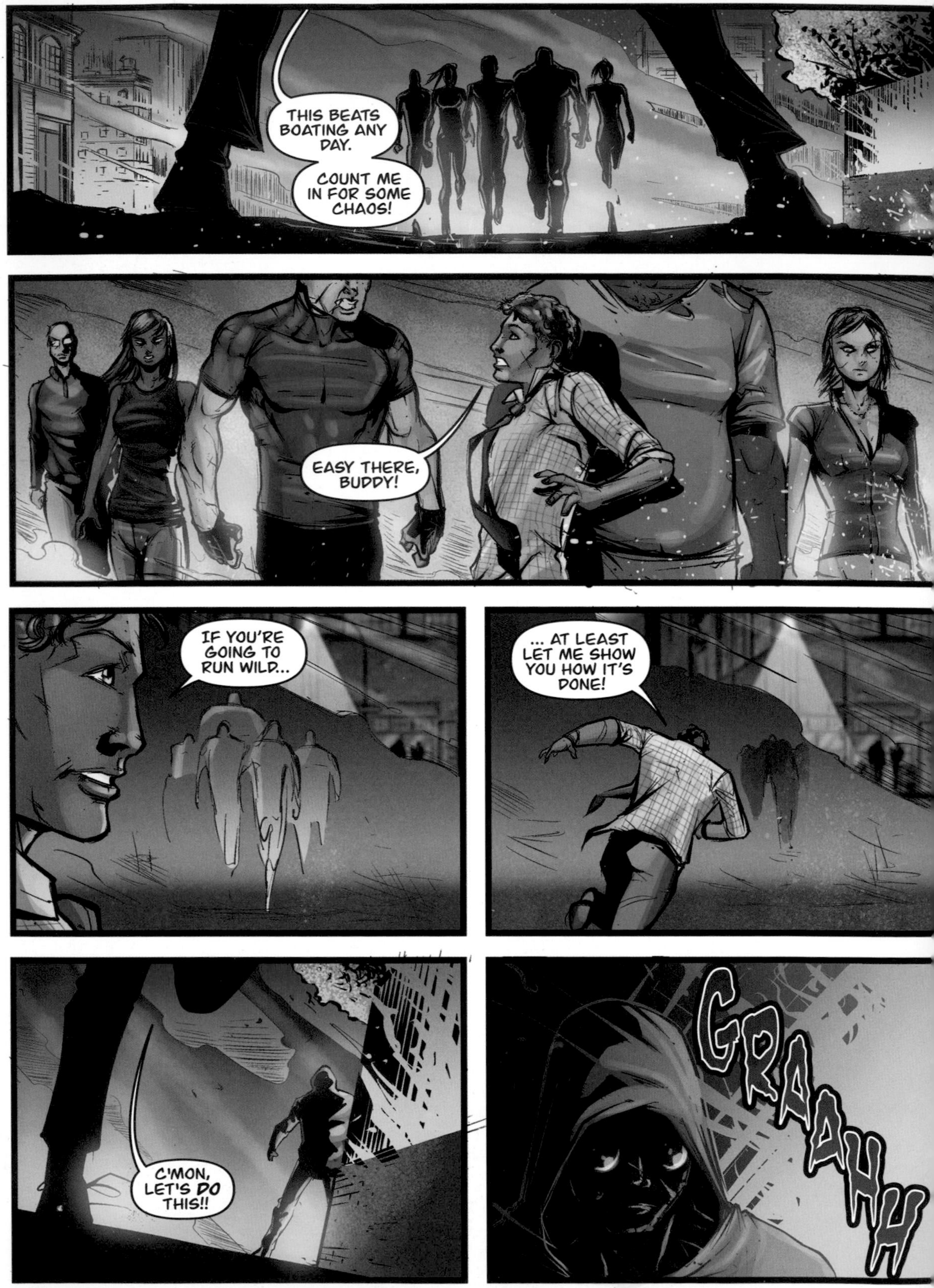
THIS BEATS BOATING ANY DAY.
COUNT ME IN FOR SOME CHAOS!
EASY THERE, BUDDY!
IF YOU'RE GOING TO RUN WILD...
... AT LEAST LET ME SHOW YOU HOW IT'S DONE!
C'MON, LET'S DO THIS!!
GRAAHH

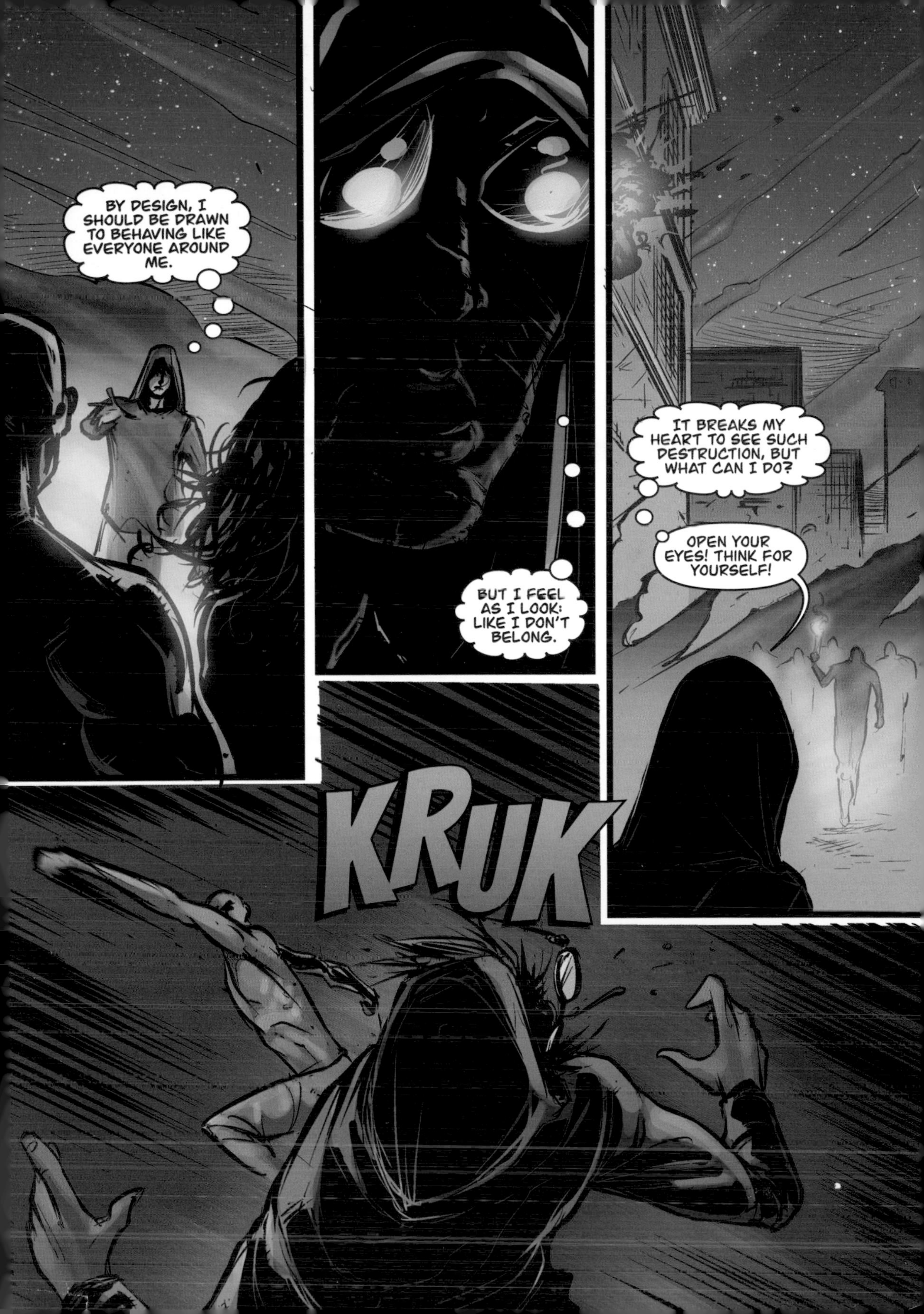

BY DESIGN, I SHOULD BE DRAWN TO BEHAVING LIKE EVERYONE AROUND ME.
BUT I FEEL AS I LOOK: LIKE I DON'T BELONG.
IT BREAKS MY HEART TO SEE SUCH DESTRUCTION, BUT WHAT CAN I DO?
OPEN YOUR EYES! THINK FOR YOURSELF!
KRUK

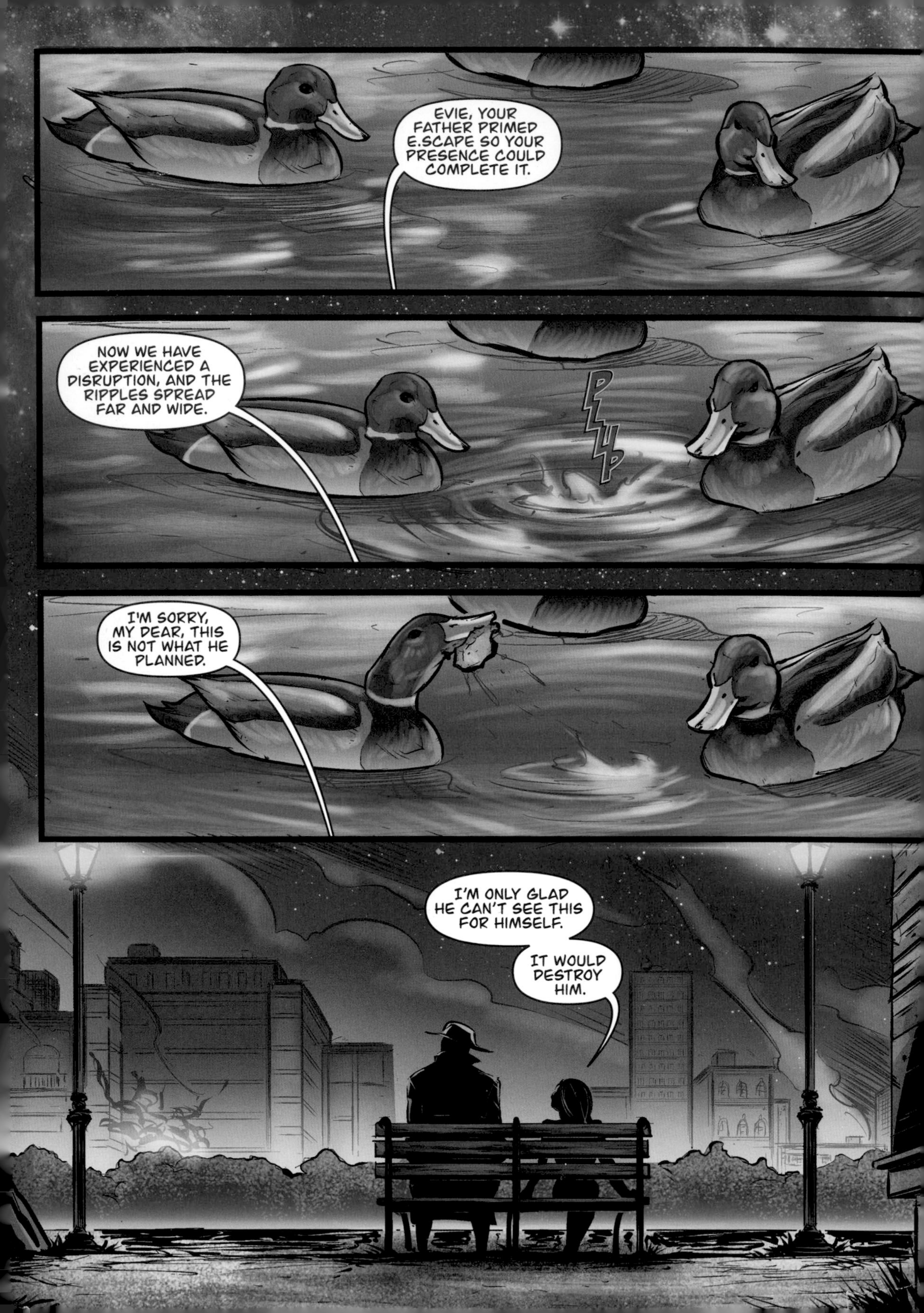
EVIE, YOUR FATHER PRIMED E.SCAPE SO YOUR PRESENCE COULD COMPLETE IT.
NOW WE HAVE EXPERIENCED A DISRUPTION, AND THE RIPPLES SPREAD FAR AND WIDE.
PLUP
I'M SORRY, MY DEAR, THIS IS NOT WHAT HE PLANNED.
I'M ONLY GLAD HE CAN'T SEE THIS FOR HIMSELF.
IT WOULD DESTROY HIM.

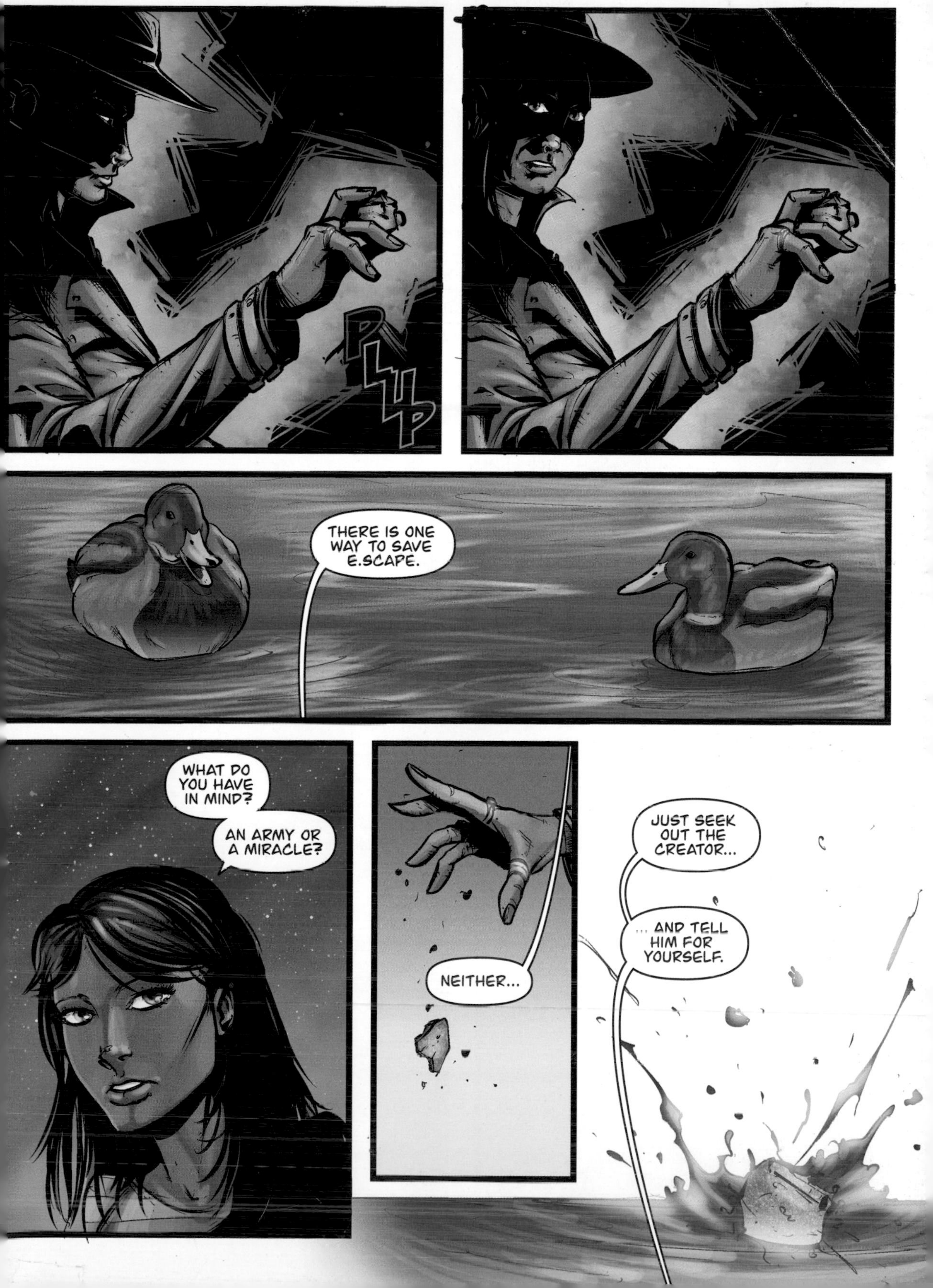
PLUP
THERE IS ONE WAY TO SAVE E.SCAPE.
WHAT DO YOU HAVE IN MIND?
AN ARMY OR A MIRACLE?
NEITHER...
JUST SEEK OUT THE CREATOR...
... AND TELL HIM FOR YOURSELF.

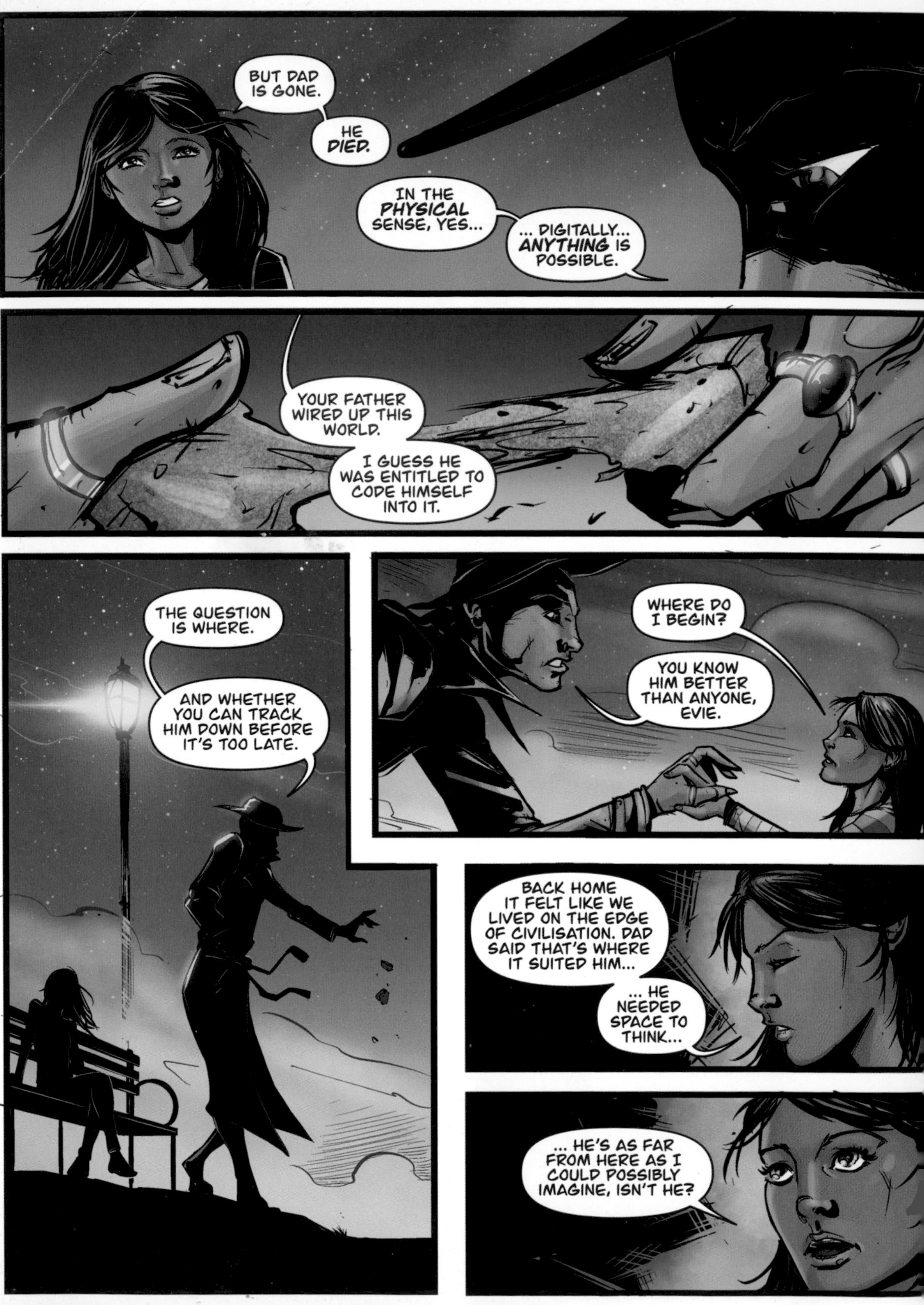

BUT DAD IS GONE.
HE DIED.
IN THE PHYSICAL SENSE, YES...
... DIGITALLY... ANYTHING IS POSSIBLE.
YOUR FATHER WIRED UP THIS WORLD.
I GUESS HE WAS ENTITLED TO CODE HIMSELF INTO IT.
THE QUESTION IS WHERE.
AND WHETHER YOU CAN TRACK HIM DOWN BEFORE IT'S TOO LATE.
WHERE DO I BEGIN?
YOU KNOW HIM BETTER THAN ANYONE, EVIE.
BACK HOME IT FELT LIKE WE LIVED ON THE EDGE OF CIVILISATION. DAD SAID THAT'S WHERE IT SUITED HIM...
... HE NEEDED SPACE TO THINK...
... HE'S AS FAR FROM HERE AS I COULD POSSIBLY IMAGINE, ISN'T HE?

I HAVE EVERY FAITH YOU'LL FIND HIM.

IT WON'T BE EASY, BUT THEN YOU'RE NO STRANGER TO A HOSTILE LANDSCAPE.

BACK HOME, IT CAN FEEL LIKE EVERYONE AT SCHOOL IS OUT TO GET ME...

... HERE, IT'S A WHOLE *PLANET*!

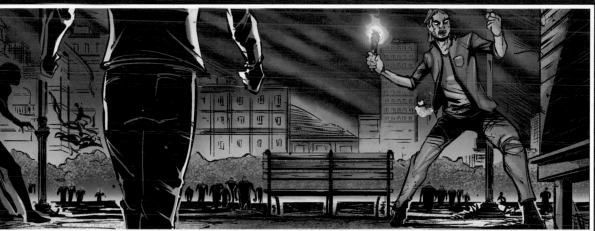

YOU'LL FIND A WAY, EVIE.

IT WON'T BE EASY, BUT I SENSE YOU'RE FAMILIAR WITH FEELING LIKE THE ODDS ARE STACKED AGAINST YOU...

... EVERY SETBACK IS A CHALLENGE, EVERY TRIAL A POTENTIAL TRIUMPH, EVERY—

UNITY, WERE YOU A SPORTS COACH IN A FORMER LIFE?

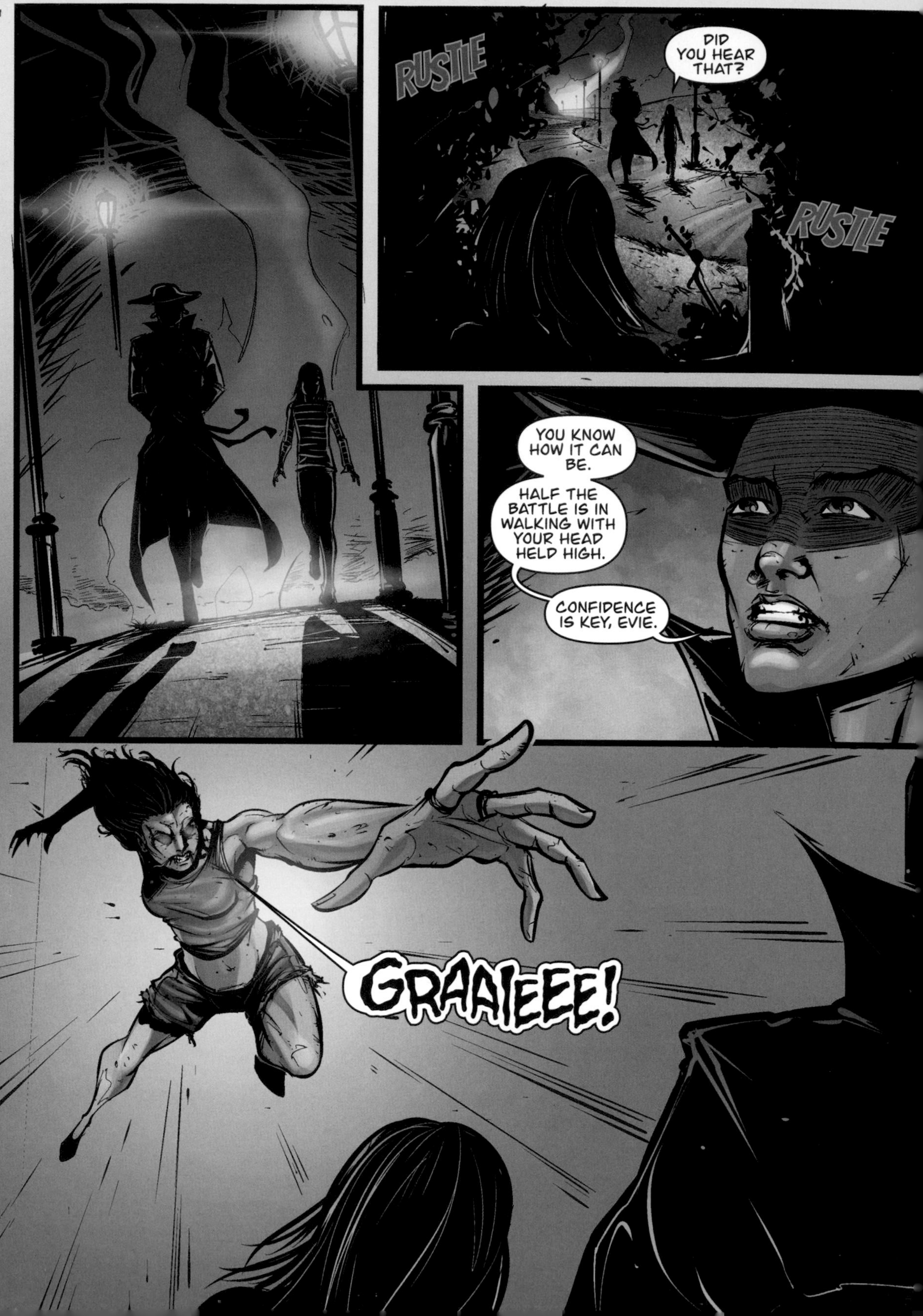
RUSTLE
DID YOU HEAR THAT?
RUSTLE
YOU KNOW HOW IT CAN BE.
HALF THE BATTLE IS IN WALKING WITH YOUR HEAD HELD HIGH.
CONFIDENCE IS KEY, EVIE.
GRAAIEEE!

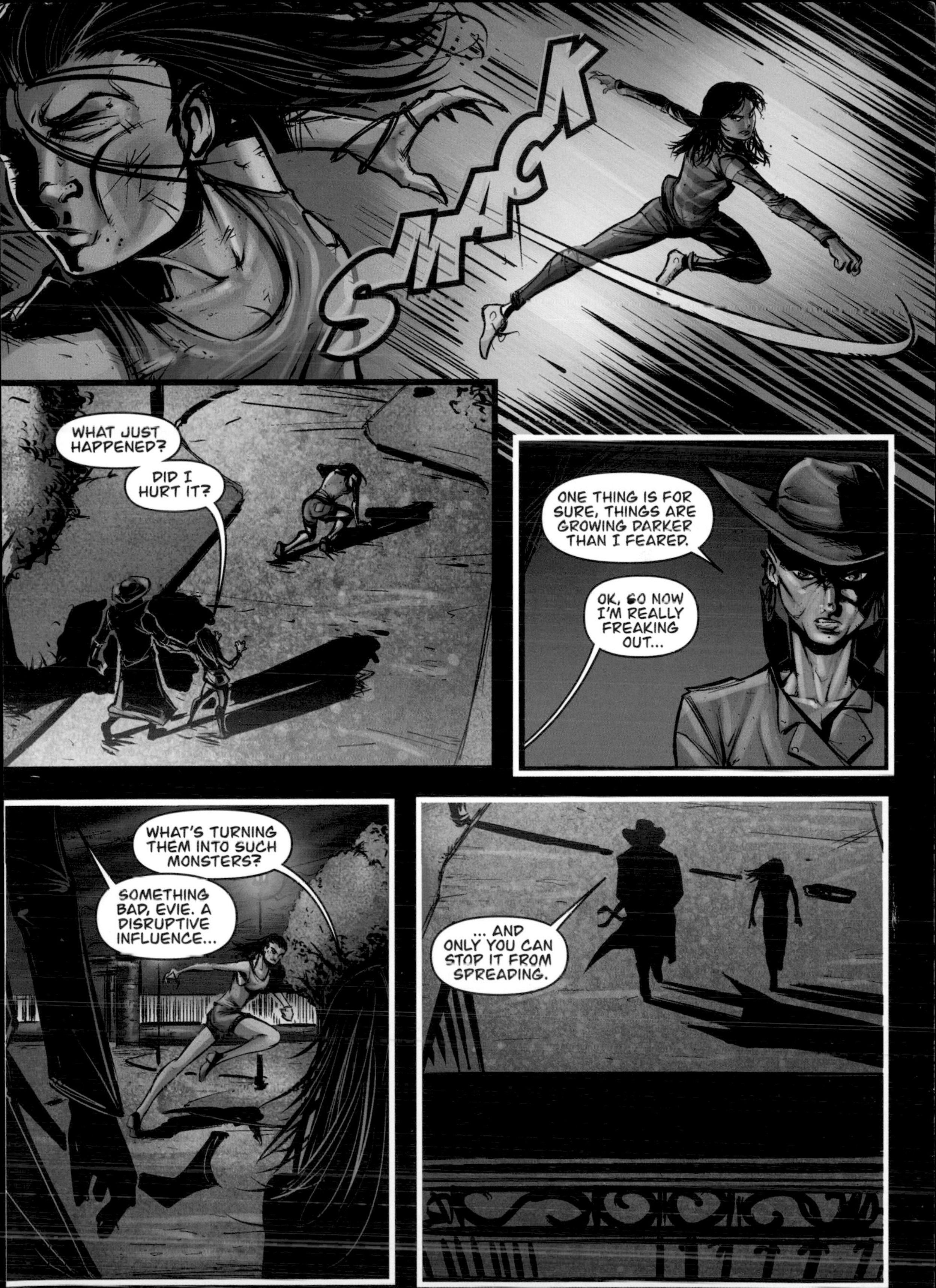
SMACK
WHAT JUST HAPPENED?
DID I HURT IT?
ONE THING IS FOR SURE, THINGS ARE GROWING DARKER THAN I FEARED.
OK, SO NOW I'M REALLY FREAKING OUT...
WHAT'S TURNING THEM INTO SUCH MONSTERS?
SOMETHING BAD, EVIE. A DISRUPTIVE INFLUENCE...
... AND ONLY YOU CAN STOP IT FROM SPREADING.

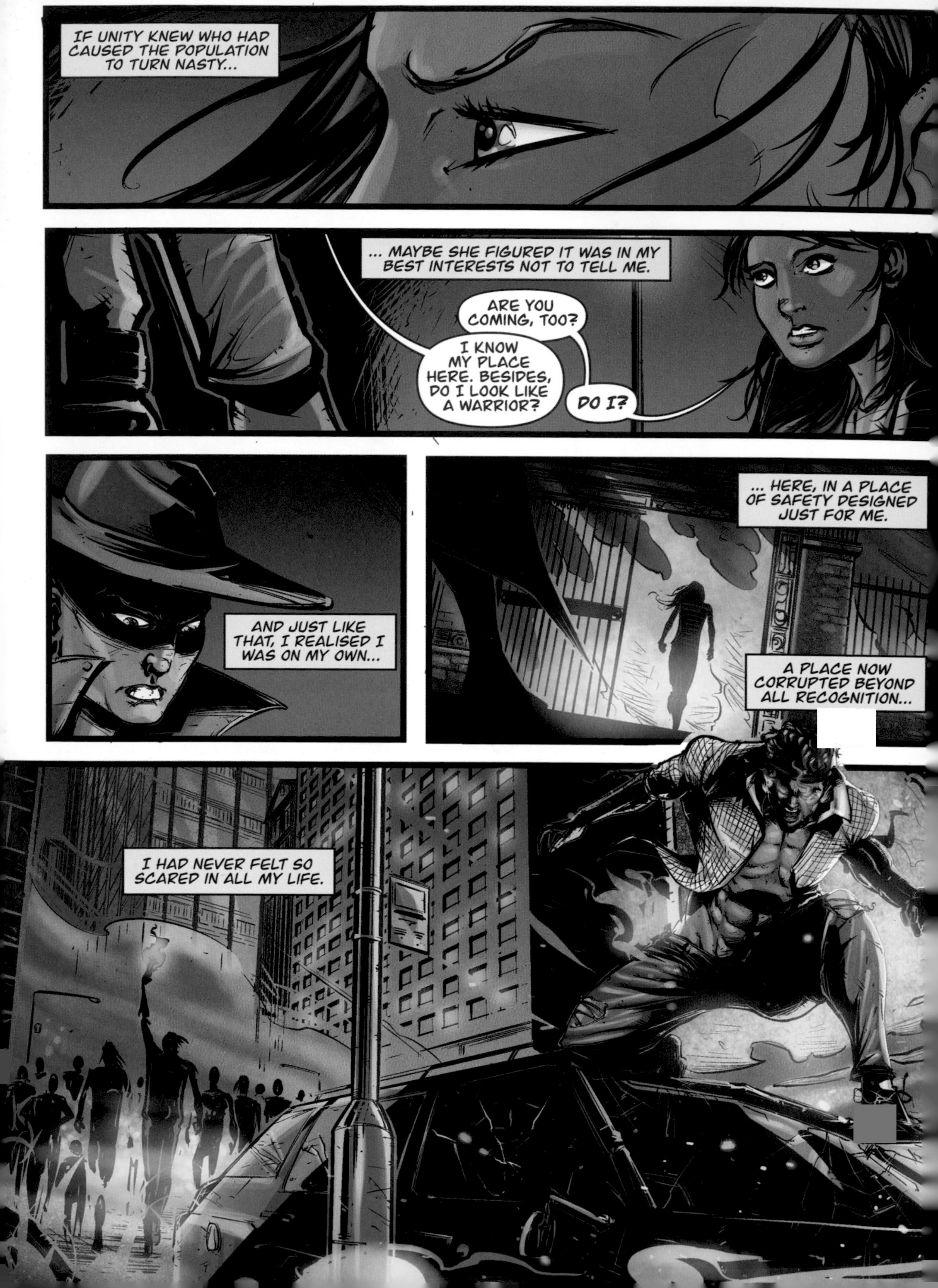
IF UNITY KNEW WHO HAD CAUSED THE POPULATION TO TURN NASTY...
... MAYBE SHE FIGURED IT WAS IN MY BEST INTERESTS NOT TO TELL ME.
ARE YOU COMING, TOO?
I KNOW MY PLACE HERE. BESIDES, DO I LOOK LIKE A WARRIOR?
DO I?
AND JUST LIKE THAT, I REALISED I WAS ON MY OWN...
... HERE, IN A PLACE OF SAFETY DESIGNED JUST FOR ME.
A PLACE NOW CORRUPTED BEYOND ALL RECOGNITION...
I HAD NEVER FELT SO SCARED IN ALL MY LIFE.

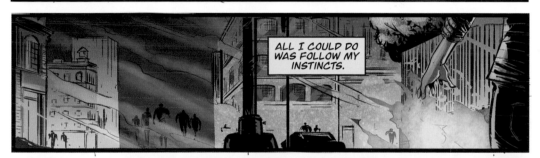

SO, I HAD NO MAP TO FIND MY DAD. NO WAY OF KNOWING WHAT DIRECTION TO HEAD.

ALL I COULD DO WAS FOLLOW MY INSTINCTS.

HEAD AS FAR AS MY FEET WOULD TAKE ME, AND HOPE FOR THE BEST.

DON'T JOIN THEM...

≷GASP≷

PLEASE! IT'S SO SENSELESS.

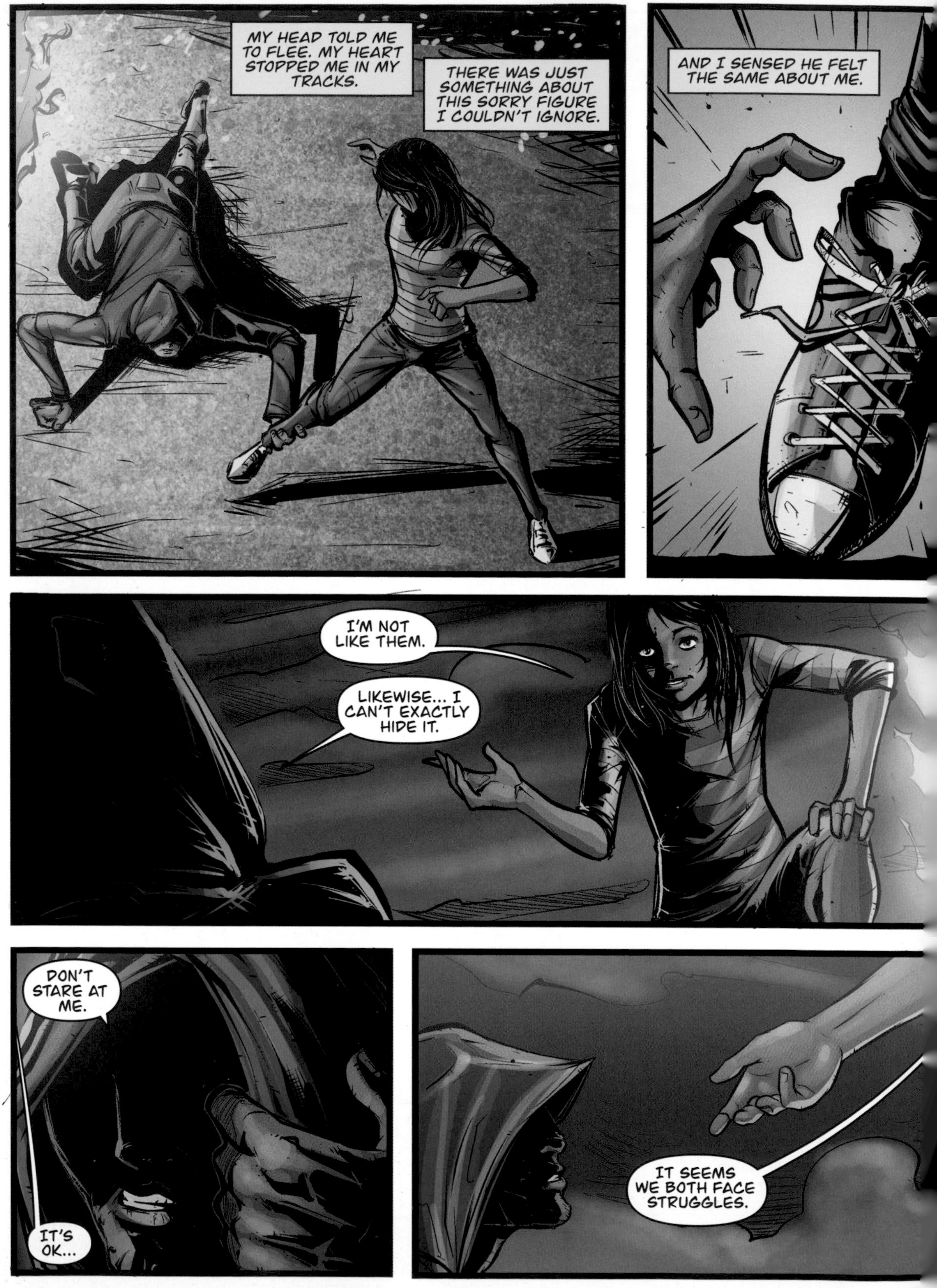
MY HEAD TOLD ME TO FLEE. MY HEART STOPPED ME IN MY TRACKS.
THERE WAS JUST SOMETHING ABOUT THIS SORRY FIGURE I COULDN'T IGNORE.
AND I SENSED HE FELT THE SAME ABOUT ME.
I'M NOT LIKE THEM.
LIKEWISE... I CAN'T EXACTLY HIDE IT.
DON'T STARE AT ME.
IT'S OK...
IT SEEMS WE BOTH FACE STRUGGLES.

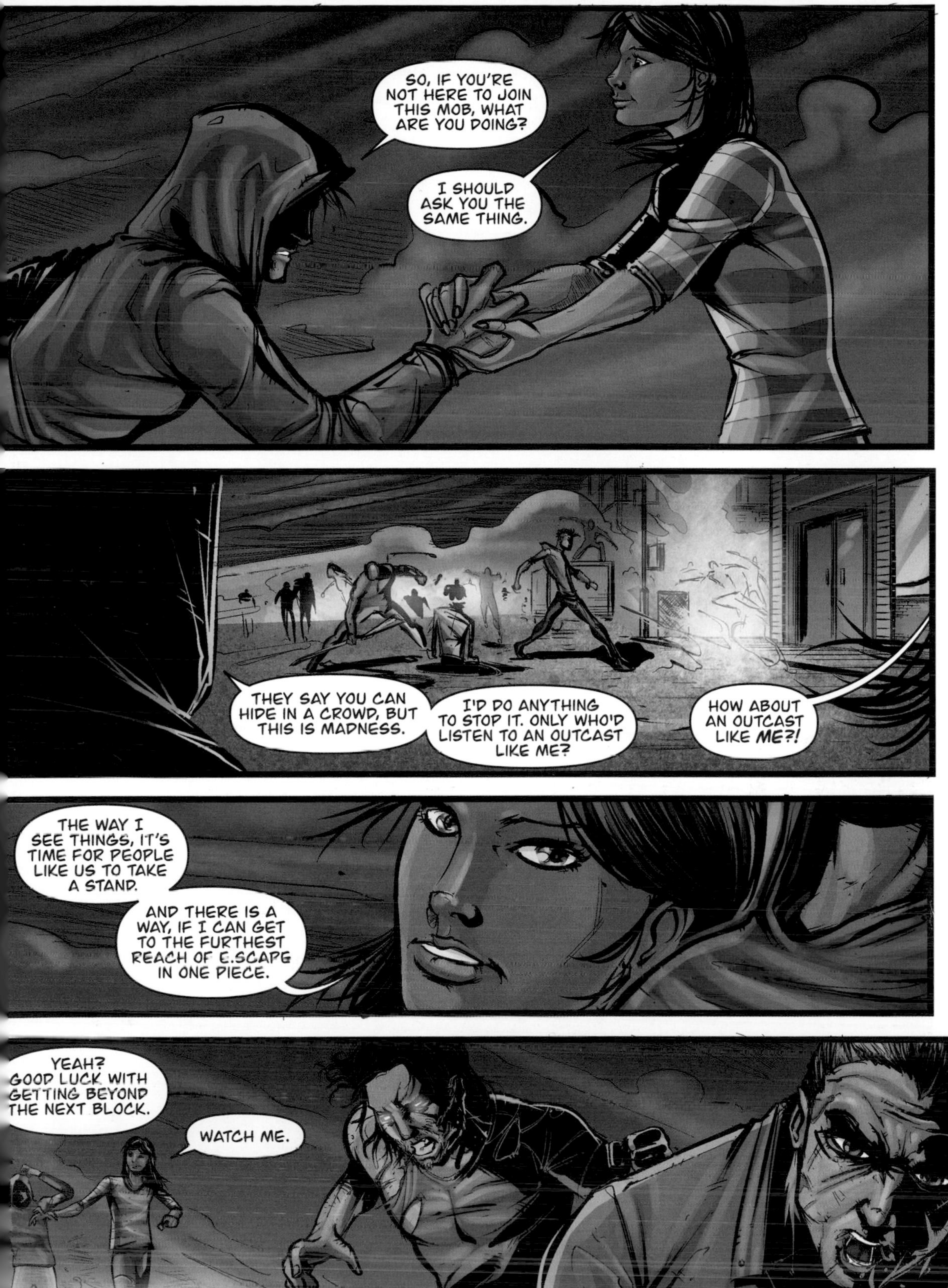
SO, IF YOU'RE NOT HERE TO JOIN THIS MOB, WHAT ARE YOU DOING?
I SHOULD ASK YOU THE SAME THING.
THEY SAY YOU CAN HIDE IN A CROWD, BUT THIS IS MADNESS.
I'D DO ANYTHING TO STOP IT. ONLY WHO'D LISTEN TO AN OUTCAST LIKE ME?
HOW ABOUT AN OUTCAST LIKE ***ME?!***
THE WAY I SEE THINGS, IT'S TIME FOR PEOPLE LIKE US TO TAKE A STAND.
AND THERE IS A WAY, IF I CAN GET TO THE FURTHEST REACH OF E.SCAPE IN ONE PIECE.
YEAH? GOOD LUCK WITH GETTING BEYOND THE NEXT BLOCK.
WATCH ME.

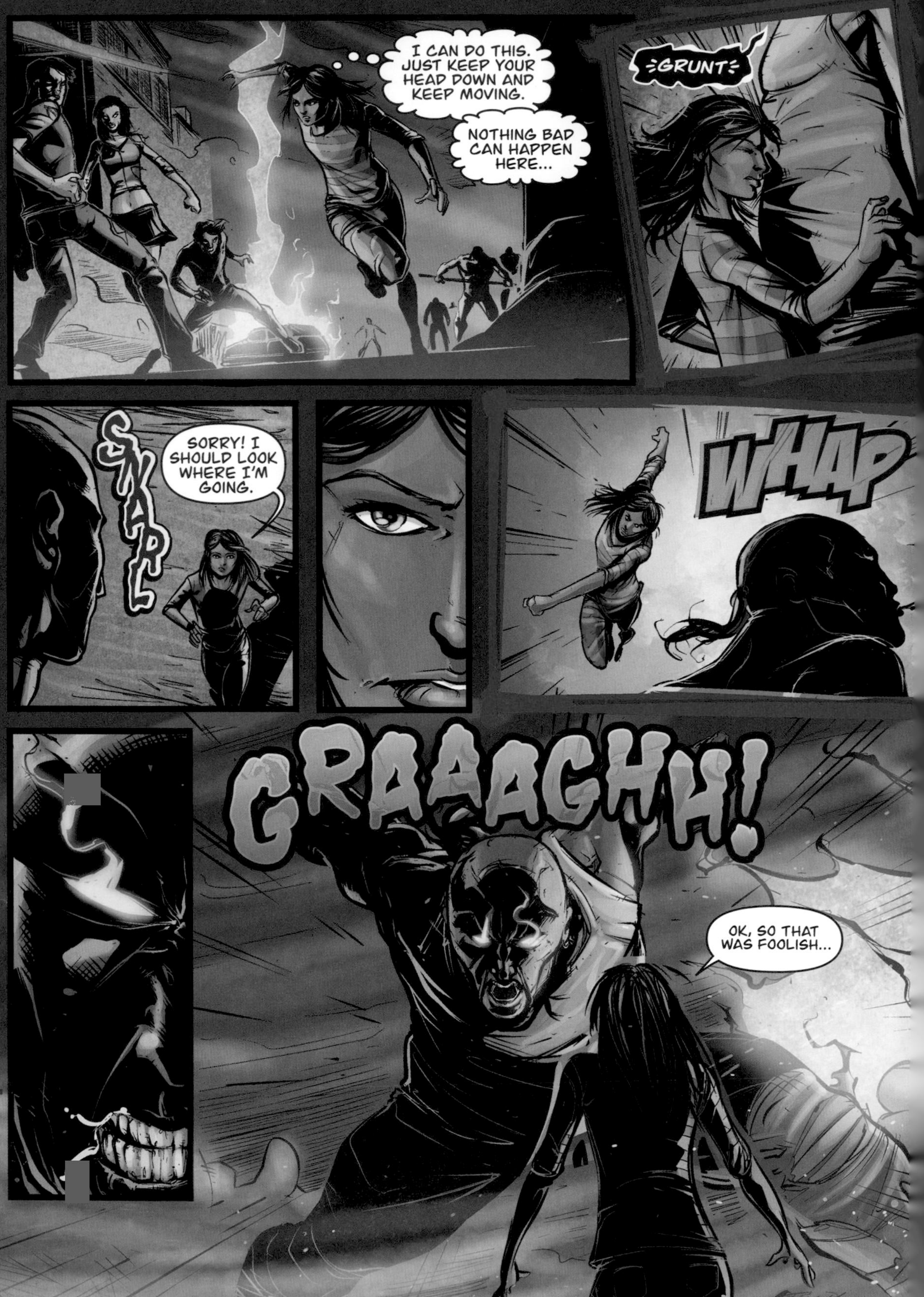
I CAN DO THIS. JUST KEEP YOUR HEAD DOWN AND KEEP MOVING.
NOTHING BAD CAN HAPPEN HERE...
GRUNT
SNARL
SORRY! I SHOULD LOOK WHERE I'M GOING.
WHAP
GRAAAGHH!
OK, SO THAT WAS FOOLISH...

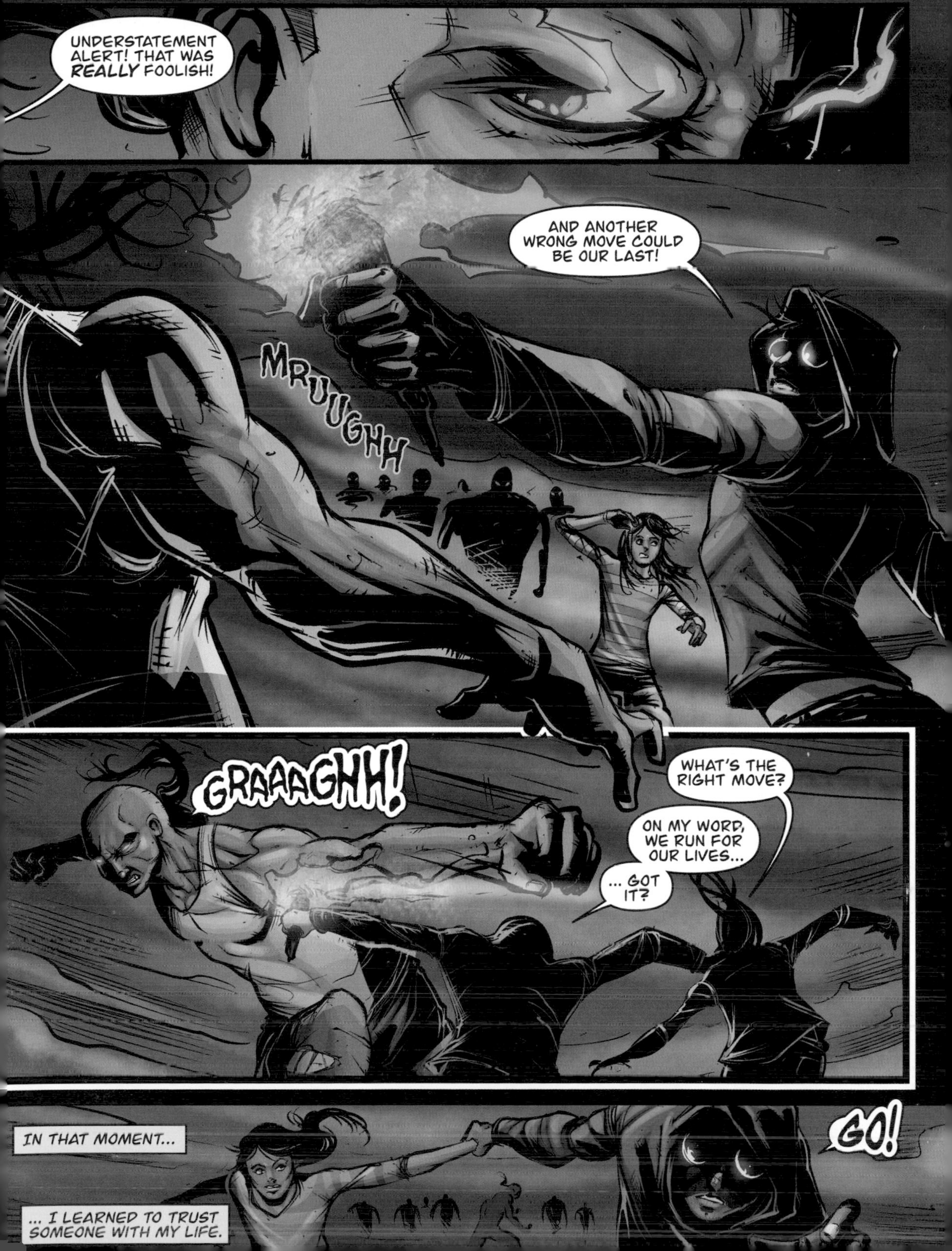
UNDERSTATEMENT ALERT! THAT WAS REALLY FOOLISH!
AND ANOTHER WRONG MOVE COULD BE OUR LAST!
MRUUGHH
GRAAAGHH!
WHAT'S THE RIGHT MOVE?
ON MY WORD, WE RUN FOR OUR LIVES...
... GOT IT?
IN THAT MOMENT...
GO!
... I LEARNED TO TRUST SOMEONE WITH MY LIFE.

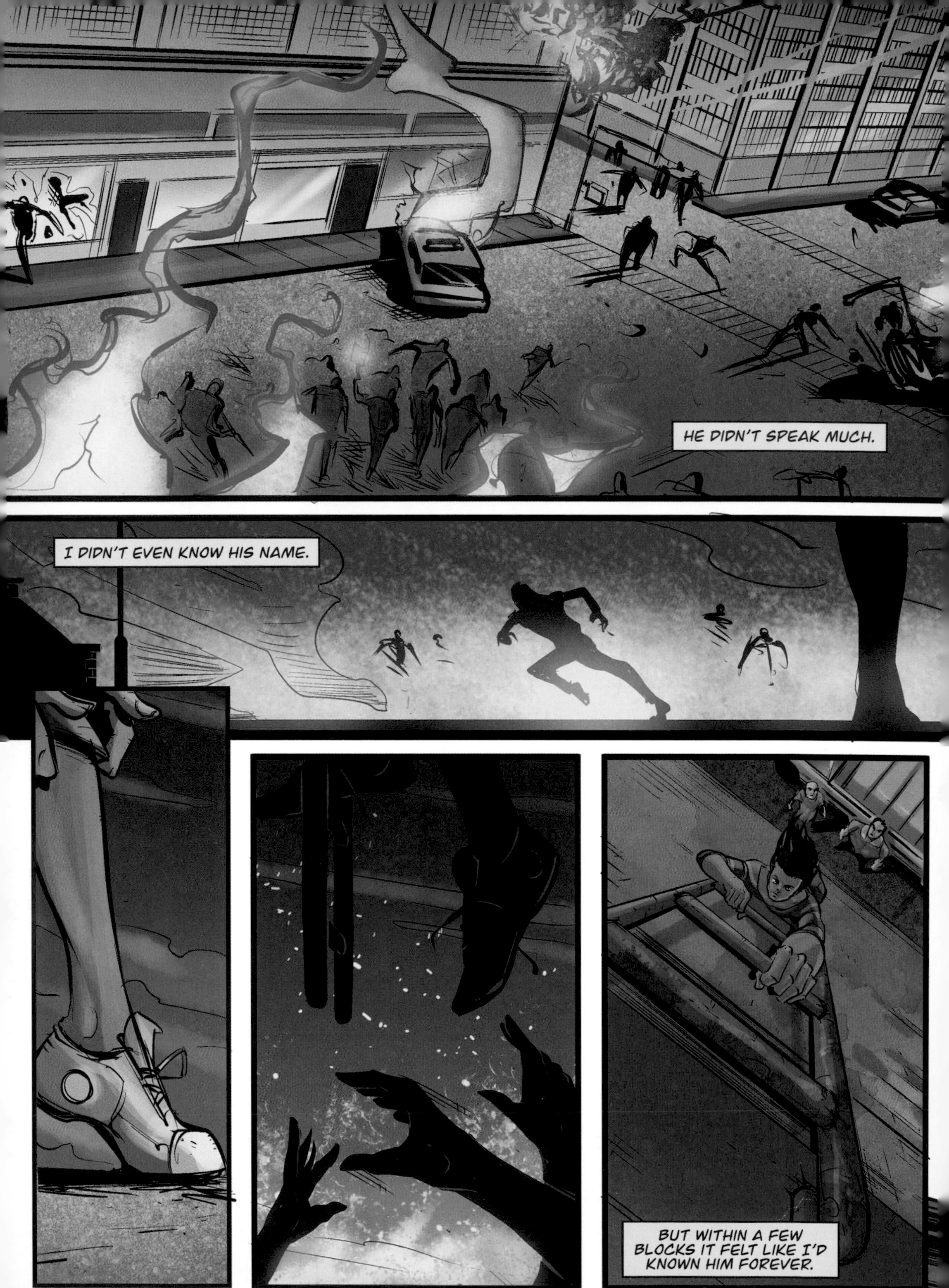
HE DIDN'T SPEAK MUCH.
I DIDN'T EVEN KNOW HIS NAME.
BUT WITHIN A FEW BLOCKS IT FELT LIKE I'D KNOWN HIM FOREVER.

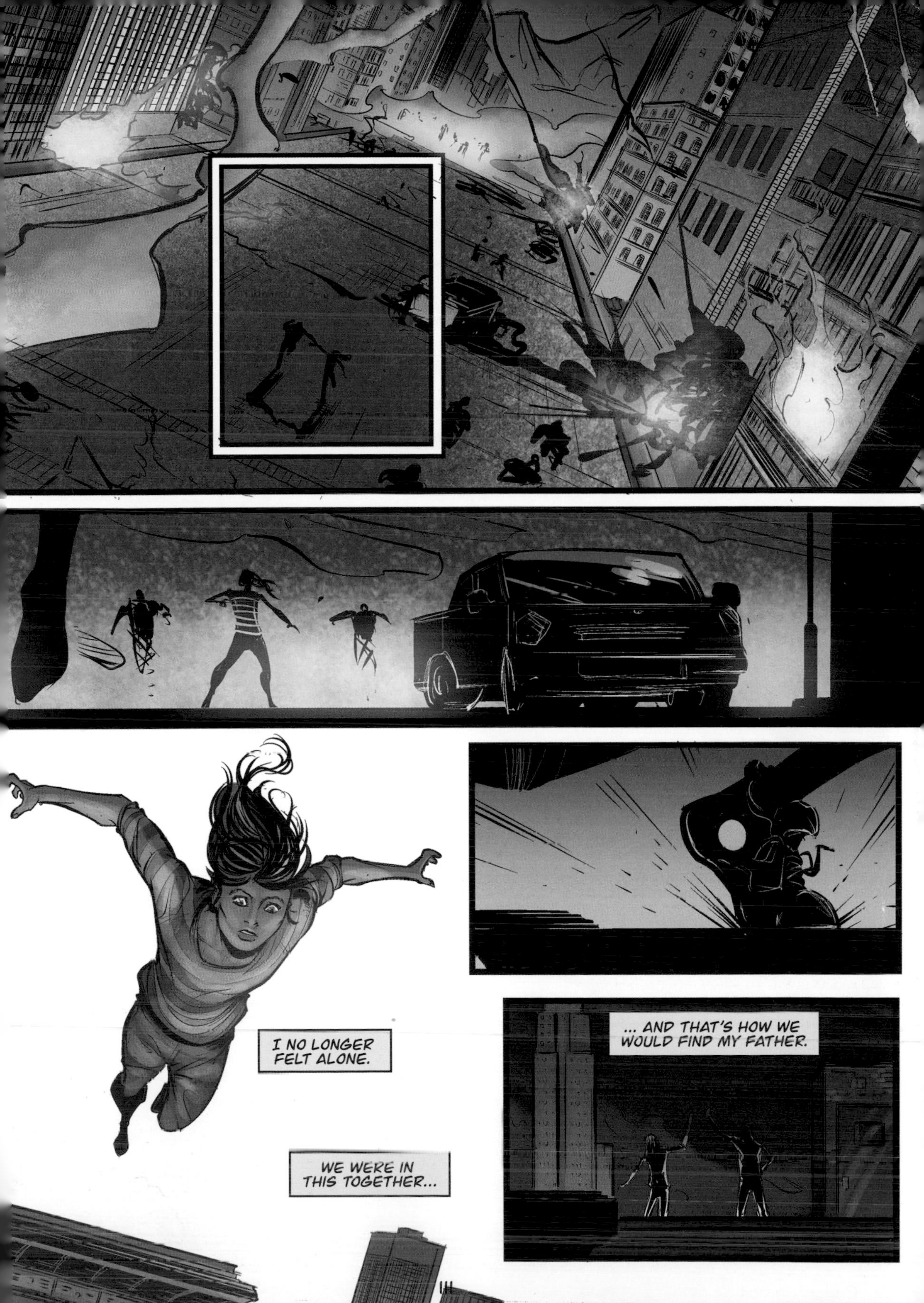
I NO LONGER
FELT ALONE.
WE WERE IN
THIS TOGETHER...
... AND THAT'S HOW WE
WOULD FIND MY FATHER.

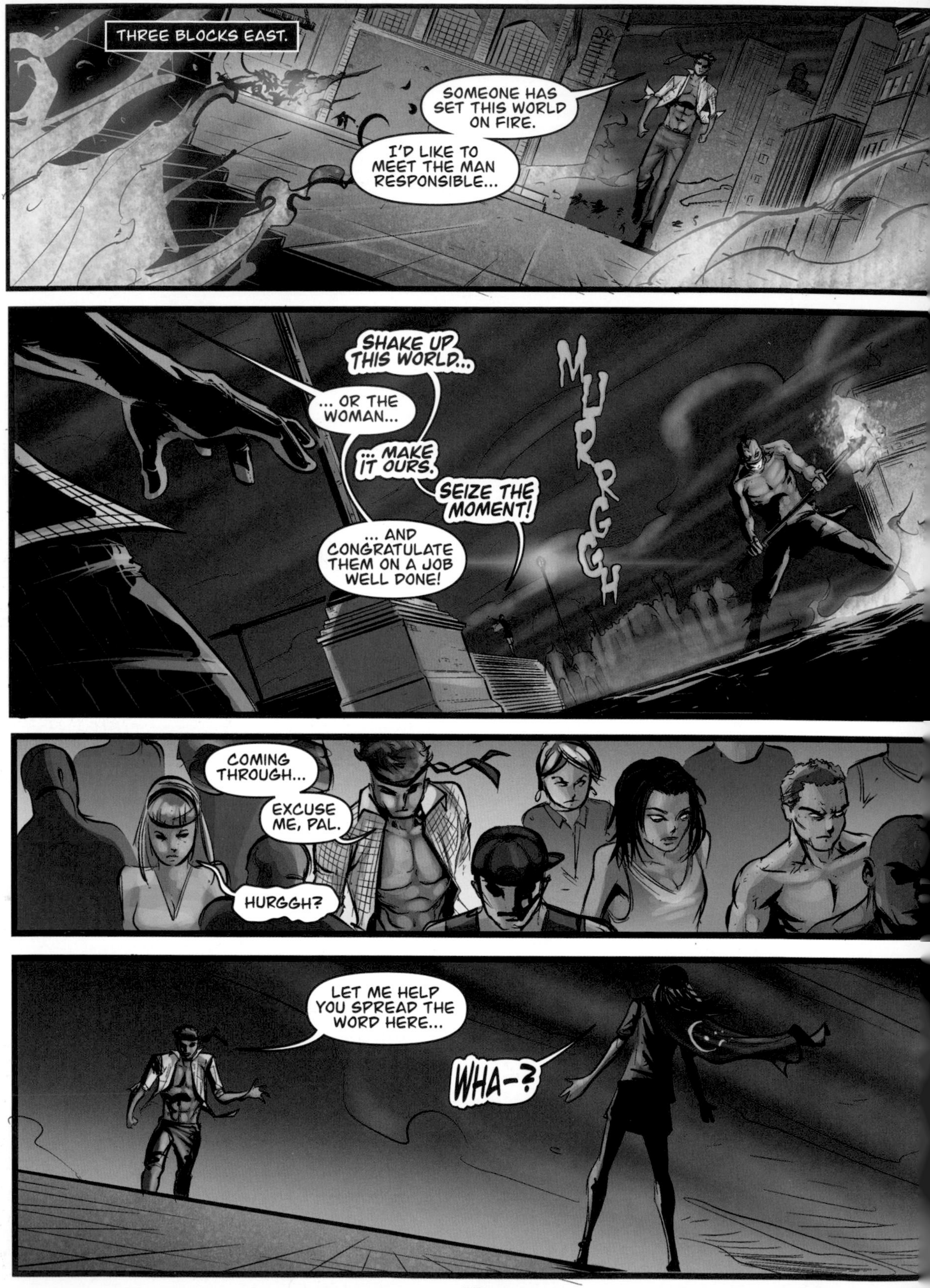
THREE BLOCKS EAST.
SOMEONE HAS SET THIS WORLD ON FIRE.
I'D LIKE TO MEET THE MAN RESPONSIBLE...
SHAKE UP THIS WORLD...
... OR THE WOMAN...
... MAKE IT OURS.
SEIZE THE MOMENT!
... AND CONGRATULATE THEM ON A JOB WELL DONE!
MURRGGH
COMING THROUGH...
EXCUSE ME, PAL.
HURGGH?
LET ME HELP YOU SPREAD THE WORD HERE...
WHA-?

IF YOU'LL ALLOW ME TO STEAL THE SPOTLIGHT FOR A MOMENT...

... AND CAN I SAY HOW *HOT* YOU LOOK, ALL FIRED UP.

MRRHHHH?

LISTEN UP, PEOPLE.

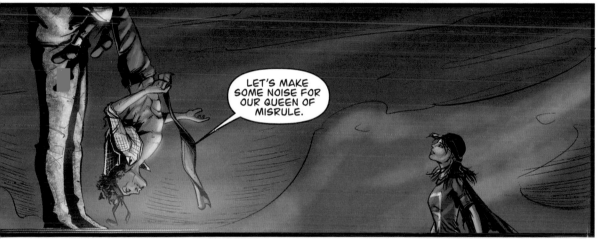

LET'S MAKE SOME NOISE FOR OUR QUEEN OF MISRULE.

THE OTHER VISITOR WOULD NEVER DREAM OF TAKING THINGS THIS FAR.

NOW MAKE SOME *NOISE!*

HRUGGHH!

HRUGGHH!

MRAWW

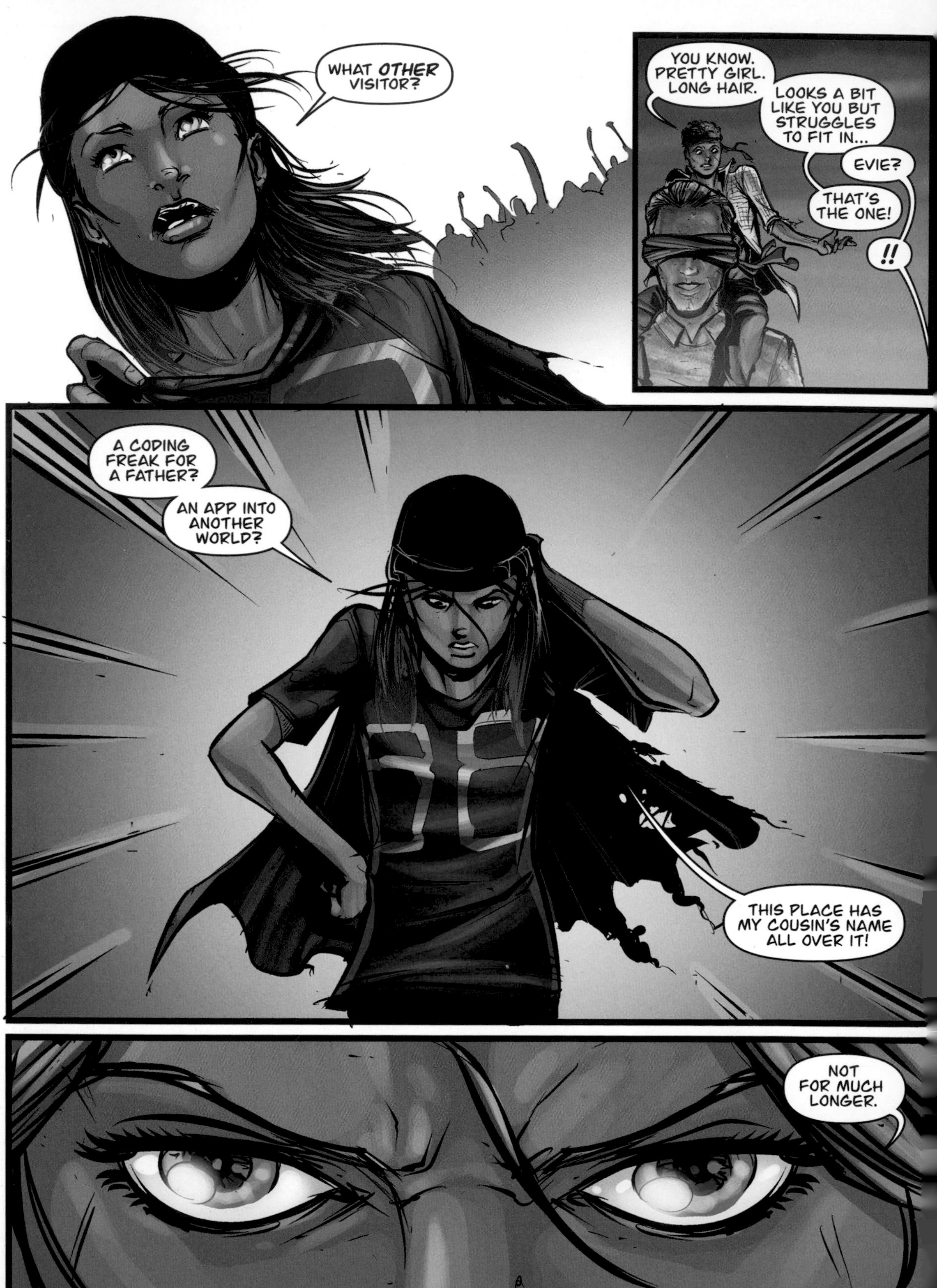
WHAT OTHER VISITOR?
YOU KNOW. PRETTY GIRL. LONG HAIR.
LOOKS A BIT LIKE YOU BUT STRUGGLES TO FIT IN...
EVIE?
THAT'S THE ONE!
!!
A CODING FREAK FOR A FATHER?
AN APP INTO ANOTHER WORLD?
THIS PLACE HAS MY COUSIN'S NAME ALL OVER IT!
NOT FOR MUCH LONGER.

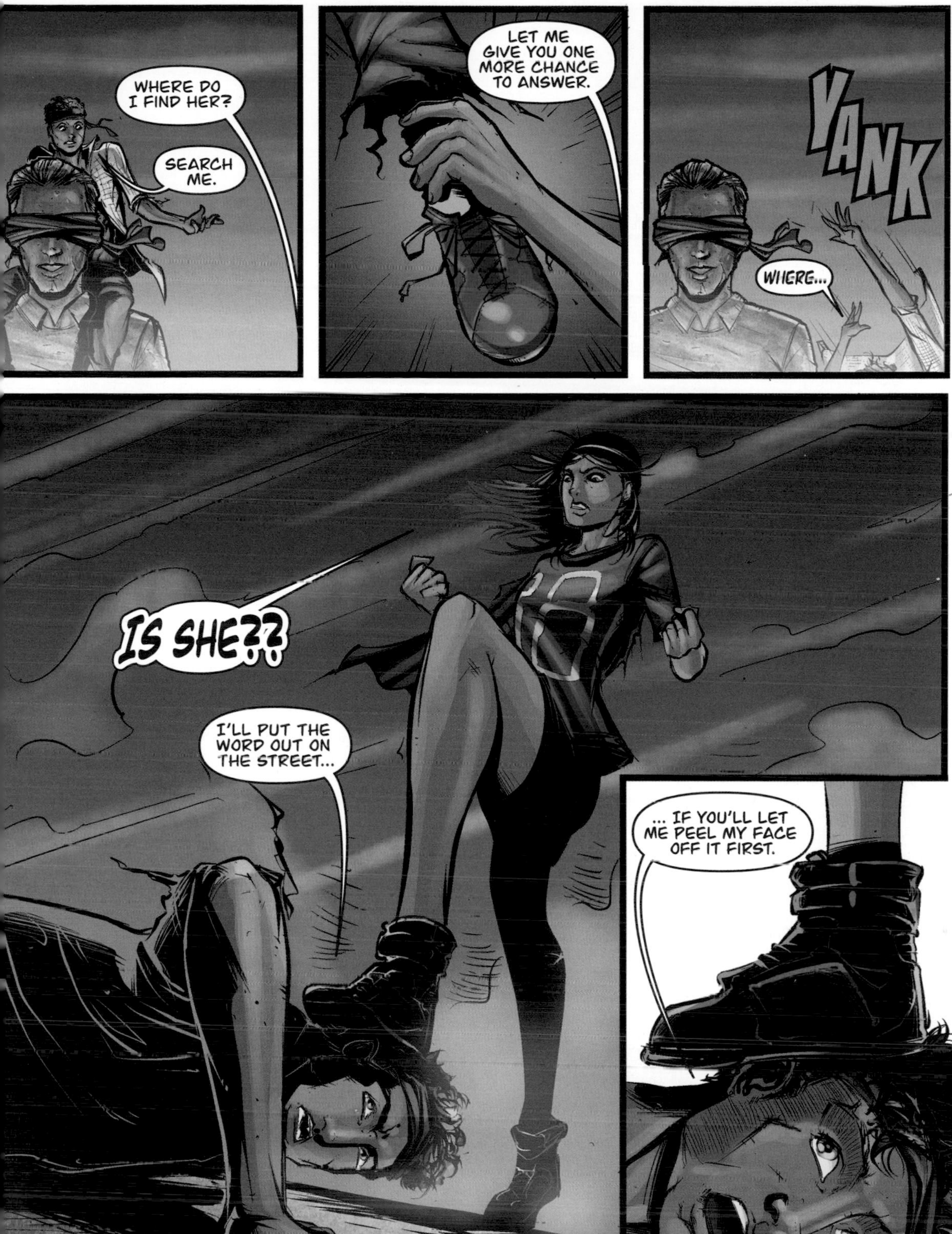
WHERE DO I FIND HER?
SEARCH ME.
LET ME GIVE YOU ONE MORE CHANCE TO ANSWER.
YANK
WHERE...
IS SHE??
I'LL PUT THE WORD OUT ON THE STREET...
... IF YOU'LL LET ME PEEL MY FACE OFF IT FIRST.

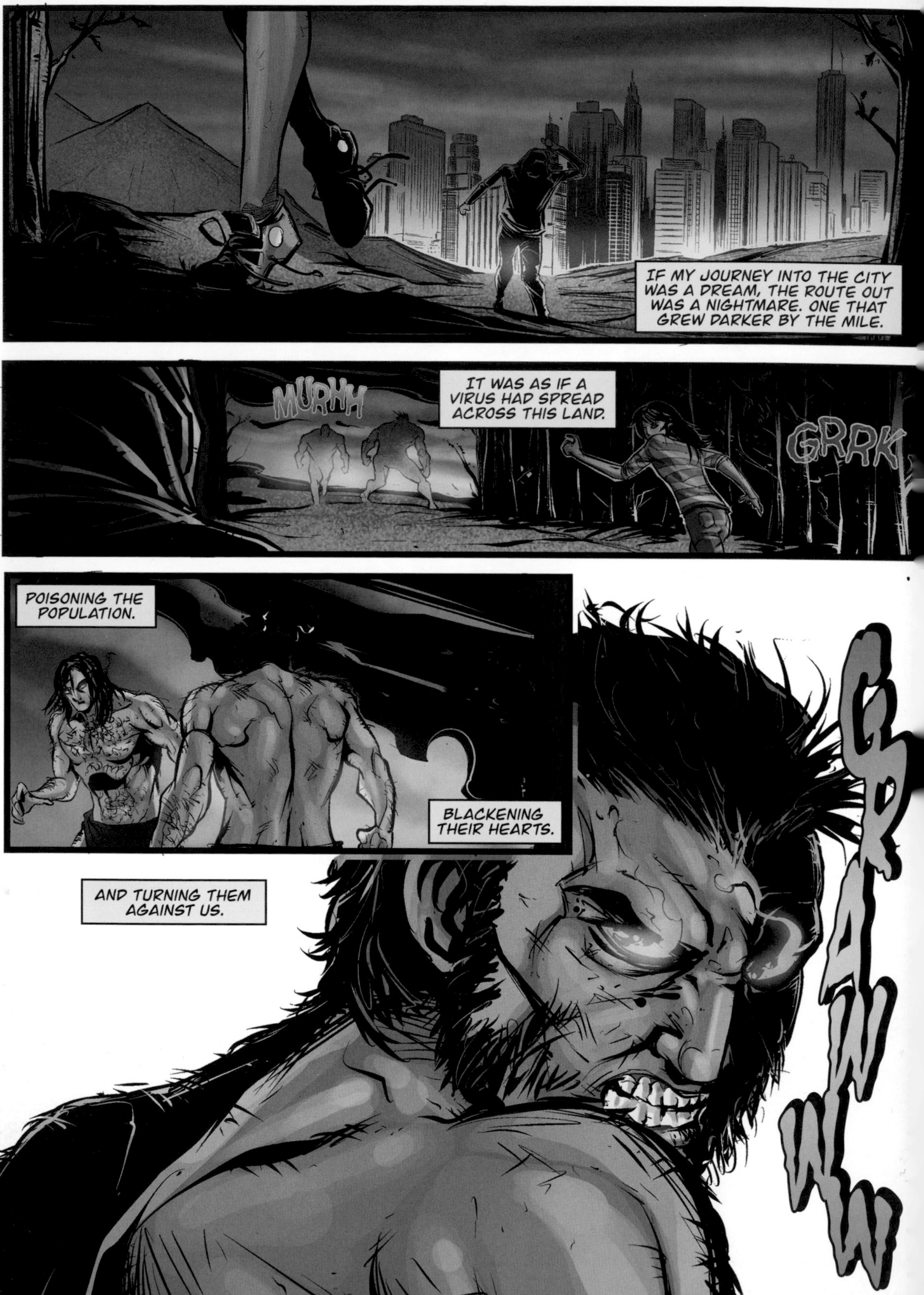
IF MY JOURNEY INTO THE CITY WAS A DREAM, THE ROUTE OUT WAS A NIGHTMARE. ONE THAT GREW DARKER BY THE MILE.
MURHH
IT WAS AS IF A VIRUS HAD SPREAD ACROSS THIS LAND.
GRRK
POISONING THE POPULATION.
BLACKENING THEIR HEARTS.
AND TURNING THEM AGAINST US.
GRAWWW

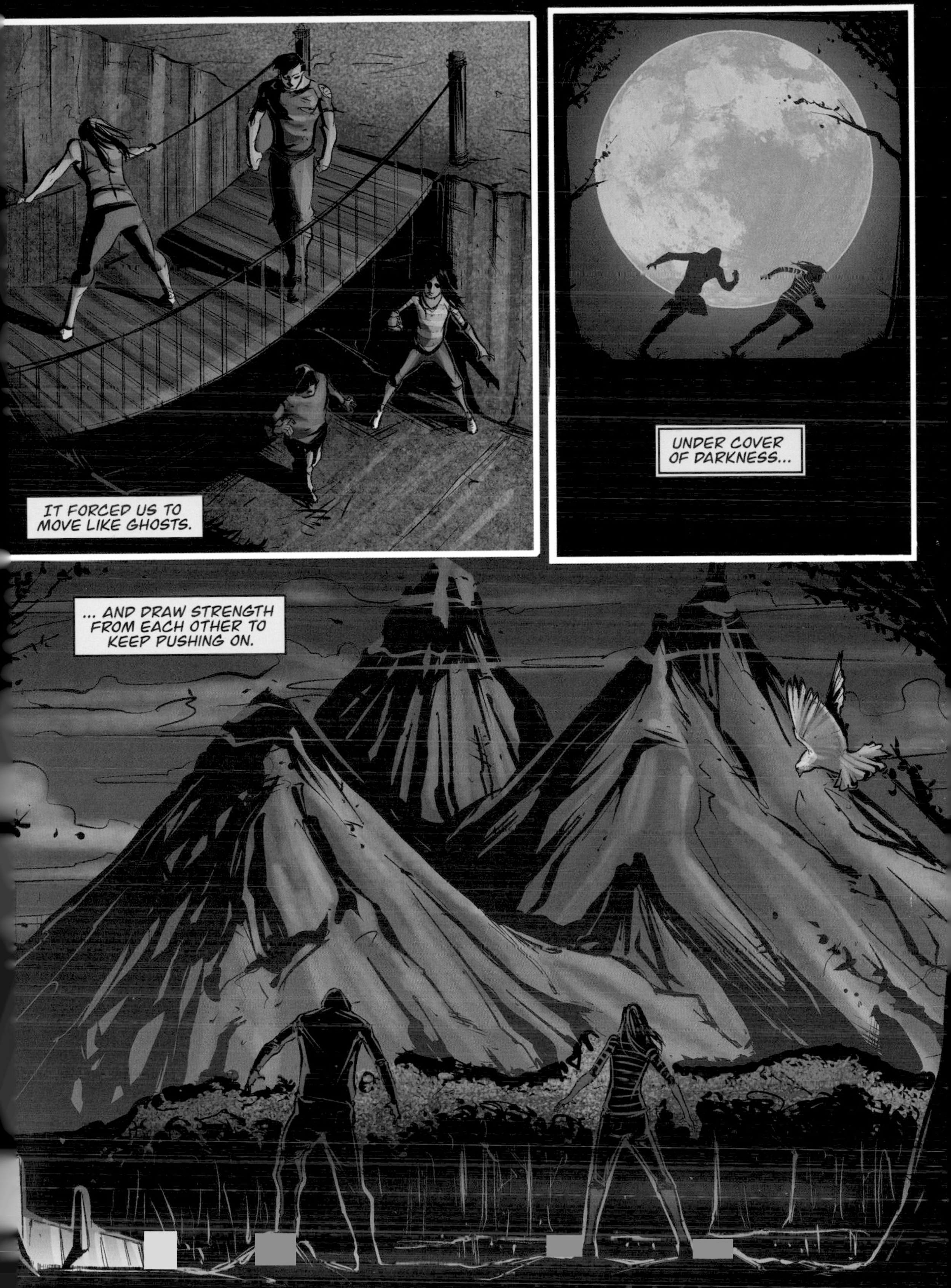
IT FORCED US TO MOVE LIKE GHOSTS.
UNDER COVER OF DARKNESS...
... AND DRAW STRENGTH FROM EACH OTHER TO KEEP PUSHING ON.

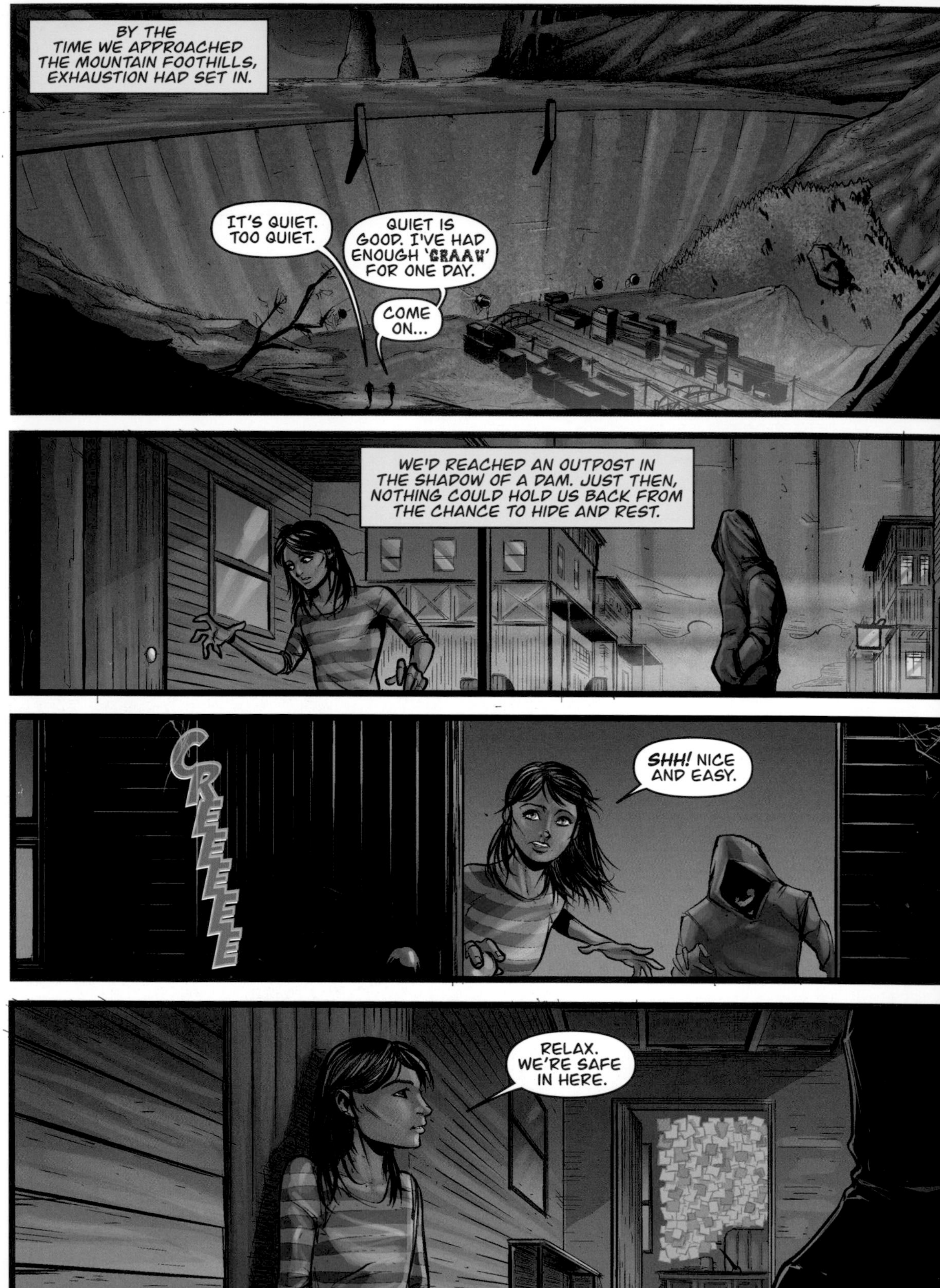
BY THE TIME WE APPROACHED THE MOUNTAIN FOOTHILLS, EXHAUSTION HAD SET IN.
IT'S QUIET. TOO QUIET.
QUIET IS GOOD. I'VE HAD ENOUGH 'GRAAW' FOR ONE DAY.
COME ON...
WE'D REACHED AN OUTPOST IN THE SHADOW OF A DAM. JUST THEN, NOTHING COULD HOLD US BACK FROM THE CHANCE TO HIDE AND REST.
CREEEEEE
SHH! NICE AND EASY.
RELAX. WE'RE SAFE IN HERE.

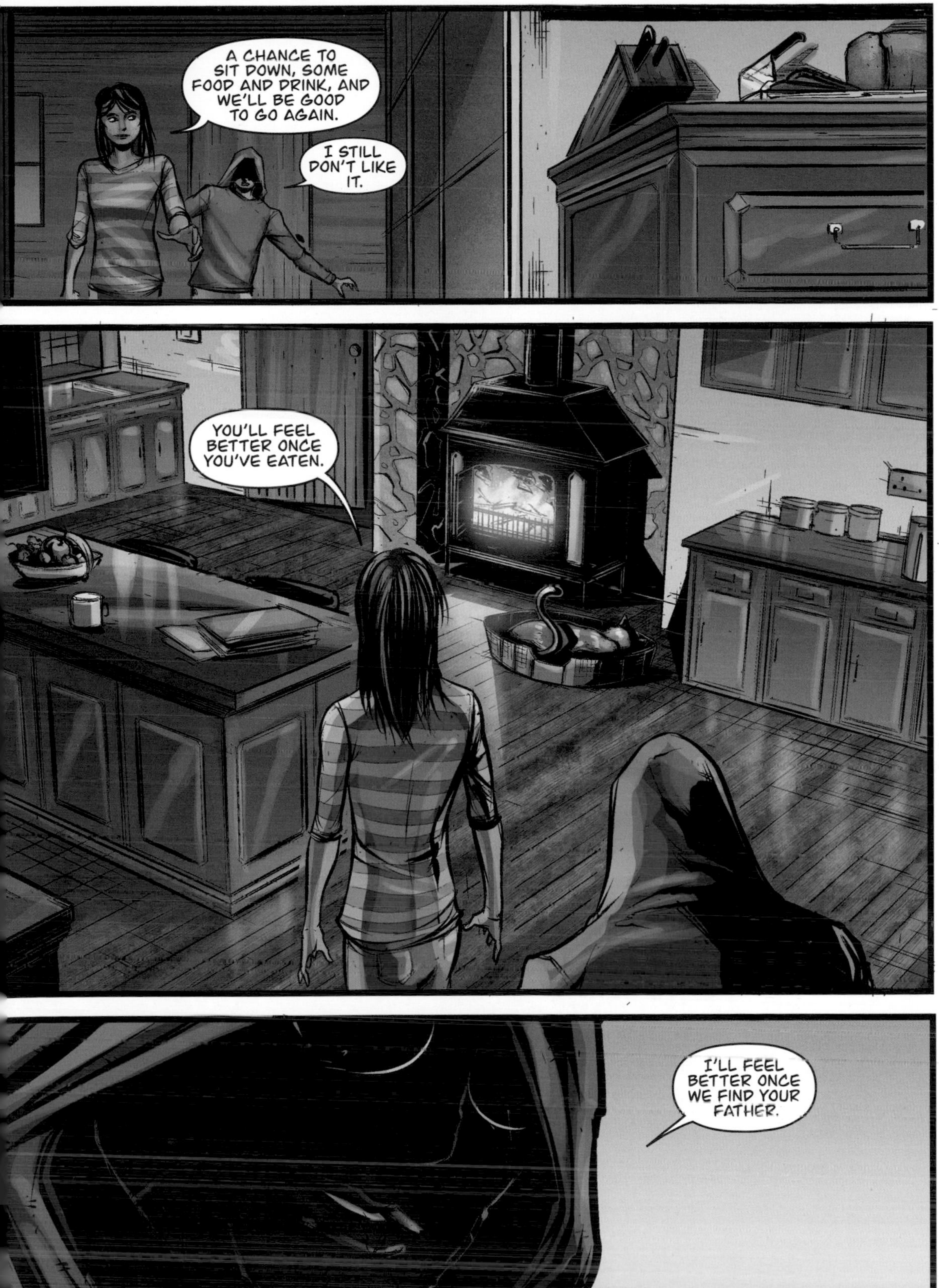

A CHANCE TO SIT DOWN, SOME FOOD AND DRINK, AND WE'LL BE GOOD TO GO AGAIN.
I STILL DON'T LIKE IT.
YOU'LL FEEL BETTER ONCE YOU'VE EATEN.
I'LL FEEL BETTER ONCE WE FIND YOUR FATHER.

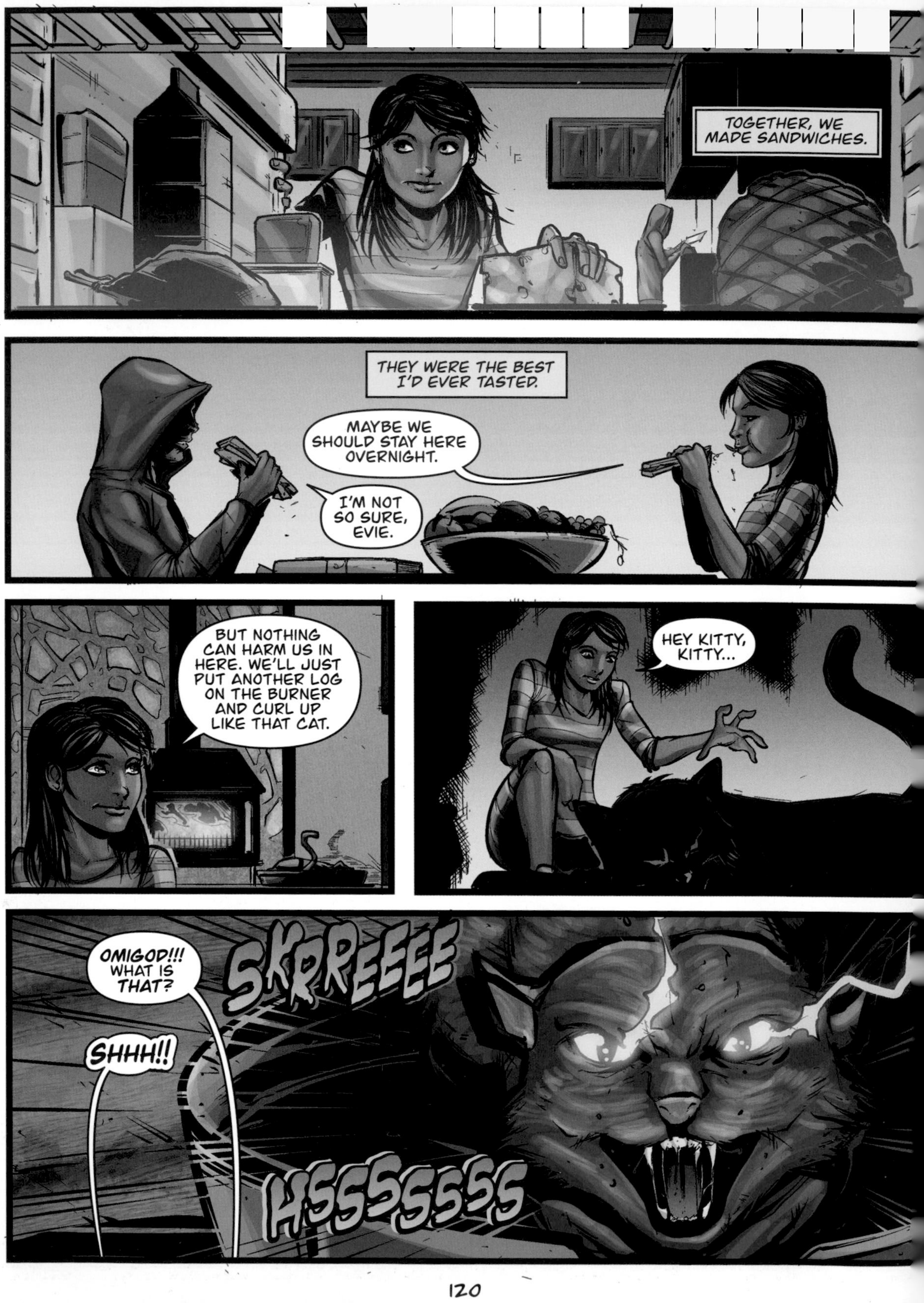
TOGETHER, WE MADE SANDWICHES.
THEY WERE THE BEST I'D EVER TASTED.
MAYBE WE SHOULD STAY HERE OVERNIGHT.
I'M NOT SO SURE, EVIE.
BUT NOTHING CAN HARM US IN HERE. WE'LL JUST PUT ANOTHER LOG ON THE BURNER AND CURL UP LIKE THAT CAT.
HEY KITTY, KITTY...
OMIGOD!!! WHAT IS THAT?
SKREEEEE
SHHH!!
HSSSSSSS

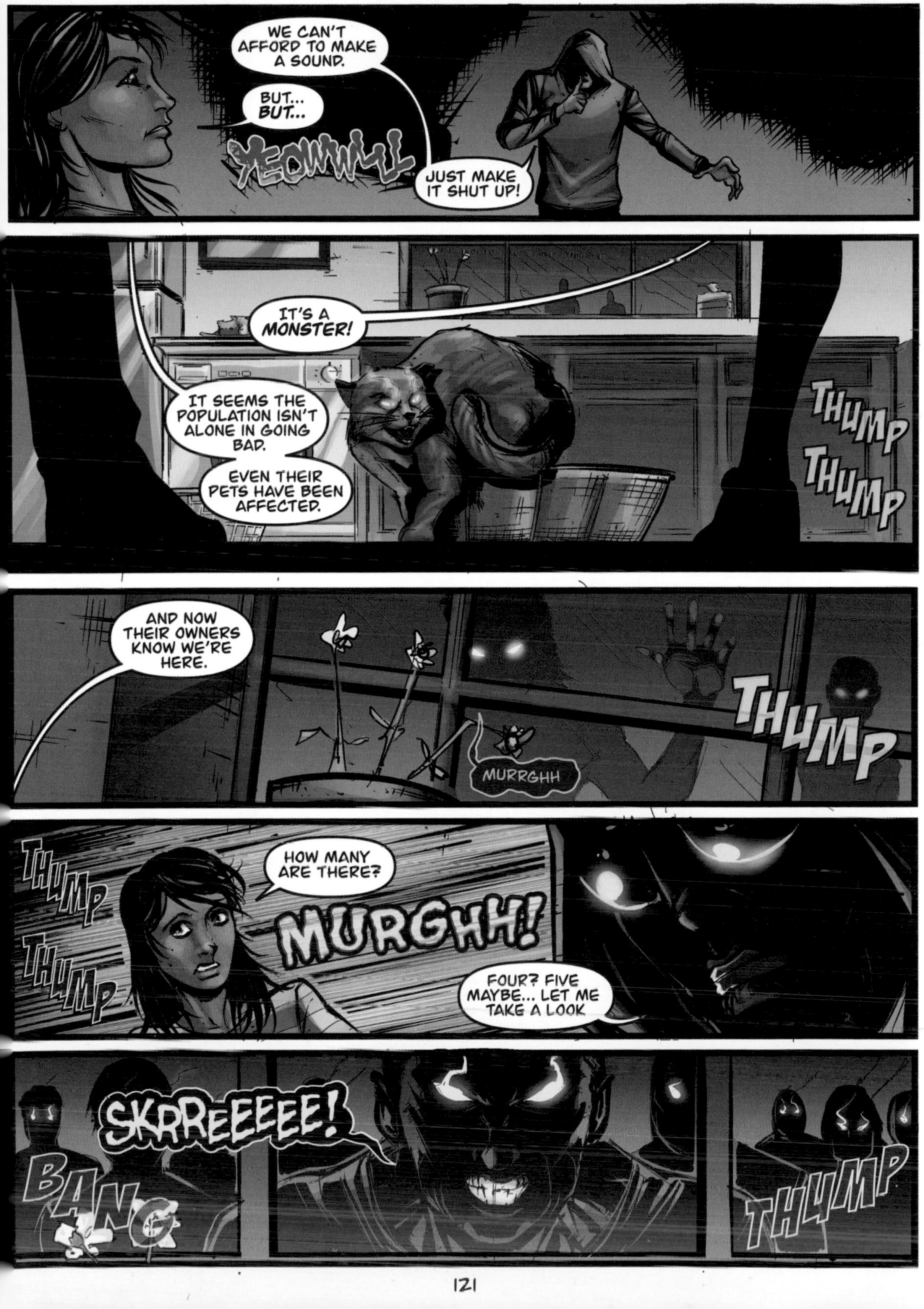
WE CAN'T AFFORD TO MAKE A SOUND.
BUT... BUT...
YEOWWLL
JUST MAKE IT SHUT UP!
IT'S A MONSTER!
IT SEEMS THE POPULATION ISN'T ALONE IN GOING BAD.
EVEN THEIR PETS HAVE BEEN AFFECTED.
THUMP
THUMP
AND NOW THEIR OWNERS KNOW WE'RE HERE.
THUMP
MURRGHH
THUMP
THUMP
HOW MANY ARE THERE?
MURGHH!
FOUR? FIVE MAYBE... LET ME TAKE A LOOK
SKRREEEEEE!
BANG
THUMP

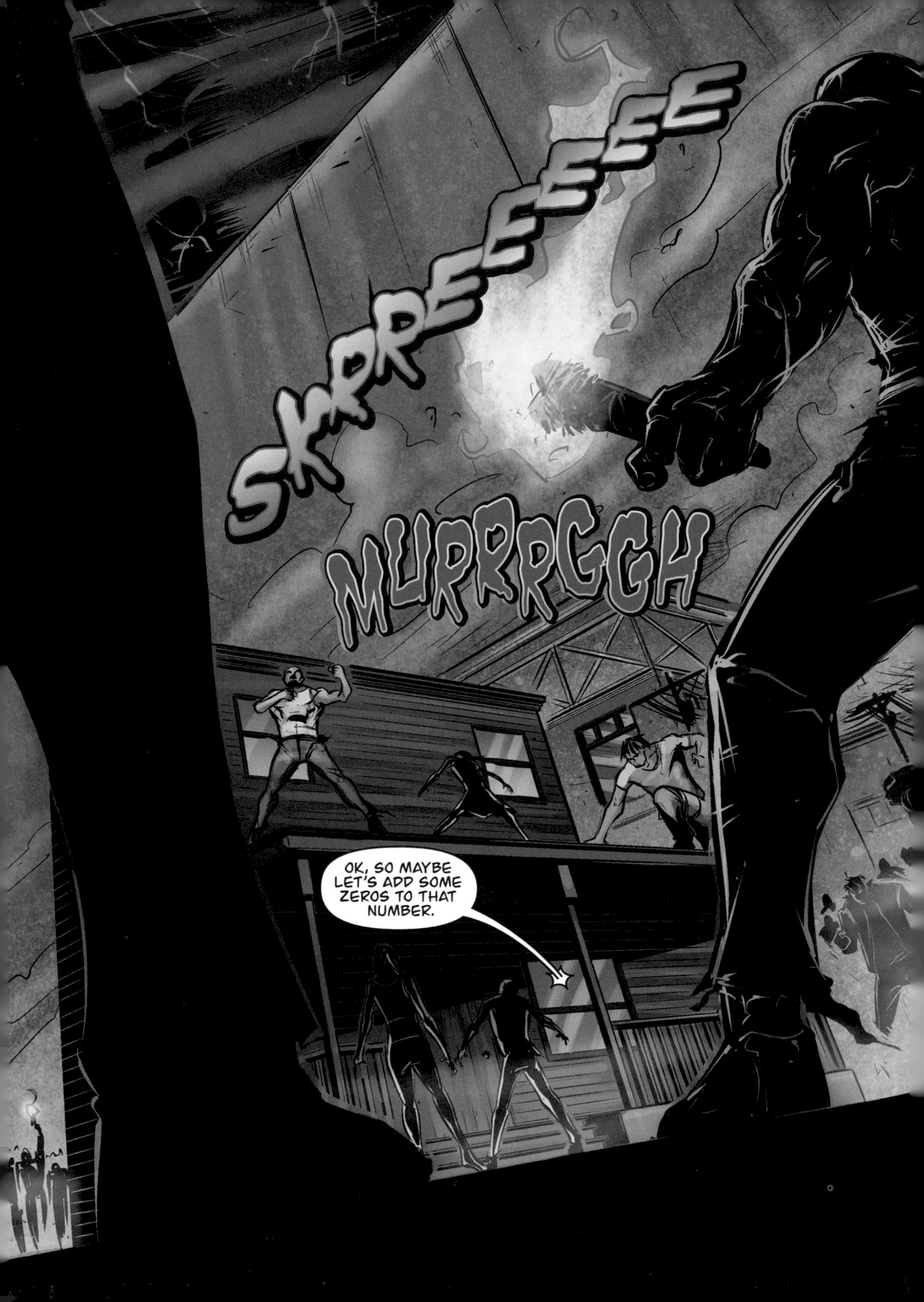
SKRREEEEEEE
MURRRGGH
OK, SO MAYBE LET'S ADD SOME ZEROS TO THAT NUMBER.

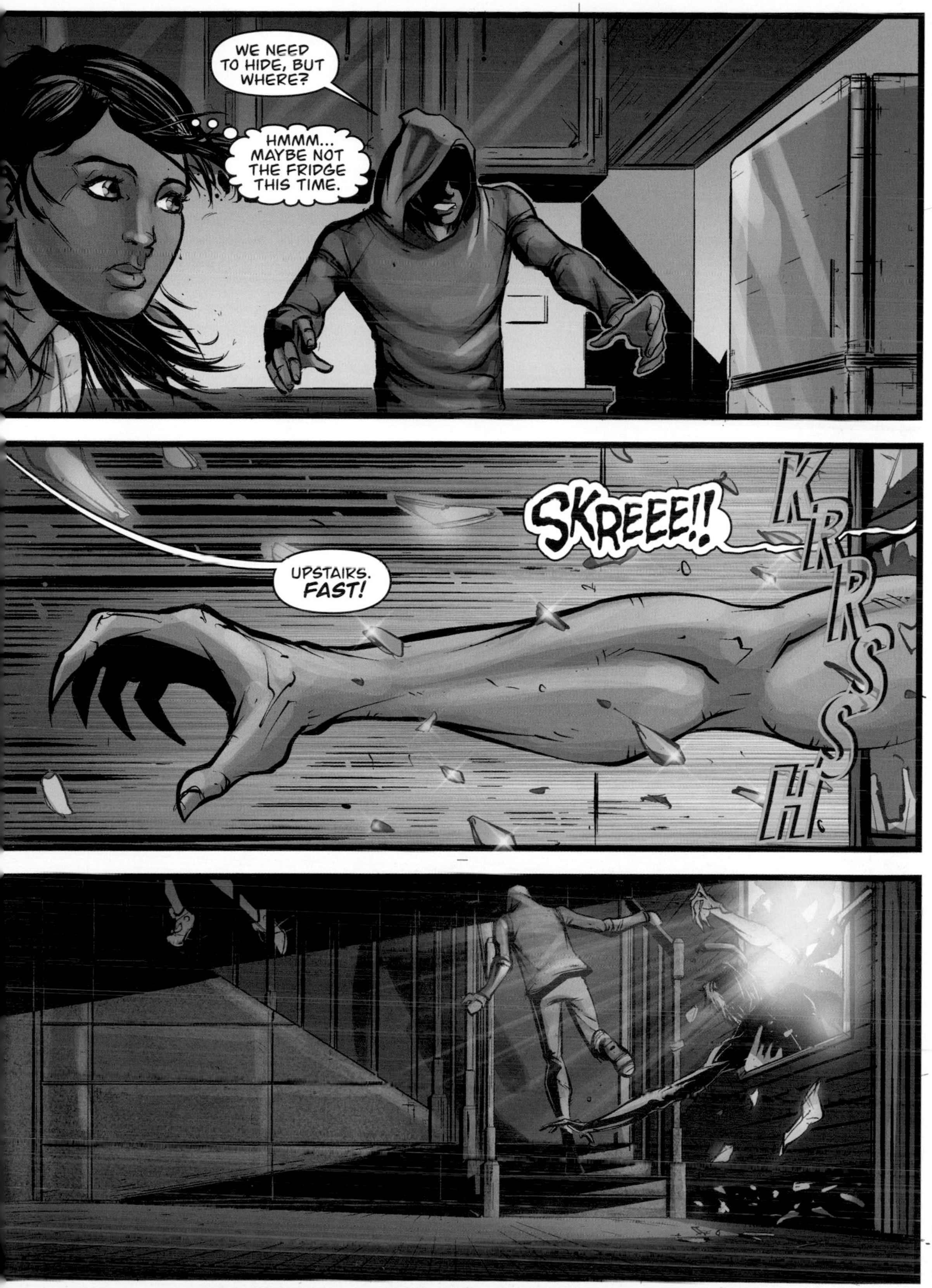
WE NEED TO HIDE, BUT WHERE?
HMMM... MAYBE NOT THE FRIDGE THIS TIME.
UPSTAIRS. FAST!
SKREEE!!
KRRSSH

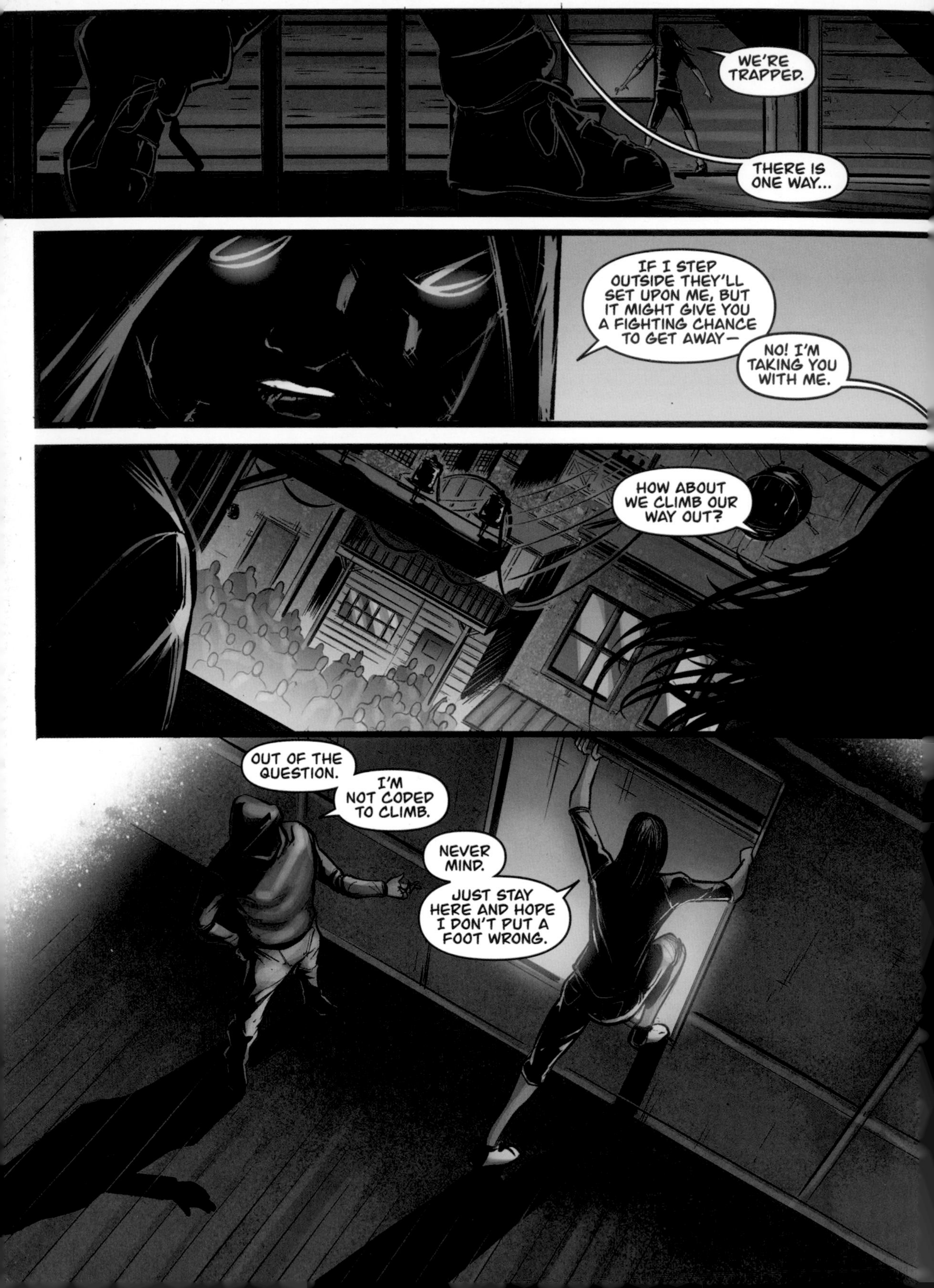
WE'RE TRAPPED.
THERE IS ONE WAY...
IF I STEP OUTSIDE THEY'LL SET UPON ME, BUT IT MIGHT GIVE YOU A FIGHTING CHANCE TO GET AWAY—
NO! I'M TAKING YOU WITH ME.
HOW ABOUT WE CLIMB OUR WAY OUT?
OUT OF THE QUESTION.
I'M NOT CODED TO CLIMB.
NEVER MIND.
JUST STAY HERE AND HOPE I DON'T PUT A FOOT WRONG.

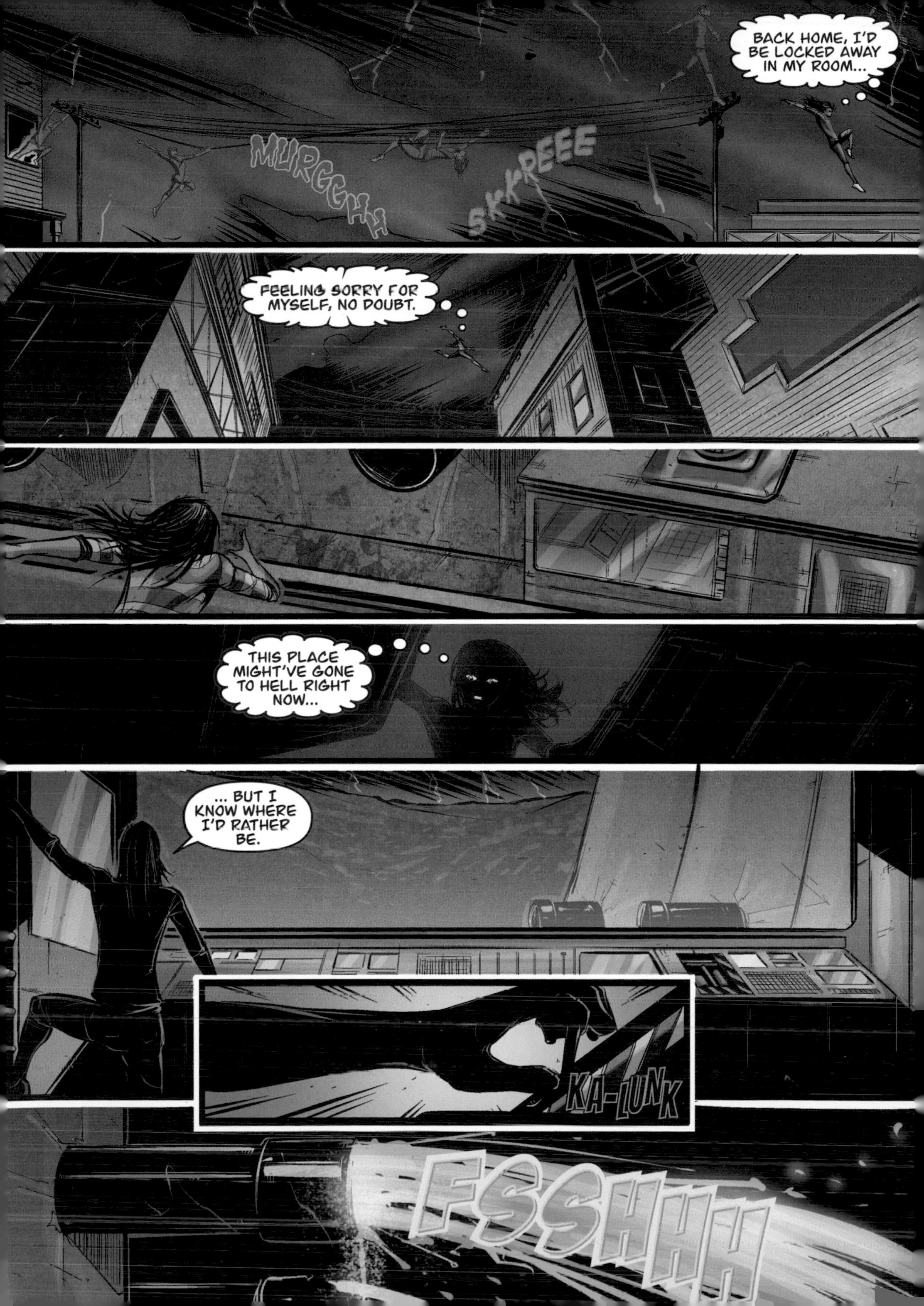
BACK HOME, I'D BE LOCKED AWAY IN MY ROOM...
MURGGHH
SKKREEE
FEELING SORRY FOR MYSELF, NO DOUBT.
THIS PLACE MIGHT'VE GONE TO HELL RIGHT NOW...
... BUT I KNOW WHERE I'D RATHER BE.
KA-LUNK
FSSHHH

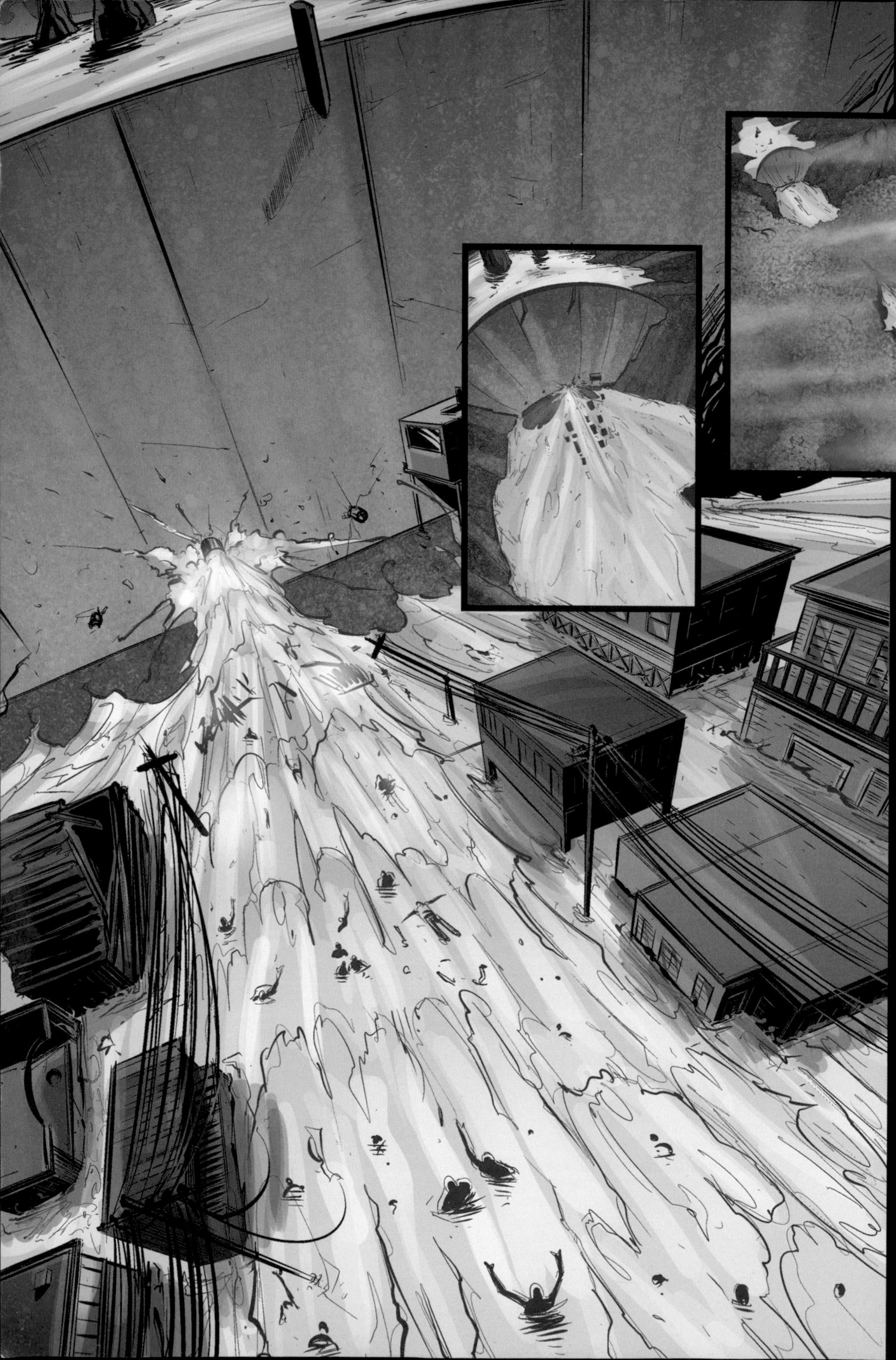

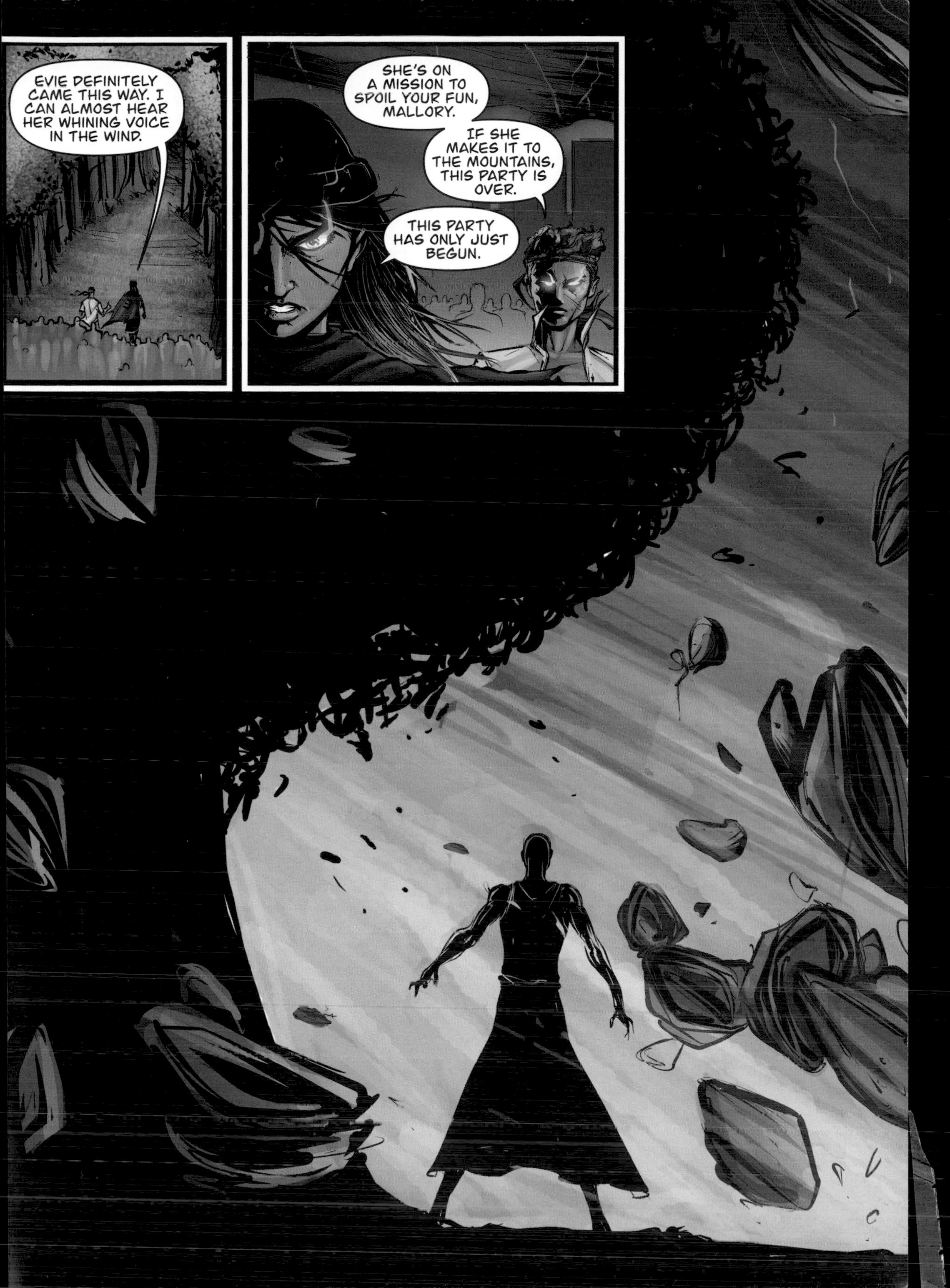
EVIE DEFINITELY CAME THIS WAY. I CAN ALMOST HEAR HER WHINING VOICE IN THE WIND.
SHE'S ON A MISSION TO SPOIL YOUR FUN, MALLORY.
IF SHE MAKES IT TO THE MOUNTAINS, THIS PARTY IS OVER.
THIS PARTY HAS ONLY JUST BEGUN.

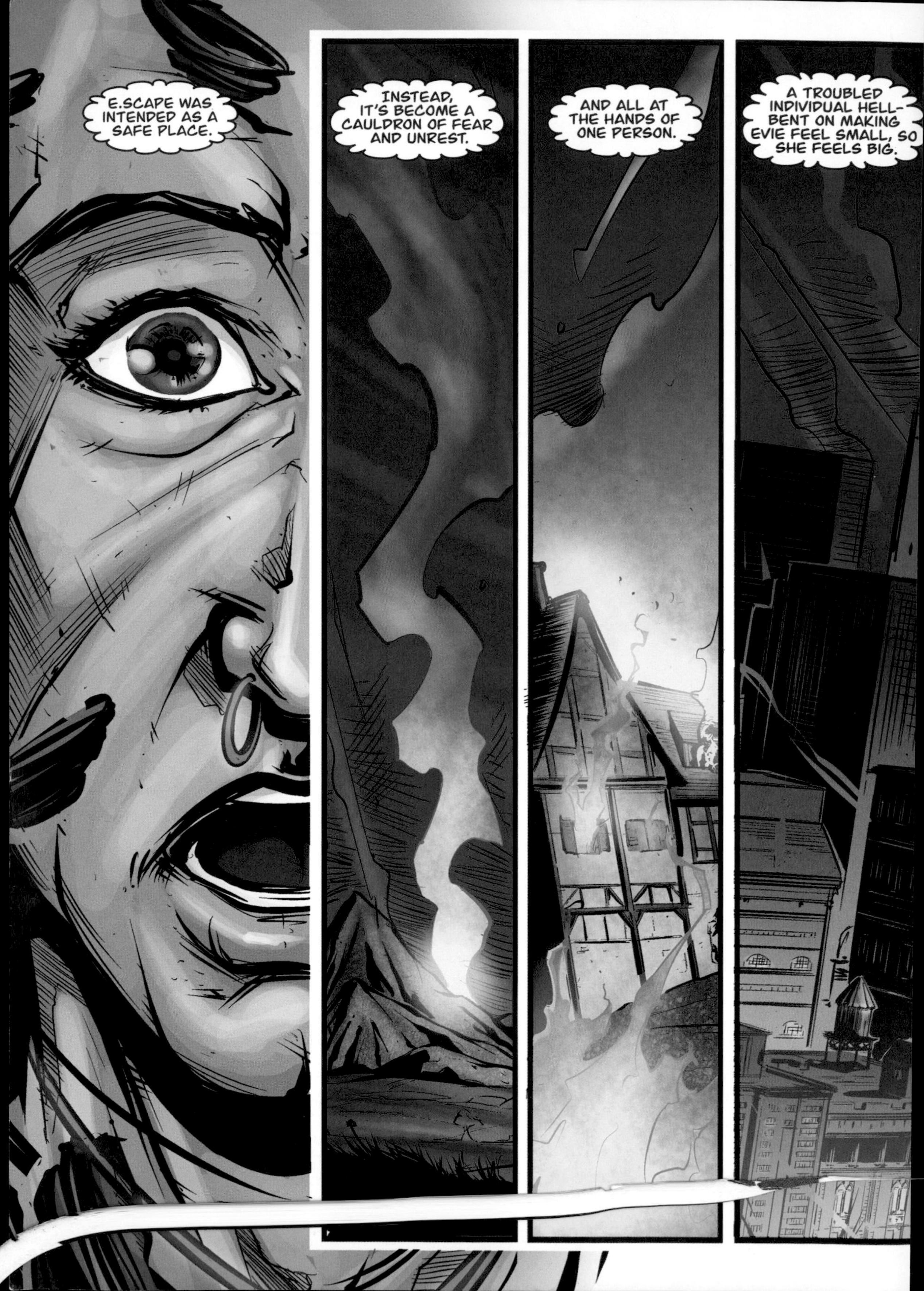
E.SCAPE WAS INTENDED AS A SAFE PLACE.
INSTEAD, IT'S BECOME A CAULDRON OF FEAR AND UNREST.
AND ALL AT THE HANDS OF ONE PERSON.
A TROUBLED INDIVIDUAL HELL-BENT ON MAKING EVIE FEEL SMALL, SO SHE FEELS BIG.

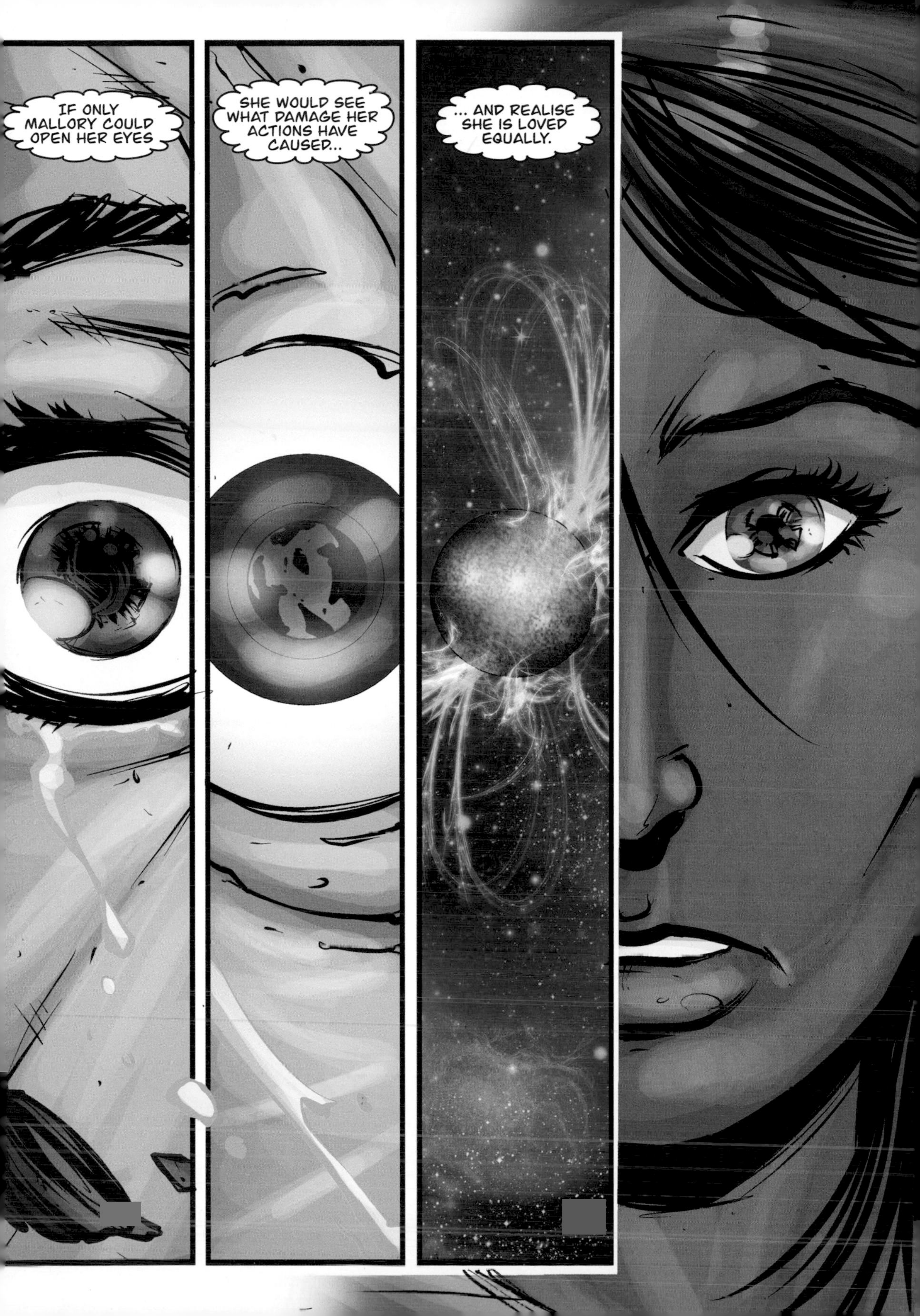
IF ONLY MALLORY COULD OPEN HER EYES
SHE WOULD SEE WHAT DAMAGE HER ACTIONS HAVE CAUSED...
... AND REALISE SHE IS LOVED EQUALLY.

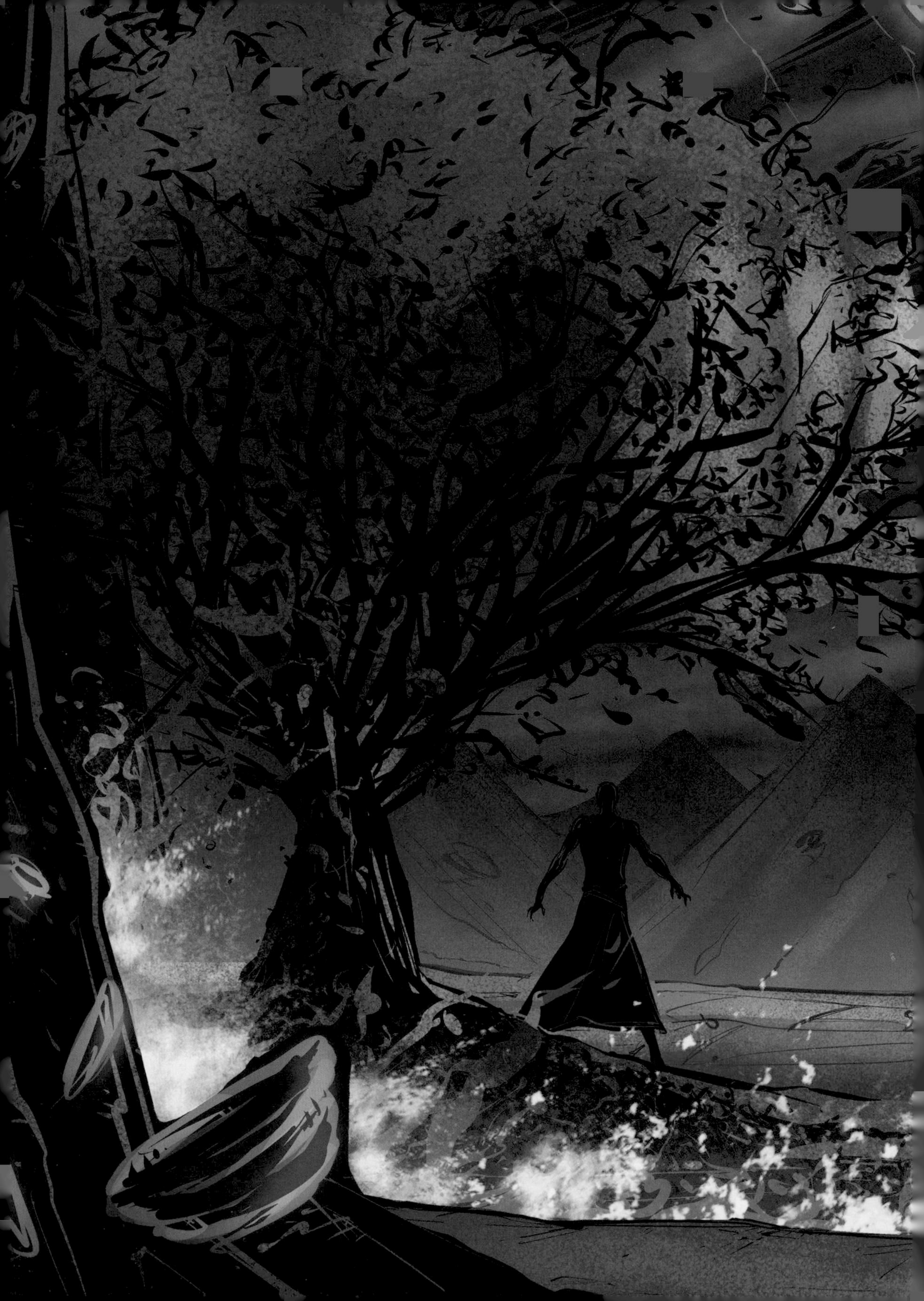

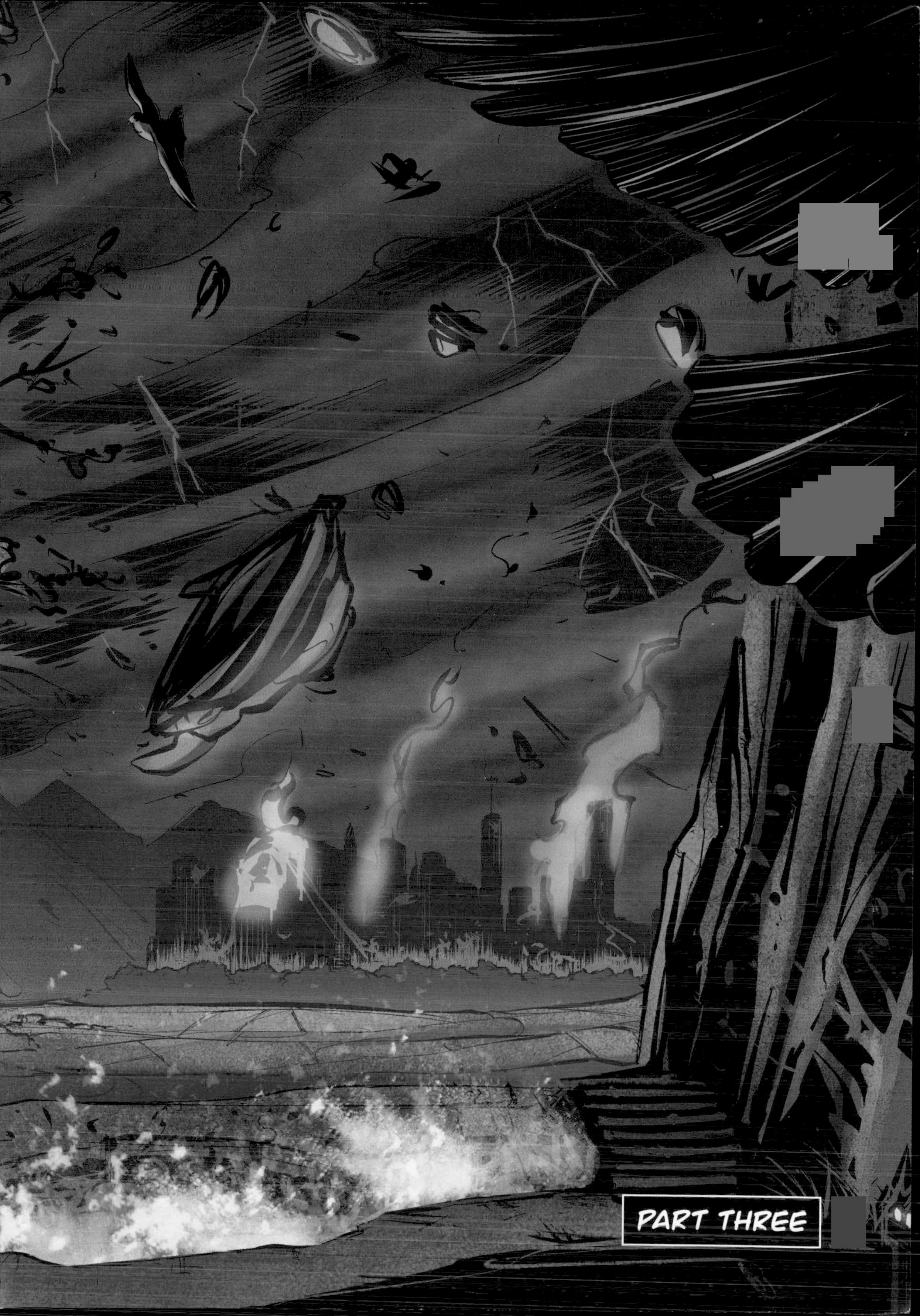
PART THREE

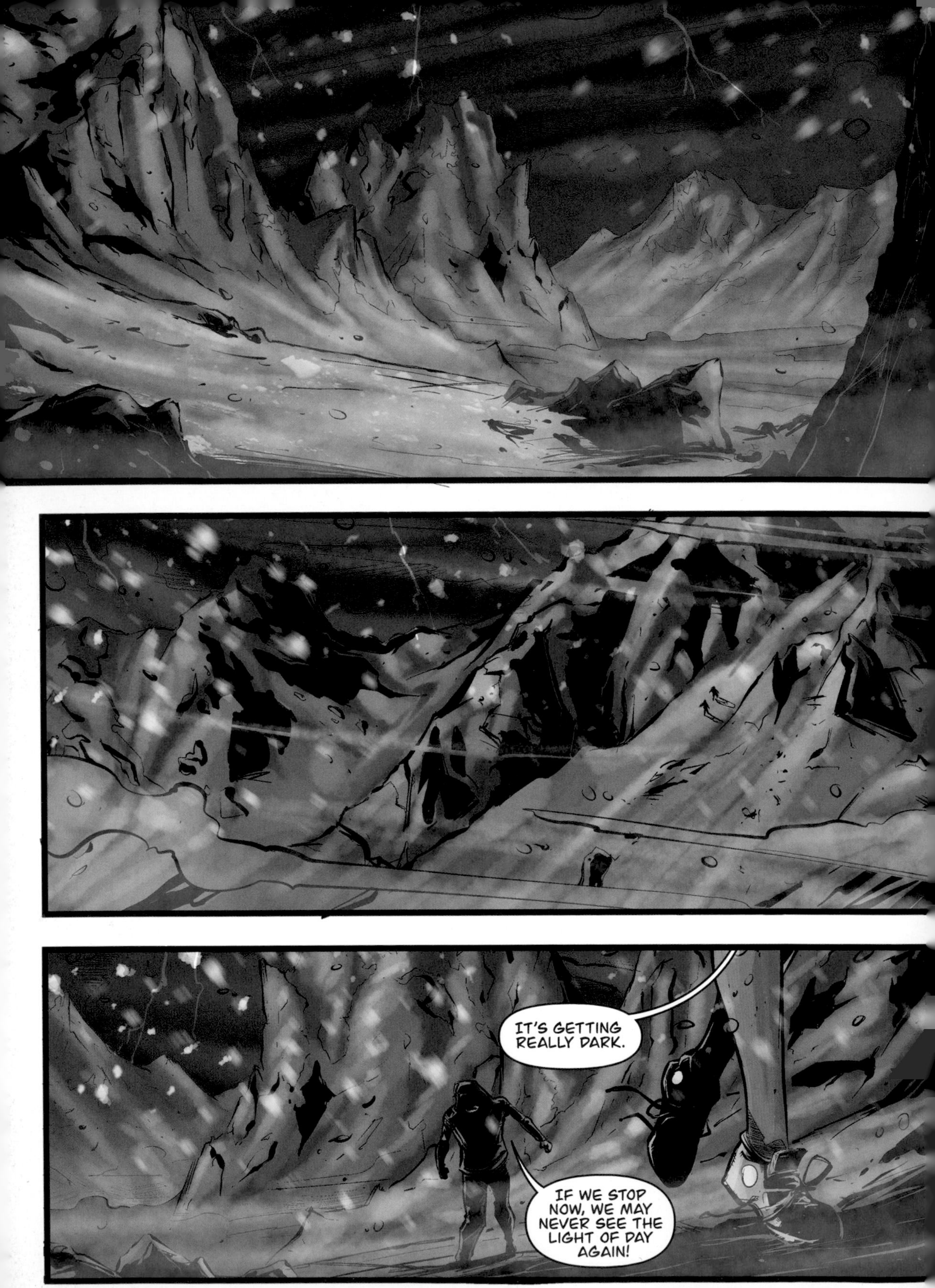
IT'S GETTING REALLY DARK.
IF WE STOP NOW, WE MAY NEVER SEE THE LIGHT OF DAY AGAIN!

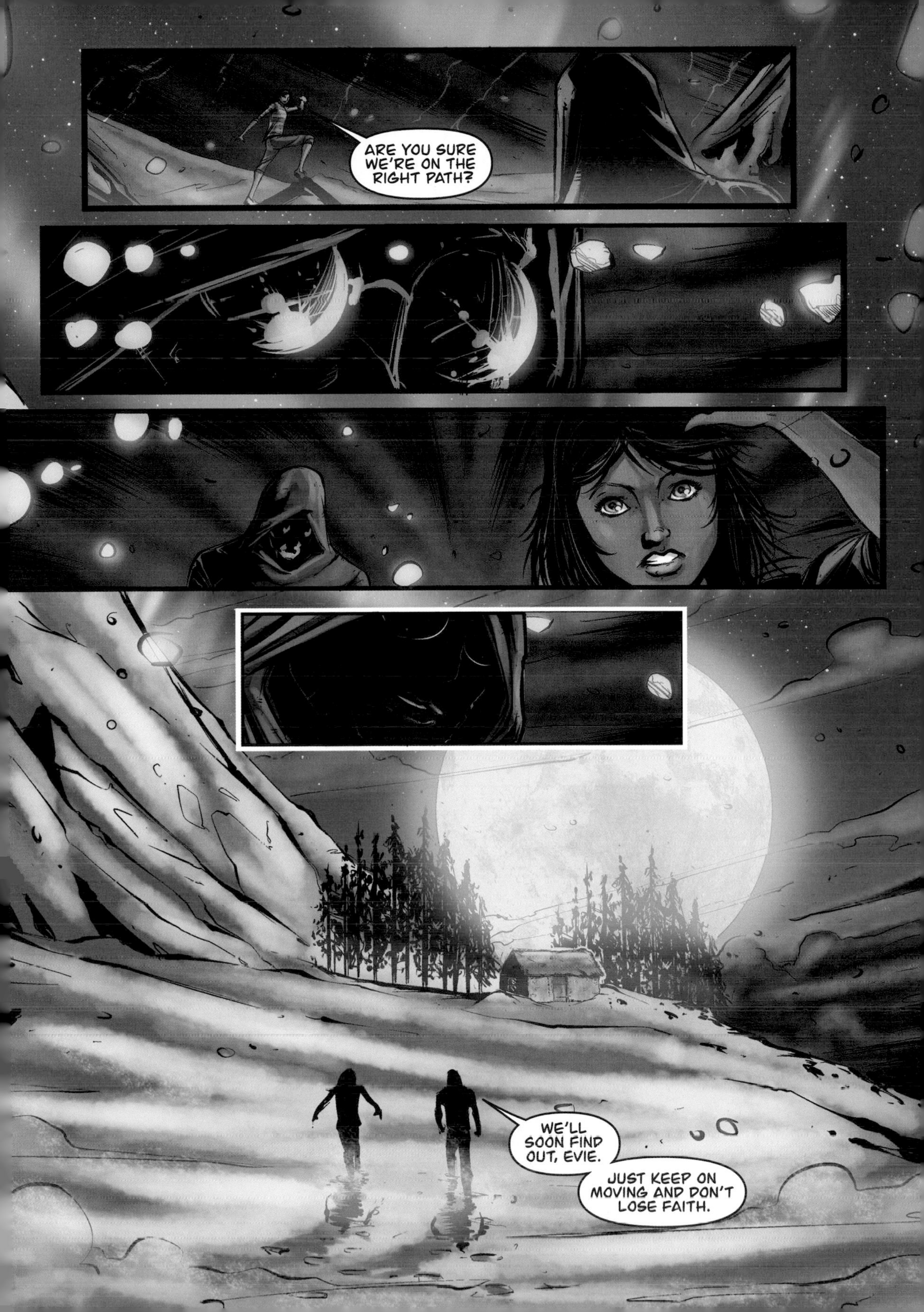
ARE YOU SURE WE'RE ON THE RIGHT PATH?
WE'LL SOON FIND OUT, EVIE.
JUST KEEP ON MOVING AND DON'T LOSE FAITH.

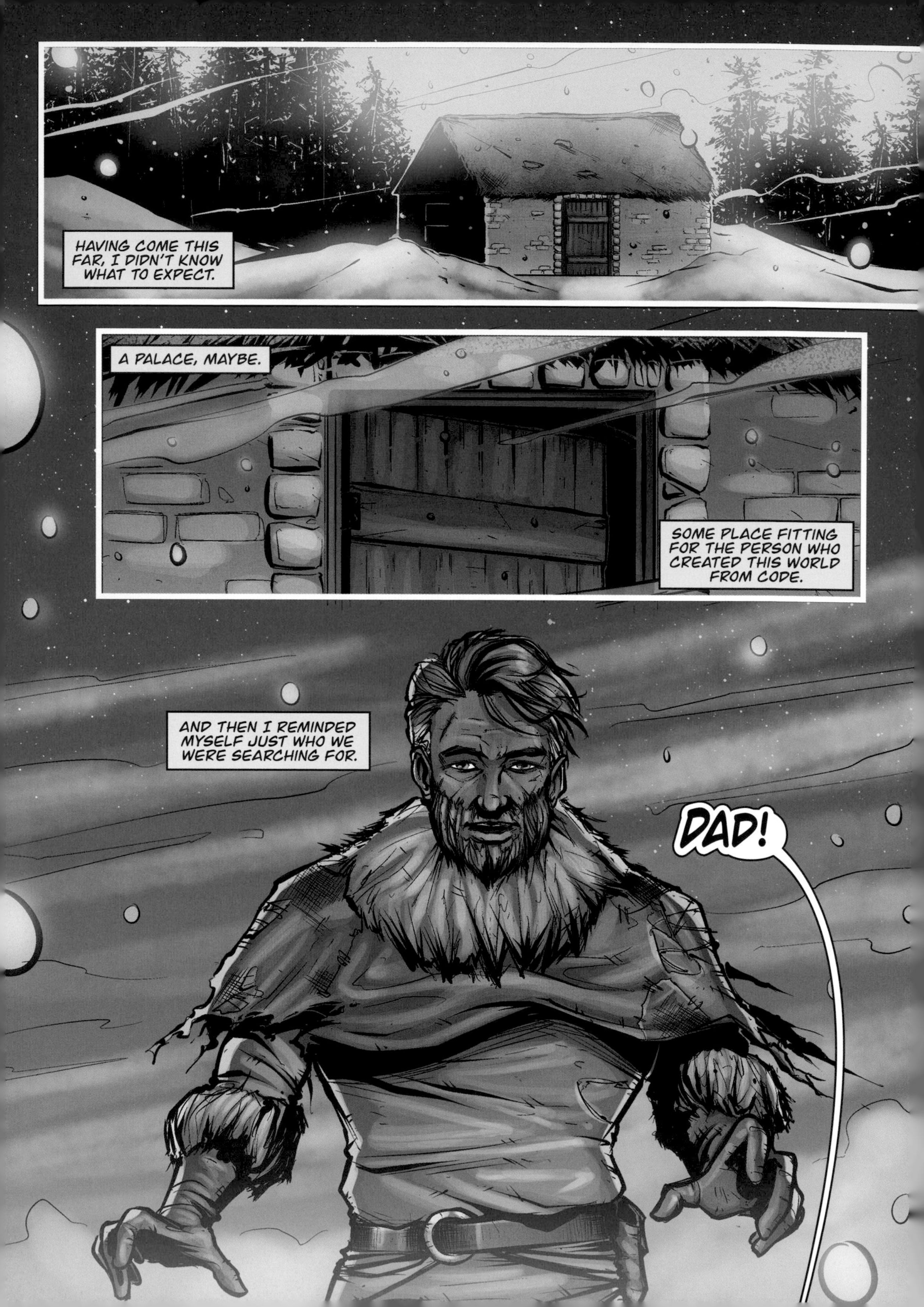
HAVING COME THIS FAR, I DIDN'T KNOW WHAT TO EXPECT.
A PALACE, MAYBE.
SOME PLACE FITTING FOR THE PERSON WHO CREATED THIS WORLD FROM CODE.
AND THEN I REMINDED MYSELF JUST WHO WE WERE SEARCHING FOR.
DAD!

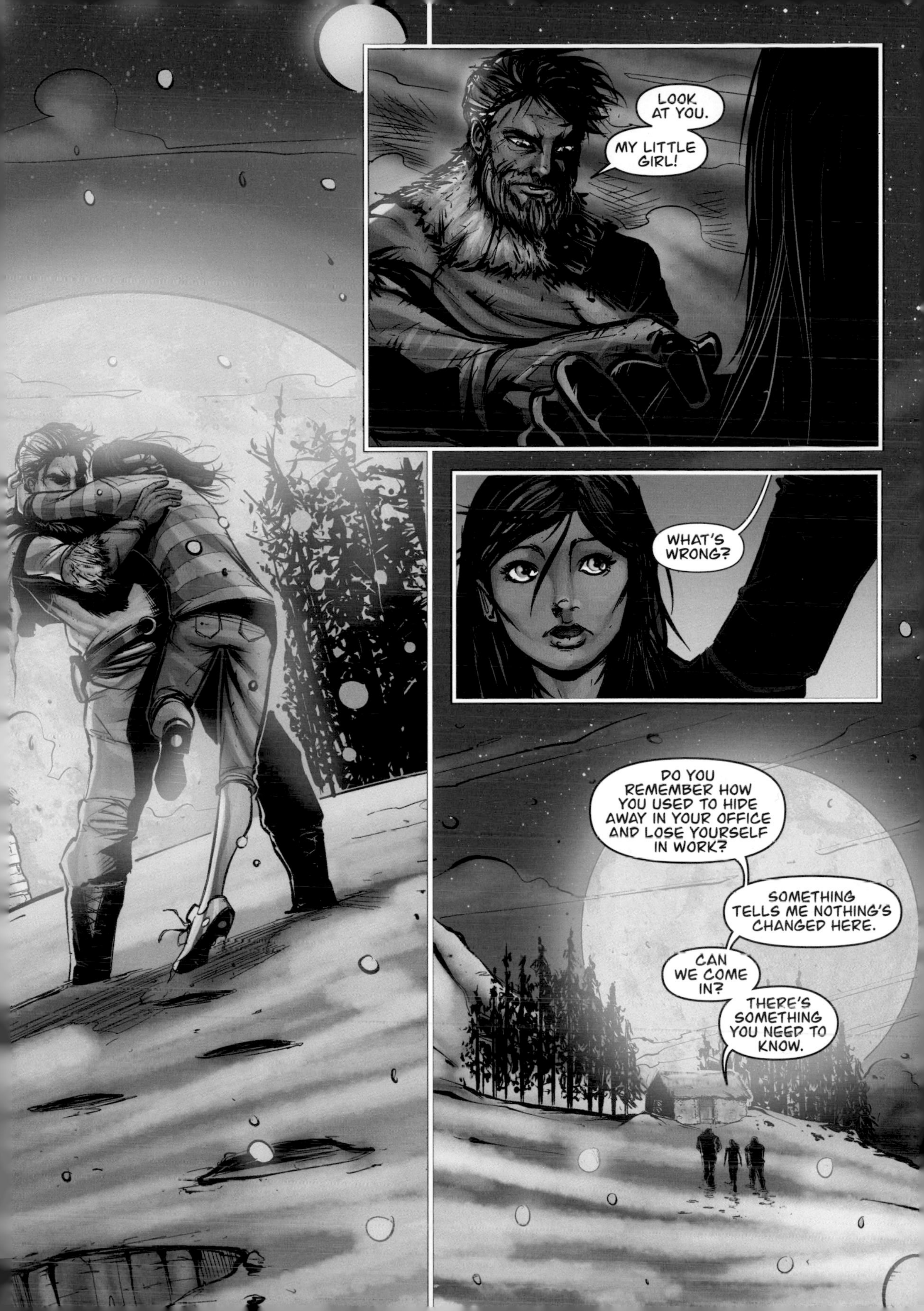
LOOK AT YOU.
MY LITTLE GIRL!
WHAT'S WRONG?
DO YOU REMEMBER HOW YOU USED TO HIDE AWAY IN YOUR OFFICE AND LOSE YOURSELF IN WORK?
SOMETHING TELLS ME NOTHING'S CHANGED HERE.
CAN WE COME IN?
THERE'S SOMETHING YOU NEED TO KNOW.

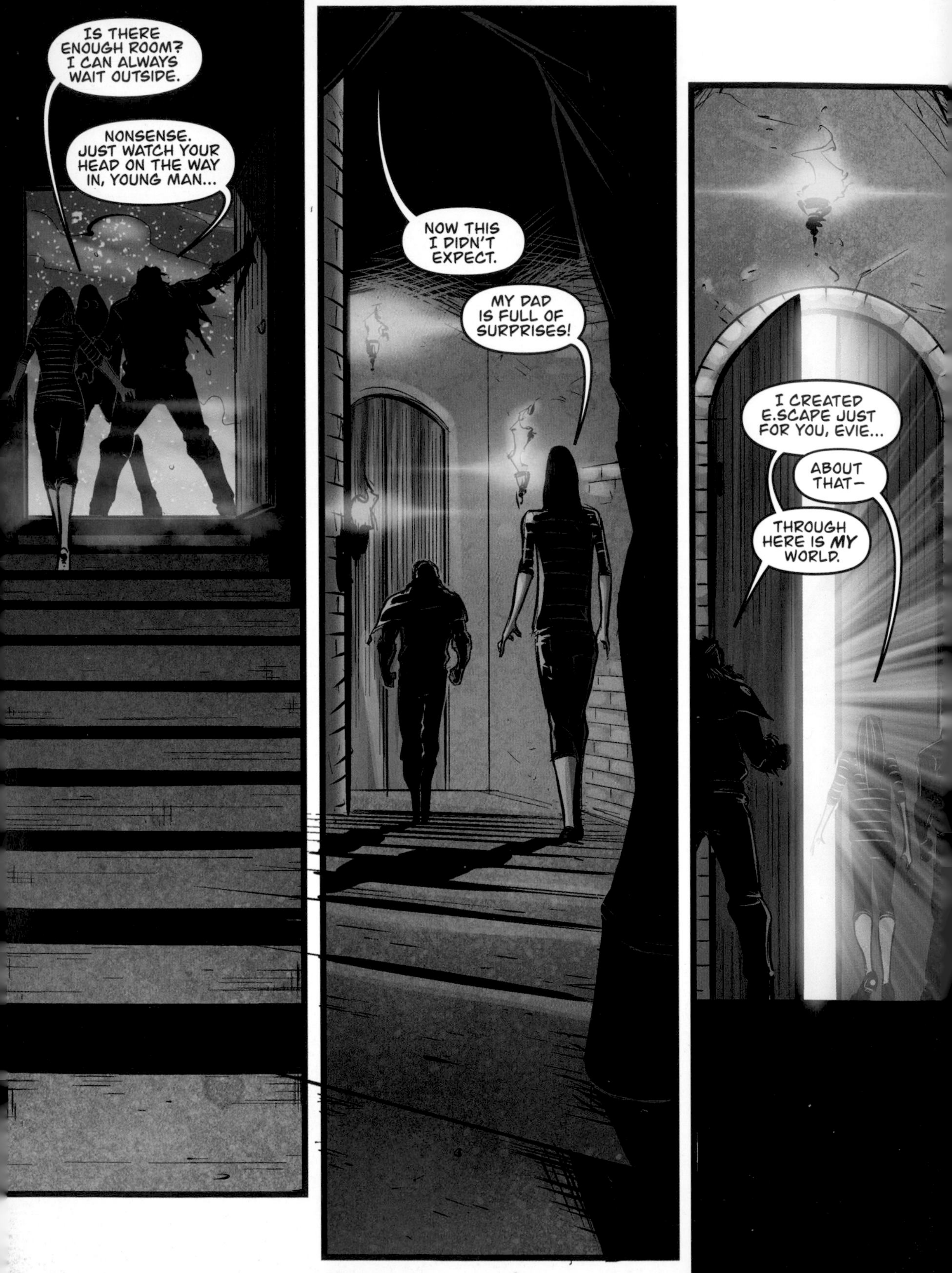
IS THERE ENOUGH ROOM? I CAN ALWAYS WAIT OUTSIDE.
NONSENSE. JUST WATCH YOUR HEAD ON THE WAY IN, YOUNG MAN...
NOW THIS I DIDN'T EXPECT.
MY DAD IS FULL OF SURPRISES!
I CREATED E.SCAPE JUST FOR YOU, EVIE...
ABOUT THAT—
THROUGH HERE IS MY WORLD.

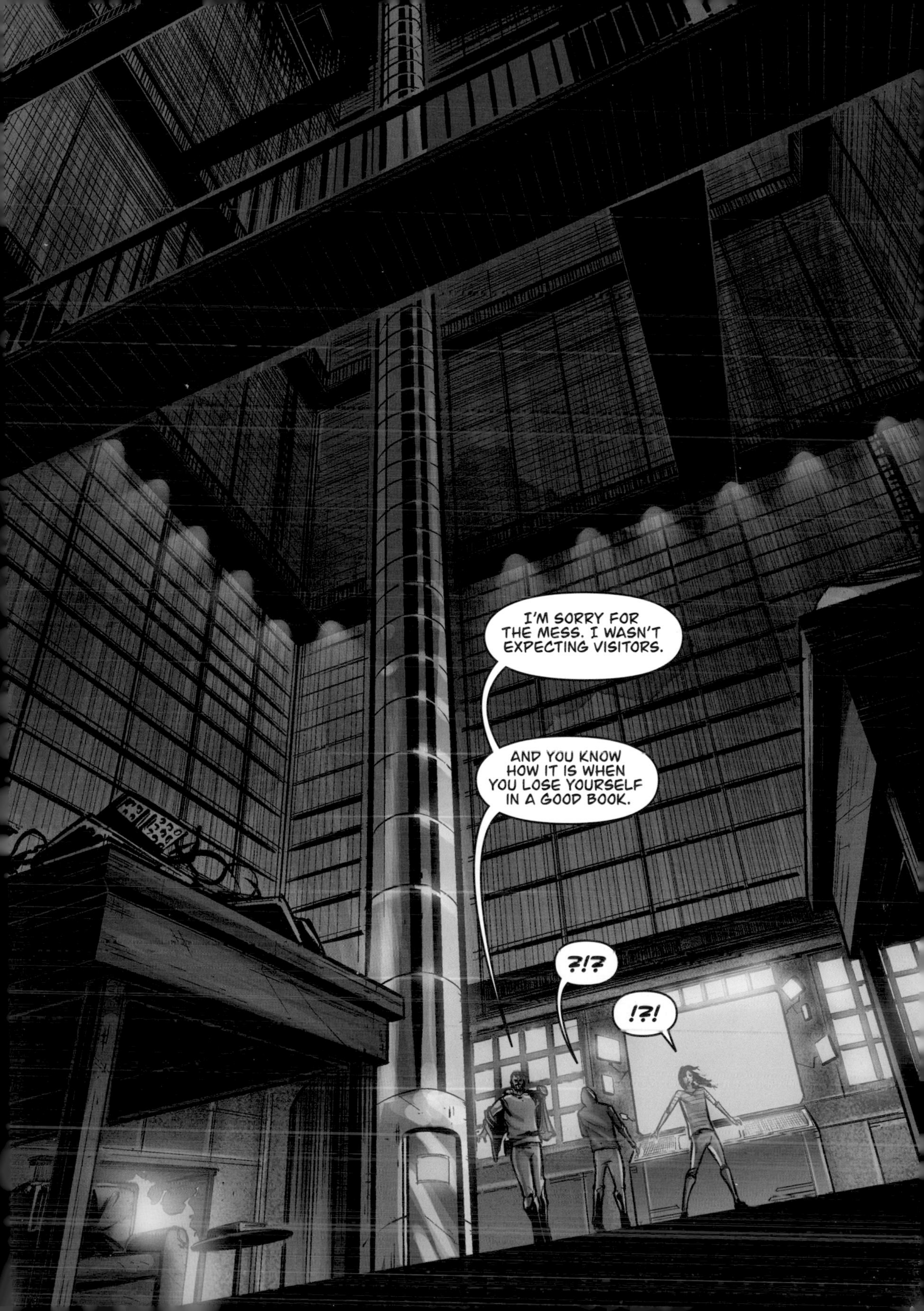
I'M SORRY FOR THE MESS. I WASN'T EXPECTING VISITORS.
AND YOU KNOW HOW IT IS WHEN YOU LOSE YOURSELF IN A GOOD BOOK.
?!?
!?!

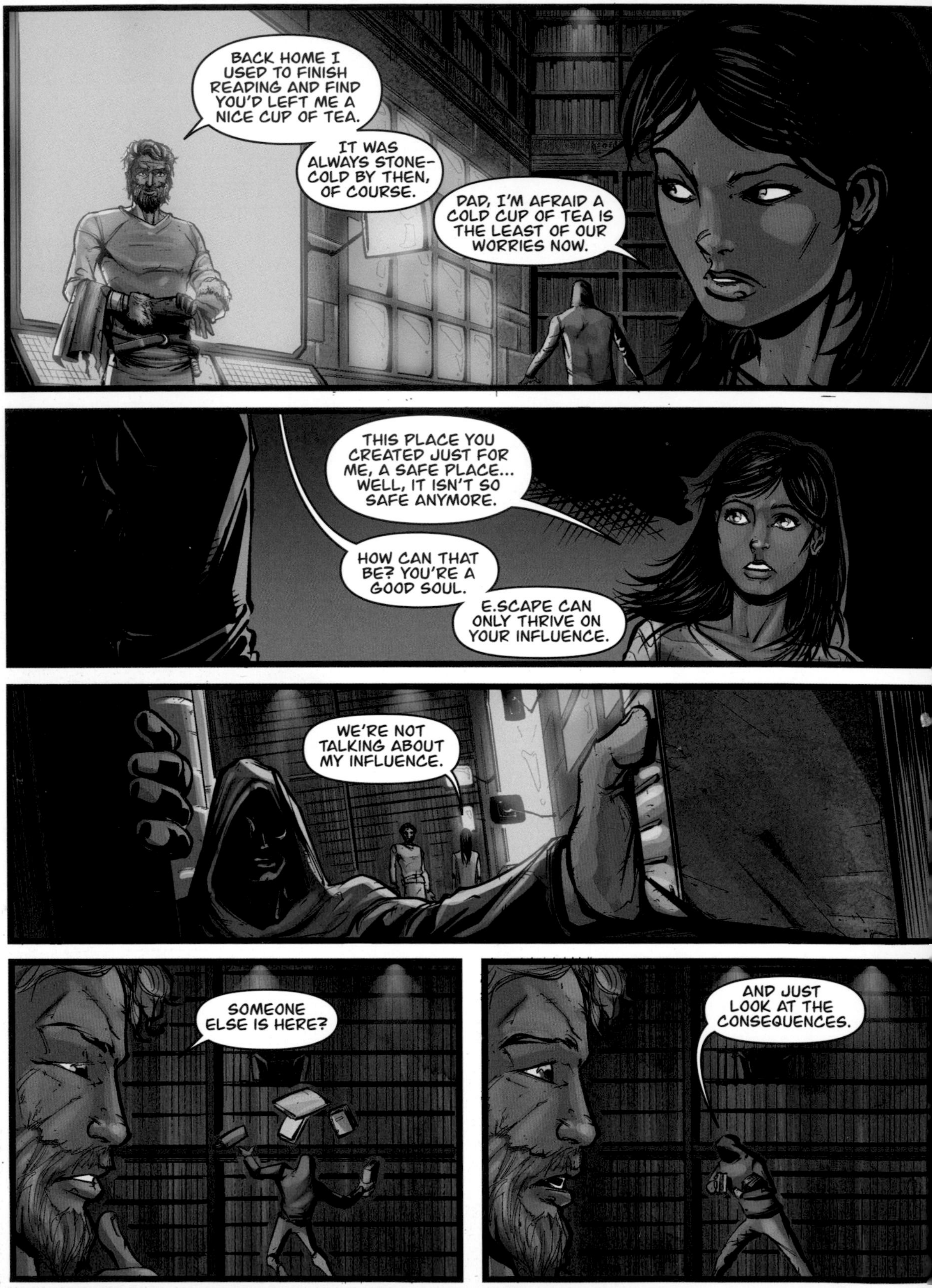
BACK HOME I USED TO FINISH READING AND FIND YOU'D LEFT ME A NICE CUP OF TEA.
IT WAS ALWAYS STONE-COLD BY THEN, OF COURSE.
DAD, I'M AFRAID A COLD CUP OF TEA IS THE LEAST OF OUR WORRIES NOW.
THIS PLACE YOU CREATED JUST FOR ME, A SAFE PLACE... WELL, IT ISN'T SO SAFE ANYMORE.
HOW CAN THAT BE? YOU'RE A GOOD SOUL.
E.SCAPE CAN ONLY THRIVE ON YOUR INFLUENCE.
WE'RE NOT TALKING ABOUT MY INFLUENCE.
SOMEONE ELSE IS HERE?
AND JUST LOOK AT THE CONSEQUENCES.

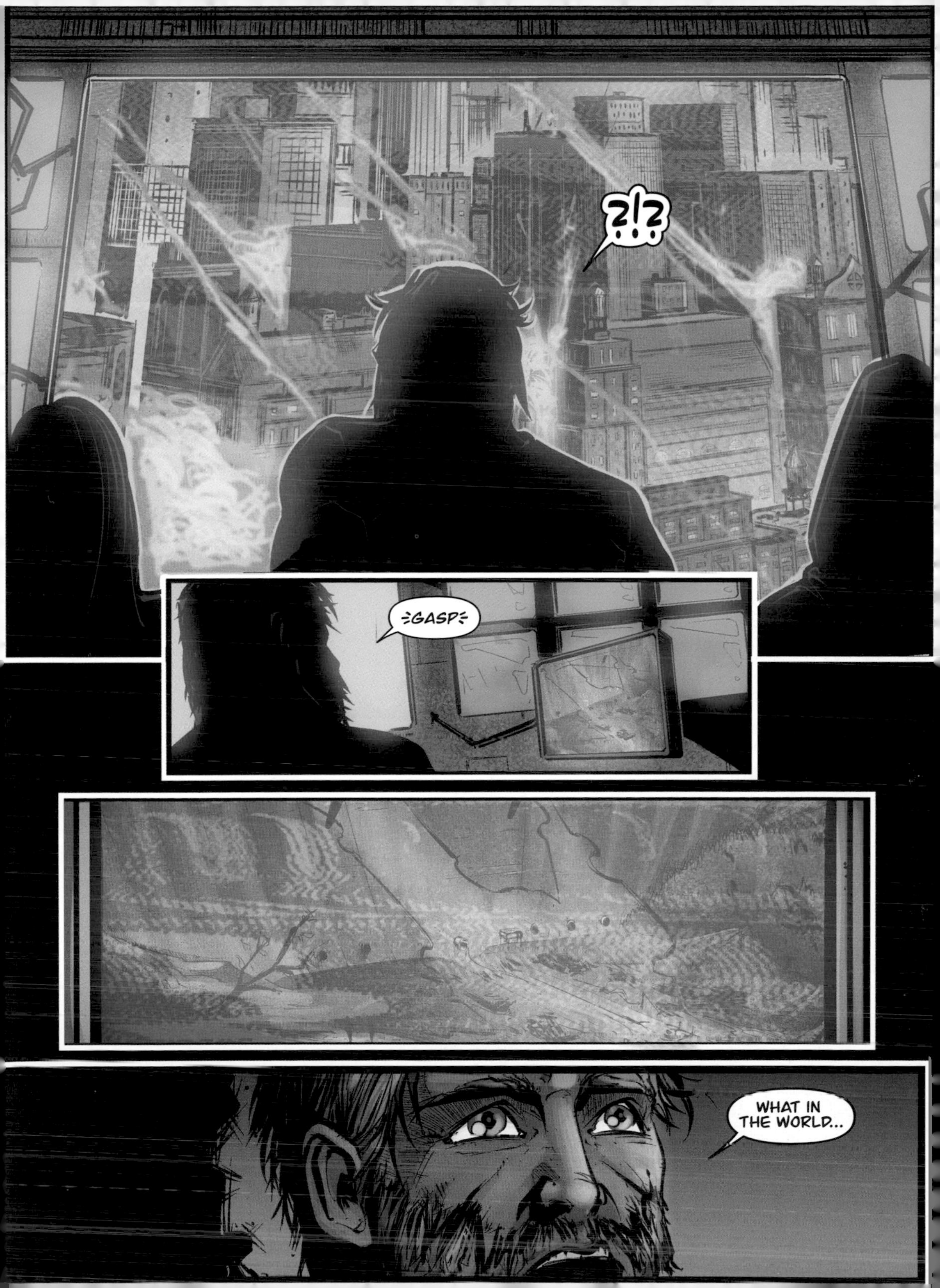
?!?
GASP
WHAT IN THE WORLD...

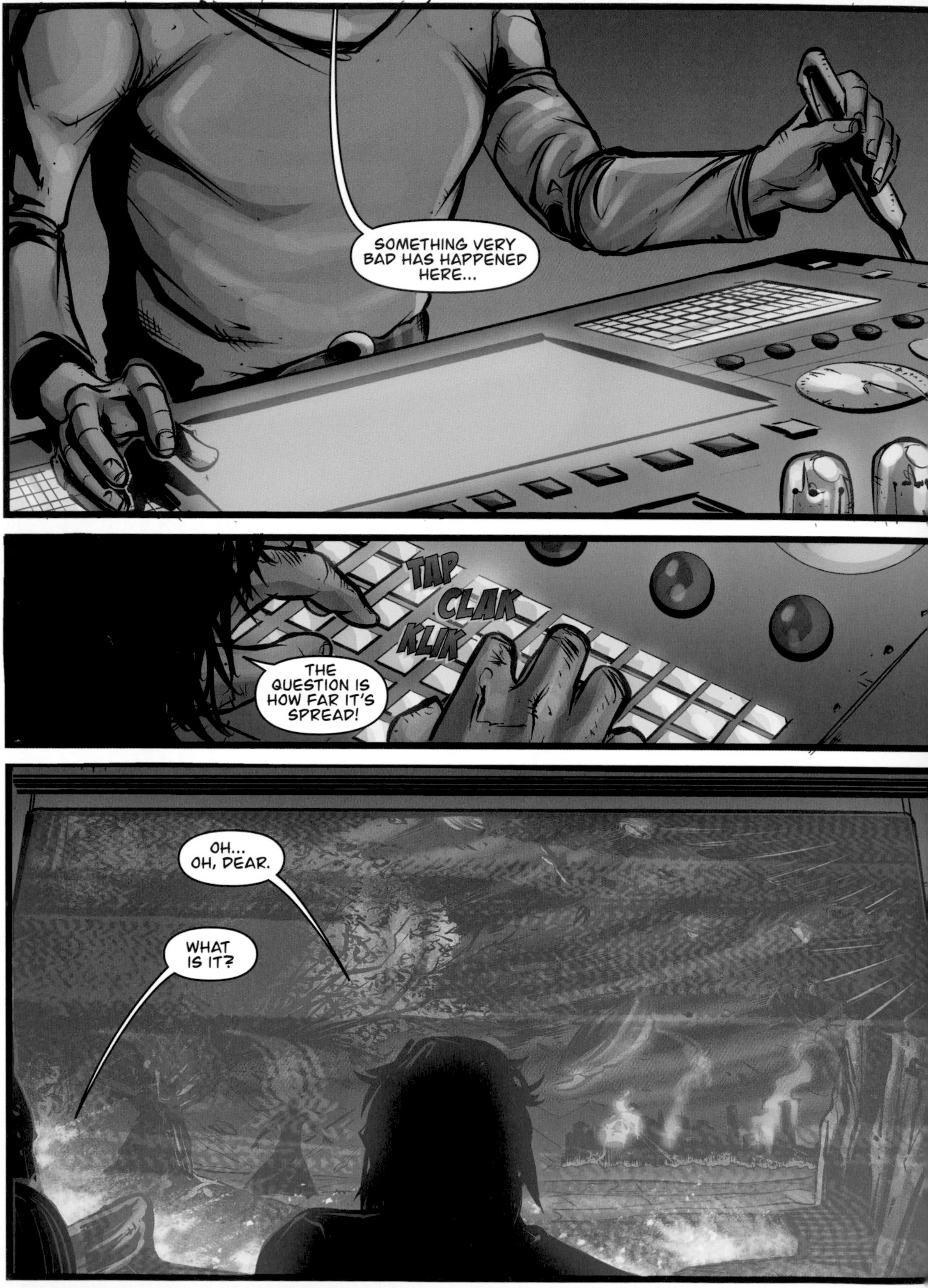
SOMETHING VERY BAD HAS HAPPENED HERE...
TAP
CLAK
KLIK
THE QUESTION IS HOW FAR IT'S SPREAD!
OH... OH, DEAR.
WHAT IS IT?

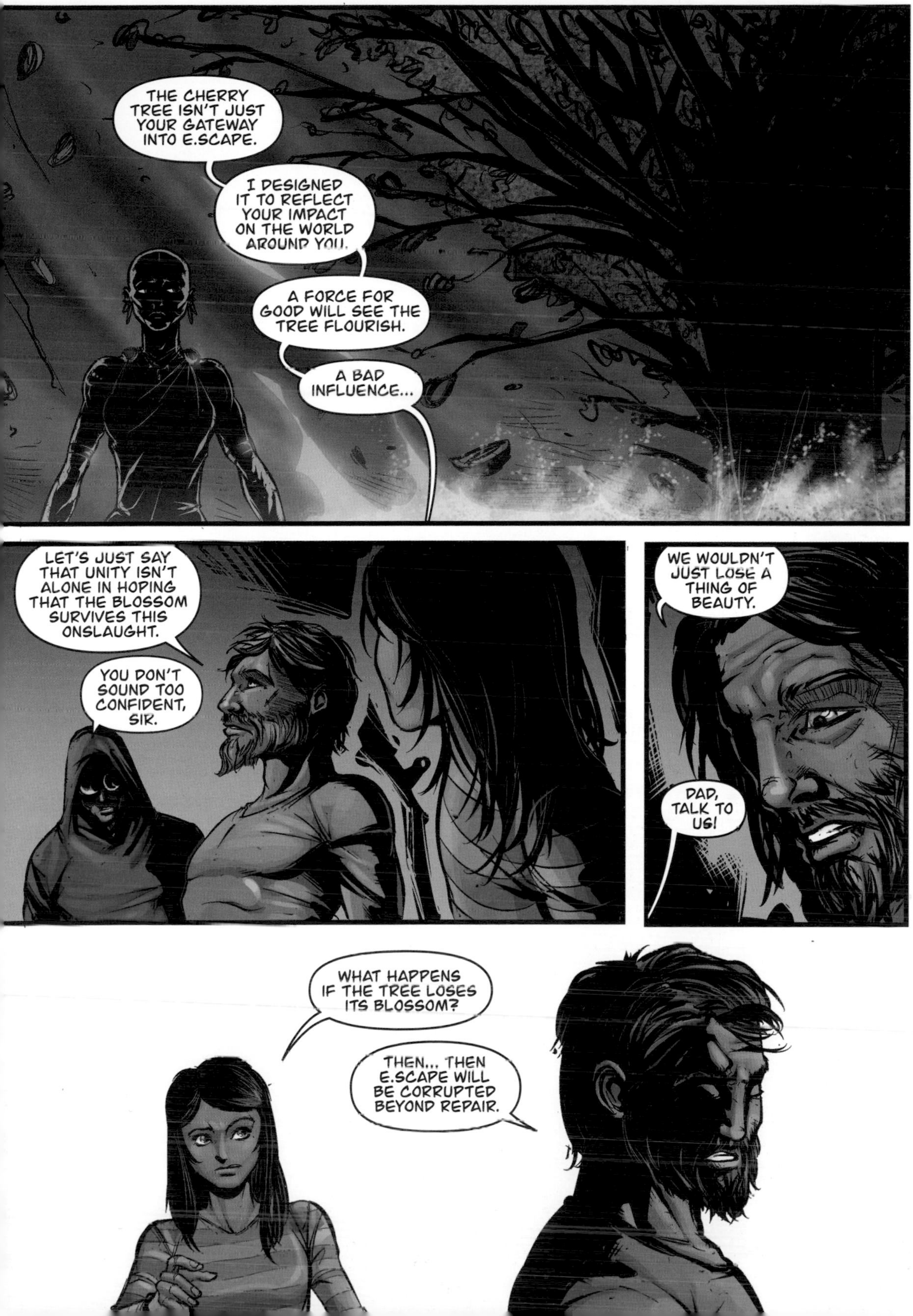
THE CHERRY TREE ISN'T JUST YOUR GATEWAY INTO E.SCAPE.
I DESIGNED IT TO REFLECT YOUR IMPACT ON THE WORLD AROUND YOU.
A FORCE FOR GOOD WILL SEE THE TREE FLOURISH.
A BAD INFLUENCE...
LET'S JUST SAY THAT UNITY ISN'T ALONE IN HOPING THAT THE BLOSSOM SURVIVES THIS ONSLAUGHT.
YOU DON'T SOUND TOO CONFIDENT, SIR.
WE WOULDN'T JUST LOSE A THING OF BEAUTY.
DAD, TALK TO US!
WHAT HAPPENS IF THE TREE LOSES ITS BLOSSOM?
THEN... THEN E.SCAPE WILL BE CORRUPTED BEYOND REPAIR.

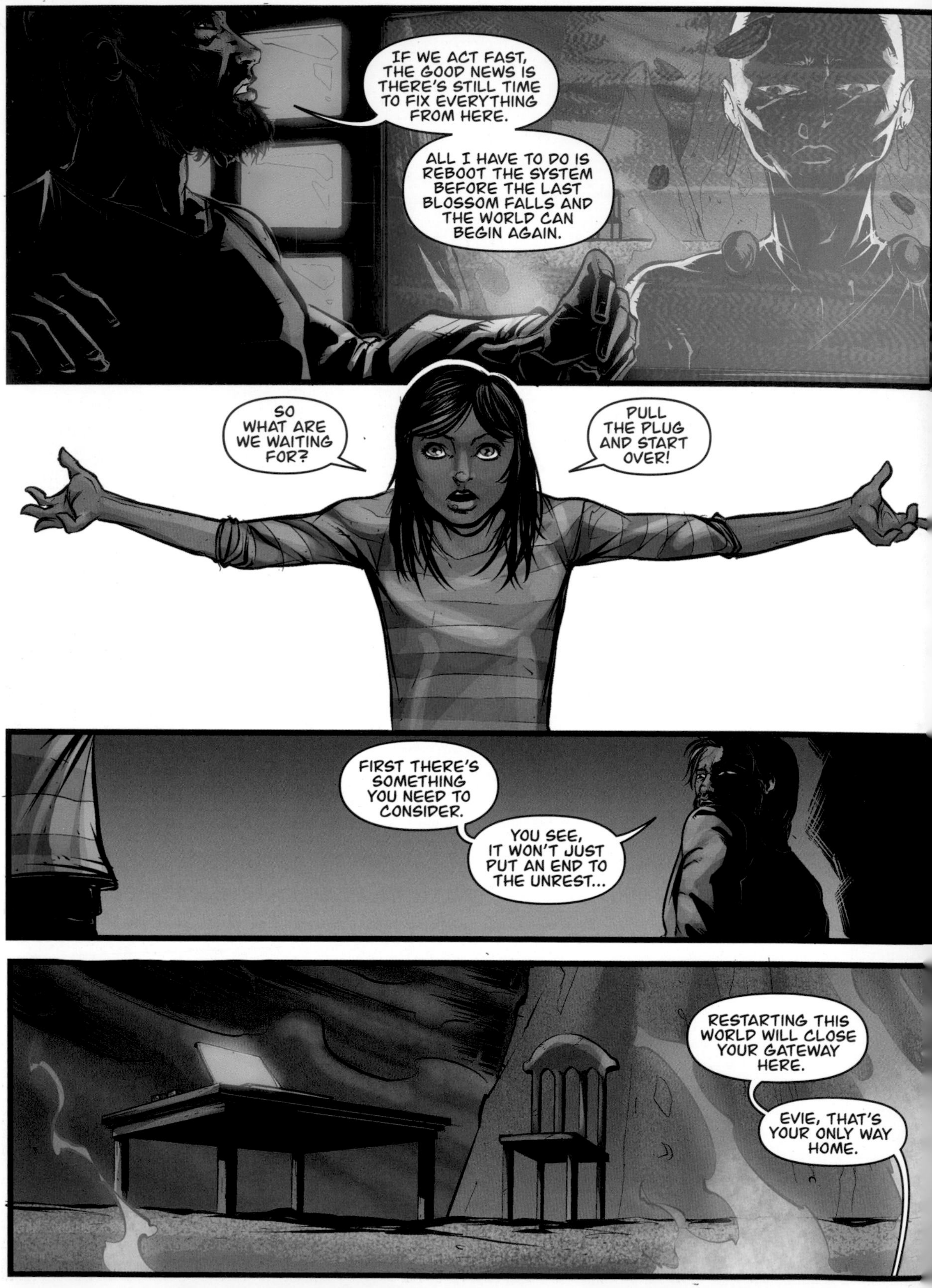

IF WE ACT FAST, THE GOOD NEWS IS THERE'S STILL TIME TO FIX EVERYTHING FROM HERE.
ALL I HAVE TO DO IS REBOOT THE SYSTEM BEFORE THE LAST BLOSSOM FALLS AND THE WORLD CAN BEGIN AGAIN.
SO WHAT ARE WE WAITING FOR?
PULL THE PLUG AND START OVER!
FIRST THERE'S SOMETHING YOU NEED TO CONSIDER.
YOU SEE, IT WON'T JUST PUT AN END TO THE UNREST...
RESTARTING THIS WORLD WILL CLOSE YOUR GATEWAY HERE.
EVIE, THAT'S YOUR ONLY WAY HOME.

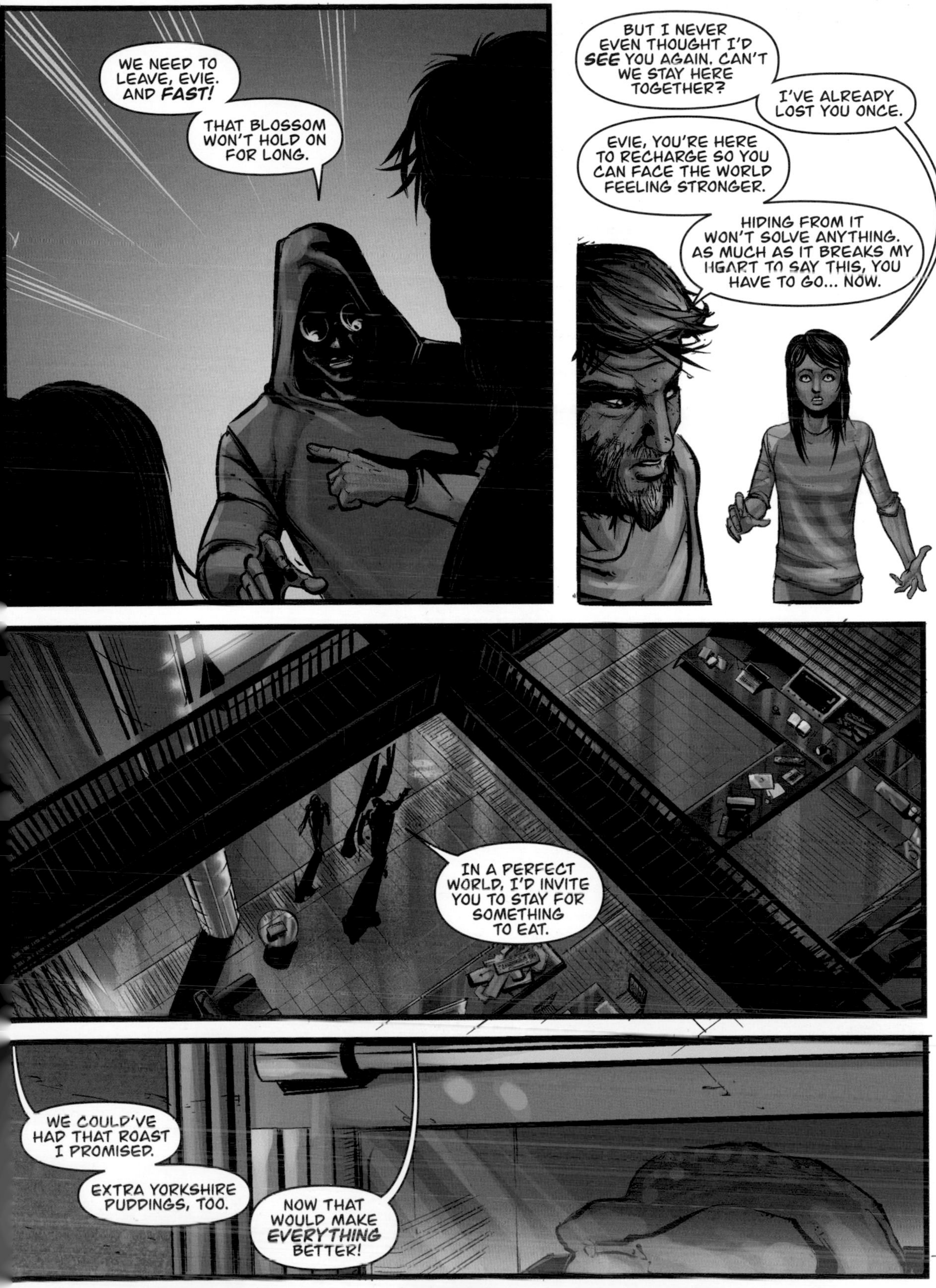
WE NEED TO LEAVE, EVIE. AND *FAST!*
THAT BLOSSOM WON'T HOLD ON FOR LONG.
BUT I NEVER EVEN THOUGHT I'D *SEE* YOU AGAIN. CAN'T WE STAY HERE TOGETHER?
I'VE ALREADY LOST YOU ONCE.
EVIE, YOU'RE HERE TO RECHARGE SO YOU CAN FACE THE WORLD FEELING STRONGER.
HIDING FROM IT WON'T SOLVE ANYTHING. AS MUCH AS IT BREAKS MY HEART TO SAY THIS, YOU HAVE TO GO... NOW.
IN A PERFECT WORLD, I'D INVITE YOU TO STAY FOR SOMETHING TO EAT.
WE COULD'VE HAD THAT ROAST I PROMISED.
EXTRA YORKSHIRE PUDDINGS, TOO.
NOW THAT WOULD MAKE *EVERYTHING* BETTER!

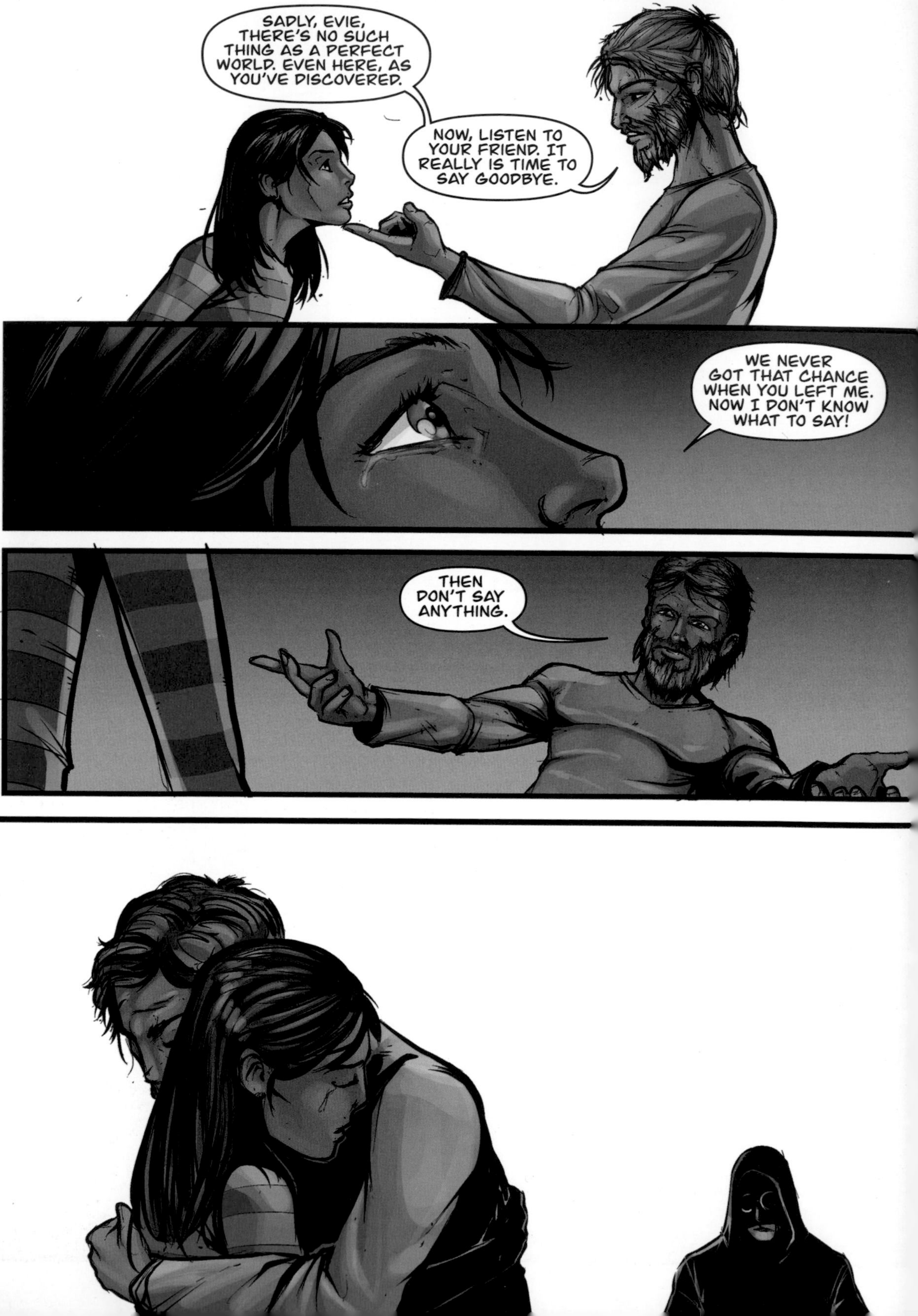
SADLY, EVIE, THERE'S NO SUCH THING AS A PERFECT WORLD. EVEN HERE, AS YOU'VE DISCOVERED.
NOW, LISTEN TO YOUR FRIEND. IT REALLY IS TIME TO SAY GOODBYE.
WE NEVER GOT THAT CHANCE WHEN YOU LEFT ME. NOW I DON'T KNOW WHAT TO SAY!
THEN DON'T SAY ANYTHING.

SO, THIS IS WHAT IT MUST MEAN TO BE LOVED.

EVEN WHEN THE WORLD IS CRASHING DOWN AROUND US, A SIMPLE HUG PROVIDES SUCH COMFORT AND STRENGTH.

≠SNIFF≠

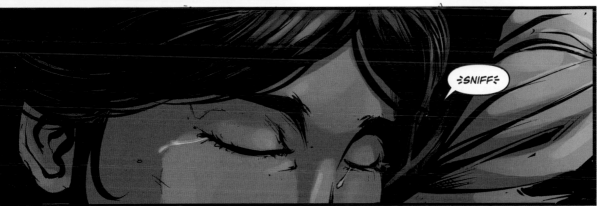

MAYBE ONE DAY I'LL KNOW HOW THAT FEELS. RIGHT NOW, I'M HAPPY FOR EVIE.

FATHER AND DAUGHTER REUNITED. MY WORK HERE IS DONE.

THANK YOU.

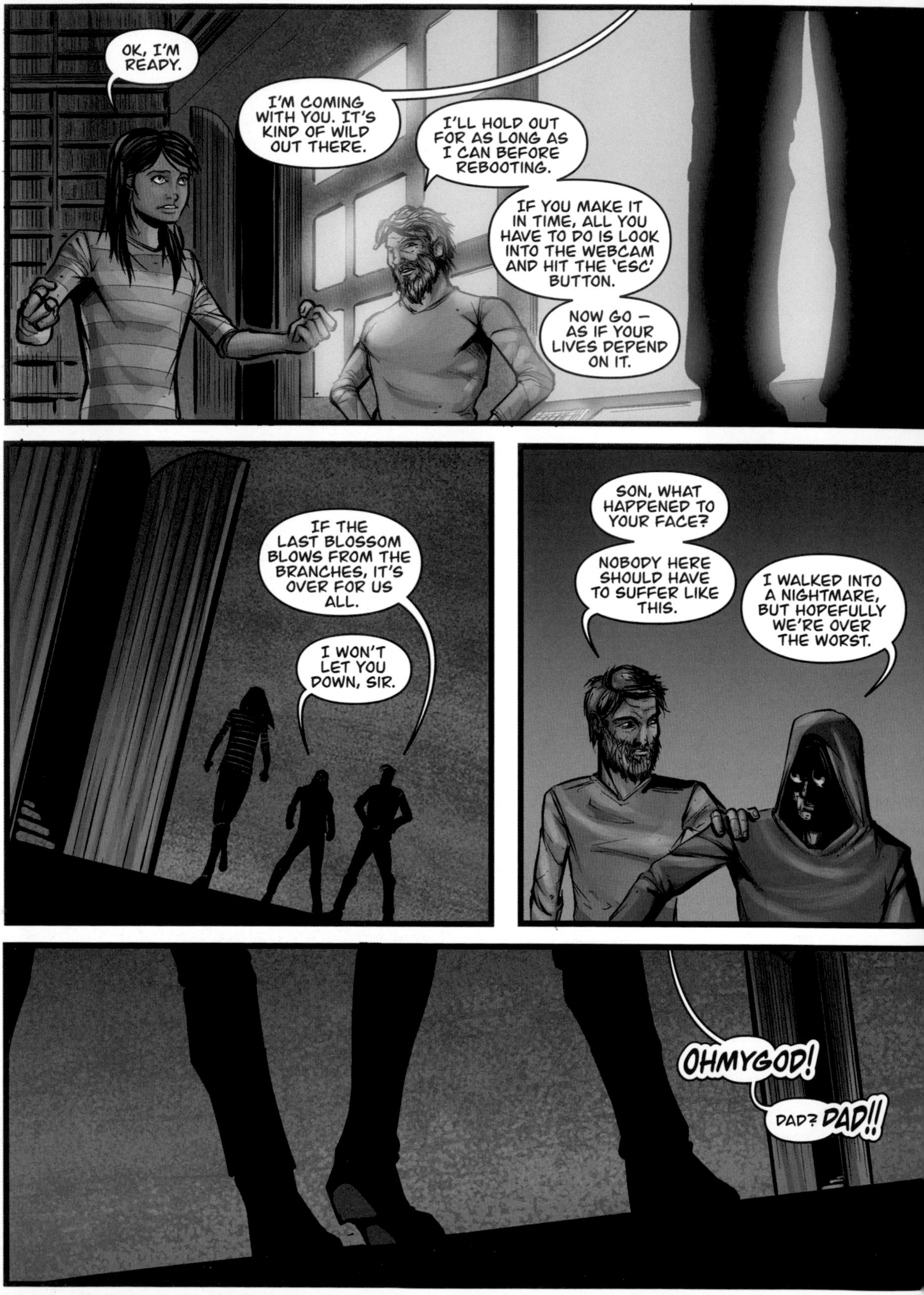
OK, I'M READY.
I'M COMING WITH YOU. IT'S KIND OF WILD OUT THERE.
I'LL HOLD OUT FOR AS LONG AS I CAN BEFORE REBOOTING.
IF YOU MAKE IT IN TIME, ALL YOU HAVE TO DO IS LOOK INTO THE WEBCAM AND HIT THE 'ESC' BUTTON.
NOW GO — AS IF YOUR LIVES DEPEND ON IT.
IF THE LAST BLOSSOM BLOWS FROM THE BRANCHES, IT'S OVER FOR US ALL.
I WON'T LET YOU DOWN, SIR.
SON, WHAT HAPPENED TO YOUR FACE?
NOBODY HERE SHOULD HAVE TO SUFFER LIKE THIS.
I WALKED INTO A NIGHTMARE, BUT HOPEFULLY WE'RE OVER THE WORST.
OHMYGOD!
DAD? DAD!!

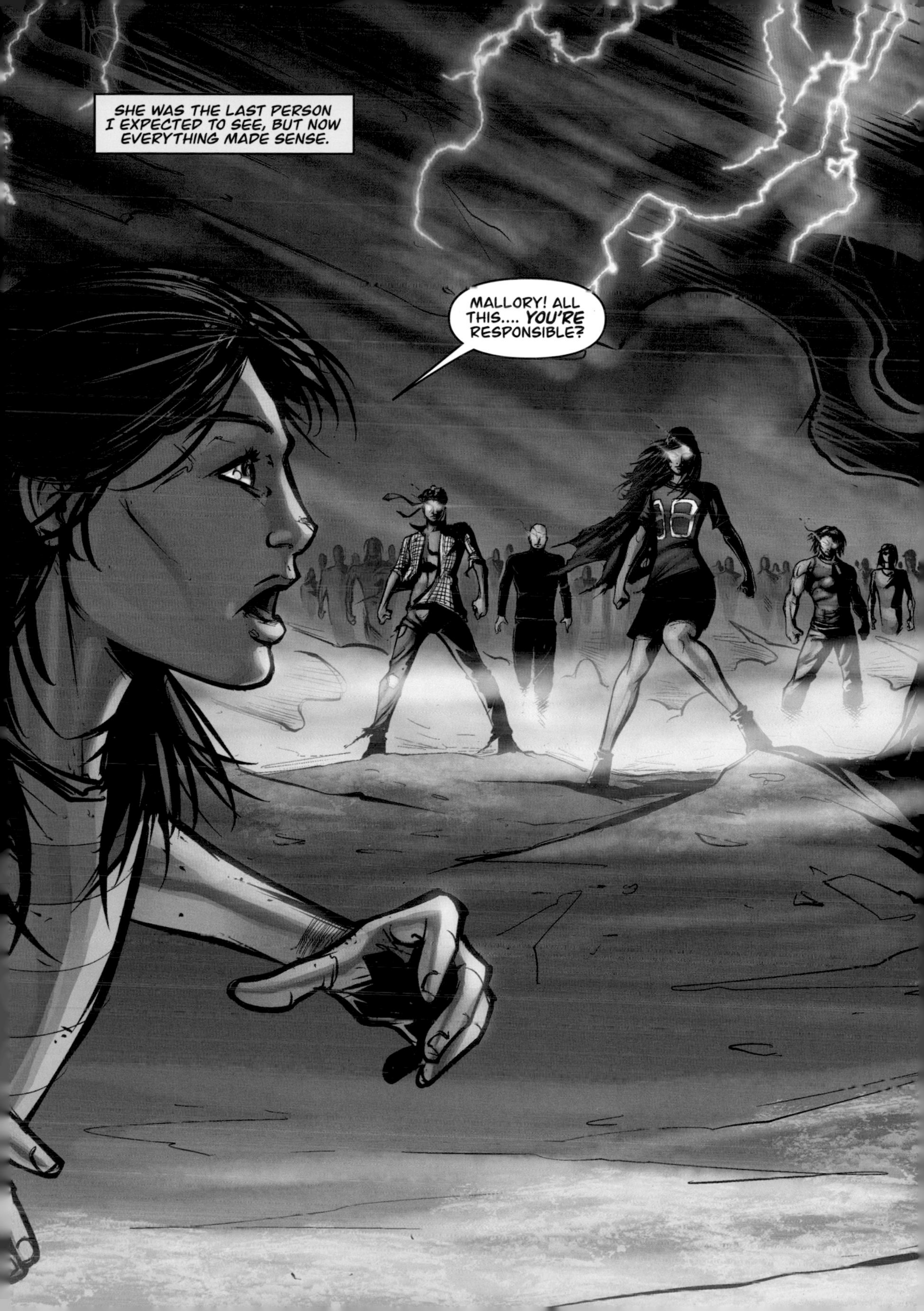
SHE WAS THE LAST PERSON I EXPECTED TO SEE, BUT NOW EVERYTHING MADE SENSE.
MALLORY! ALL THIS.... *YOU'RE* RESPONSIBLE?

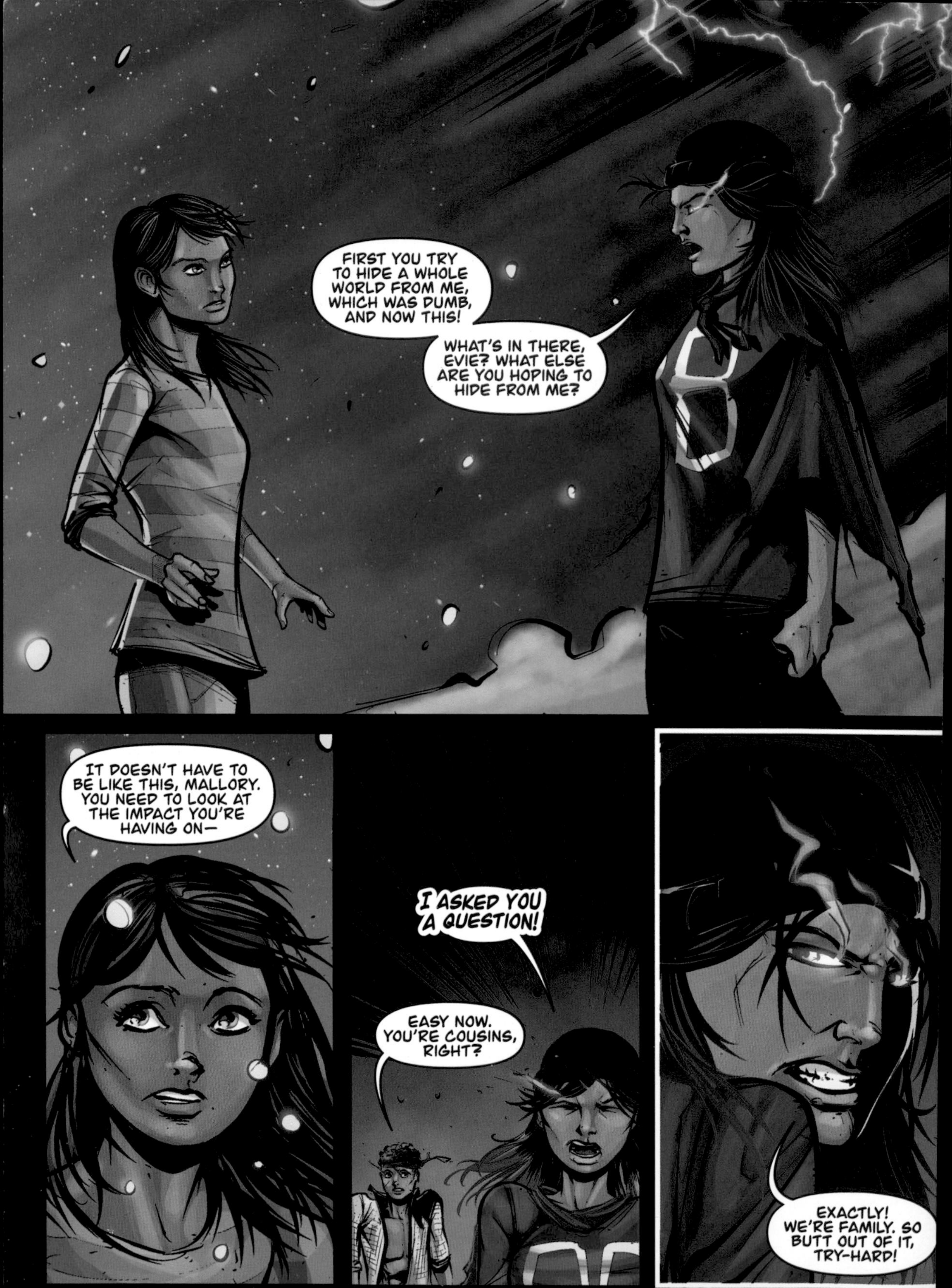
FIRST YOU TRY TO HIDE A WHOLE WORLD FROM ME, WHICH WAS DUMB, AND NOW THIS!
WHAT'S IN THERE, EVIE? WHAT ELSE ARE YOU HOPING TO HIDE FROM ME?
IT DOESN'T HAVE TO BE LIKE THIS, MALLORY. YOU NEED TO LOOK AT THE IMPACT YOU'RE HAVING ON—
I ASKED YOU A QUESTION!
EASY NOW. YOU'RE COUSINS, RIGHT?
EXACTLY! WE'RE FAMILY. SO BUTT OUT OF IT, TRY-HARD!

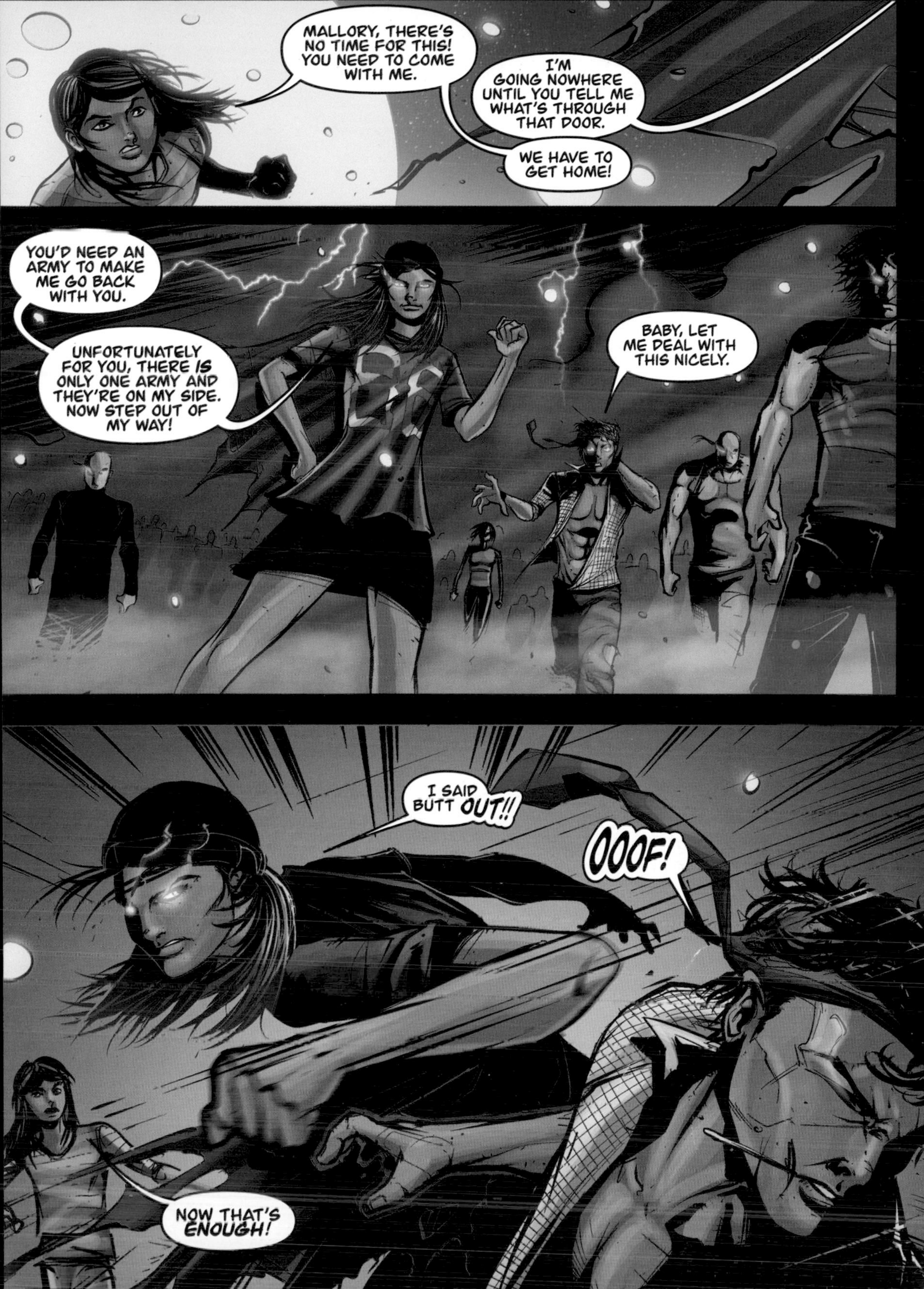
MALLORY, THERE'S NO TIME FOR THIS! YOU NEED TO COME WITH ME.
I'M GOING NOWHERE UNTIL YOU TELL ME WHAT'S THROUGH THAT DOOR.
WE HAVE TO GET HOME!
YOU'D NEED AN ARMY TO MAKE ME GO BACK WITH YOU.
UNFORTUNATELY FOR YOU, THERE *IS* ONLY ONE ARMY AND THEY'RE ON MY SIDE. NOW STEP OUT OF MY WAY!
BABY, LET ME DEAL WITH THIS NICELY.
I SAID BUTT **OUT**!!
OOOF!
NOW THAT'S **ENOUGH**!

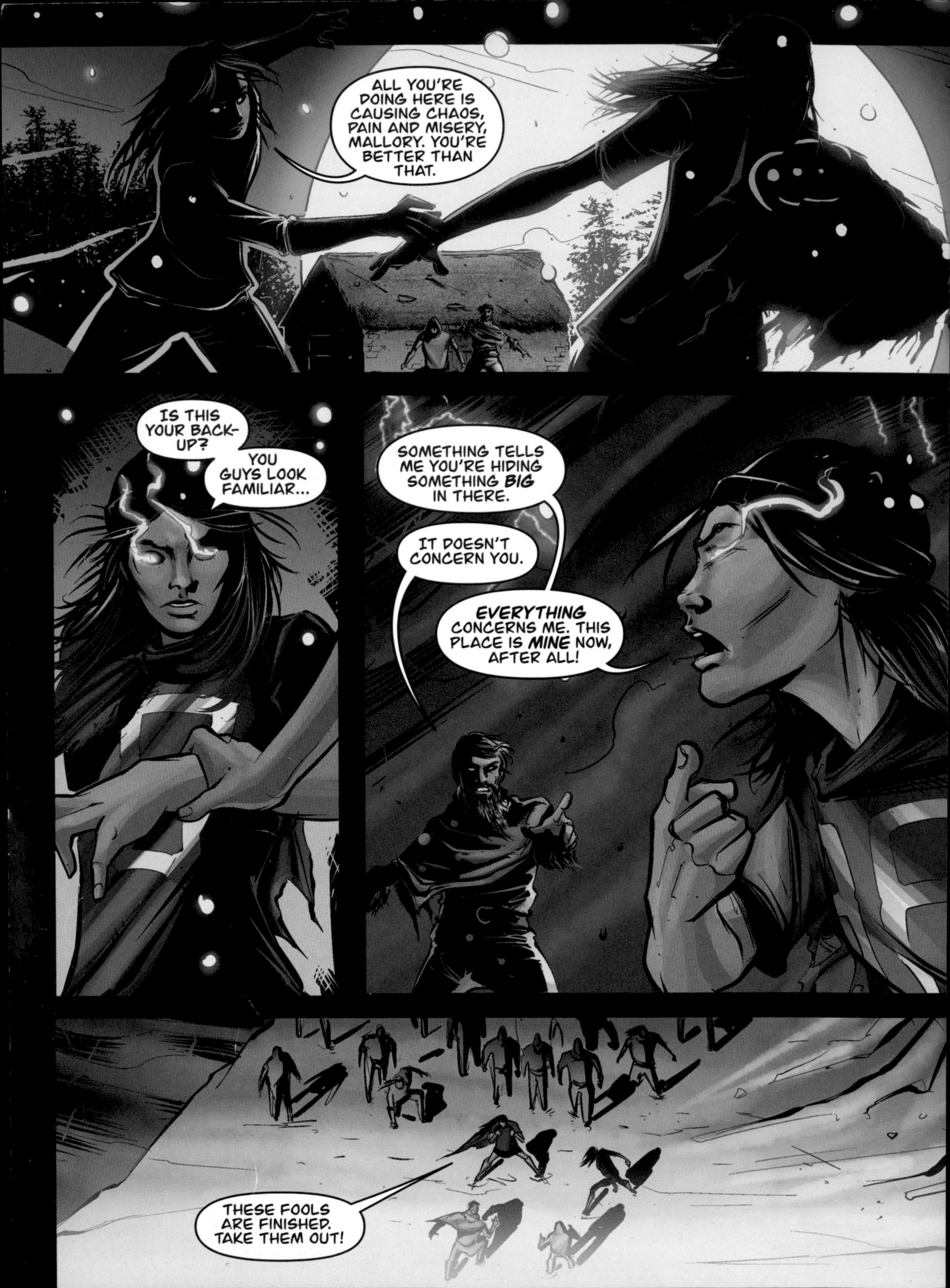
ALL YOU'RE DOING HERE IS CAUSING CHAOS, PAIN AND MISERY, MALLORY. YOU'RE BETTER THAN THAT.
IS THIS YOUR BACK-UP?
YOU GUYS LOOK FAMILIAR...
SOMETHING TELLS ME YOU'RE HIDING SOMETHING BIG IN THERE.
IT DOESN'T CONCERN YOU.
EVERYTHING CONCERNS ME. THIS PLACE IS MINE NOW, AFTER ALL!
THESE FOOLS ARE FINISHED. TAKE THEM OUT!

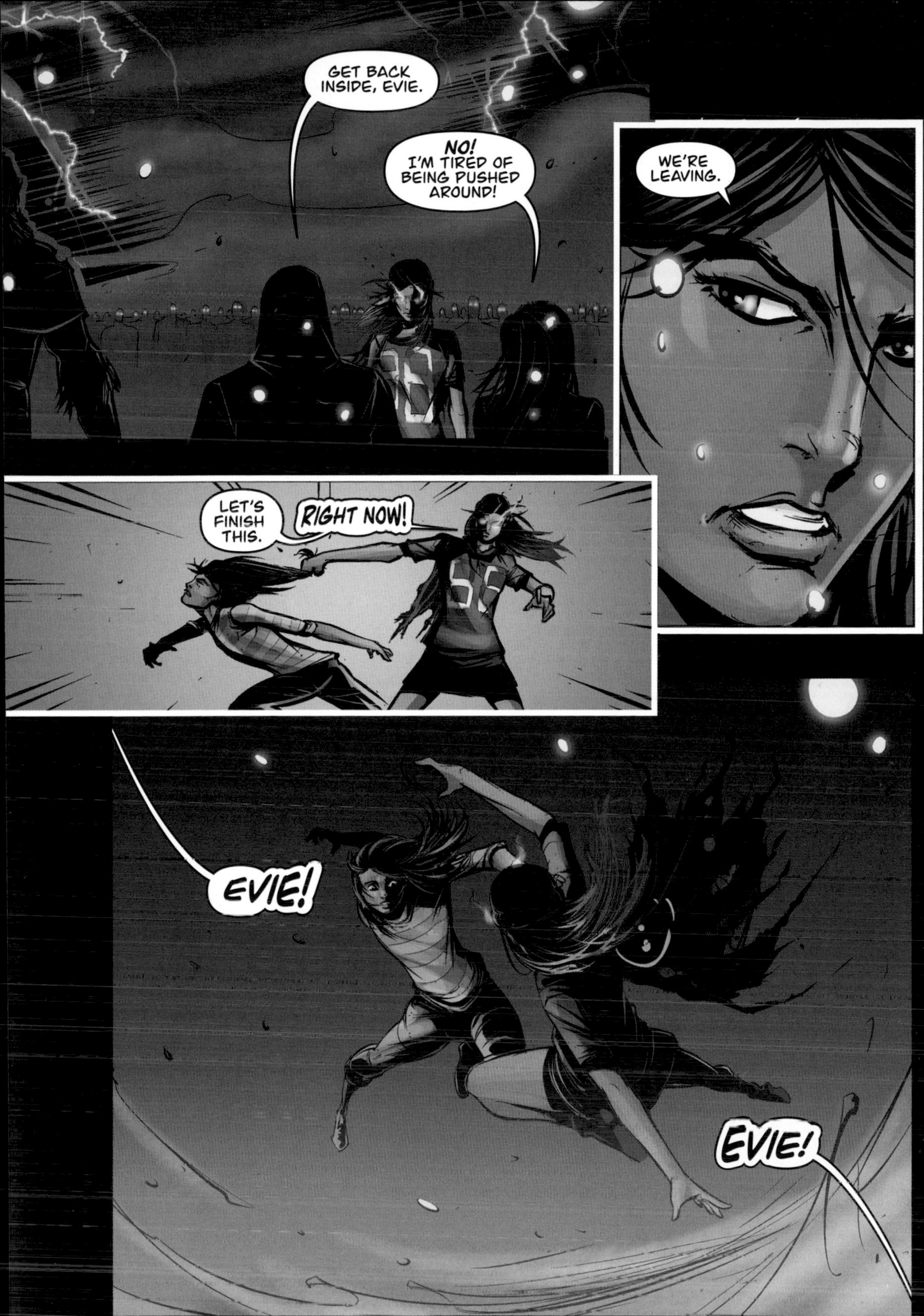
GET BACK INSIDE, EVIE.
NO! I'M TIRED OF BEING PUSHED AROUND!
WE'RE LEAVING.
LET'S FINISH THIS.
RIGHT NOW!
EVIE!
EVIE!

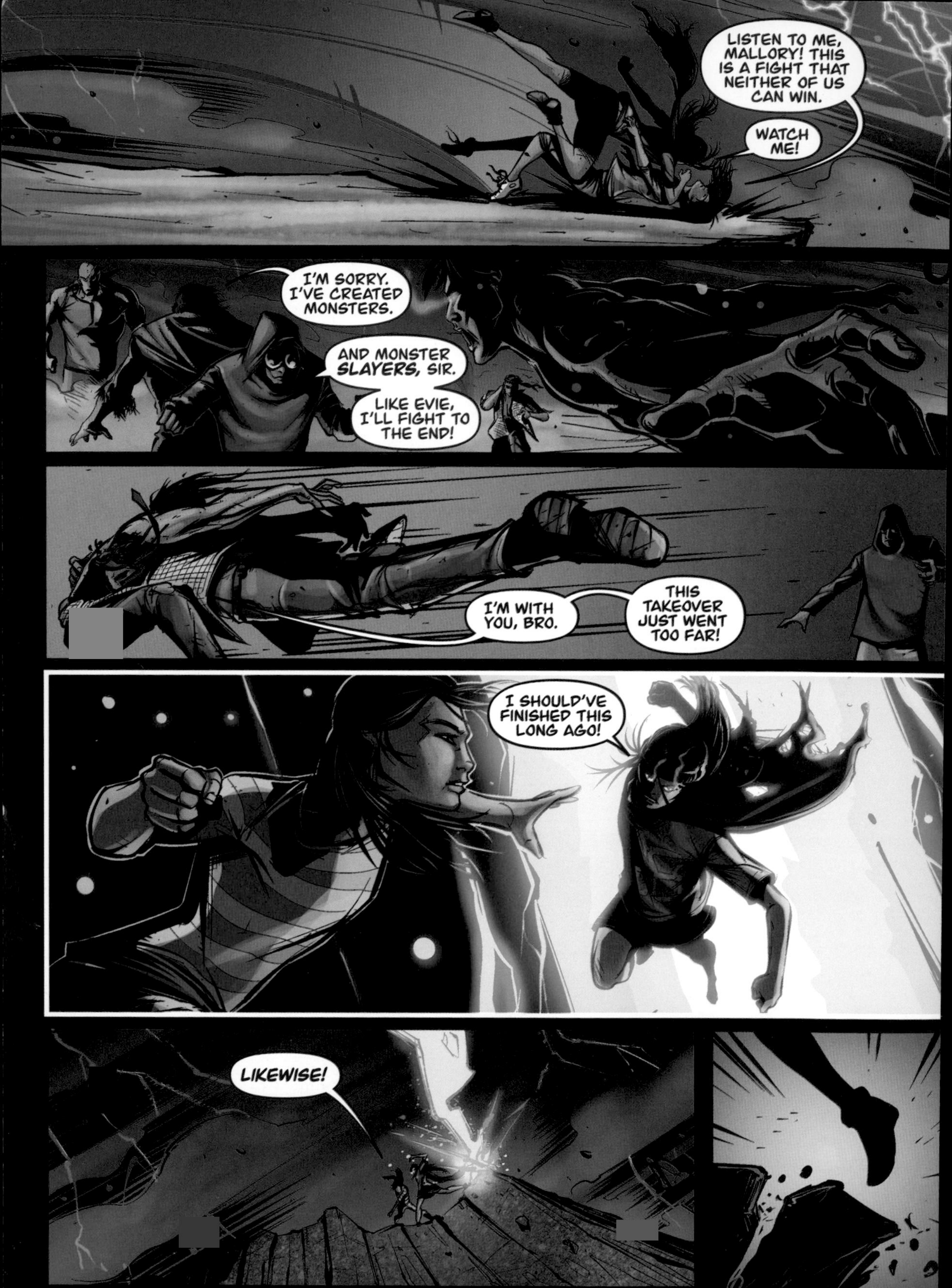
LISTEN TO ME, MALLORY! THIS IS A FIGHT THAT NEITHER OF US CAN WIN.
WATCH ME!
I'M SORRY. I'VE CREATED MONSTERS.
AND MONSTER SLAYERS, SIR.
LIKE EVIE, I'LL FIGHT TO THE END!
I'M WITH YOU, BRO.
THIS TAKEOVER JUST WENT TOO FAR!
I SHOULD'VE FINISHED THIS LONG AGO!
LIKEWISE!

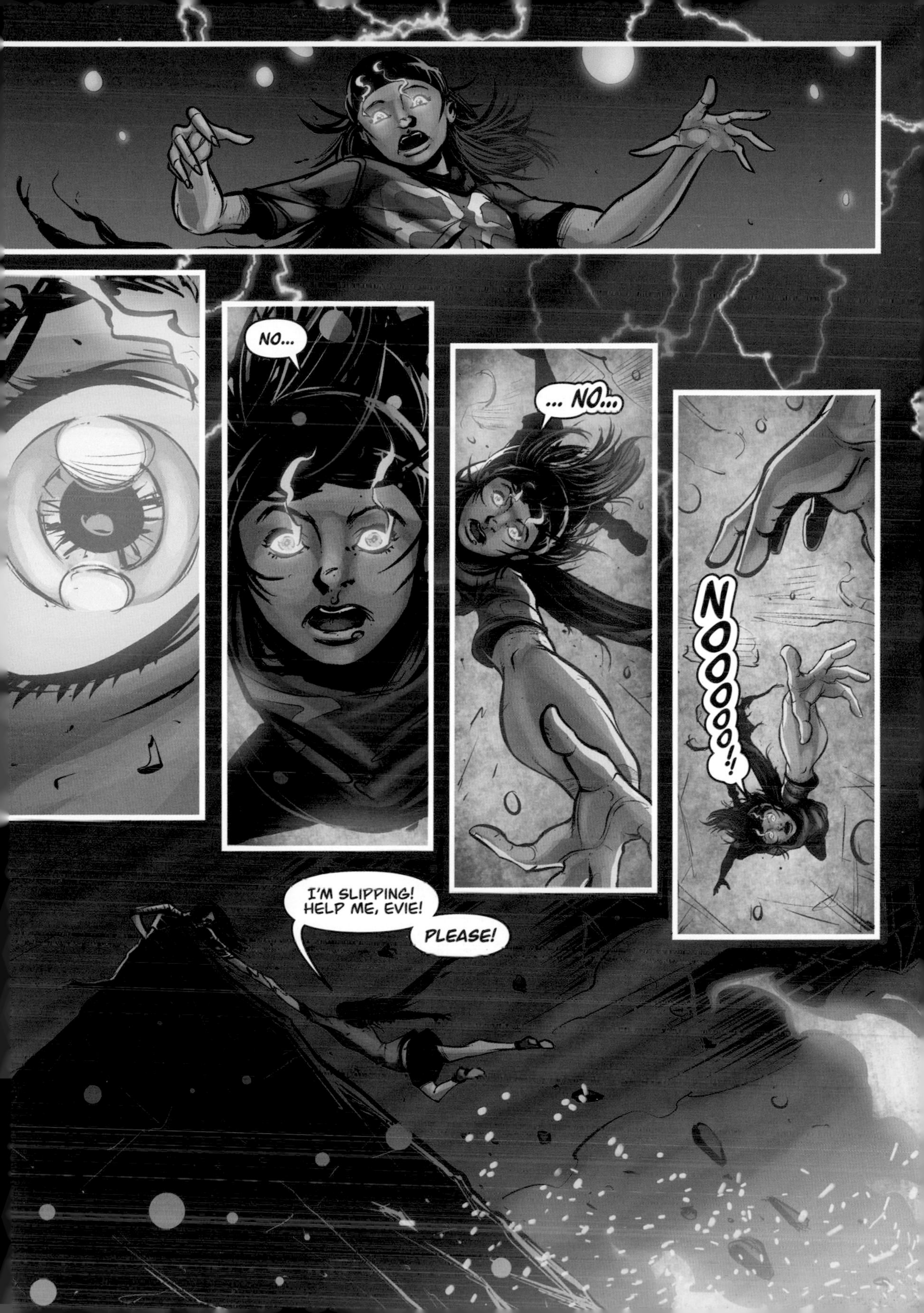
NO...
... NO...
NOOOOO!!
I'M SLIPPING! HELP ME, EVIE!
PLEASE!

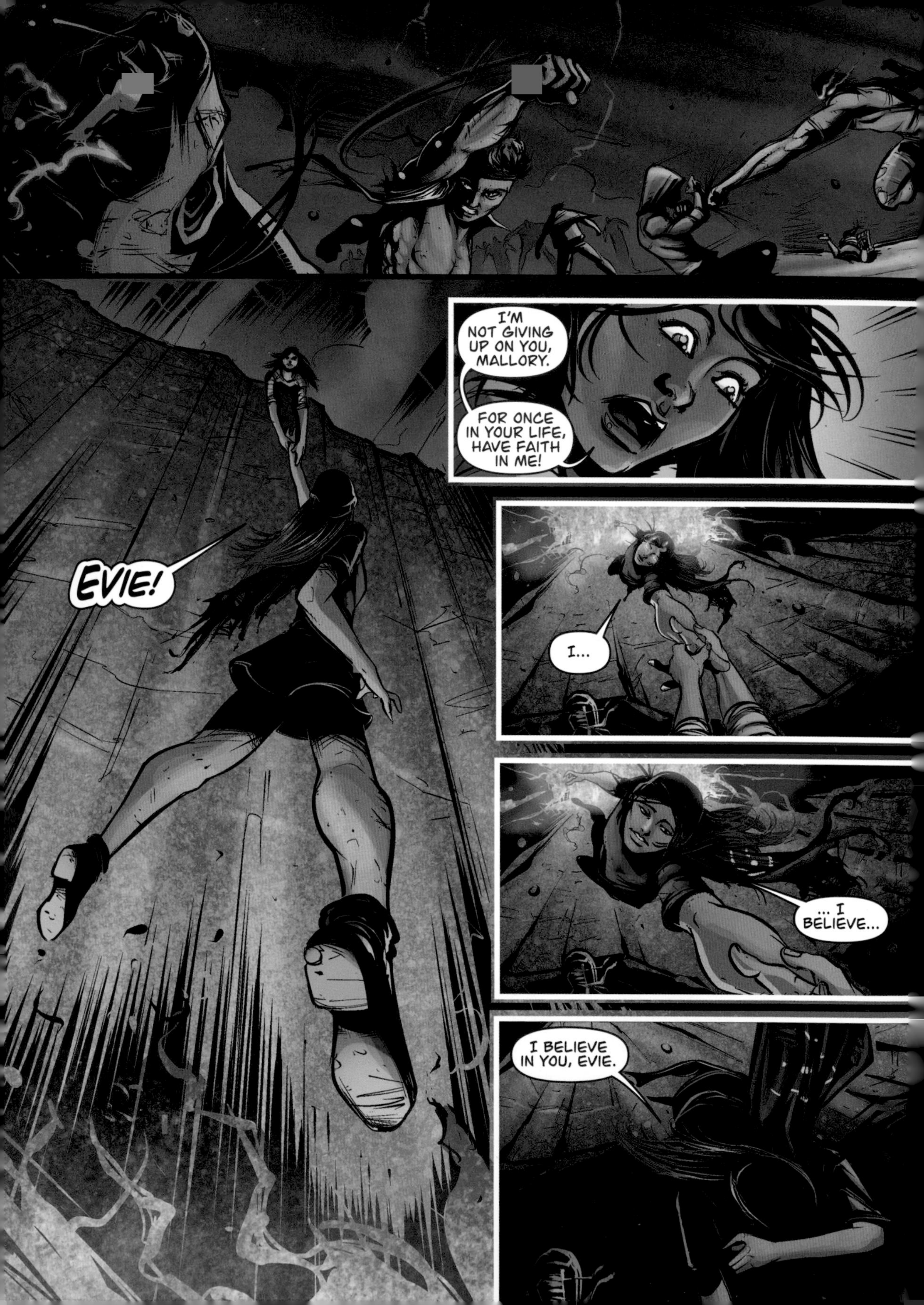
EVIE!
I'M NOT GIVING UP ON YOU, MALLORY.
FOR ONCE IN YOUR LIFE, HAVE FAITH IN ME!
I...
... I BELIEVE...
I BELIEVE IN YOU, EVIE.

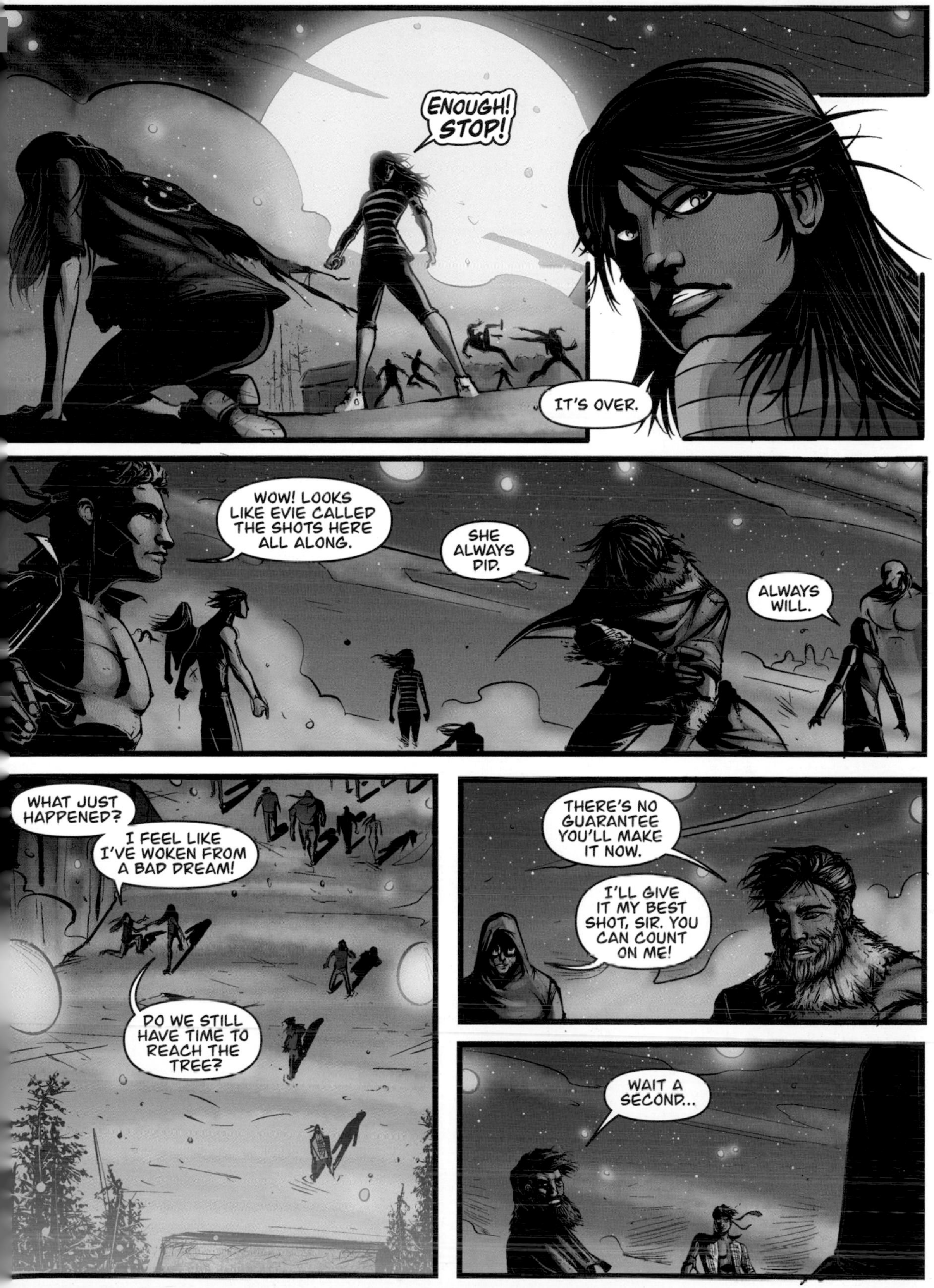
ENOUGH! STOP!
IT'S OVER.
WOW! LOOKS LIKE EVIE CALLED THE SHOTS HERE ALL ALONG.
SHE ALWAYS DID.
ALWAYS WILL.
WHAT JUST HAPPENED?
I FEEL LIKE I'VE WOKEN FROM A BAD DREAM!
DO WE STILL HAVE TIME TO REACH THE TREE?
THERE'S NO GUARANTEE YOU'LL MAKE IT NOW.
I'LL GIVE IT MY BEST SHOT, SIR. YOU CAN COUNT ON ME!
WAIT A SECOND...

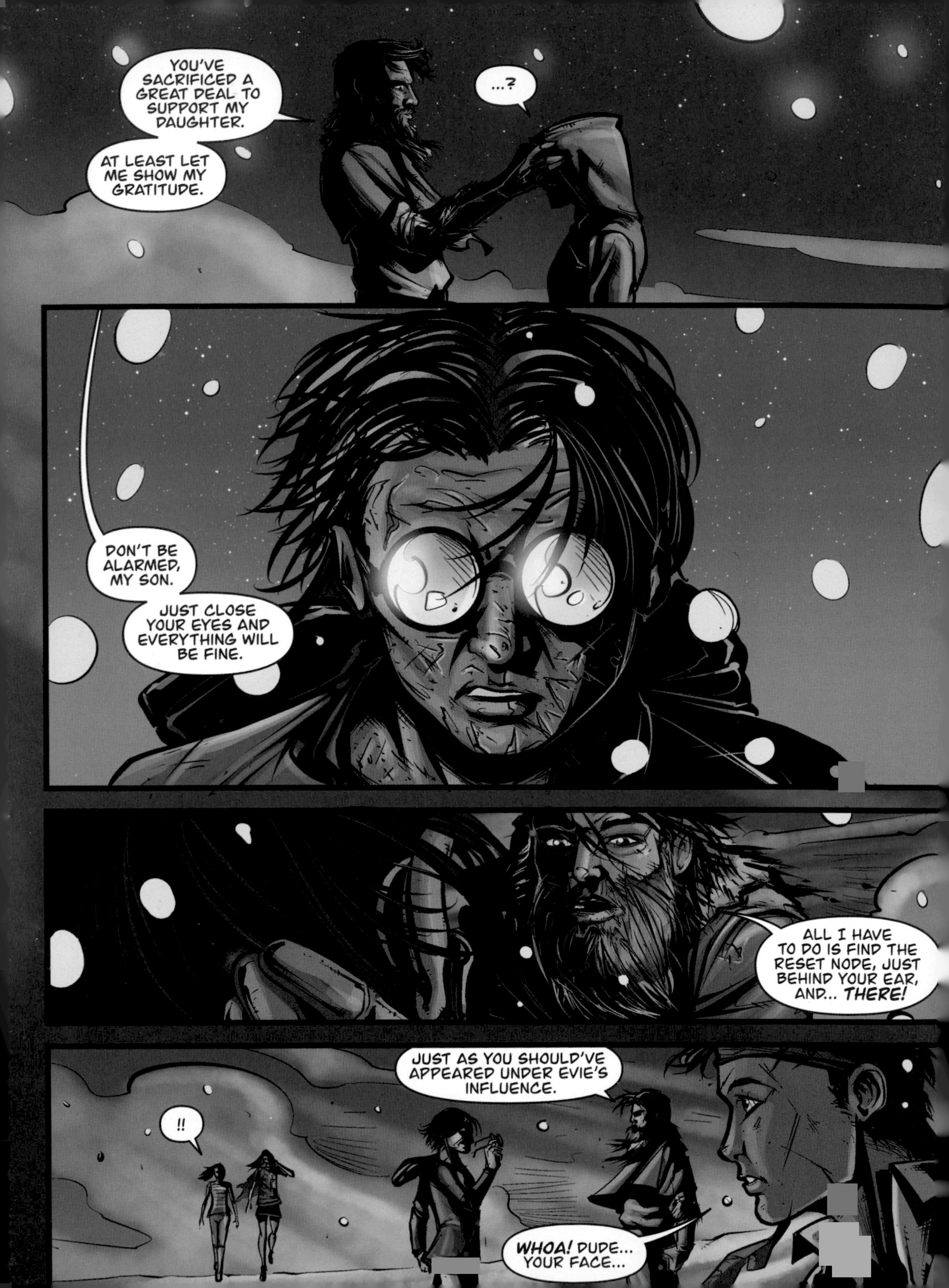
YOU'VE SACRIFICED A GREAT DEAL TO SUPPORT MY DAUGHTER.
AT LEAST LET ME SHOW MY GRATITUDE.
...?
DON'T BE ALARMED, MY SON.
JUST CLOSE YOUR EYES AND EVERYTHING WILL BE FINE.
ALL I HAVE TO DO IS FIND THE RESET NODE, JUST BEHIND YOUR EAR, AND... *THERE!*
JUST AS YOU SHOULD'VE APPEARED UNDER EVIE'S INFLUENCE.
!!
WHOA! DUDE... YOUR FACE...

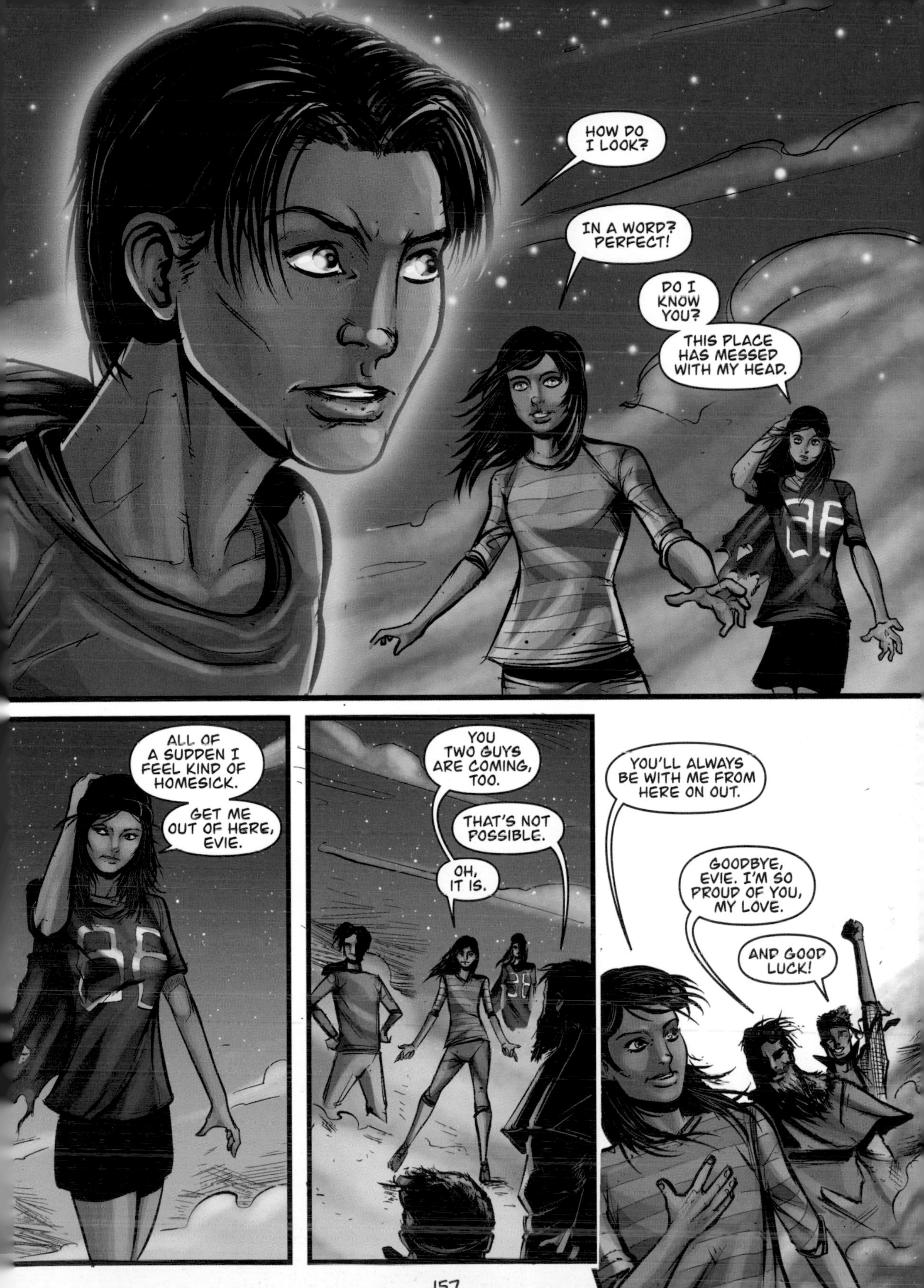
HOW DO I LOOK?
IN A WORD? PERFECT!
DO I KNOW YOU?
THIS PLACE HAS MESSED WITH MY HEAD.
ALL OF A SUDDEN I FEEL KIND OF HOMESICK.
GET ME OUT OF HERE, EVIE.
YOU TWO GUYS ARE COMING, TOO.
THAT'S NOT POSSIBLE.
OH, IT IS.
YOU'LL ALWAYS BE WITH ME FROM HERE ON OUT.
GOODBYE, EVIE. I'M SO PROUD OF YOU, MY LOVE.
AND GOOD LUCK!

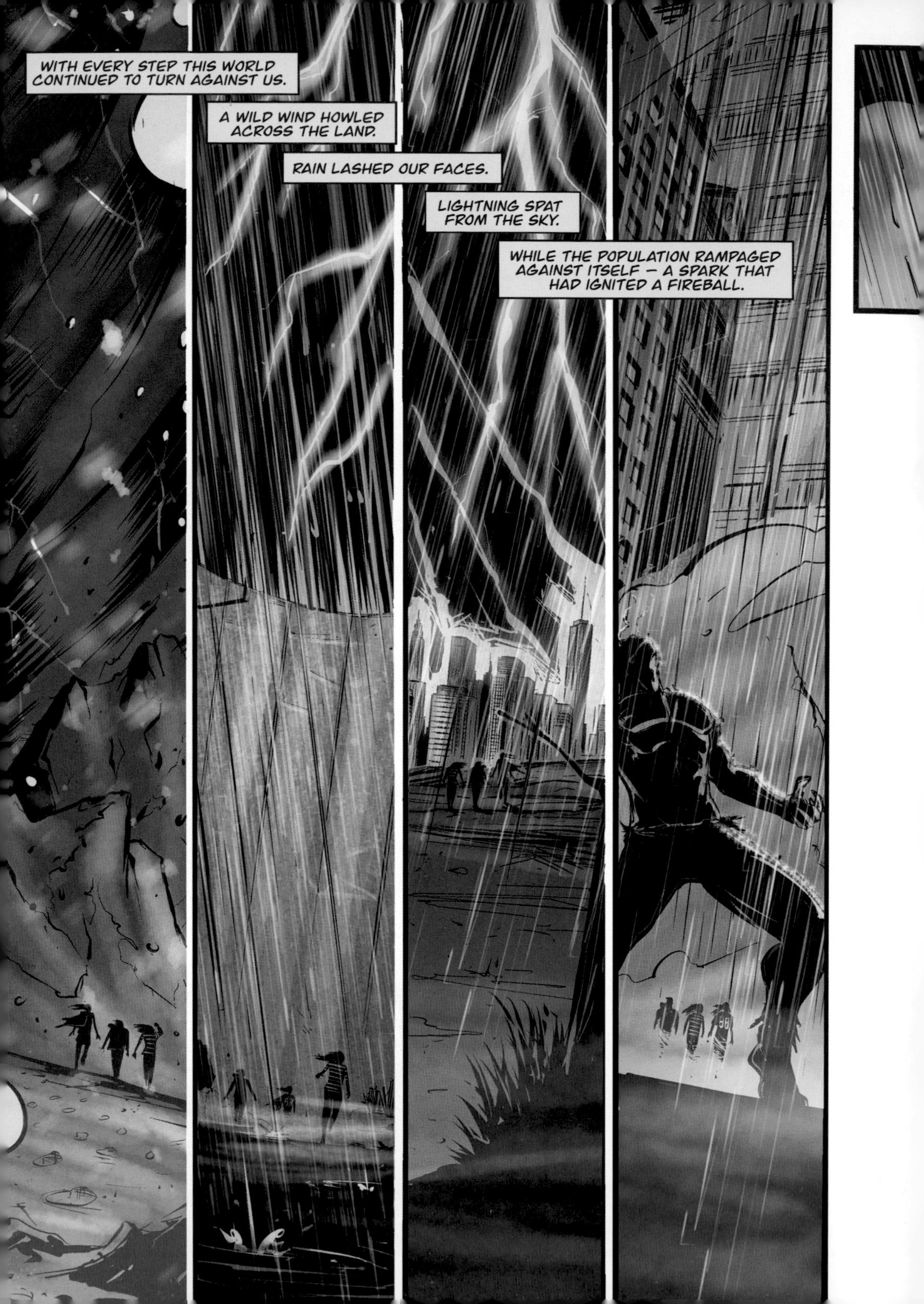
WITH EVERY STEP THIS WORLD CONTINUED TO TURN AGAINST US.
A WILD WIND HOWLED ACROSS THE LAND.
RAIN LASHED OUR FACES.
LIGHTNING SPAT FROM THE SKY.
WHILE THE POPULATION RAMPAGED AGAINST ITSELF — A SPARK THAT HAD IGNITED A FIREBALL.

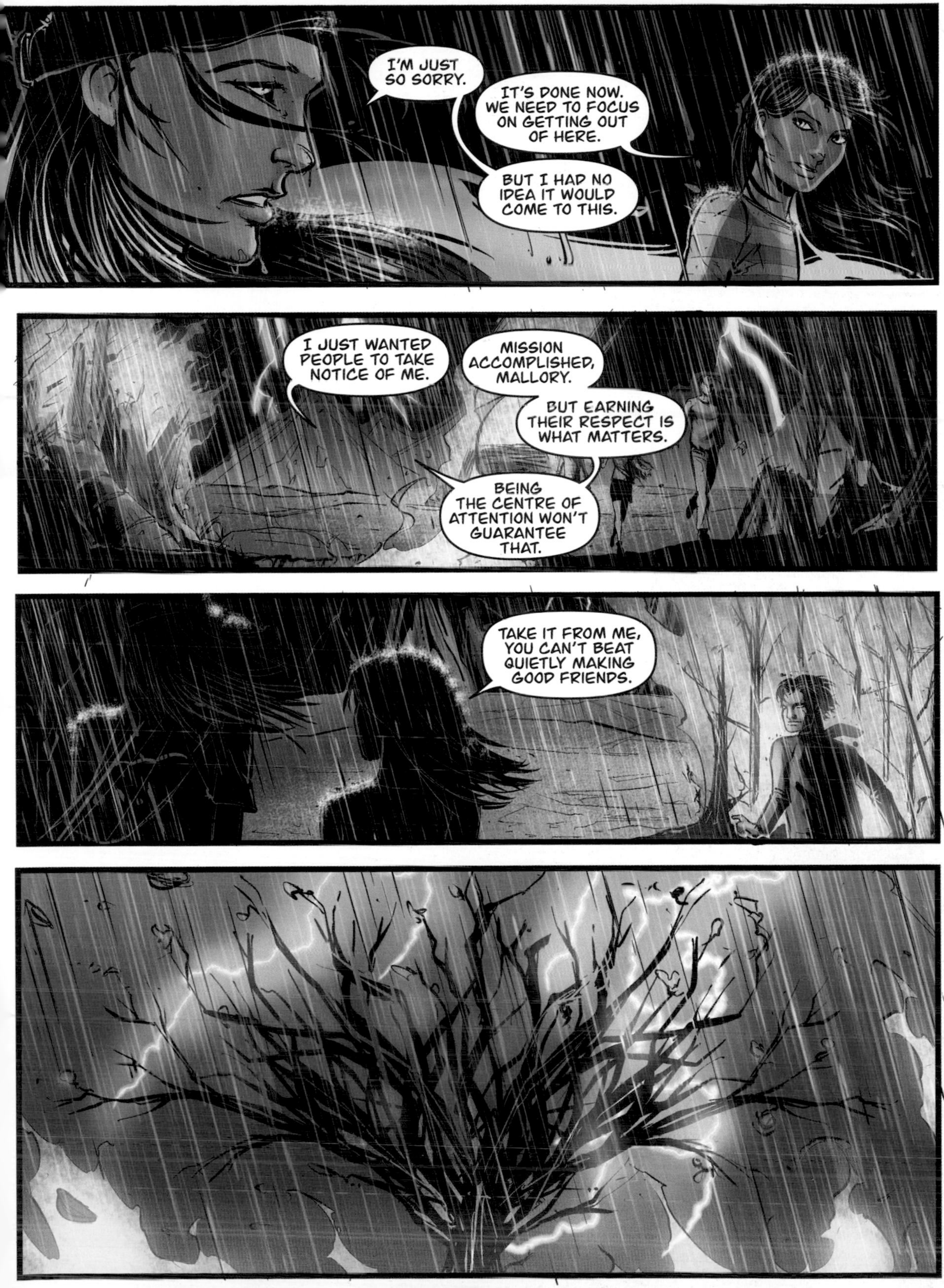
I'M JUST SO SORRY.
IT'S DONE NOW. WE NEED TO FOCUS ON GETTING OUT OF HERE.
BUT I HAD NO IDEA IT WOULD COME TO THIS.
I JUST WANTED PEOPLE TO TAKE NOTICE OF ME.
MISSION ACCOMPLISHED, MALLORY.
BUT EARNING THEIR RESPECT IS WHAT MATTERS.
BEING THE CENTRE OF ATTENTION WON'T GUARANTEE THAT.
TAKE IT FROM ME, YOU CAN'T BEAT QUIETLY MAKING GOOD FRIENDS.

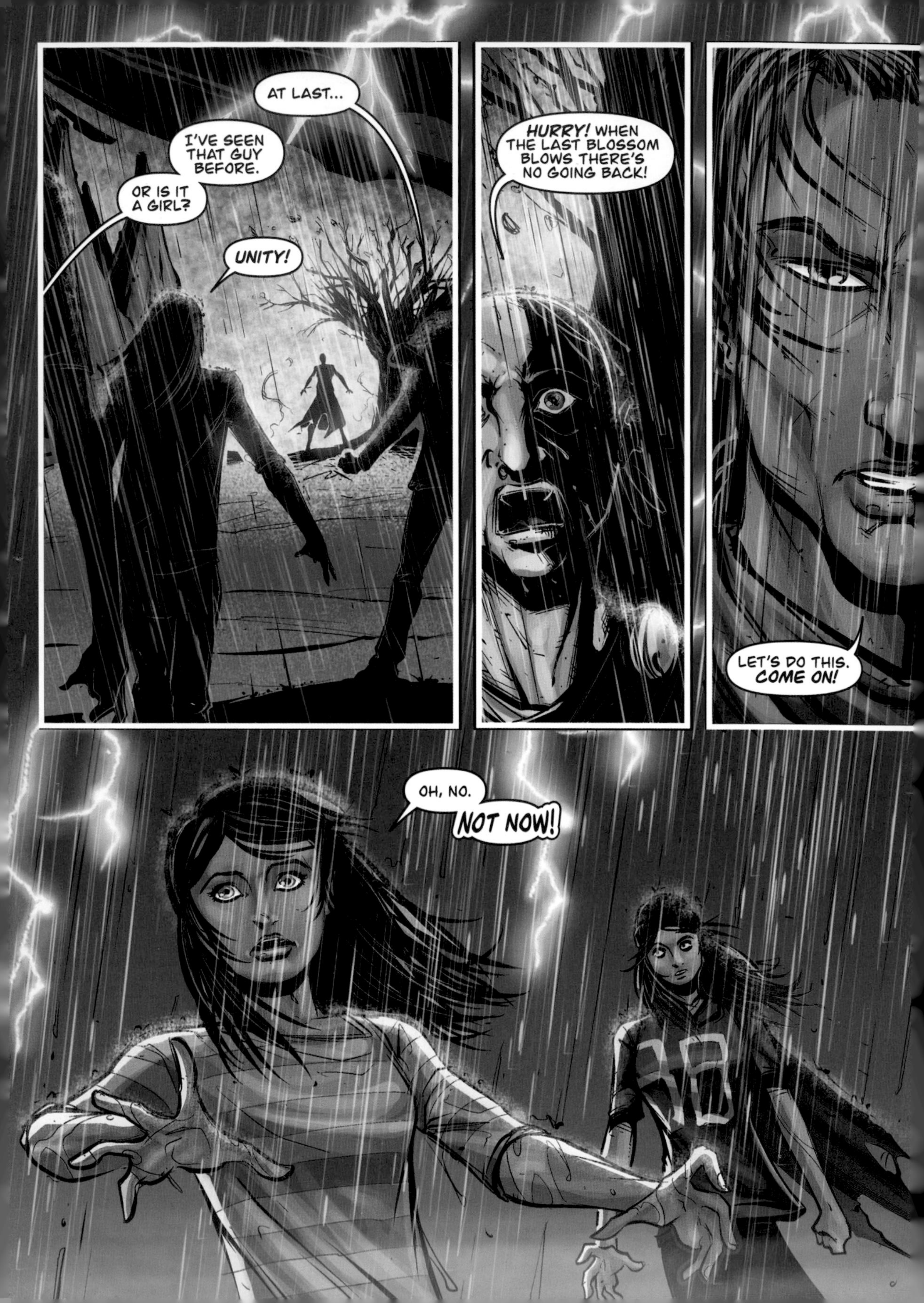
AT LAST...
I'VE SEEN THAT GUY BEFORE.
OR IS IT A GIRL?
UNITY!
HURRY! WHEN THE LAST BLOSSOM BLOWS THERE'S NO GOING BACK!
LET'S DO THIS. COME ON!
OH, NO. NOT NOW!

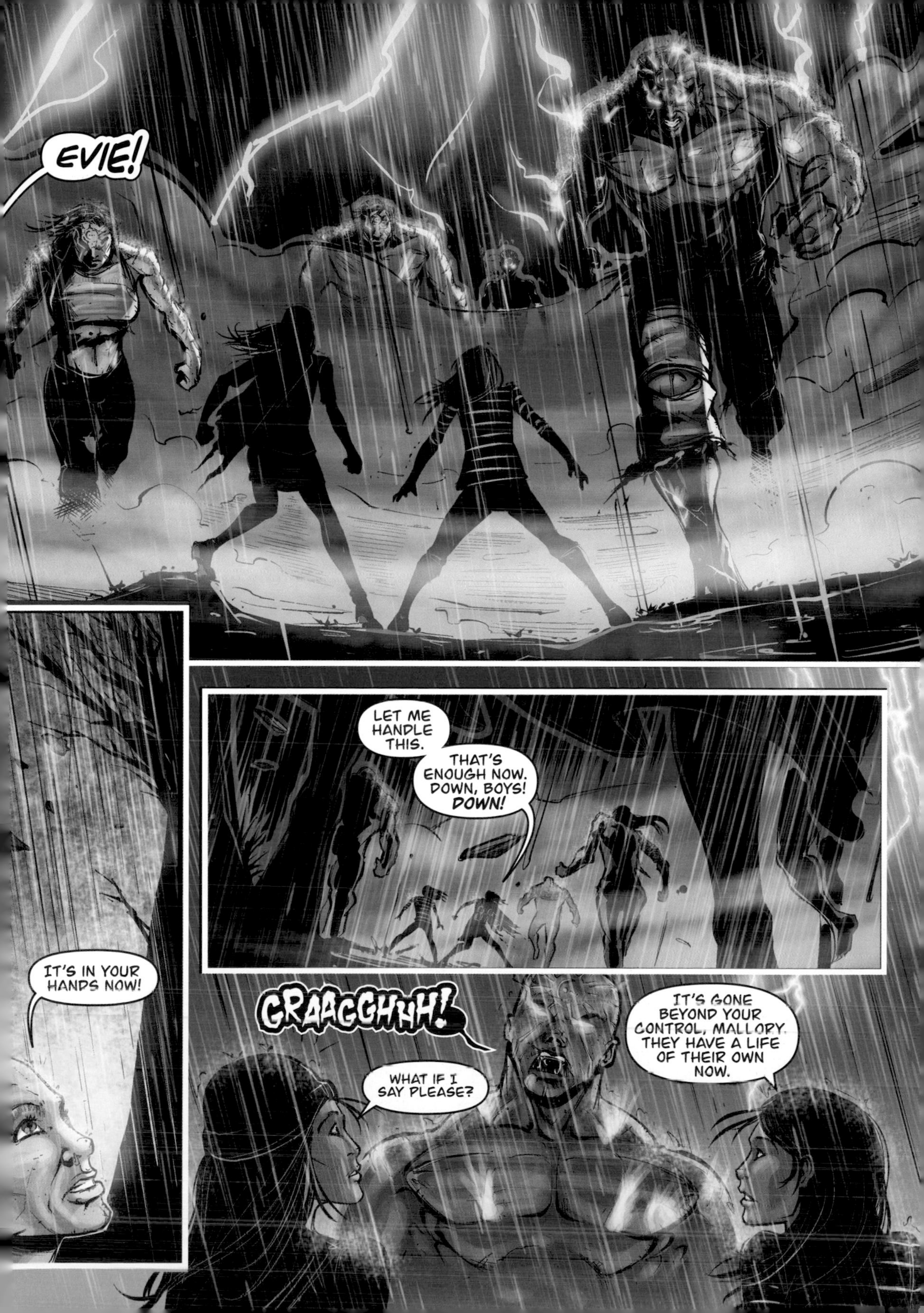
EVIE!
LET ME HANDLE THIS.
THAT'S ENOUGH NOW. DOWN, BOYS! DOWN!
IT'S IN YOUR HANDS NOW!
GRAAGGHHH!
WHAT IF I SAY PLEASE?
IT'S GONE BEYOND YOUR CONTROL, MALLORY. THEY HAVE A LIFE OF THEIR OWN NOW.

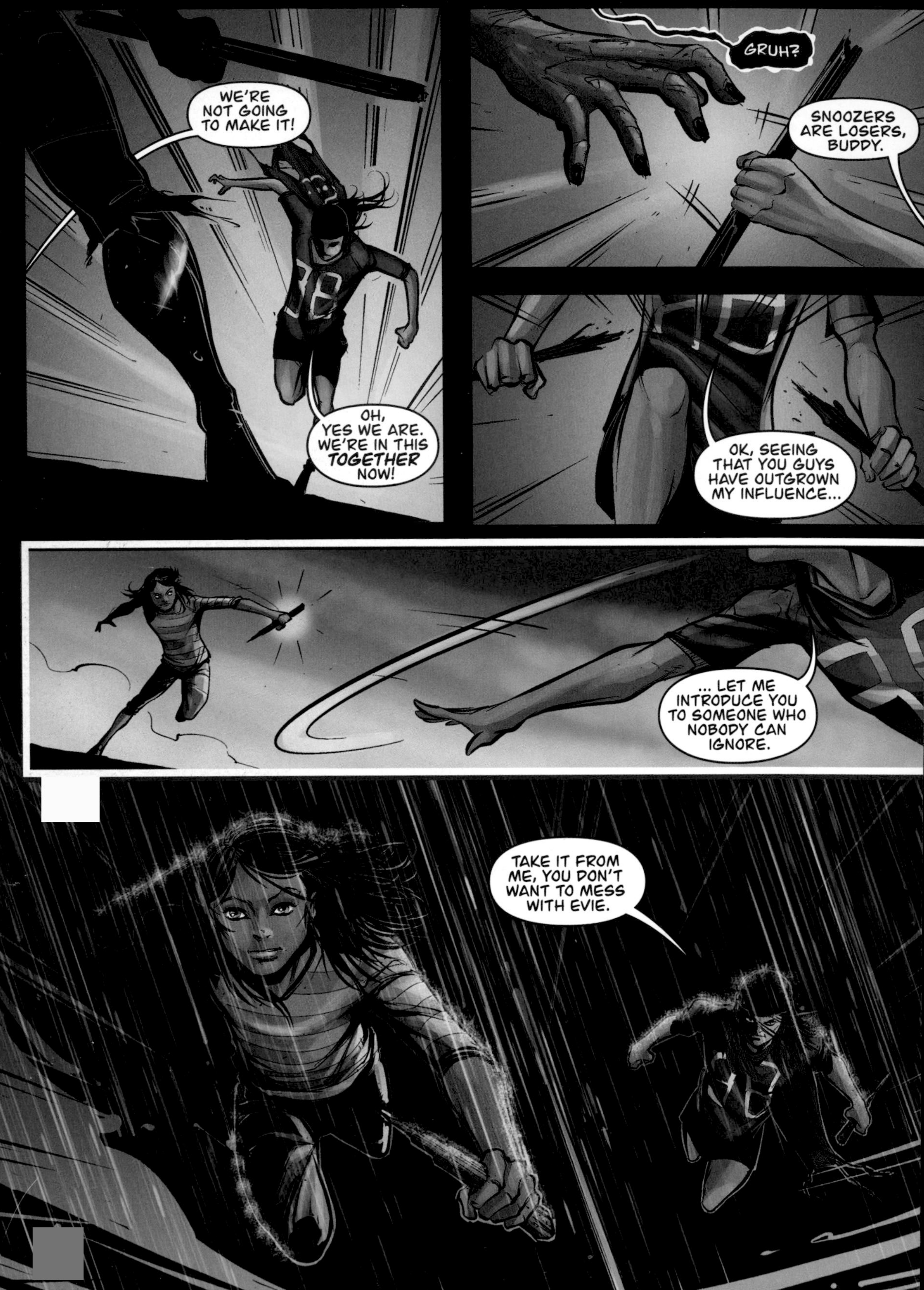
WE'RE NOT GOING TO MAKE IT!
OH, YES WE ARE. WE'RE IN THIS TOGETHER NOW!
GRUH?
SNOOZERS ARE LOSERS, BUDDY.
OK, SEEING THAT YOU GUYS HAVE OUTGROWN MY INFLUENCE...
... LET ME INTRODUCE YOU TO SOMEONE WHO NOBODY CAN IGNORE.
TAKE IT FROM ME, YOU DON'T WANT TO MESS WITH EVIE.

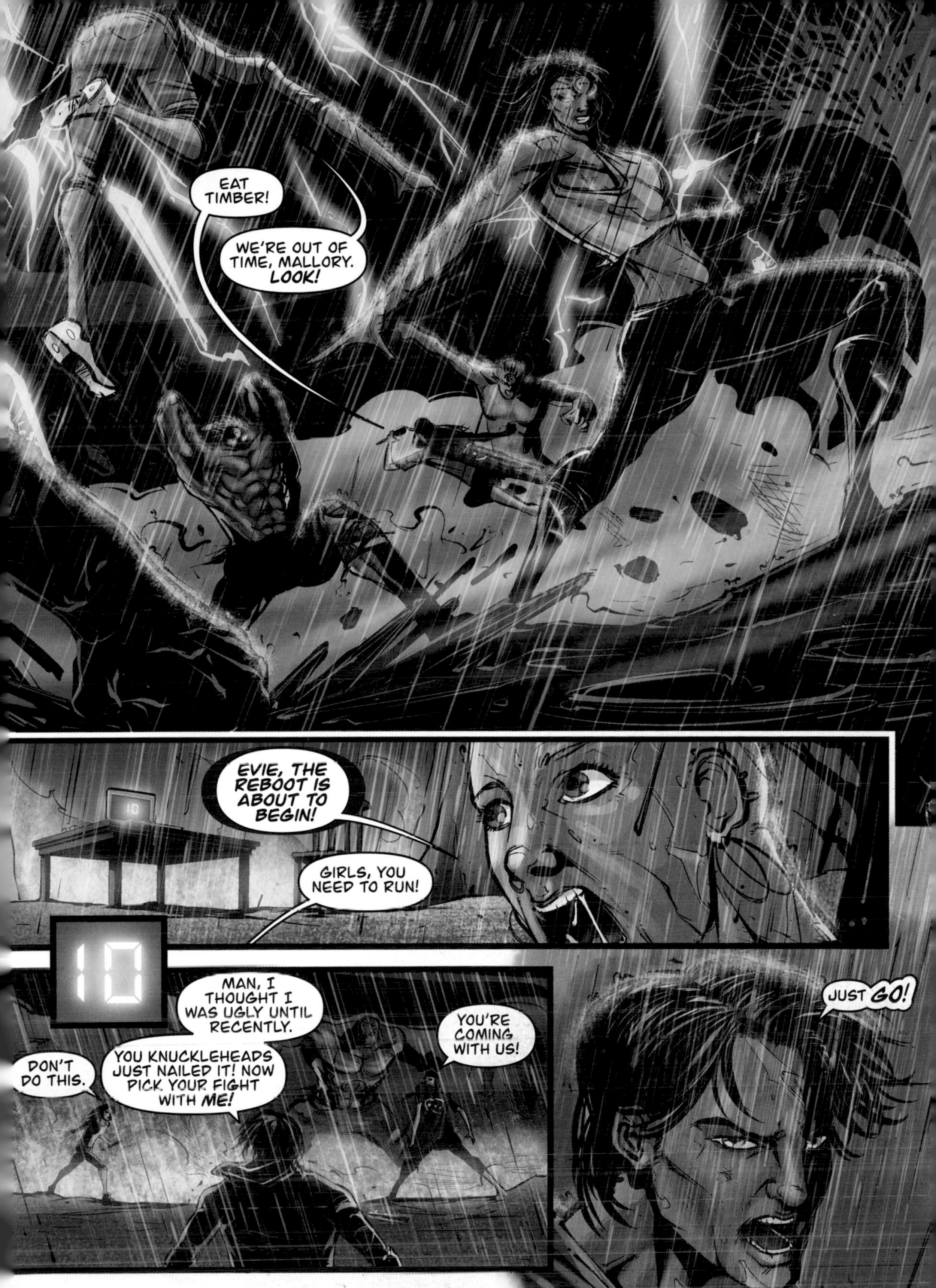
EAT TIMBER!
WE'RE OUT OF TIME, MALLORY. LOOK!
EVIE, THE REBOOT IS ABOUT TO BEGIN!
GIRLS, YOU NEED TO RUN!
10
MAN, I THOUGHT I WAS UGLY UNTIL RECENTLY.
DON'T DO THIS.
YOU KNUCKLEHEADS JUST NAILED IT! NOW PICK YOUR FIGHT WITH ME!
YOU'RE COMING WITH US!
JUST GO!

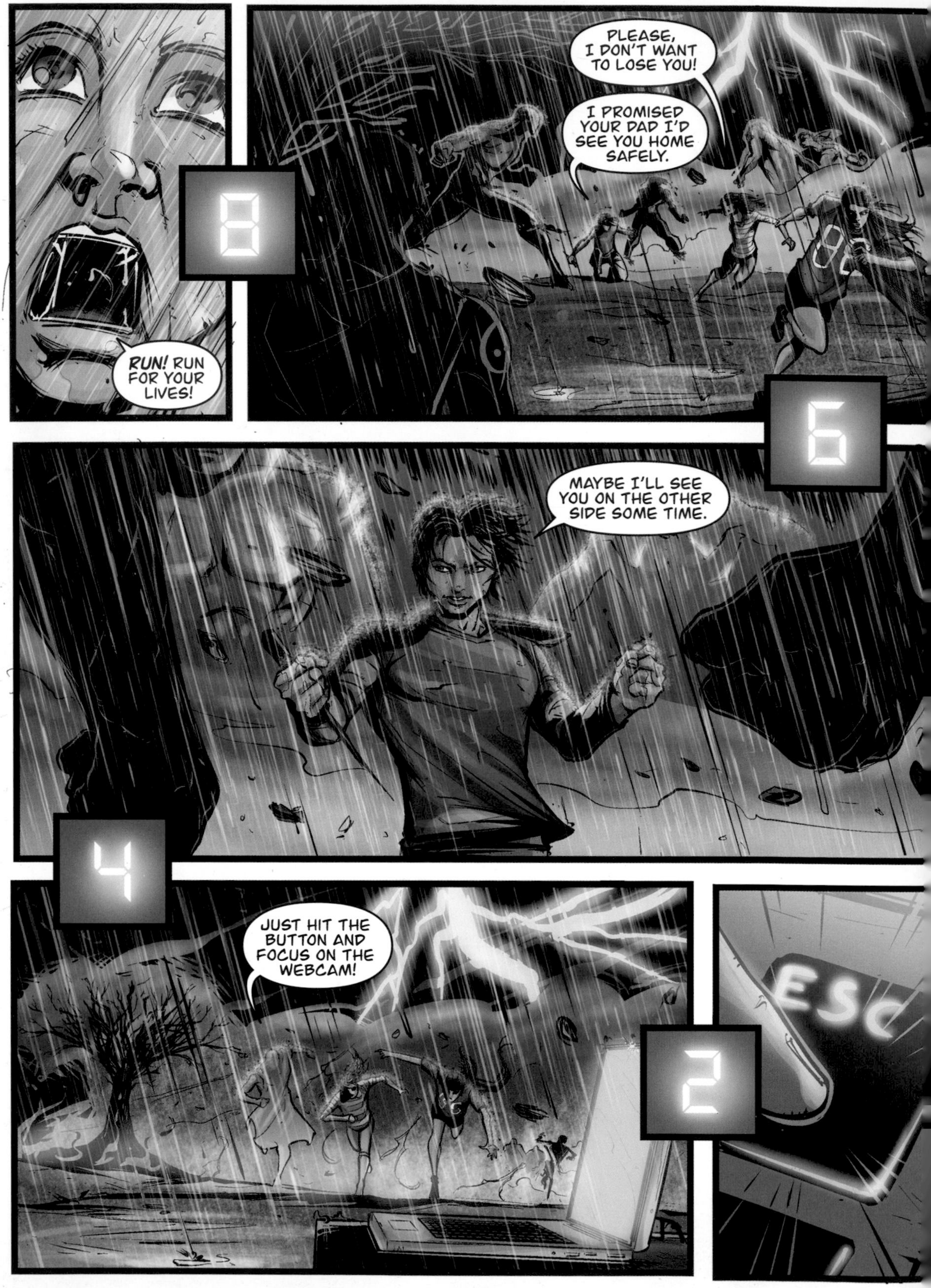
8
RUN! RUN FOR YOUR LIVES!
PLEASE, I DON'T WANT TO LOSE YOU!
I PROMISED YOUR DAD I'D SEE YOU HOME SAFELY.
6
MAYBE I'LL SEE YOU ON THE OTHER SIDE SOME TIME.
4
JUST HIT THE BUTTON AND FOCUS ON THE WEBCAM!
2
ESC

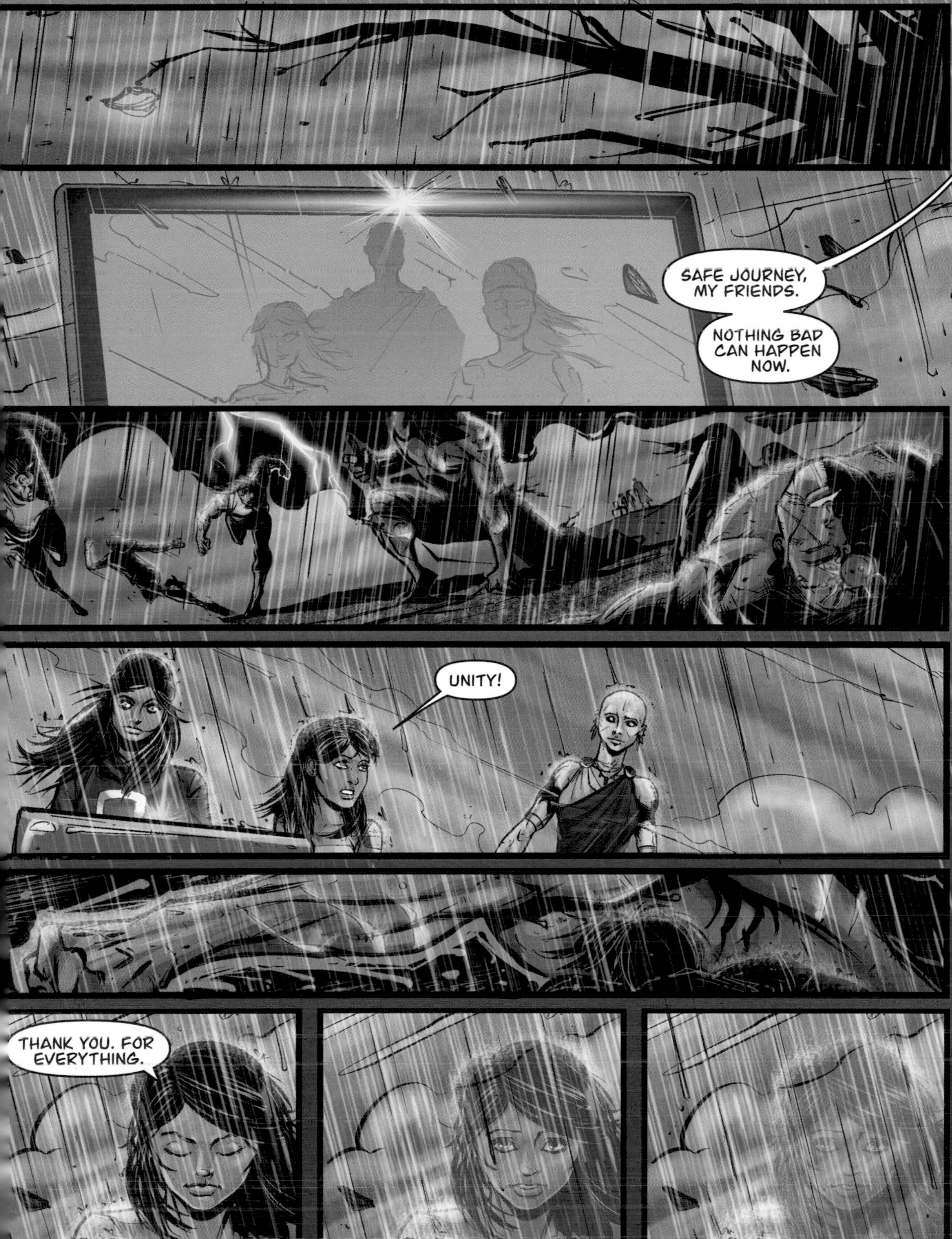
SAFE JOURNEY, MY FRIENDS.
NOTHING BAD CAN HAPPEN NOW.
UNITY!
THANK YOU. FOR EVERYTHING.

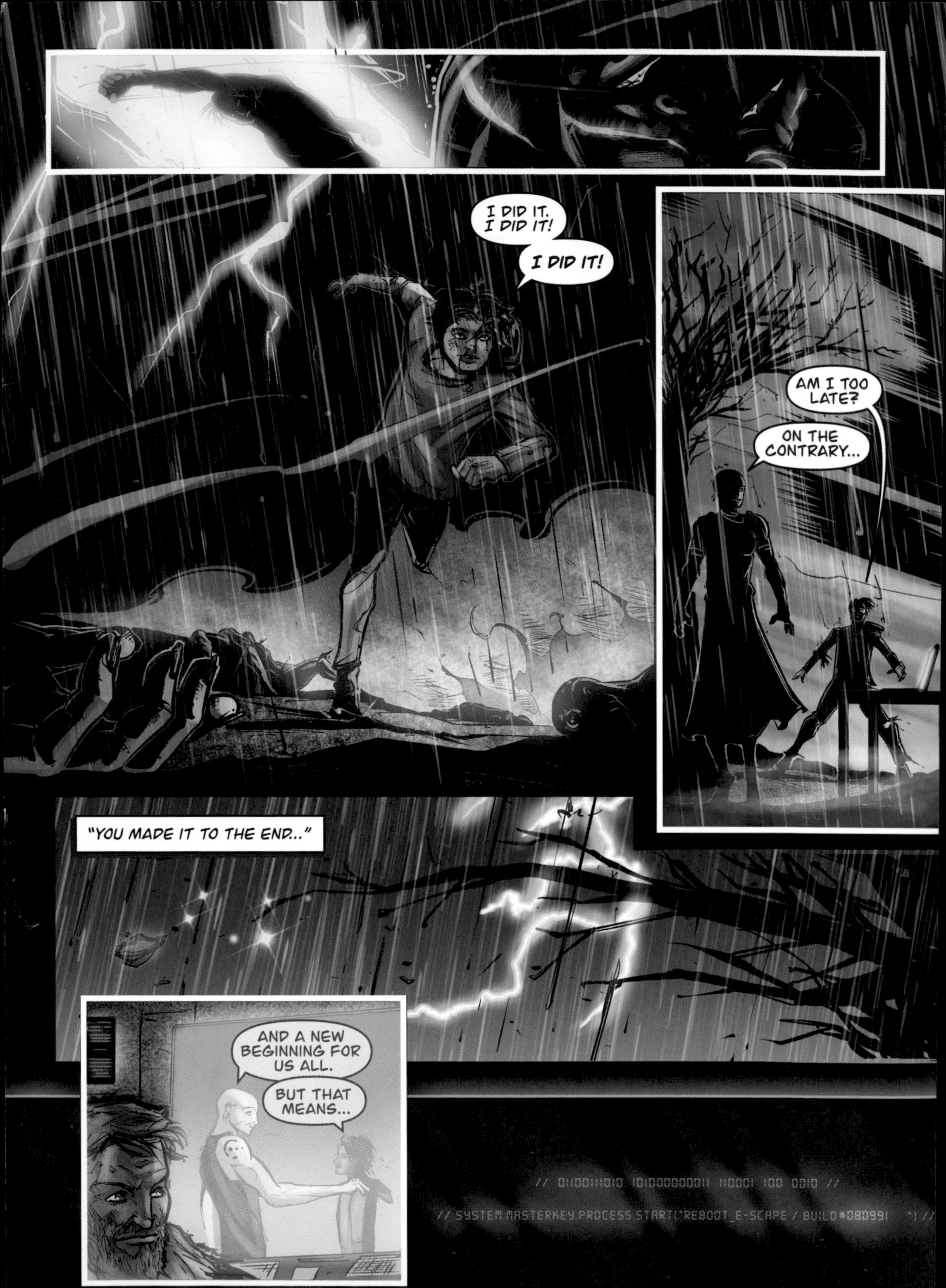
I DID IT. I DID IT!
I DID IT!
AM I TOO LATE?
ON THE CONTRARY...
"YOU MADE IT TO THE END..."
AND A NEW BEGINNING FOR US ALL.
BUT THAT MEANS...
// 0110011010 10100000011 110001 100 0010 //
// SYSTEM.MASTERKEY.PROCESS.START("REBOOT_E-SCAPE / BUILD #080991 ") //

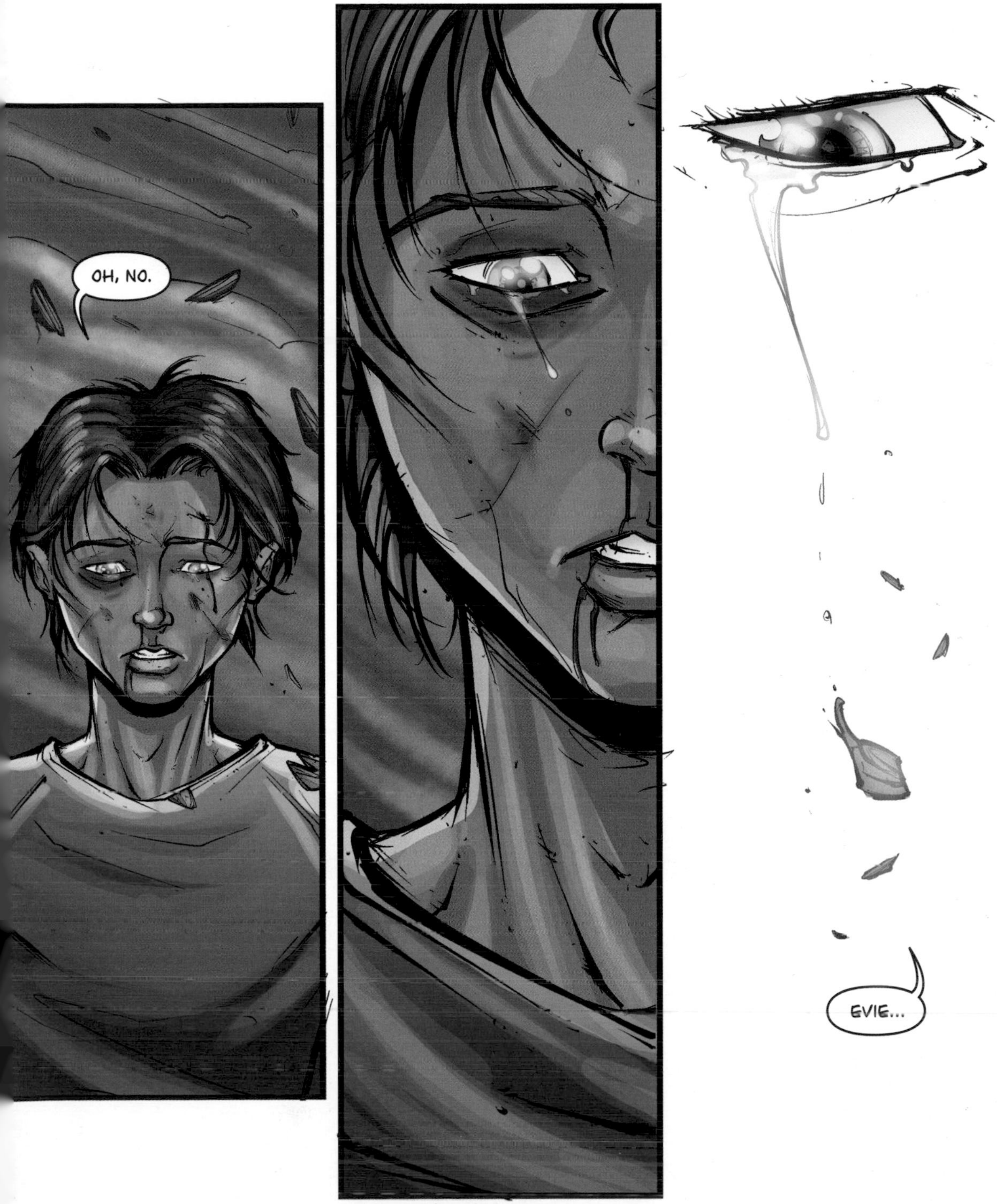
OH, NO.
EVIE...

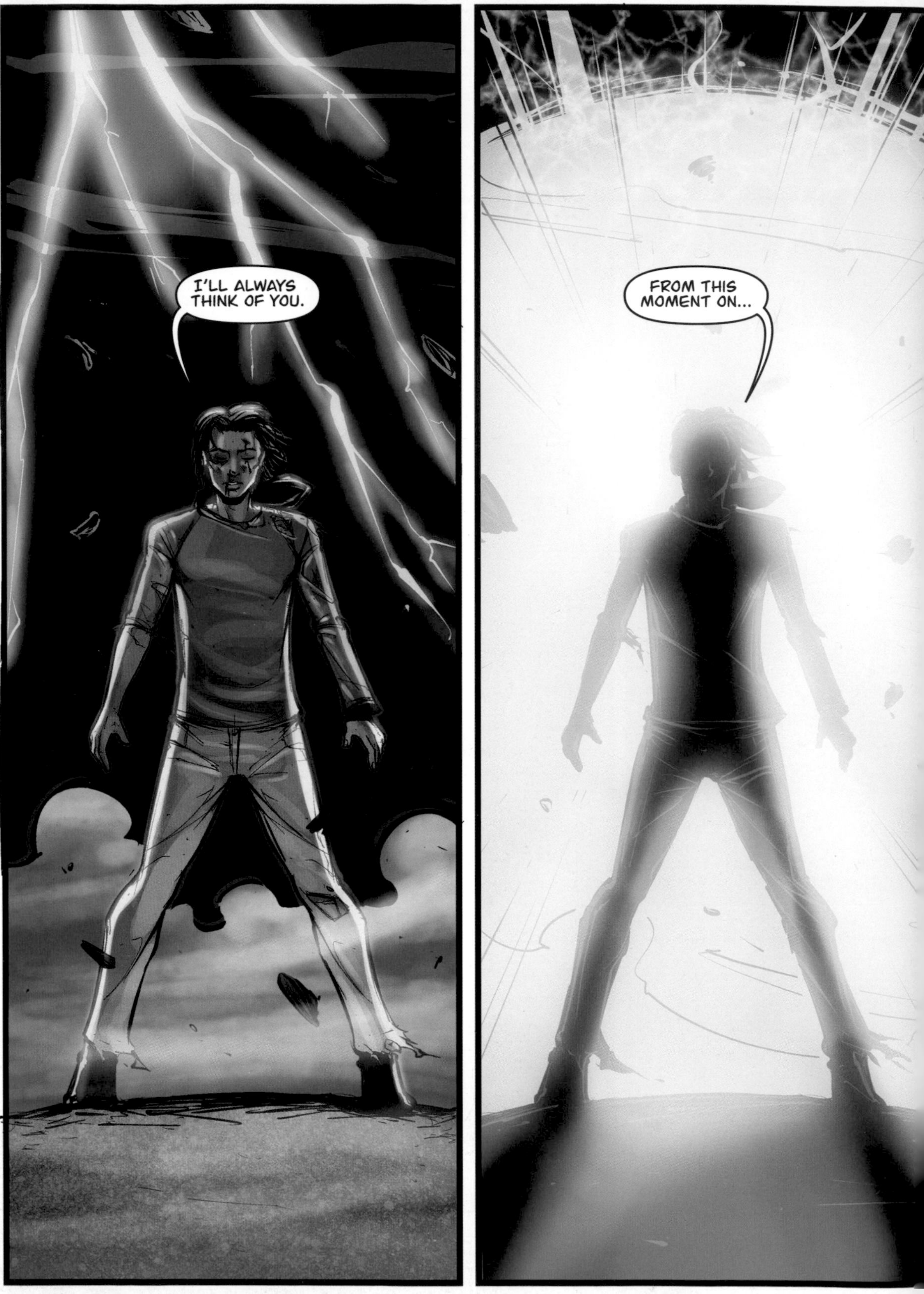
I'LL ALWAYS THINK OF YOU.
FROM THIS MOMENT ON...

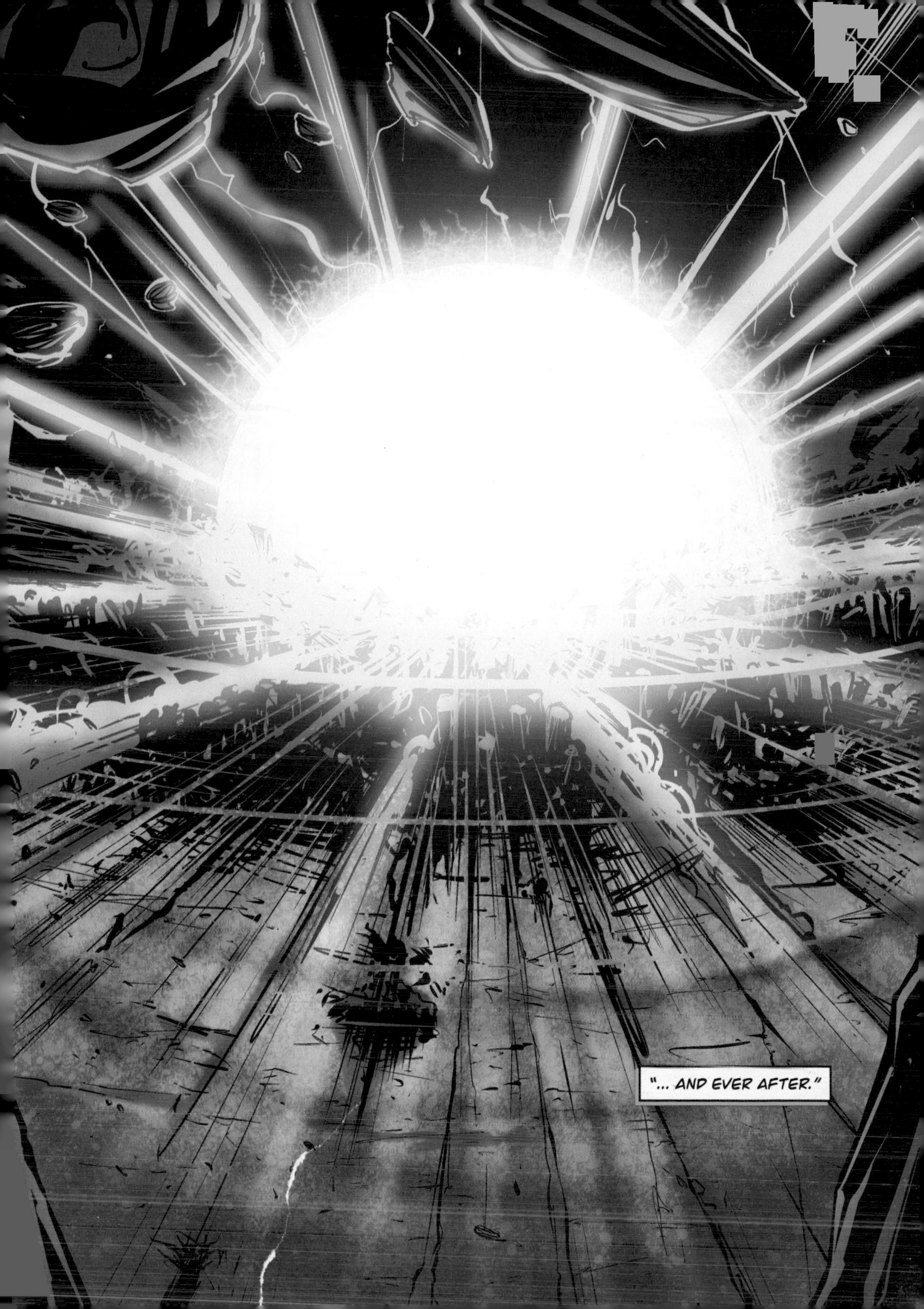
"... AND EVER AFTER."

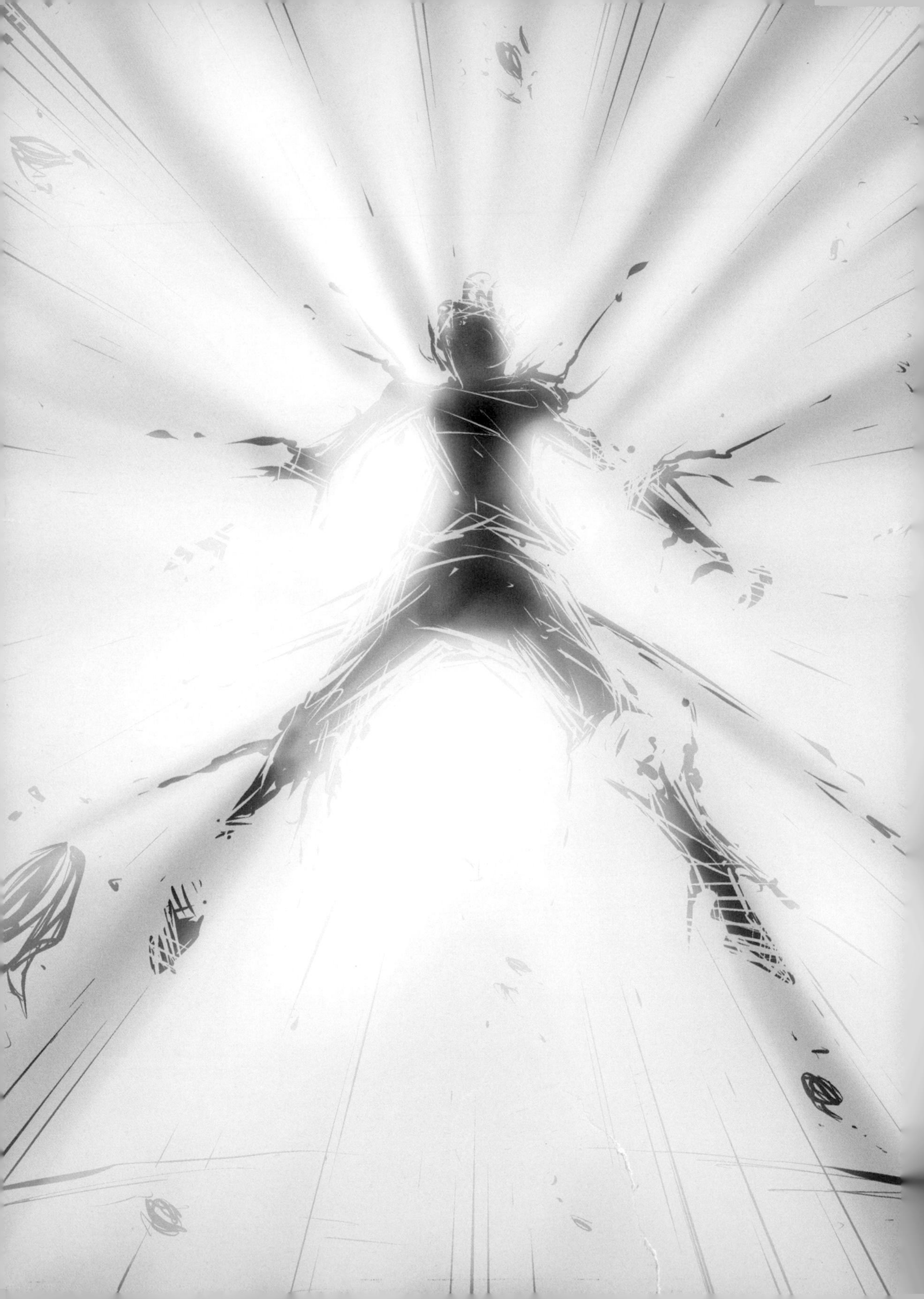

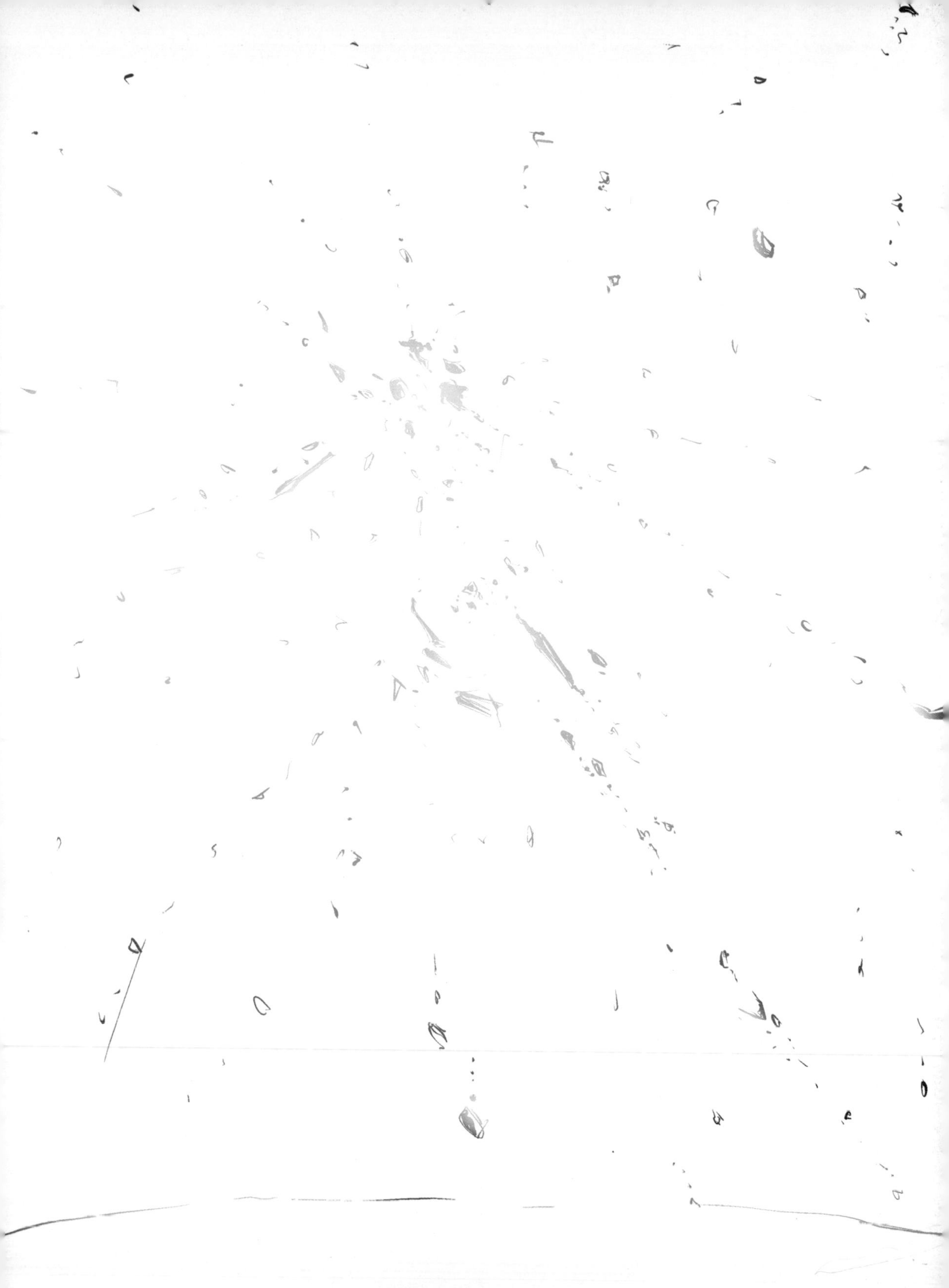

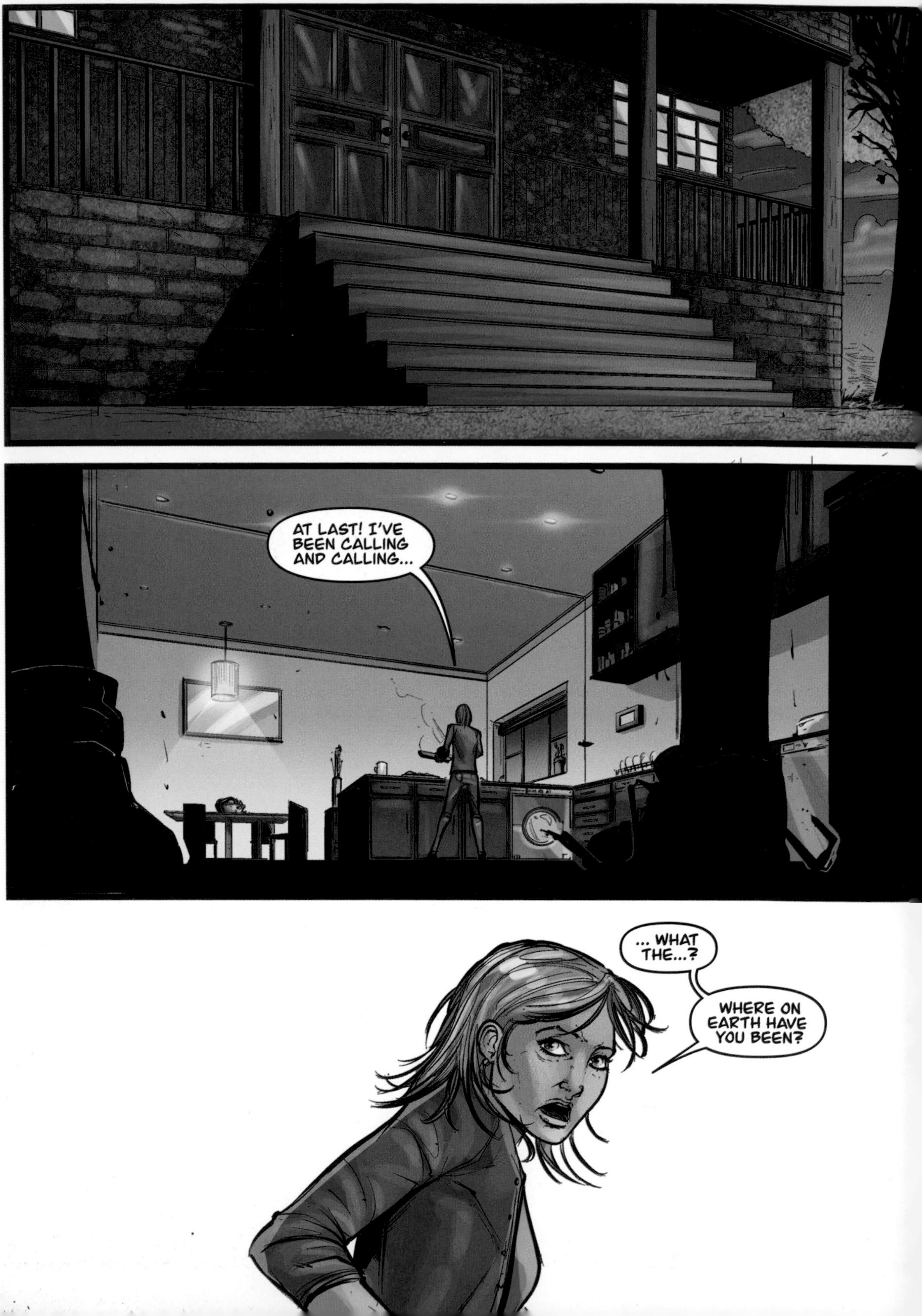
AT LAST! I'VE BEEN CALLING AND CALLING...
... WHAT THE...?
WHERE ON EARTH HAVE YOU BEEN?

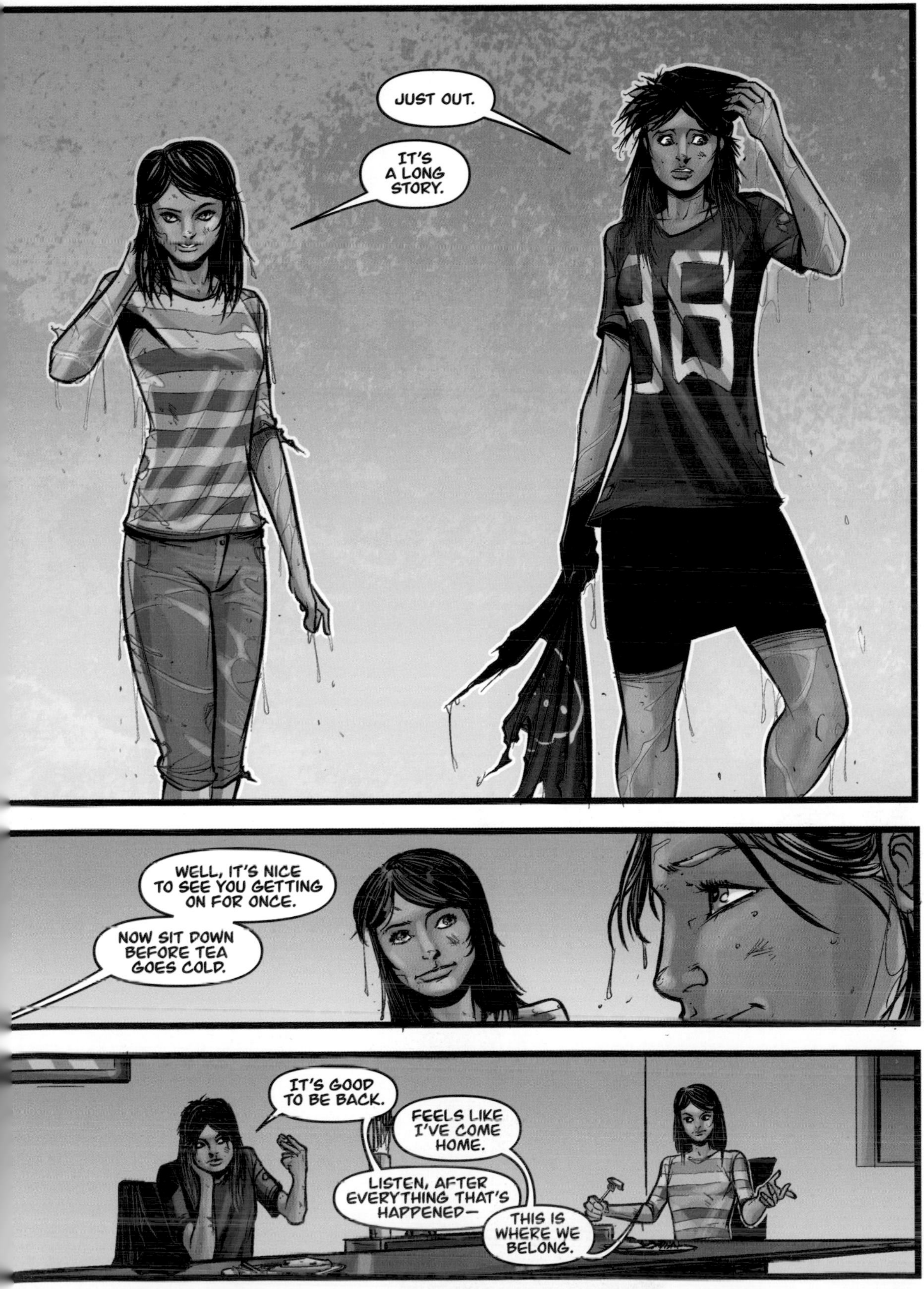
JUST OUT.
IT'S A LONG STORY.
WELL, IT'S NICE TO SEE YOU GETTING ON FOR ONCE.
NOW SIT DOWN BEFORE TEA GOES COLD.
IT'S GOOD TO BE BACK.
FEELS LIKE I'VE COME HOME.
LISTEN, AFTER EVERYTHING THAT'S HAPPENED—
THIS IS WHERE WE BELONG.

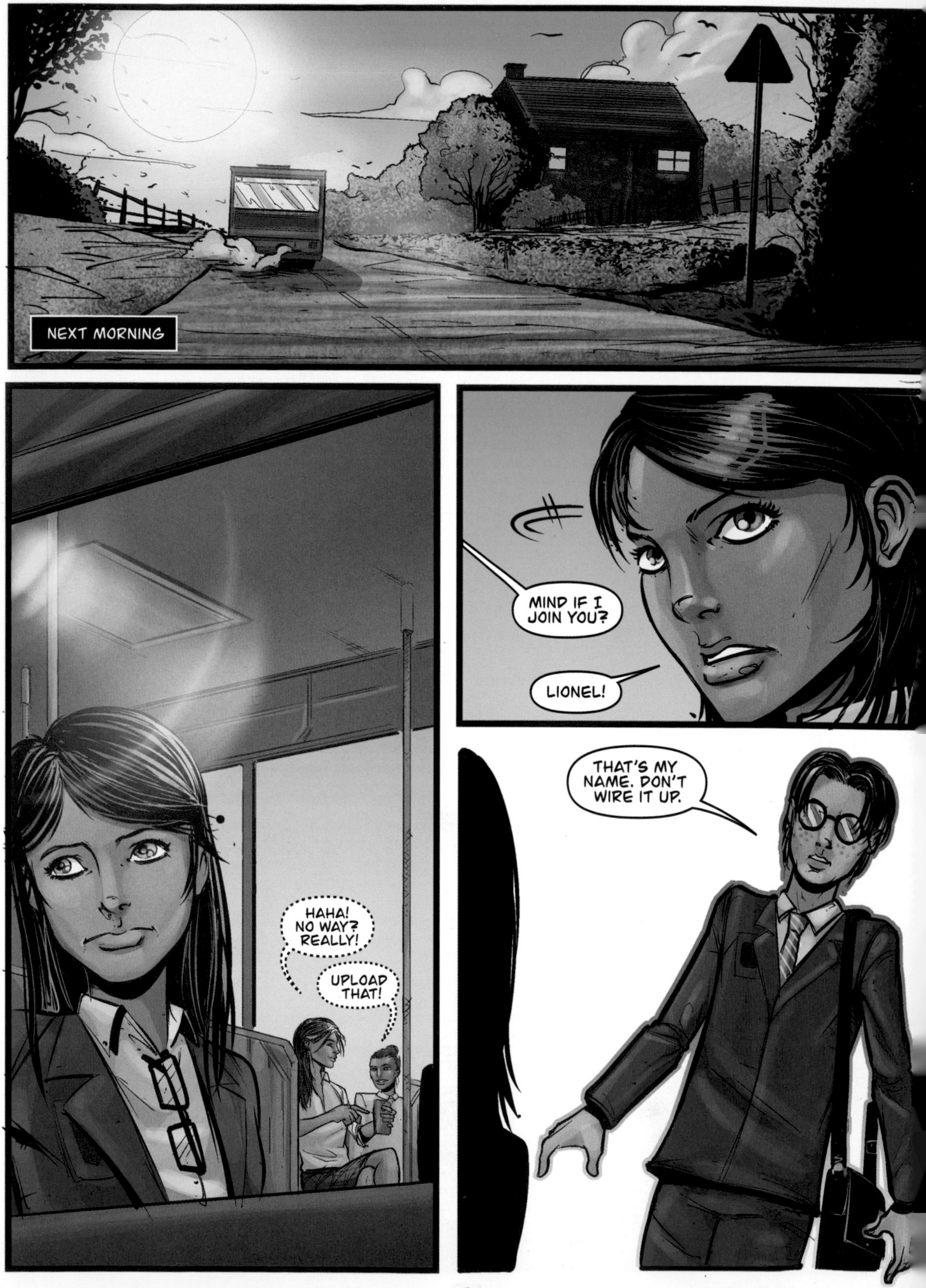
NEXT MORNING
HAHA! NO WAY? REALLY!
UPLOAD THAT!
MIND IF I JOIN YOU?
LIONEL!
THAT'S MY NAME. DON'T WIRE IT UP.

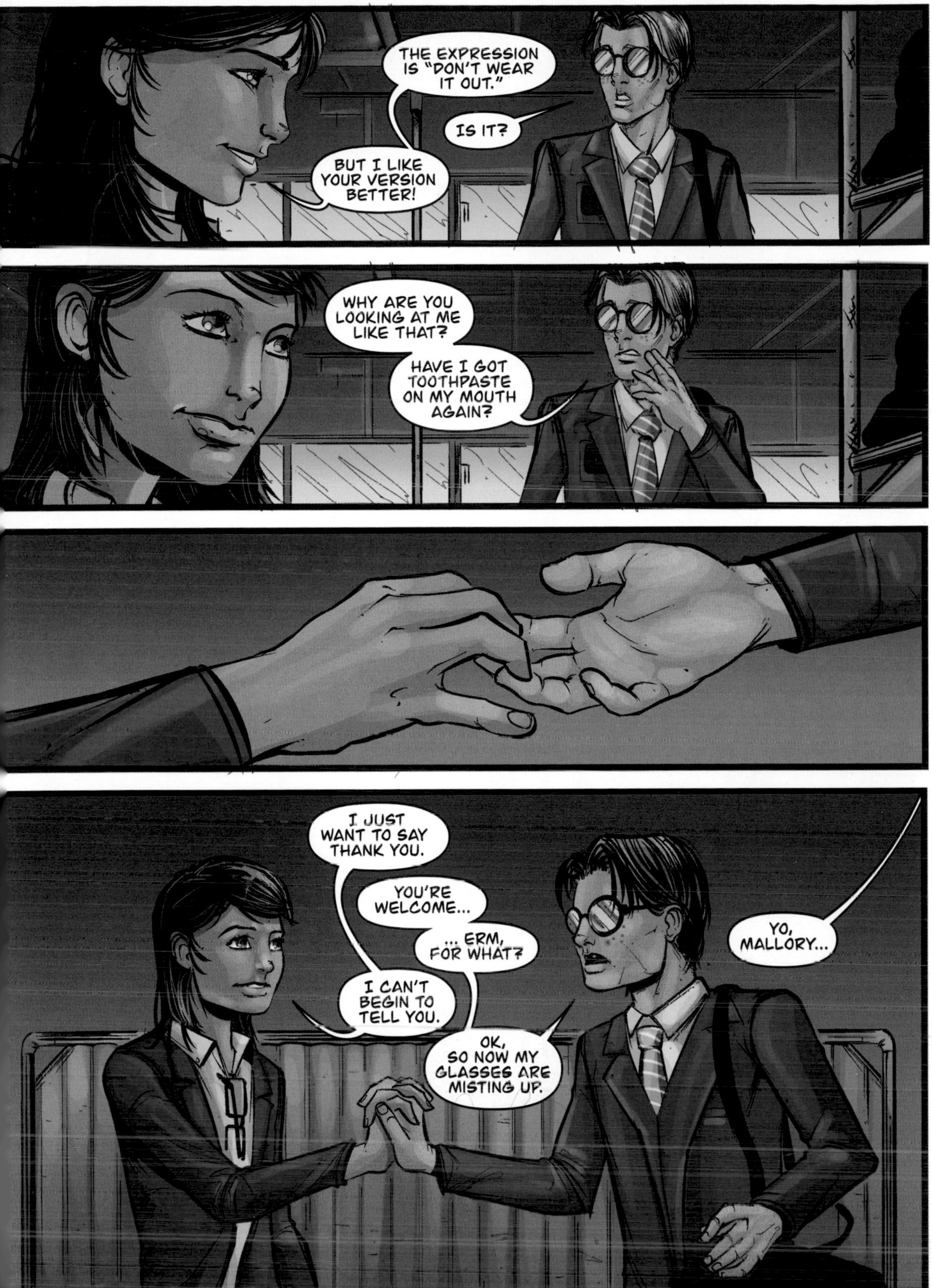
THE EXPRESSION IS "DON'T WEAR IT OUT."
IS IT?
BUT I LIKE YOUR VERSION BETTER!
WHY ARE YOU LOOKING AT ME LIKE THAT?
HAVE I GOT TOOTHPASTE ON MY MOUTH AGAIN?
I JUST WANT TO SAY THANK YOU.
YOU'RE WELCOME...
... ERM, FOR WHAT?
I CAN'T BEGIN TO TELL YOU.
OK, SO NOW MY GLASSES ARE MISTING UP.
YO, MALLORY...

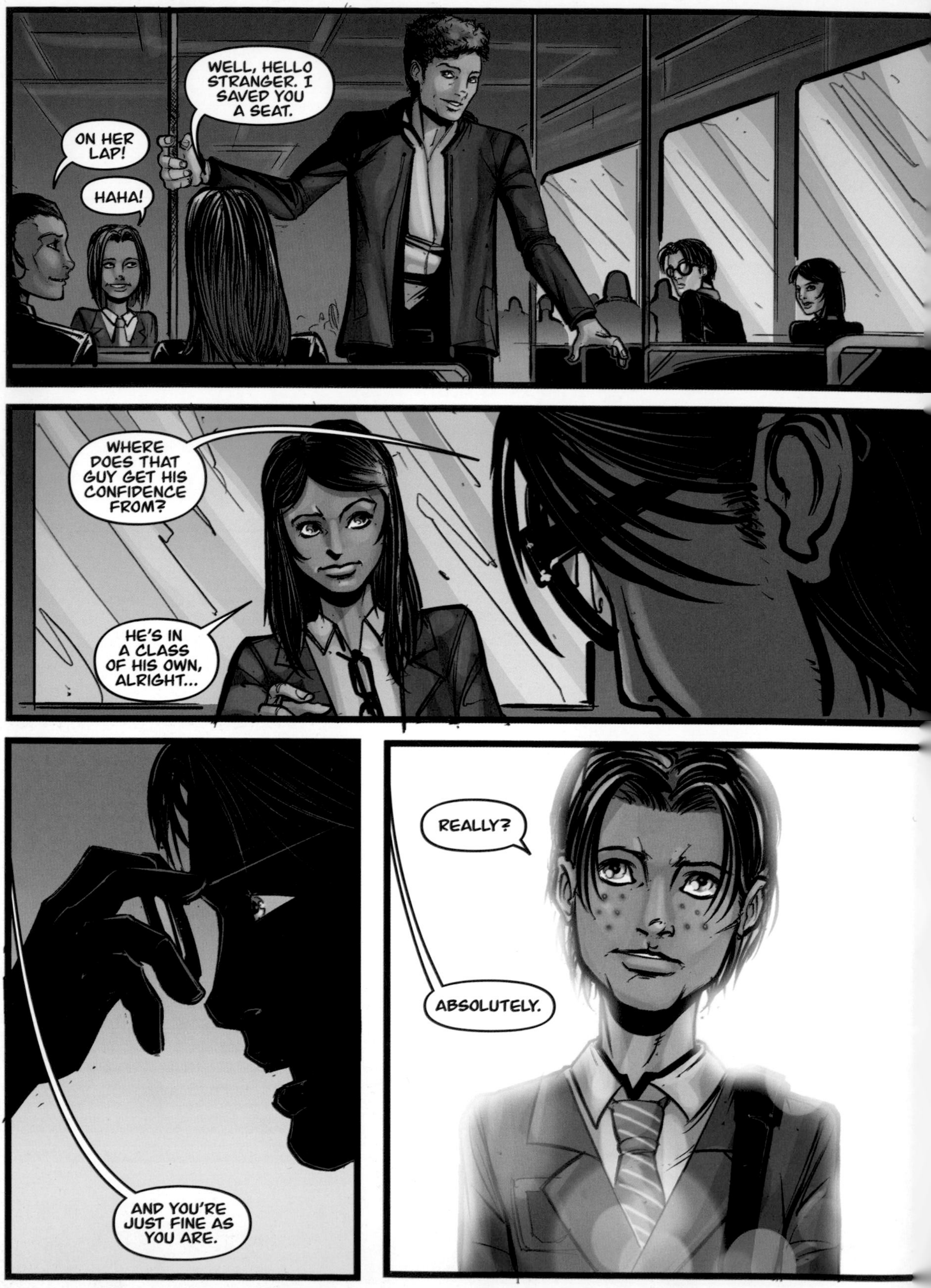
WELL, HELLO STRANGER. I SAVED YOU A SEAT.
ON HER LAP!
HAHA!
WHERE DOES THAT GUY GET HIS CONFIDENCE FROM?
HE'S IN A CLASS OF HIS OWN, ALRIGHT...
REALLY?
ABSOLUTELY.
AND YOU'RE JUST FINE AS YOU ARE.

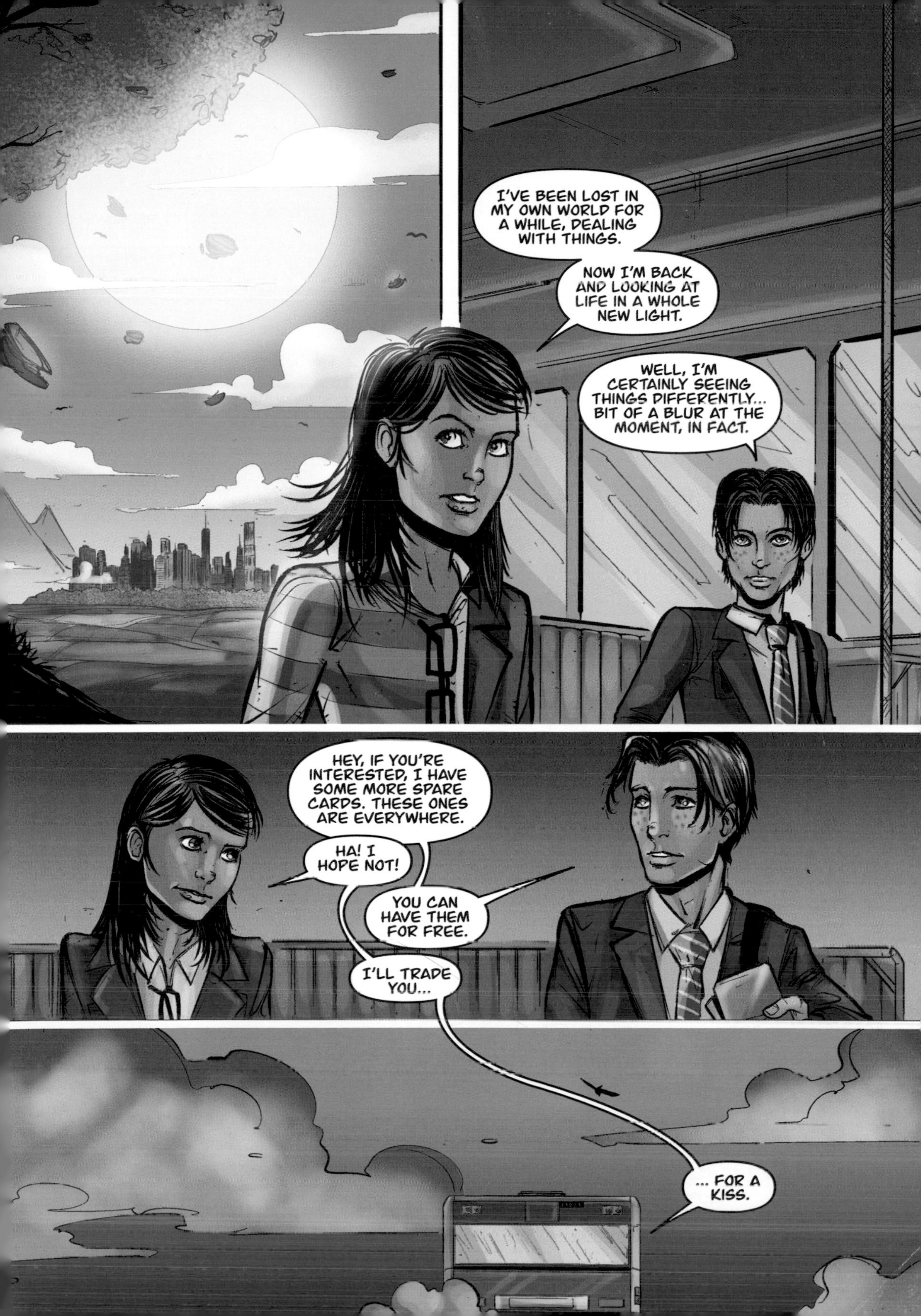
I'VE BEEN LOST IN MY OWN WORLD FOR A WHILE, DEALING WITH THINGS.
NOW I'M BACK AND LOOKING AT LIFE IN A WHOLE NEW LIGHT.
WELL, I'M CERTAINLY SEEING THINGS DIFFERENTLY... BIT OF A BLUR AT THE MOMENT, IN FACT.
HEY, IF YOU'RE INTERESTED, I HAVE SOME MORE SPARE CARDS. THESE ONES ARE EVERYWHERE.
HA! I HOPE NOT!
YOU CAN HAVE THEM FOR FREE.
I'LL TRADE YOU...
... FOR A KISS.

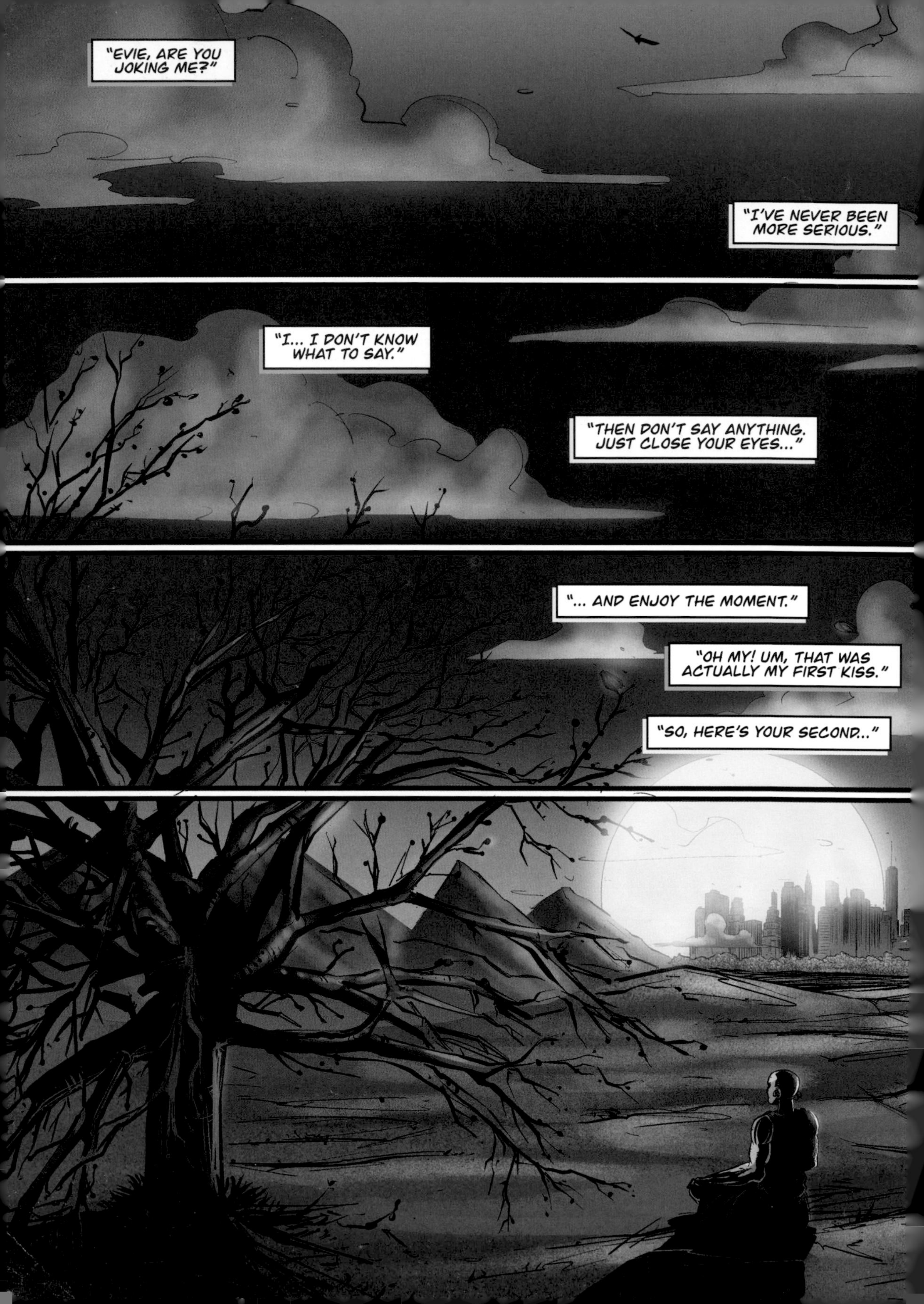
"EVIE, ARE YOU JOKING ME?"
"I'VE NEVER BEEN MORE SERIOUS."
"I... I DON'T KNOW WHAT TO SAY."
"THEN DON'T SAY ANYTHING. JUST CLOSE YOUR EYES..."
"... AND ENJOY THE MOMENT."
"OH MY! UM, THAT WAS ACTUALLY MY FIRST KISS."
"SO, HERE'S YOUR SECOND..."

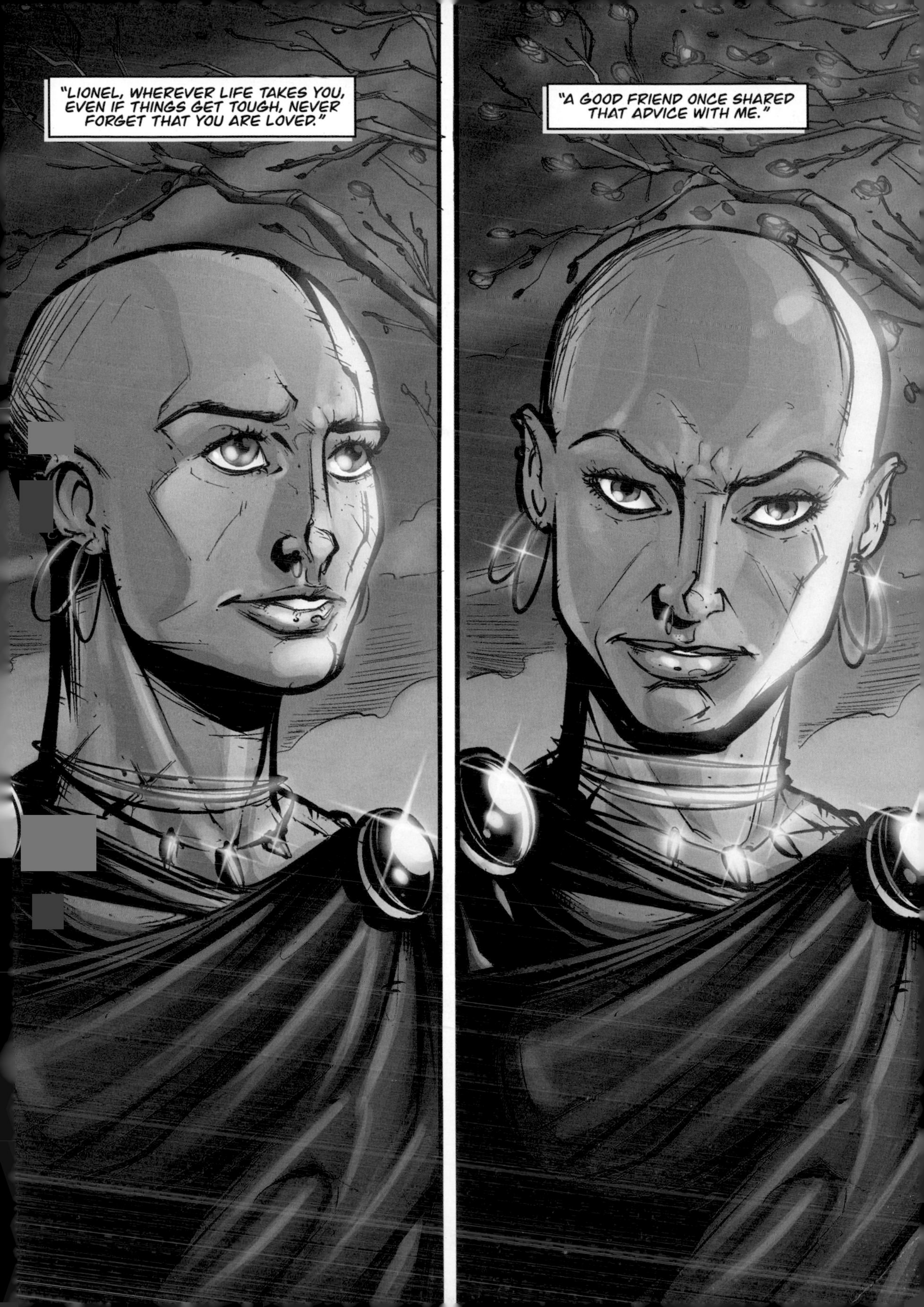
"LIONEL, WHEREVER LIFE TAKES YOU, EVEN IF THINGS GET TOUGH, NEVER FORGET THAT YOU ARE LOVED."
"A GOOD FRIEND ONCE SHARED THAT ADVICE WITH ME."

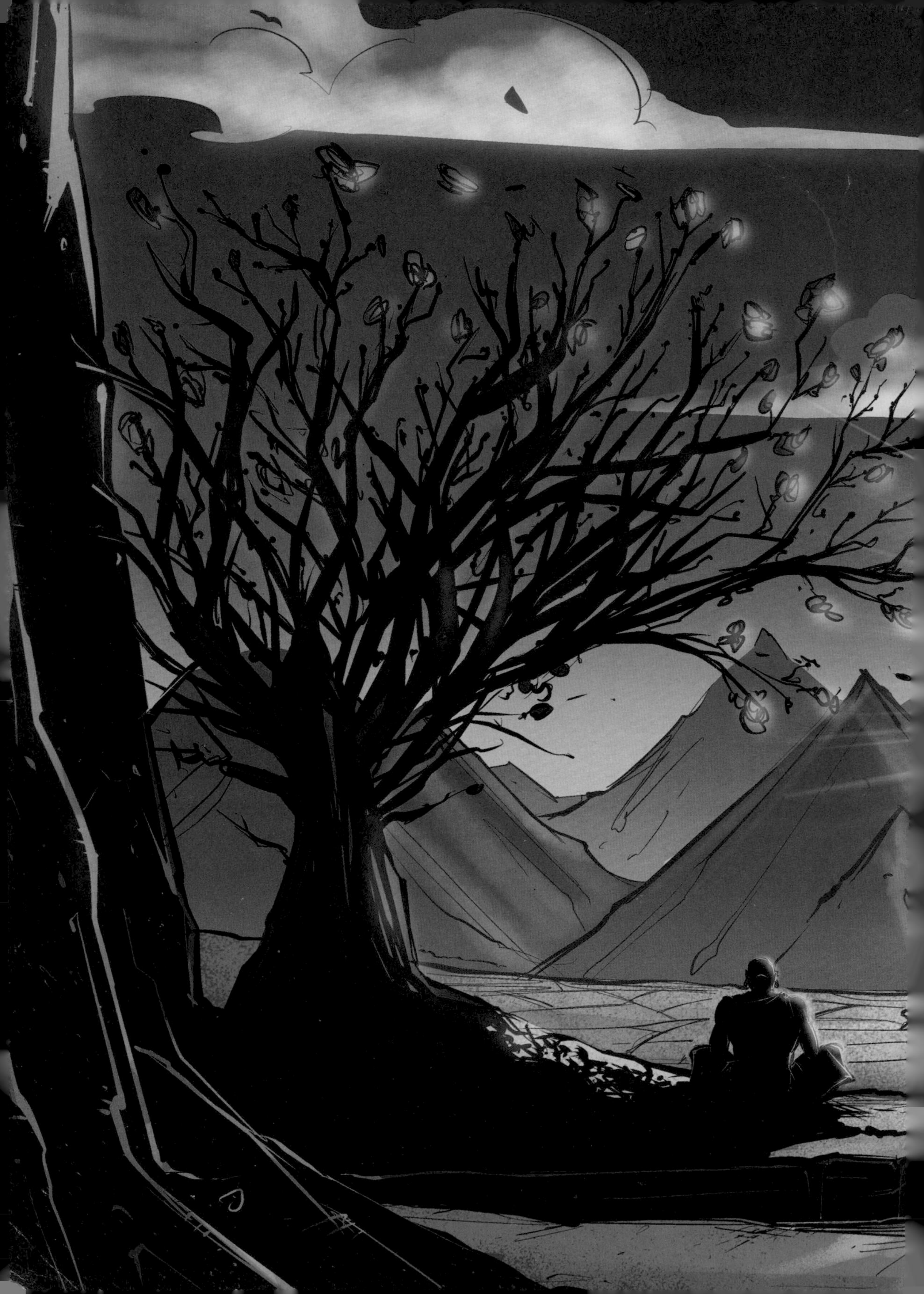

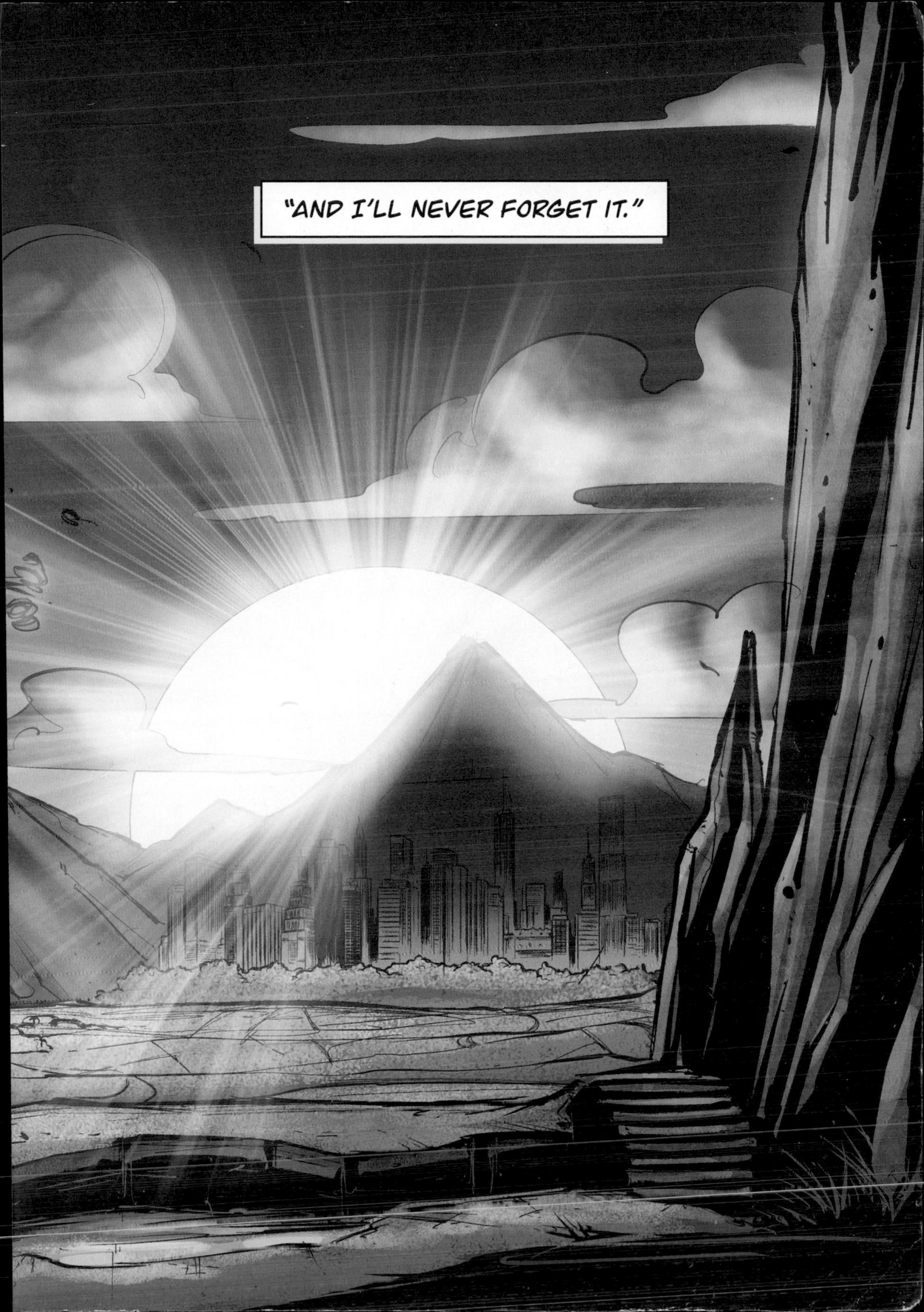
"AND I'LL NEVER FORGET IT."

THANK YOUs

FIRST AND FOREMOST I'D LIKE TO THANK **YOU** FOR READING THIS RIGHT NOW, AND FOR YOUR AMAZING SUPPORT. IT MEANS THE WORLD TO ME THAT YOU LOVE WHAT I DO SO MUCH :)

ALSO BIG UP BRIONY, LENI AND THE REST OF HODDER FOR BEING THE BEST/MOST PATIENT PUBLISHER CREW I COULD ASK FOR. ENORMOUS THANKS TO THE REST OF THE SUGG SQUAD, MATT WHYMAN & AMRIT BIRDI. TOGETHER, WE HAVE CREATED SOMETHING VERY SPECIAL TO ME.

A MASSIVE THANK YOU TO LUCY LENDREM, ALEX CLARKE AND DOM SMALES AT GLEAM FOR PUTTING UP WITH ME. SHOUT OUT TO MY YOUTUBE BUDDIES — YOU KNOW WHO YOU ALL ARE! THANKS TO CASPAR LEE & OLI WHITE FOR JUST BEING GENERAL LEGENDS AND NOT HURTING ME AFTER I CONSTANTLY PRANK AND WIND THEM UP.

THANKS TO ALL MY FRIENDS BACK HOME IN WILTSHIRE FOR THE SUPPORT AND REMINDING ME THAT I MAY BE DOING ALL THIS COOL STUFF, BUT I'M STILL USELESS AT DOWNING A PINT.

THANKS TO BOTH MY NANS AND GRANDDAD, MY MUM AND DAD, AND OF COURSE, LAST BUT NOT LEAST...

THANKS TO MY BIG SIS, ZOE. YOU FILMED AND EDITED MY FIRST TWO VIDEOS, GAVE ME ALL YOUR HAND-ME-DOWN LAPTOPS AND FILMING EQUIPMENT TO HELP ME START MY YOUTUBE CHANNEL, AND HAVE GIVEN ME SOME OF THE BEST SISTERLY ADVICE ONLINE AND OFFLINE. BUT, ABOVE ALL THAT, YOU'RE JUST A PRETTY GREAT SISTER. WELL DONE, MATE.

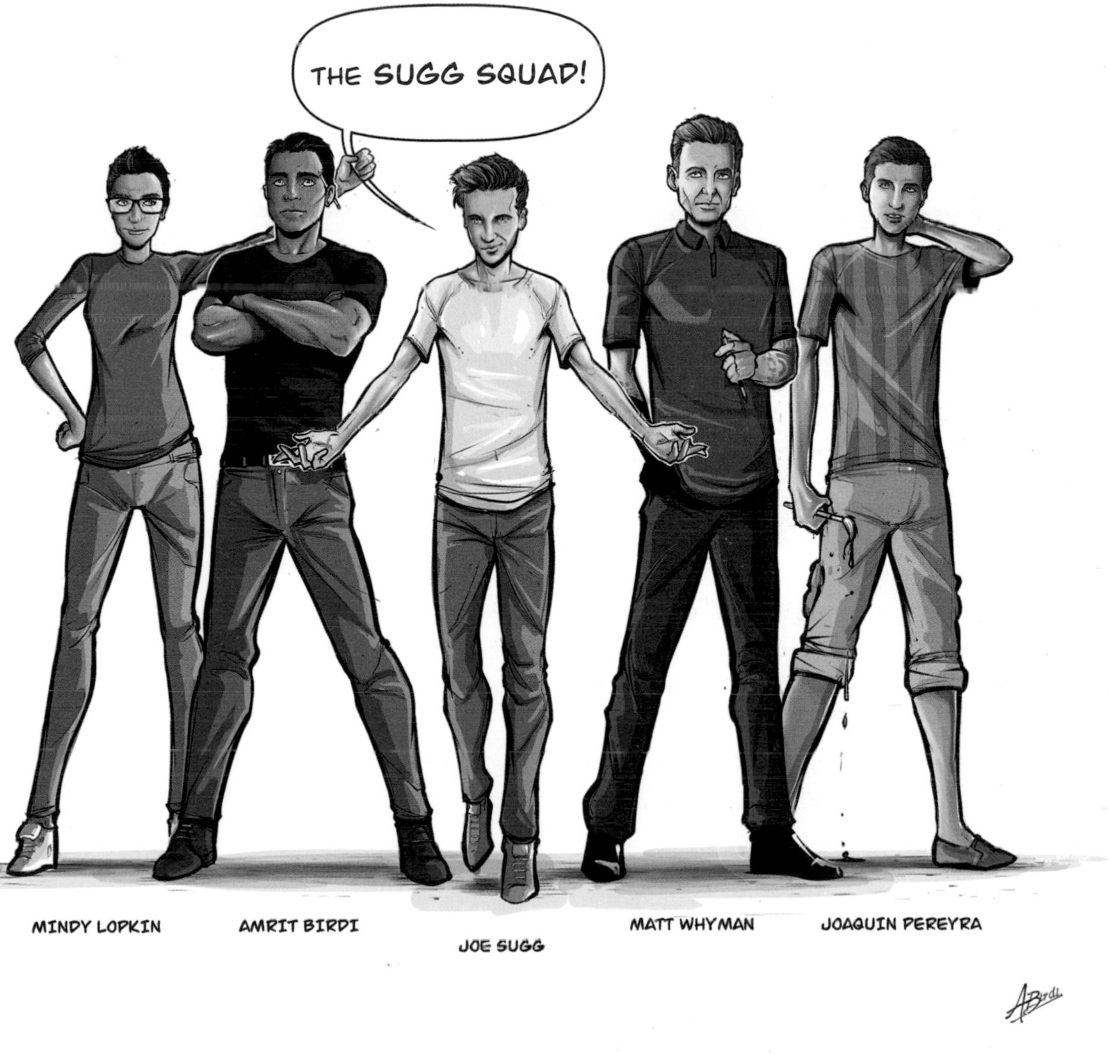
THE SUGG SQUAD!
MINDY LOPKIN
AMRIT BIRDI
JOE SUGG
MATT WHYMAN
JOAQUIN PEREYRA
A Birdi